Using Art Therapy with
Diverse Populations

of related interest

Art Therapy in Asia
To the Bone or Wrapped in Silk
Edited by Debra Kalmanowitz, Jordan S. Potash and Siu Mei Chan
Forewords by Shaun McNiff and William Fan
ISBN 978 1 84905 210 8
eISBN 978 0 85700 449 9

Art Therapy, Race and Culture
Edited by Jean Campbell, Marian Liebmann, Frederica Brooks, Jenny Jones and Cathy Ward
Foreword by Suman Fernando
ISBN 978 1 85302 578 5
eISBN 978 0 85700 234 1

Art Therapy Techniques and Applications
Susan I. Buchalter
ISBN 978 1 84905 806 3
eISBN 978 1 84642 961 3

Art Therapy and Anger
Edited by Marian Liebmann
ISBN 978 1 84310 425 4
eISBN 978 1 84642 810 4

Spirituality and Art Therapy
Living the Connection
Edited by Mimi Farrelly-Hansen
Foreword by Deborah Bowman
ISBN 978 1 85302 952 3
eISBN 978 1 84642 219 5

Art in Action
Expressive Arts Therapy and Social Change
Edited by Ellen G. Levine and Stephen K. Levine
Foreword by Michelle LeBaron
ISBN 978 1 84905 820 9
eISBN 978 0 85700 270 9

Using Art Therapy with Diverse Populations

Crossing Cultures and Abilities

Edited by Paula Howie, Sangeeta Prasad, and Jennie Kristel

Foreword by Mercedes B. ter Maat and Gaelynn Bordonaro

Jessica Kingsley *Publishers*
London and Philadelphia

First published in 2013
by Jessica Kingsley Publishers
73 Collier Street
London N1 9BE, UK
and
400 Market Street, Suite 400
Philadelphia, PA 19106, USA

www.jkp.com

Library of Congress Cataloging in Publication Data
Using art therapy with diverse populations : crossing cultures and abilities / [edited by] Paula Howie,
Sangeeta Prasad and Jennie Kristel ; foreword by Mercedes B. ter Maat and Gaelynn P. Wolf
Bordonaro.
    p. ; cm.
  Includes bibliographical references and index.
  ISBN 978-1-84905-916-9 (alk. paper)
  I. Howie, Paula, editor of compilation. II. Prasad, Sangeeta, editor of compilation. III. Kristel, Jennie,
editor of compilation.
  [DNLM: 1. Art Therapy--methods. 2. Cultural Diversity. WM 450.5.A8]
  RC489.A7
  616.89'1656--dc23
                        2013012278

British Library Cataloguing in Publication Data
A CIP catalogue record for this book is available from the British Library

ISBN 978 1 84905 916 9
eISBN 978 0 85700 694 3

Printed and bound in Great Britain

Contents

List of Figures

List of Figures in the Color Insert

Foreword

Confronted with the challenge of acculturating the field in diverse contexts, art therapists are contributing to the global growth of the profession. We have the responsibility to do so in ways that are appropriate, valuable, and ethical, and to develop coping skills and competence for working in each new culture.

Indeed, art therapists are well positioned to answer the call to assist the mental health needs of every person in a way that is sensitive to their personal struggle with the human experience. For the therapeutic encounter to succeed, we must understand how our clients identify themselves, define their culture, and engage in their struggle. If we cannot touch our clients' cultural souls, can we help them at all?

As the field expands across the globe, individuals in countries with a burgeoning interest in the formal applications of art therapy reach out for support from the more than two dozen countries with established art therapy associations. Professional, credentialed art therapists with training in multicultural constructs can offer unique assistance in the cross-cultural application of art therapy as well as inform educational criteria and standards of practice for new and innovative training programs on the international stage.

Success in global growth will require more than just a broad repertoire of culturally sensitive therapeutic approaches. We will have to explore our own biases and prejudices. It is imperative that we acknowledge the cultural diversity that exists between clients and clinicians in ways that enhance therapeutic outcomes. How will we do this? The answer is that we do this by utilizing resources such as *Using Art Therapy with Diverse Populations: Crossing Cultures and Abilities.*

This book is strategically and sequentially laid out to provide the reader with the basis for understanding art therapy as practiced in a culturally diverse society. Editors Paula Howie, Sangeeta Prasad, and Jennie Kristel have accomplished a unique contribution to the global growth of art therapy. The book compiles writings from the three editors and 27 authors experienced in culturally sensitive and competent practice. We are fortunate to have these art therapists—these leaders—both because our profession calls for truth and evidence in practice and because each of our clients deserves an art therapist able to assist him/her with the lifelong struggle to answer the question, "Who am I?"

The reader is introduced to art therapy theory, best practices, contemporary programming, cross-cultural applications, ethical principles, thoughtful choice and use of art media, and clinical work of art therapists treating diverse special populations. Furthermore, the chapters present challenges, considerations, and cultural implications for art therapists working in community, private, public, institutional, hospital, educational, and medical settings.

Each chapter is grounded in the author's area of expertise and ethical foundations of art therapy. Importantly, the reader is charged with building his or her own multi- and cross-cultural competence, scholarly curiosity, and reverence for cultural perspectives, perceptions, customs, and aesthetic expression. We recommend that each of you utilize this book for your personal and professional art therapy growth and cultural awareness. It is a book to be appreciated, valued, and referenced by students, educators, practitioners, and individuals from various parts of the world in which there is a growing interest in the field of art therapy.

Mercedes B. ter Maat, PhD, ATR-BC, LPC,
Associate Professor, Nova Southeastern University,
President, American Art Therapy Association,
and Gaelynn Bordonaro, PhD, ATR-BC,
Director, Art Therapy Program,
Associate Professor, Emporia State University,
Clinical Director, Communities Healing Through Art

Acknowledgments

There are many ways to name those who guide us. Guru, maestro, sensei, lehrer, onderwyser are all translated "teacher." We would like to thank all of our wise teachers for what they have inspired us to learn about art therapy in all its complexities. They gave us a love and a belief in the process of this work, which has helped us to have the confidence to bring art therapy into locations that have never had services before, to utilize its therapeutic interventions in challenging circumstances, and to bring together the ideas for this book.

We want to acknowledge the many art, expressive arts, and arts-based therapists who believe in the arts in therapy and who daily bring it into the lives of many individuals. They are as much part of this book as are the authors of each chapter, since each writer not only draws on his/her own experience, but also on the unique experiences of those around us who inspire us.

A very big *thank you* to the 27 authors willing to share their experiences, thoughts, and visions of art therapy from their own unique perspective. Each one worked diligently to impart his/her thoughts and cultural experiences, making this book a special pleasure to read.

We wish to thank our families for their support in making this a reality and tolerating our long hours at the computer. We could not have done this without their help and the help of friends and others who have inspired us, believed in our quest, and helped us edit and shape each chapter into its present form. Many thanks to Crystal Campbell, Richard Hilker, Michael Watson, Tony and Marilyn Lloyd, Radha and Tara Patel, Hugh, Rachael, Chris and Lauren Marr, Linda Gantt, and Louis Tinnin. To Supna, Sangeeta's daughter, for her inspiring artwork on the cover, and to Sangeeta's mother-in-law who made delicious food when we had our editorial meetings. Our minds and palettes will be forever grateful. We are sure our authors have special people whom they would like to thank. We salute them all!

A special acknowledgment goes to Latha Ramalingam for her patience and wonderful editorial expertise, which made the finished product much tighter and better organized. Our special thanks to the staff at Jessica Kingsley Publishers— Bethany Gower, Lisa Clark, and Victoria Peters, and those many whose names we do not know; they were with us through each aspect of the evolution of this manuscript. They tirelessly helped translate the world of publishing for us, answering a myriad of questions with patience and clarity, supporting us in our work, and having faith in the fact that such this book is needed at this time.

To the clients and students with whom we work, we owe a most profound debt. Without them, a clinical book such as this could not be written. Thank you for what you have taught us over the years. We know that when we are able to listen with our hearts and our humanity rather than being constrained by the lens of our culture, social class, gender, orientation, or race, we are able to attune to the power of relationship and more fully access the depth of resilience our clients possess.

A vision remains just an ephemeral idea until it is implemented. It took many hours of discussion and planning to put together a book that reflected the diversity of the field. Due to the limitation of space, we had to focus on certain aspects of art therapy and leave out others. This is always a challenging task as there are so many ways to approach the diverse topics covered. We are grateful to have found one another in the process of compiling this book. It was wonderful to experience how three people were able to work together in such harmony, to utilize each other's expertise, and to complement their strengths. Our gratitude and appreciation for one another is boundless.

Preface

Anthropologist Conrad Kottak (2004) defines culture as "traditions or customs, transmitted through learning, that guide the beliefs and behavior of the people exposed to them" (p. 5). He further asserts that all human beings learn cultural norms through enculturation. Culture is learned, shared, and symbolic, and can be either adaptive or maladaptive. There have been many writings on understanding culture from the unique perspective of art therapists by writers such as Case and Dalley (2006); Gil and Drewes (2005); Gussak and Virshup (1997); Malchiodi (1998); Rubin (2001); and Talwar, Iyer, and Doby-Copeland (2004), to name a few.

In 1985, Sangeeta Prasad began her studies in art therapy in the United States. She most often wore a traditional salwar kameez (Indian dress) to work since that was what she had worn in India. She had a bindi (dot on the forehead) and a nose ring, things seldom seen in the United States at that time. Her hair was long. As her supervisor was orienting her to the work site, a child stopped her, looked at her face, and said, "Are you from God?" and "Is there a hole in your head?" She was taken aback by this reaction. In India, everyone has a bindi. Why did he think she was from God? This was one of her first introductions to cultural sensitivity and how our appearance and reactions may affect the way we are seen or the way we view others. In supervision, Sangeeta remembered talking about her own biases, her nascent knowledge about the United States, how she was becoming aware of how others may perceive a person from a different culture, and how this knowledge could be used to inform therapy. This instance exemplifies a certain cultural innocence, where the therapist and client are confronting a new experience and must be open to learning from it. From the first meeting, our appearance, speech, and demeanor carry the cultural imprint of our history.

Sangeeta's cultural education continued when she worked the following year at a military hospital with Paula Howie. Both felt their individual, interpersonal, and cross-cultural experiences were especially riveting in that they had impact on patients and staff and on supervisory relationships developed against the backdrop of military culture. For Sangeeta, understanding one's view of oneself and one's surroundings was a continuous discussion in supervision at the university and with Paula at the worksite. It was not surprising that Paula learned as much as did Sangeeta as a result of their interchanges.

In 2009, as Sangeeta continued to make her home in the United States, she had begun to explore the possibilities of starting an art therapy program in India. She quickly realized that to understand the art therapy books from the West one needs to have a background in psychology or counseling. It would also be difficult and expensive to purchase these books since they were not available in India. She felt the need for one comprehensive book to address the various settings in which art therapists work. It was with this in mind that Sangeeta approached Paula Howie to join her in writing a book on how art therapy is used with different populations; however, due to their personal experiences in the United States and in other countries where they had taught, this seemed too confining a topic. Expanding their thinking to include the perspectives of cultural understanding and sensitivity for those with whom they work, they began to consider including their global cultural perceptions as well as those of their workplace settings.

Gomez Carlier and Salom (2012) entreat art therapists as a whole to help raise cultural awareness so that those carrying art therapy to other parts of the world can adapt it to their respective cultures. Those with whom we work are best served if we understand ourselves, the impact of our culture, and the limitations of our understanding and if we continue to strive to respect and learn from one another.

With this in mind, as Sangeeta and Paula began working, they decided that they needed another perspective from someone who had worked in the burgeoning educational setting of South Asia. Jennie Kristel, an expressive therapist, was invited to join this endeavor. We then felt that we had a wonderful team that brought together various experiences, backgrounds, and interests.

A note about the terminology used in this book: throughout the text, the reader will see the words *expressive therapies*, *arts-based therapies*, and *arts therapies* used, at times interchangeably. This reflects the varied backgrounds of our contributors. For example, a person with a degree in expressive therapies or expressive arts therapy has been trained in multiple art forms to be used individually or in concert with one another, whereas an art therapy degree relies more on the visual arts as the main modality of treatment. All the arts, however, are looked upon as valuable options for healing. No one degree is better than another; they are simply different. All individuals who are formally trained through accredited programs learn about psychology and the arts as well as the theory and practice of clinical training.

Each author brings his or her unique perspective to the theory and practice of art therapy. It is important to remember that what has been written is only a slice of what is possible to cover. We have provided an introduction into understanding the influence a particular environment has on the approach one uses for the novice as well as for experienced clinicians who are interested in using art in therapy.

While we are trained as arts or expressive therapists, we have to translate our training to be effective with various populations and settings. This poses unique challenges since many times we are the first to bring art therapy into that particular setting. We wanted this book to be useful to art therapists in the United States and to be a resource for art therapists who are beginning programs around the world, and for students who are interested in the field of art therapy. We felt it had to be a book that people with English as a second language could understand.

Many of the contributors to this book have worked in other countries, have faced cultural challenges, and have had to work through their own cultural bias in exploring the myriad ways that art therapy can be and is useful on an intercultural level. In writing this text, the editors hope to honor the complexity of one's cultural heritage as something important and ubiquitous to which all therapists must attend. The editors are themselves from very different cultural backgrounds, which accounts for a variation in and sensitivity to different cultural issues in this text. It is our hope that the unique perspectives all the authors bring to this book provide the reader with a clearer understanding of a variety of cultures from different art therapist experiences.

In addition to looking at cultural influences in a traditional way, it is also our intention to highlight the unique "micro-culture" of the facility in which the therapist works and its influence upon the treatment. It is our hope that everyone reading this book will come away with a unique understanding of the particular setting in which our contributors provide art therapy services and how this affects every aspect of their work. We see culture in today's world as a large patchwork quilt of lines, forms, and shapes that make up who we are individually and which connect us in our own unique ways to one another. One looks not only at the individual patterns and patches of the quilt, but also at the quilt as a whole, the entire gestalt of the quilt (Figure P.1).

Figure P.1 A collage of the artwork in the book representing the quilt

Positive awareness of one's cultural heritage acts as a connection to the past and contributes to health and well-being. Negative feelings that the individual has may represent a cutoff from his/her family or culture. It may also indicate traumatic events which have led to a suppression of his/her personal history (McGoldrick

2003). Clients from marginalized cultures, including, for example, people who are deaf or being raised in a deaf culture, have probably internalized society's prejudices about them, although this can be ameliorated by the strength of cultural ties. Those from the dominant culture might have internalized a sense of superiority and of their right to be privileged (McGoldrick 2003). Most significant for those of us in mental health is that cultural, class, religious, and political background influence how an individual views his/her problems; this therefore gives insights into his/her view of the meaning of suffering and the means of its mitigation.

McGoldrick asserts that "mental health professionals are being challenged to develop treatment responses and services that are more responsive to ethnic, racial, and religious identities" (p.235). Cultural background (ethnicity) is profoundly influenced by social class, religion, migration, geography, gender oppression, and racism. In working from a perspective of curiosity and humility around cultural differences we are able to relate to others in a more meaningful way.

Thus, this book grew out of a wish to give voice to the experience of various art therapists and their clients from around the world. It was our intention, as editors, to reach out to people from other countries who are well versed in the field of art therapy and expressive therapies so that our book would support and reflect the international essence of what art therapy means around the globe.

Through the technological wizardry of computers, including Skype, email, and of course face-to-face discussions, this book unfolded among the three of us and 27 authors based around the world. From working on "live" documents that allowed us to edit together online, to being able to email responses back and forth within minutes, it truly was an amazing process of learning the "art" of new ways to think about writing, from a technical perspective.

Richard Schwartz (1995) has pointed to the changing demography of culture in the United States. He views culture as ethnicity or the common ancestry through which individuals have evolved and through which they share values and customs. He describes culture as identity and cultural context as the ongoing social context within which our lives have evolved. In this book, the authors add to this list, in that the art therapist must also keep in mind the unique aspects of cultural influence on color use, color preference, the importance of symbols, choice of materials, the forms art therapy intervention will take, and the unique settings in which we work (prisons, the military, homeless shelters, hospitals, etc.).

So it is with profound respect to those whose work we build upon that we endeavor to extend the art therapy literature with this book, acknowledging the influence of culture on each participant in the therapeutic relationship. We hope you will enjoy our exploration and realize that such a book will forever be a work in progress.

References

Case, C. and Dalley, T. (2006) *The Handbook of Art Therapy*. New York: Routledge.

Gil, E. and Drewes, A. (2005) *Cultural Issues in Play Therapy*. New York: The Guilford Press.

Gomez Carlier, N. and Salom, A. (2012) "When Art Therapy Migrates: The Accumulation Challenge of Sojourner Art Therapists." *Art Therapy: Journal of the American Art Therapy Association 29*, 1, 4–10.

Gussak, D. and Virshup, E. (1997) *Drawing Time*. Chicago: Magnolia Street Publishers.

Kottak, C. (2004) *Cultural Anthropology, Tenth Edition*. Boston: McGraw-Hill.

Malchiodi, C. (1998) *The Art Therapy Sourcebook*. Los Angeles: NTC/Contemporary Publishing Group.

McGoldrick, M. (2003) "Culture: A Challenge to Concepts of Normalcy." In F. Walsh (ed.) *Normal Family Processes, Third Edition*. New York: The Guilford Press.

Rubin, J. (ed.) (2001) *Approaches to Art Therapy: Theory and Technique*. New York: Brunner-Routledge.

Schwartz, R. (1995) *Internal Family Systems Therapy*. New York: The Guilford Press.

Talwar, S., Iyer, J., and Doby-Copeland, C. (2004) "The invisible veil: Changing paradigms in the art therapy profession." *Art Therapy: Journal of the American Art Therapy Association 21*, 1, 44–48.

Introduction

In their book *Cultural Issues and Play Therapy*, Gil and Drewes (2005) assert that creating conscious attention to culture is a therapeutic imperative. In the same book, Cathy Malchiodi (p.96) points to art therapists who have addressed the implications of cultural sensitivity for clinical work. This mirrors what has been said in other mental health fields about the importance of understanding the culture of the client and therapist in order to understand the interaction of the two.

Art therapy is expanding in different countries exponentially. There are, now more than ever, multiple avenues for trained art therapists to work in other countries. Frances Anderson, Doris Arrington, Catherine Moon, Yasmine Awais, and many others point this out through their own personal and professional experiences. To do art therapy well, there needs to be thoughtful attention to details. This is the ethic we bring to this work, which involves a deep knowledge of the process and materials, and a keen sense of listening to and sharing in the culture of the setting and/or country we are in. One needs to have the willingness to be open and flexible, and to work toward a deepening attunement with those with whom we work. We begin to see the places of alignment as well as the places in which art therapy as a practice needs to weave between cultures and ideologies. In thinking about what we wanted as the focus of this book, we knew that we wanted to reach beyond the comfortable. We have tried to write from a wide variety of sources about things that matter to people, whether they are in Asia, the United States, Europe, or Africa. This of course was a fairly daunting task. Essentially the book could have been written in a myriad of ways. According to McGoldrick, "Cultural competence requires not a cookbook approach to cultural differences but an appreciation for the often hidden cultural aspects of our psychological, spiritual and physical selves, a profound respect for the limitations of our own cultural perspective and an ability to deal respectfully with those whose values differ from our own" (McGoldrick 2003, p.239). In this statement, she is referring to true multiculturalism, which can guide us to more effective treatment and with which we constantly grapple in order to overcome our own limitations and cultural biases.

The Structure of This Book

In the first chapter of Part I, Jennie Kristel begins with a history of art therapy, how it began, and the impact of culture on art therapy practice. Louis Tinnin and Paula Howie then explain how art therapy works and the mechanisms of the verbal and nonverbal brain that clarify our understanding of this process. They separate cultural orientation from brain-based theory. This is followed by Donna Betts's write-up on current assessments, which contains excerpts from the authors of each diagnostic technique. It highlights the need for research when introducing assessments into various environments. Audrey Di Maria Nankervis introduces us to ethical issues that pertain to the art therapist at work. Different countries have a wide variety of ways of looking at the issue of ethics. As art therapy is mostly a Western-based practice, the ethics have been structured around guidelines developed by the prevalent thinking in the psychological and medical communities of these countries. Supervision can be challenging when people come from different perspectives and backgrounds. Lisa Garlock, through her work as a student and field supervisor, points out the various nuances involved in supervision.

In understanding what it takes to be a culturally aware and sensitive art therapist, the editors felt it would be important to explore this topic from a visual emotional viewpoint. Sangeeta Prasad opens this discussion in Part II by examining the ways in which culture impacts the choices and uses of materials. In writing about attunement, Jennie investigates the deeper connections that encircle the therapeutic alliance and allow the clinician and client to be in a truly authentic relationship with each other. Paula explores the potential and expansive nature of color and how intertwined culture, science, and art really are. Mimi Farrelly-Hansen looks at the process of spirituality in our work as art therapists. Cheryl Doby-Copeland reminds us of our responsibility to social awareness, engagement, and integrative awareness around race and culture issues. Her narrative comes from an African-American perspective, imploring that it is imperative for every student or practitioner, no matter where they are from, to have training in multicultural competency. This theme comes up in many places within this book.

Art therapy has been used widely in educational settings in several countries. In Part III, Emmy Lou Glassman and Sangeeta describe how art therapy was developed in various schools to suit the needs of their particular setting and culture. Audrey Di Maria Nankervis looks back at her work with children at risk and describes how culture played into the art therapy process and her identity as an art therapist. In her chapter on art therapy with autistic children, Deni Brancheau highlights the role of nonverbal means of communication in therapy. Emmy Lou Glassman outlines her experience in balancing the needs of an art curriculum within a high school setting. She addresses the fine line between art education and art therapy with this population. While working with adolescents in a school may seem similar to working in a residential or group home setting, Charlotte Boston brings out the many unique considerations for art therapists in a school environment.

Hospitals and rehabilitation units are very different settings from educational facilities or schools. Here art therapists need to be acutely aware of the medical aspects of the culture, which has its own vocabulary, therapeutic interventions, and ways of viewing illness and health. Depending on the country and culture, faith, social norms, and societal expectations play a role in these settings as well. We begin Part IV with the culture of a military hospital where Paula introduces us to the military and to what the art therapist needs to understand of this culture in order to function in this environment. Tracy Councill and Katharine Phlegar describe how art therapy is used for children with major medical illnesses as well as how families and individuals react to the diagnosis of cancer. Their approach helps to illuminate methods for empowering children and their families in order to benefit from their inpatient stay. Yasmine Awais gives us an overview of the very beginnings of art therapy work in Saudi Arabia within a medical hospital. She takes an introspective look at her experience from various points of view. Shanthi Ranganathan and Reshma Malick outline how they have incorporated arts-based therapy (ABT) into their family-based award-winning substance abuse and rehabilitation program.

There is a wide variety of clinical and nonclinical settings in which art therapy can be found; we wanted to include the role of art therapy in other outpatient treatment programs. Linda Gantt begins Part V with a careful observation of the deep impact of trauma and abuse and the urgent need for cultural understanding when treating people with trauma. How we perceive art and artistic endeavors is often placed within a cultural lens that either mars or enhances our perceptions. She outlines the Initial Trauma Response (ITR) process and the brain-based theory of understanding trauma. Barbara Sobol and Paula examine this further in looking at family constellations and approaching family art therapy through the "8 Ways Paradigm," a method to reflect on family through the lens of differing theoretical perspectives that are translated into artistic methodologies in order to embrace perspectives from a wide variety of artistically intrinsic markers. Through their case discussion, the reader is made aware of how grief and loss are a part of everyday development given the aging of parents and the maturing of the family system. Loss and grief are inherently a part of life in every global community. Heidi Bardot gently shows us ways to work with children experiencing loss from deaths in family and times when communities at large have to deal with disasters. This leads to a need for a discussion of living with dignity and full awareness of the prospect of death, and the realization that by doing so one lives a much fuller and more enriched life. Daniel Blausey and Yasmine Awais further this by offering a historical account and exploration of people living with HIV/AIDS in New York City and the vital need for a paradigmatic change in how society perceives this population. Our last chapter in this part relates directly to how art therapy is useful in examining symbolic work as an important part of cultural understanding, particularly around the increasingly common experience of eating disorders. In this discussion, Michelle Dean probes the multitude of factors influencing why some populations are more prone than others to eating disorders and in what ways society is and needs to be held responsible. In all the chapters in this part, then, understanding the historical contexts, constructs, and social conserves of our cultural selves is the background collage to bringing together the artistic arena of color, texture, line, form, and symbolic representations that help us make sense of ourselves and the world around us.

In Part VI, we attempt to look at the multicultural influences that occur in community-based art therapy work. Each country we work in has a multiple level of cultural constructs and influences. Within this part, we look at different approaches that need to be acknowledged within the art therapy relationship. We look at ways in which people meet others on a one-to-one or a group level, and then at a community level in which all are accepted and welcome, making it very accessible for those who need and desire these types of services. All have points of validity and often work in concert with one another. We begin in Chapter 25 with two of the editors describing some of what they considered when opening a practice in the United States and the ethical issues they faced. The next chapter looks at the role of a community art studio, another venue for art therapy that allows a more expansive approach to work and yet remains inherently therapeutic. Catherine Moon and Valery Shuman look at the role of social engagement and how it has influenced their thinking around the open studio format, claiming a committed stake in inclusive thinking and a collaborative process way to think about the art therapy processes that occur within the studio itself among the clientele that utilize it. By taking this approach, the work within the studio inherently becomes socially engaged among the community members who are there. Following this, we take a look at how art therapy is used in another community setting, that of the community of people lacking adequate shelter. In this community studio, more than art is created. As Kate Baasch eloquently describes, this community art studio is about the members being able to simply "be" and to be accepted, no matter what their external circumstances are. From here, we look at another community, that of elders living in independent, assisted, or nursing care. Linda Levine Madori describes her experience in developing a Therapeutic Thematic Arts Programming (TTAP) theme-based award-winning approach in art therapy with seniors and persons with Alzheimer's and other forms of dementia. She outlines how using the arts in a thematically based way can spark important neural and social connections for people who often struggle with simple and basic activities. She provides through the artistic process a means to explore aging and acceptance of one's situation. In looking at the cultural needs of others and of ourselves, we do not desire to create a homogeneous experience: instead, we work very hard to engage with and support our uniqueness and diversity, allowing these to be present within the therapeutic art processes. It is in this way, then, that we are supporting ourselves and others to truly "be" and accepting one another on a wide variety of levels.

In Part VII, the editors decided that it would be important to look at the cultural implications of practicing art therapy in various settings. Some settings are more difficult than others and involve a wide array of different ways to think about using the arts in therapy. Some methods necessitate more or less structure and frames in order for them to be effective therapy. We begin this analysis with David Gussak's chapter on working in prisons using art therapy. He addresses the uniqueness of bringing art therapy to this antitherapeutic environment. Art here plays a different role, and the art therapist's awareness of psychological boundaries becomes an integral part of therapy. In working with asylum seekers and refugees, Marian Liebmann discusses the importance of practicing the deep acceptance and understanding that is needed by therapists, as well as clients, of the process of assimilation and integration into another country. Looking at the dark world of human trafficking, Doris Arrington brings the light of art therapy to disadvantaged young adults and children in orphanages, who are at risk due to their backgrounds and environment. Frances Anderson helps us to think through ways to bring art therapy overseas and shares what she has learned from doing so herself. We conclude this part by looking at a program co-created by Catherine Moon and African artists and social workers in Tanzania and Kenya. This ties together many of the earlier chapters by looking at the role of collaboration, at assumptions that people make around cultural awareness, and at how, even with the best of intentions, our cultural empathy can be limited.

We hope that this book will stimulate discussions on culture and art therapy and provide insights into how art therapy is used in various settings and what some of the cultural considerations are for particular populations. Our authors have also provided extensive references and sometimes further resources to help you explore the topic of your interest. Our hope is that you will continue to use this book as you work, whether in a prison or in a school, and whether that be in Burlington, NYC, Plymouth in the UK, Dubai, Chennai, or Seoul.

References

Gil, E. and Drewes, A. (2005) *Cultural Issues in Play Therapy.* New York: The Guilford Press.

McGoldrick, M. (2003) "Culture: A Challenge to Concepts of Normalcy." In F. Walsh (ed.) *Normal Family Processes, Third Edition.* New York: The Guilford Press.

Part I

Art Therapy
and Culture

Chapter 1

Exploring Outside the Box
Art Therapy in Practice
Jennie Kristel

Using the arts as a form of personal expression is certainly not new. For centuries, all the arts have been explored by individuals to communicate with each other and other communities. Creating art has been an expressive way for people to understand the world around them. Using color, form, and symbols allows us to record history and give meaning to the world. To this day, this continues to be true. Art is around us, and integrated into the many parts of our lives, including our homes, our places of worship, our shops, and our landscapes. "It is widely acknowledged that the ability to communicate is an essential human characteristic" (Dalley 1984, p.xi). We paint, write, dance, and give voice to make sense of our world and what is going on within it.

While the idea of self-discovery through art is an old one, the concept of art therapy is relatively new. For years, artists of all kinds have been growing, learning, and expressing themselves through their respective media, but only in the last century or so have the arts as a potential tool for healing been taken more seriously.

Historical Perspective

Clinicians first began to consider the usefulness of the arts for healing in the 1860s. At that time, psychiatrists began experimenting with introducing the arts into "insane" asylums. MacGregor (1989) reflects on the intertwining of art and psychology going back centuries. Hans Prinzhorn, a German psychiatrist, documented artistic productions of those in insane asylums throughout Europe, culminating in *The Artistry of the Mentally Ill*, published in 1922 (Malchiodi 2012). His collection of art, known as the Prinzhorn Collection, is still shown in museums around the world and considered one of the earliest and largest collections of artwork by residents of the asylums. During his own illness, artist Adrian Hill used art as part of his healing while in a tuberculosis sanatorium. This experience obviously left a deep impression on him, as he later practiced as an art therapist and was instrumental in many ways in defining the term "art therapy" in Britain (Hogan 2001).

It is through the work of psychiatrists such as Prinzhorn and others, including Fritz Mohr (1874–1966), that people have begun to look at art created by the mentally ill, known as "Outsider Art" or "Art Brut" (ugly art), as poignant and valuable in its own right. It offers the viewer the opportunity to move from fear of the mentally ill to exploring art as a tool for healing and treatment. In the nineteenth century, Fritz Mohr began using art as an assessment tool. He first documented this in 1906 (Malchiodi 1998).

Sigmund Freud was not an art therapist, but his theories became the base for the evolution of what we now consider art therapy. "His theories of repression, projection, the unconscious and symbolism in dreams identified the importance of visual images to understanding mental illness" (Brooke 2006, p.4). Carl Jung brought his own theories of archetypes, symbolism, universal imagery, and the collective unconscious, as well as his own sense of artistry, to the field of psychotherapy. Jung saw the symbolic as present in everything we do and everywhere we go. He believed that through our understanding of these symbols we understand our internal worlds and ourselves as individuals and communities (Jung and Von Franz 1964).

Art therapy has been found to be deeply beneficial for soldiers returning from war and their families, helping them to deal with the traumas of combat, isolation, and reentry. Sangeeta Prasad (2008) states the need for art therapy in this situation: "Psychiatrists and artists recognized the deep connection between the mind, body and spirit as patients, soldiers, veterans, and prisoners were spontaneously creating art as a form of healing, expression and survival" (p.53).

Art Therapy Today

We are surrounded by art whether we know or think about it. As we walk down a street or through a park we experience art made by both nature and humans. We often connect through artistic mediums—dancing, playing music, or painting. In many countries, the world of the museum has been deeply important as a way of preserving and keeping history through art. For centuries, women have collected in sacred circles to sew, knit, and create. As they gather, they talk about their lives, their families, and the world at large. These circles were often the history keepers.

The arts can transform our lives: they can tell challenging and dark truths, resolve conflict, bring communities together, and express what is often inexpressible in words. We also know that art therapy can be used to promote positive social change and social justice. Art therapy aims to heal individuals and groups and promote positive social change. For many, it is in fact a form of coping with their world, a way to understand the chaos of their minds and of the world around them.

As exemplified here, the expressive arts therapies use visual arts and other modalities like writing, music, drama, and dance to help people of all ages and backgrounds to express themselves in ways that might not be possible with other forms of therapy. Based on the idea that the arts communicate unconscious and even archetypal material, and that images and symbols carry meaning that can transform experience, art therapy involves not only the creation of art but also the reflection and discovery of its meaning. The art-based therapies also allow unconscious material to arise when verbalizing issues is too difficult. Art therapy is typically practiced with individuals, groups, and families and is often very effective with individuals who are limited verbally or speak a different language. Many different kinds of populations benefit from the art therapy process. For example, Kate, a woman in her early 40s, came to art therapy to explore long-standing issues related to childhood sexual and emotional abuse. Kate continues to experience secondary traumatic symptoms related to abuse that she experienced between the ages of 8 and 16.

A person who finds writing an accessible way of communicating, she began keeping a journal and bringing it to therapy with her. She is used to shouldering tremendous responsibility, both in her family and at work, often at her own expense. Kate often found it difficult to say "no" when asked to do things and frequently felt that her family expected her to carry the emotional load within the family system. Through specific art assessments and techniques, Kate found and created a safe place, observed her relationships, using a creative genogram assessment, and used visual art and psychodrama to channel the negative feelings that she still had toward her abuser.

In one session, to help release these feelings, Kate threw wet clay at a target on the wall. Each time she threw the clay, she made statements to the wall, which repesented her abuser, about her feelings toward him. At first, it was challenging for her to put words to what she felt and instead made wordless sounds that described her feelings. She felt this was an easier way to express herself and, in the end, was able to find the right words she wanted to say to him. She stopped the exercise when she felt a shift within herself signaling that she was done and had no more to say to him. Afterward, she took the clay off the wall and shaped it into a new form, signifying a new inner relationship for herself, releasing and excluding the lingering effects of the abuse. Through a process of physically expressing her need and desire for release, she was able to explore her anger and rage at her abuser. In addition, she integrated important aspects of her verbal and nonverbal brain and released the deep emotions that remained a part of her body memory.

Along with painting and other expressive arts media, Kate also explored and got clarity about her own needs—her need for self-expression and for finding personal balance between family and work. In discovering this balance, she was able to understand the links between her experiences of being abused and the resulting feeling of being overly responsible and driven. By externalizing her feelings through a creative process, she was able to increase her self-esteem and let go of her need to be responsible for everyone.

Hannah, 29, a young woman on the autism spectrum (PDD-NOS), came to the art studio to work on improving and increasing her social skills. Hannah was aware that she had trouble moderating her emotions, especially at work, and was hoping to change this. When she arrived, she was not comfortable using art materials. With guidance from the therapist she hesitantly drew with pencils and sometimes pastels. Her lines were rigid and straight in a very linear formation. She also kept a journal where she wrote down positive exchanges with people. While working on her issues of low self-esteem, Hannah's lines became more fluid and less rigid. She began to paint using tempera. In doing this, her lines became more abstract. At the same time, she reported less conflict at work and at home.

Christine is a 12-year-old adopted child living in the United States, originally from Korea. Referred by her school for acting-out behavior, she arrived with her mother very quiet and unwilling to engage. In the first session, she complained of being bored and not caring about what people thought of her. She refused to look at me or her mother and instead stared at the design on the rug where we were sitting. She appeared defensive about her behavior.

In her first session she was asked to do a genogram in order for me to understand her relationships. In her genogram she listed her mother, father, brother (also adopted), and her birth parents whom she had no contact with and had never met. Through art assessments that included psychological testing such as the House–Tree–Person (Buck 1948) and Kinetic Family Drawing, and art therapy assessments such as the PPAT (Person Picking an Apple from a Tree; Gantt in Malchiodi 2012) and the Family Art Evaluation as developed by Kwiatkowska (Kwiatkowska 1978), among others, we looked at how she experienced herself, her attachments, her family life, and the coping and resiliency skills that she felt she had at the time. She was able to explore through a variety of expressive modalities, including psychodrama, keeping a journal, and art, her relationships and her attachments to these relationships. By using the expressive arts, she ultimately was able to understand more of herself, relax rather than being defensive, creatively restructure her primary relationships in a different way, and make needed changes both at school and at home.

There are two ways to approach art within the therapeutic context. The first is art *in* therapy, a means to gain psychological insight, and the second is art *as* therapy, the process of art making.

In art *in* therapy, Margaret Naumburg, who promoted art therapy from a psychoanalytical perspective in the United States, suggested this was the best way to utilize art therapy. The therapist works to guide the client to explore what her/his unconscious is revealing through her/his artwork. The focus then is on the symbolism of the art and exploring the meaning. In this case, the art making is specifically to understand unconscious material—the act of art making is then secondary to the overall process.

In art *as* therapy, the act of creating art is the focus. That is, the activity itself is the primary vehicle to understanding unconscious material, so it is very process based. In this form of therapy we pay careful attention to what the person is consciously or unconsciously expressing through their art and how they are using the materials to make that expression. There may or may not be a verbal exchange, then, within this model.

Edith Kramer focused on using art therapy as healing for children. Her use of art in schools is psychologically based—she very much believed that the act of creating art was therapy in itself. When teachers focus on the artistic quality of the student's work, the act of creation as well as a child's self-esteem is raised as he/she is supported in feeling competent.

It is this type of art as therapy that lends itself well to use in education as a form of expression. Utilizing art therapy with children to explore and assist in self-expression, both in nonclinical settings such as schools and after-school programs and in clinical settings such as hospitals and mental health facilities, is becoming more known and accepted. Art therapy can also be utilized in places like a psychotherapy office, a classroom, or a designated art therapy studio, where the focus is on the creation of the art itself. Whether with individuals, families, or groups, or in larger community settings, art has the power to heal and to profoundly impact one's life. In addition, whether it is clinically based or not, art supports clients in being able to communicate their confusing emotions as well as their interludes of calm; it may also help some individuals to forget symptoms of an illness (Prasad 2008).

Art therapy as a field has grown in the last 50 years. There are multiple undergraduate and graduate programs in art therapy in Canada, Britain, and the United States and ethical guidelines specific to the use of art therapy. The American Art Therapy Association (AATA), the British Association of Art Therapy (BAAT), ANZATA of Australia, and YAHA in Israel offer ways for people to network, develop collaborative projects, and create ethical guidelines. Art therapy assessment tools have been created, some of which have been incorporated into the larger field of mental health in the United States. Guidelines about using these assessments are clearly demarcated in the mental health profession as well as the AATA art therapy ethical guidelines.

Recently, art therapy has been widely recognized for its healing power in coping with traumatic disasters such as the tsunami of 2008 in Southeast Asia or the earthquake in Japan in 2011.

While art therapy began from a Western psychological basis (Malchiodi 2012), it is now being used in countries around the world. For instance, the use of expressive arts as therapy has been growing in Asia and reflects the strong cultural, artistic, and ethnic roots of each country in which it is practiced. Other forms of therapy exist in many of these countries with ethical guidelines of their own that respond to the societal, religious, and individual needs of that country. Because of this, there is a need for continuing education consistent with the cultural needs of each country, as well as an understanding of the ways of Eastern philosophy and spiritual practices to inform clinical practice.

Arts-based therapists are by their very nature multifaceted and encourage others to "think outside the box." Many art therapists look to dreams, creativity studies, and other explorations to help clients access their creativity. In her research of art therapy and myth making, Paula Howie observes (Wilson et al. 2003, p.208):

> In the short history of art therapy, our "cultural" incompatibility between the artist and therapist has helped to define the field. It has certainly led to the synthetic view proposed by Ulman that anything that was to be considered art therapy had to genuinely partake of both art and therapy and to have become part of our art therapy mythological journey. When we call ourselves art therapists, creative arts therapists, or art psychotherapists the question about our multi-sided nature is vividly portrayed.

As art therapists, we test the boundaries and limits of what is artistically possible in a safe and ethical way in order to help individuals access their deeper selves, to calm the places within that are hurting, to change and reframe their understanding of themselves physically, emotionally, and spiritually. We utilize images, narrative, and a deep connection between the therapist and client to empower and strengthen individuals to find their voice, and themselves, in a co-creative journey.

Conclusion

Art therapy is a growing field. There has been a cascade of writing about art therapy. There is also a strong need for more continued research about using the arts in various populations as well as using the arts therapies in other cultures. For practitioners, there continues to be a need to develop more resources, as art therapy grows and spreads around the world. This book is intended to be a resource for people to begin to explore the use of art therapy as well as supporting those who are already working as art therapists and would like more insight about using it in other cultures. Art therapy does not and cannot look the same in all cultures. Attention to nuance and culture-specific ways of living requires us to be particularly careful about how a process such as art therapy, which was developed in the West, can be integrated into non-Western cultures. For instance, in looking at integrating art and therapy in Asia, Kalmanowitz, Potash, and Chan state: "To maintain integrity, art therapy globally needs to maintain its links to its roots in health, the arts and the culture in which it is practised and from which it comes" (2012, p.320).

Art making and art therapy aid all of us to feel supported, increase our understanding of ourselves and our world, make connections within and with others, and transform our lives. Whether in a prison or a school, a mental health setting or a hospital, art therapy has the capacity to reach out and touch from the inside out, to bring people from a place of isolation to a place of community and to a sense of wholeness.

Artists don't make objects. Artists make mythologies.

(Anish Kapoor)

References

Brooke, S. (2006) *Creative Arts Therapy Manual: A Guide to the History, Theoretical Approaches, Assessments and Work with Special Populations, of Art, Play, Dance, Music, Drama and Poetry Therapies.* Springfield, IL: Charles C. Thomas.

Buck, J. N. (1948) "The H-T-P Technique." *Journal of Clinical Psychology 5*, 37–74.

Dalley, T. (1984) *Art as Therapy: An Introduction to the Use of Art as a Therapeutic Technique.* London: Tavistock Publications.

Hogan, S. (2001) *Healing Arts: The History of Art Therapy.* London: Jessica Kingsley Publishers.

Jung, C. and Von Franz, M. L. (eds) (1964) *Man and His Symbols.* London: Aldus Publishers.

Kalmanowitz, D., Potash, J., and Chan, S. (2012) *Art Therapy in Asia: To the Bone or Wrapped in Silk.* London: Jessica Kingsley Publishers.

Kwiatkowska, H. (1978) *Family Therapy and Evaluation Through Art.* Springfield, IL: Charles C. Thomas.

MacGregor, J. M. (1989) *The Discovery of the Art of the Insane.* Princeton, NJ: Princeton University Press.

Malchiodi, C. (1998) *Understanding Children's Drawings.* London: Jessica Kingsley Publishers.

Malchiodi, C. (2012) *Handbook of Art Therapy.* New York: Guilford Press.

Prasad, S. (2008) *Creative Expressions: Say It with Art.* Chennai, India: Author.

Wilson, L., Gantt, L., Howie, P., Rubin, J., and Williams, K. (2003) "Myths of Art Therapy: Guidelines or Straight Jackets." Panel at the 34th American Art Therapy Association Conference, Chicago, IL.

Chapter 2

Why Art Therapy Works

Louis Tinnin and Paula Howie

Art therapy is an intervention which, by its very nature, promotes interactions between a person's verbal and nonverbal minds. This can be a difficult task. The success of art therapy depends on its ability to gain access to a person's nonverbal experiences and to assimilate them into the verbal brain (Gantt and Tinnin 2007). From a brain-based perspective, this means providing access by the nonverbal brain to the contents of the verbal brain. There are three key reasons why this is difficult.

First, the intrinsic brain morphology gives rise to the force of cerebral dominance and inhibition of the nondominant brain hemisphere. Second, the verbal mind is phobic with respect to the traumatic memories held by the nonverbal mind. Third, the verbal mind is averse to the very different kind of thinking and memory of nonverbal cognition.

Intrinsic Issues: The Dual Brain

It is clear that humans have only one head. It is less clear but equally true that early in life we have two brains. These are the right and left hemispheres connected together by a bridge of immature nerves, the corpus callosum. After birth, these brains use the same body, but until the corpus callosum finally matures at around age three (Salamy 1978) there is limited exchange of their thoughts. Once the corpus callosum matures, transmission of thought brings together two distinct three-year-old minds that now must accommodate each other and determine identity and dominance. The nonverbal part of the brain is genetically programmed to be specialized for verbal thought in over 90 percent of people (Geschwind and Galaburda 1986). The verbal cerebral hemisphere takes charge by assuming the identity of this person and relegating the nonverbal hemisphere to the "it" of the brain (Tinnin 1989). For some time, the information traffic is mainly one way, flowing from the dominant verbal brain to the inhibited nonverbal mind. For many people, limited access to the nonverbal mind becomes a lasting aspect of development.

Verbal and Nonverbal Brains

The verbal brain specializes in language. The nonverbal brain specializes in body survival. Both brains think and remember, but the way they do this is very different. The logic of the verbal brain is determined by grammar and is organized around certain grammatical constructs. Nonverbal thought and memory are determined by inherited survival instincts and are not limited by grammatical constructs.

The Verbal Brain

The verbal mind communicates with others and thinks to itself in words. It remembers and retrieves memory in narrative form. Memory storage is a collection of stories. A person's self-reflection is a verbal consciousness that assumes a unique and unitary self. One's consciousness and cognition are built out of six basic verbal constructs.

The Basic Verbal Constructs

The identity of the individual holds the place of *subject* in verbal grammar. Time (past, present, future) holds the place of *tense*, volition stands for the *verb*, while body image or "me" stands as *object*. Reality perception and language complete the verbal constructs, which are further described.

- *Identity* occurs when the verbal brain speaks for the whole person and assumes it to be a unitary agent. This actually is an illusion since it excludes the silent nonverbal brain, which may have a different viewpoint. However, the illusion of unity is a necessary construct to support the person's actions as a unitary agent in the world.

- *Time* is a person's verbal subjective agreement with the culture's objective time in terms of tense (past, present, future), sequence, and duration.

- *Volition* is the shared intention and direction of action necessary for people to work together.

- *Body image* permits members of society to reflect on themselves as objects in relation to others.

- *Reality perception* is essential to differentiate reality from fantasy and to maintain self–other boundaries.

- *Symbolization*, the use of language and symbols, is essential for communication in modern society.

All these important constructs for the "normal" functioning of the individual occur in the verbal brain and allow the individual to be an effective member of his or her society and culture.

The Nonverbal Brain

The nonverbal brain normally has receptive verbal capacity despite poor speech. Its major difference from the verbal brain is the nature of thought rather than the absence of speech. The thought processes of the nonverbal brain lack the basic verbal constructs of unitary identity, objective time, volition, stable body image, reality perception, and language. The nonverbal brain is essentially the animal brain of the person. It is oriented toward survival and responds to threats with body and behavioral reactions that are determined by evolutionarily acquired survival instincts.

There are properties of the nonverbal brain that would be valuable in their own right but which would conflict if active during the usual course of verbal consciousness. These properties are revealed in some conditions involving damage to the left verbal hemisphere. For instance, some individuals labeled *idiot savant* or *autistic savant* show remarkable nonverbal talents, which generally consist of two basic features: a capacity for amazingly fast processing of large amounts of data and a special memory capacity permitting instantaneous display of eidetic imagery from vast durations of time. Commonly, savant individuals can remember, via photographic-type visual images, day-to-day events of years past and can cite the time and place of seemingly trivial incidents. Presumably, these talents would be available to most of us if not for the lifelong inhibition imposed on our nonverbal hemispheres by verbal cerebral dominance.

There is a vast amount of nonverbal function that is necessary to support a balanced or normal personality. This includes specialized nonverbal perception of space, facial recognition, holistic perspective (seeing the forest, not just the trees), emotional tone and attachment, and some aspects of creativity.

Nonverbal Memory

With respect to the storage of information, explicit memory refers to memories that are stored along with some awareness that the memory is stored. Implicit memories are stored without an associated awareness that there is such a memory (Schacter 1985). The explicit/implicit distinction can also be used to refer to encoding rather than storage (explicit = deliberate, voluntary encoding; implicit = involuntary encoding). The distinction can also be used to refer to retrieval. Retrieval of explicit memory is deliberate and effortful, whereas implicit memory emerges spontaneously or when triggered by external stimuli such as in the experience of flashbacks or traumatic experiences. It is the inhibition imposed by the verbal brain's dominance that isolates the nonverbal brain and adds to the aversion issues between the hemispheres. In simple terms, the verbal brain just doesn't speak the language of the nonverbal brain!

Trauma Phobia Issues

Individuals differ in the strength of hemispheric dominance and inhibition. Some artists, shamans, and those suffering from psychotic disorders or dementia are more able to access their nonverbal minds. The everyday inhibition of individuals usually varies and may be diminished by music or during peak emotional experience. Many people are very limited in their voluntary access to the nonverbal. This is particularly true for individuals burdened by memories of a past traumatic experience, who may have no conscious awareness of the event but who may be overwhelmed when these nonconscious memories are triggered (Scaer 2005). The effect of posttraumatic inhibition is *as if* the corpus callosum were shut down. This, in addition to the intrinsic factors, makes it difficult to get the right and left brains together and to achieve the goals of psychotherapy.

Art Therapy as Corpus Callosal Bypass

The terms *verbal* and *nonverbal* carry the same meanings as the conventional terms *conscious* and *unconscious* when referring to psychological function. Many psychotherapies describe their goal to be the bringing together of these functions and making the unconscious conscious. Traditional talk therapy methods involve the therapist interpreting the communication of the patient to reveal the implied unconscious meanings and motivations. Unconscious information may also be detected by observation of the patient's behavior and body states during the treatment session. These methods work best when the patient's disturbance is not severe. The more severely affected individuals and particularly those with posttraumatic conditions or psychosis have difficulty accessing or expressing their feelings and they usually do not respond well to talk therapy.

From the inception of art therapy, Elinor Ulman (Ulman and Dachinger 1975) spoke of the ability of art therapy to bridge the gap between a person's inner and outer worlds. Her early understanding was that the art product carries essential nonverbal information, holding it "out there" for patient and therapist to study. A dual brain model of trauma (Gantt and Tinnin 2009) regards the art product as bridging nonverbal and verbal brains while substituting for a compromised corpus callosum. Art making allows the nonverbal brain to "speak out" in its own language and to bypass the intrinsic, phobic, and avoidant resistances to nonverbal information.

Art Therapy Applied as a Procedure

From a brain-based perspective, art therapy is a method for integrating the thinking and memory of the verbal and nonverbal brains. Art therapy also provides specific procedures for particular treatment objectives. One example is the use of art therapy for trauma processing using the procedure of *graphic narrative trauma processing* (Tinnin, Bills, and Gantt 2002). This procedure applies art therapy's key method of "getting it out there." The "it" is the trauma story, or rather two trauma stories, the verbal narrative and the more important nonverbal story. Getting it out there is an essential part of therapy; it is done in this case by drawing pictures using a process similar to making a storyboard with the verbal story as the script, organized according to the underlying nonverbal plot. The verbal story tells "who, what, where, when, how," and perhaps "why." The nonverbal plot is the ever-present *instinctual trauma response* (ITR) with its crescendo of animal instincts gripping the body first in the *startle*, then the *fight/flight* arousal and the *freeze* shutdown, followed by the depersonalized *altered state of consciousness*, the *automatic obedience* of animal submission, and finally the recovery of verbal consciousness with an instinctual *self-repair*. The drawings are labeled with the appropriate phases of the ITR or as transition pictures between identified phases.

Now the usual art therapy tables are switched. The artist becomes the audience while the therapist becomes the narrator (Figure 2.1). It is the therapist's goal to merge the verbal and nonverbal stories into a single account with a beginning, middle, and end. The artist beholds the sequence of pictures pinned up on the bulletin board while listening to the dramatic narration and has the opportunity to own the entire verbal and nonverbal experience as historical memory and to finally gain closure to the trauma (Tinnin et al. 2002).

Figure 2.1 Graphic narrative processing

Verbal Brain Aversion Issues

Art therapy also increases the two-way information exchange between the verbal and nonverbal brains by reducing the defensive stance of the verbal mind. This requires safe exposure to nonverbal information without undue threat to verbal brain dominance. Art therapy applied as a method of psychotherapy provides a setting and process that secures this safety.

Art Therapy Applied as a Method

Art therapy introduces the verbal brain to the nonverbal one by combining the nonverbal images and the verbal narrative in the art product, which is studied and understood in a safe therapeutic environment. From a brain-based perspective, such an environment provides the patient with sufficient separation from the expressed nonverbal information to permit incorporation of the alien material into a familiar narrative form. The art product makes the nonverbal material available for narrative reconstruction and storage in long-term verbal memory.

Usually, the method of art therapy encourages creative expression in the art product and promotes the artist's understanding of the nonverbal information. The process often involves increasing avowal and owning of the nonverbal by the artist. Success is shown by the disappearance of the artist's aversion to nonverbal information.

Conclusion

Art therapy works because it promotes the communication of the verbal and nonverbal areas of the brain. It makes the contents of the nonverbal mind more available to the verbal mind, bypassing three interhemispheric resistances imposed by, first, the intrinsic brain morphology; second, the phobia for traumatic memory; and last, the verbal aversion to nonverbal mental processes. The art product holds the warded-off nonverbal material "out there" for joint study and processing by therapist and patient.

References

Gantt, L. M. and Tinnin, L.W. (2007) "Intensive trauma therapy of PTSD and dissociation: An outcome study." *The Arts in Psychotherapy 34*, 69–80.

Gantt, L. M. and Tinnin, L. W. (2009) "Support for a neurobiological view of trauma with implications for art therapy." *The Arts in Psychotherapy 36*, 148–153.

Geschwind, N. and Galaburda, A. M. (1986) *Cerebral Lateralization: Biological Mechanisms, Associations, and Pathology.* Cambridge, MA: MIT Press.

Salamy, A. (1978) "Commissural transmission: Maturational changes in humans." *Science 200*, 1409–1411.

Scaer, R. C. (2005) *The Trauma Spectrum: Hidden Wounds and Human Resiliency.* New York: W. W. Norton.

Schacter, D. L. (1985) "Multiple Forms of Memory in Humans and Animals." In N. M. Weinberger, J. L. McGaugh, and G. Lynch (eds) *Memory Systems of the Brain.* New York: Guilford Press.

Tinnin, L. (1989) "The anatomy of the ego." *Psychiatry 52*, 404–409.

Tinnin, L. W., Bills, L. J., and Gantt, L. M. (2002) "Short-Term Treatment of Simple and Complex PTSD." In M. B. Williams and J. G. Sommer Jr. (eds) *Simple and Complex Post-Traumatic Stress Disorder: Strategies for Comprehensive Treatment in Clinical Practice.* Binghamton: The Haworth Press.

Ulman, E. and Dachinger, P. (1975) *Art Therapy in Theory and Practice.* New York: Schocken Books.

Chapter 3

Art Therapy Assessments with Diverse Populations

Donna Betts

With the globalization of art therapy in an increasingly diverse world, art therapists are using their tools and techniques to address a variety of client needs (Betts, in press). Thus, many of the assessments familiar to art therapists in North America and internationally are being used in cross-cultural and multicultural contexts. Art therapists often approach this with consideration of the need for these tools to be adapted in order to best serve their diverse clients. This is reflected in the present chapter, which highlights the excellent and responsible work that has been undertaken in this area. I discuss the Face Stimulus Assessment (FSA) in the United States and South Korea and present anecdotes from the work of Sarah Deaver with Human Figure Drawings; Barry Cohen and Anne Mills on the Diagnostic Drawing Series; Janna Mulholland on the Person Picking an Apple from a Tree assessment; Myra Levick on the Levick Emotional and Cognitive Art Therapy Assessment; and Simone Alter-Muri on children's drawings.

Face Stimulus Assessment

Early in my career as an art therapist, I worked at a school in Washington, DC that was populated primarily by black American children and adolescents with multiple disabilities. I quickly found that while my status as an immigrant to the United States sensitized me to the experiences of people from other countries, I was nonetheless visibly different from the people with whom I had been hired to work. As a Canadian white woman, I had to draw on my life experiences and knowledge gained from multicultural trainings to work successfully in this setting.

To establish my caseload of students, I relied on a range of art therapy assessments, which I used initially to determine student eligibility for art therapy services. I worked with the clinic team and developed a treatment plan for each of my clients. Since my students had individualized education plans (IEPs), assessment also became important in the establishment of measurable treatment goals and objectives that could be tracked on a quarterly basis. To this end, I tried out a variety of established art therapy and art-based assessments. However, my clients who had severe mental retardation or developmental delay typically failed to respond to a basic directive, such as "draw a person" (Betts 2003).

Because my clients with cognitive impairments had difficulty following verbal directions, eventually I found it necessary to develop a specific method of evaluating their strengths and abilities (Betts 2003). Over time and following a few piloted versions, the FSA came about. The FSA is a series of three stimulus images presented sequentially to the client, who is asked to simply "use the markers and this piece of paper" (p.81). FSA Picture 1 consists of a standardized image of a human face; Picture 2 contains an outline of the face only; and Picture 3 is a blank page.

In my effort to be culturally sensitive, and to fairly assess my clients, I standardized the FSA with a set of eight Crayola regular markers and a set of eight Crayola multicultural markers (Betts 2003). During this process, I encountered difficulty in making a gender neutral, age neutral, and multiculturally representative face stimulus. In creating the standardized face stimulus, I consulted my Asian, black, and white colleagues to solicit their input regarding the facial features. The resulting face, although imperfect, reflects my best effort to represent various ethnic groups.

Although developed over a decade ago, efforts to validate the FSA and the FSA Rating Manual continue. Development of a valid and reliable assessment instrument takes a lifetime. An important step in the validation process of an instrument includes the establishment of normative data (or "norms"). In other words, in order to know what qualities in a drawing are not typical, it is helpful to know what typical or "normal" qualities look like. For instance, Figure 3.1 shows FSA Picture 2 completed by a normative (nonclinical) 46-year-old Korean woman in South Korea. She identified as an "artist" and had college-level art training. On the qualitative questionnaire (vital for gathering more complete information about an individual; see Betts 2012), she stated that this drawing was a self-portrait and commented, "I used yellow and orange because the person in the image is Asian. I wanted the image to look warm." In contrast, Figure 3.2 is an FSA Picture 2 drawn by a "non-normative" 21-year-old Caucasian man in the United States with autism. He was not able to provide a verbal response to his image.

Hamilton and Betts (Hamilton 2008) attempted validation of the FSA on a normative population with a convenience sample of 30 participants enrolled at a small Midwestern university in the United States. The participant groups consisted of 6 men and 24 women, ages 19 to 28. This sample contributed to the establishment of norms for further validity and reliability studies of the FSA rating system. To develop this rating system, we adapted scales from Gantt and Tabone's (1998) *Formal Elements Art Therapy Scale: The Rating Manual* (FEATS). The findings identified statistically significant results supporting the use of the modified FEATS with FSA Drawing 2. FEATS scales that differentiated the most between this normative population and clients with developmental disabilities included color fit; logic; realism; developmental level; details of objects and environment; line quality; and perseveration.

*Figure 3.1 FSA Picture 2 completed by a normative (nonclinical)
46-year-old Korean woman in South Korea*

Illustrated in the color insert

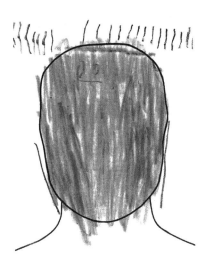

*Figure 3.2 FSA Picture 2 drawn by a "non-normative"
21-year-old Caucasian man with autism in the United States*

Illustrated in the color insert

Attempts to validate the FSA with cross-cultural groups include two South Korean samples: one study examined the FSAs of a few hundred art therapy students and practitioners (Mattson and Betts, in press), and another explored the FSAs of 240 elementary school-aged normative children, 152 children with hearing impairments, and 144 children with developmental disabilities (Kim 2010).

Human Figure Drawings

In this section, Sarah Deaver, PhD, ATR-BC, and Tess Suhyun Lee, MS, describe their work with Human Figure Drawings (HFDs) in the United States and Asia.

We, along with faculty at the Graduate Art Therapy Program at Eastern Virginia Medical School (EVMS) in Norfolk, Virginia, USA, recognized a significant problem inherent in art therapy assessment. Without contemporary examples of "normal" persons' drawings against which to compare our clients' drawings, making accurate diagnostic assumptions and planning appropriate art therapy treatment approaches was impossible (Deaver 2009, in press). To address this problem, we embarked upon a multi-year project to establish a database of normative drawings, and we started with HFDs drawn by children living in our area of southeastern Virginia.

Our collection procedure involved art therapists going to local elementary schools to collect HFDs from typical students, using standardized materials (pencils with erasers, felt-tipped markers, oil pastels, and 9" × 12" [approximately 23cm × 30cm] gray paper). We amassed two groups of HFDs: 151 from a group of younger children whose average age was about 7.5 years and 316 from a group of older children whose average age was about 9.5 years. In order to quantify aspects of the drawings, we collaborated with Linda Gantt, PhD, ATR-BC, HLM (Gantt 2001), to adapt five of the FEATS scales for use with HFDs. These scales are color prominence, color fit, space, developmental level according to Lowenfeld (Lowenfeld and Brittain 1987), and details of objects and environment. We trained a rater on the use of our scales and the rater scored all 467 HFDs. Using this method, we were able to determine that the older and younger groups' drawings were different from one another in statistically significant ways. Younger children used more color and space, and included more details, than the older children. On the other hand, the older children scored higher on the developmental-level scale than the younger children. Boys and girls differed significantly on color fit; girls were more realistic in their use of color than boys. These results have informed us regarding characteristics of HFDs drawn by "normal" or typical American children in the age ranges we studied.

In their thesis research, several students in our program have compared HFDs drawn by children in non-Western cultures to the HFDs in our database. They were interested in the impact of culture on children's drawings and in whether or not a Western-style art therapy assessment is applicable in non-Western cultures. One such student is Tess Suhyun Lee (2011), who gathered 23 HFDs, drawn with our standardized art materials in response to our standardized instructions, from students attending a school in Gyeonggi-do, South Korea. The drawings were scored by trained raters and statistically compared to 23 age- and gender-matched drawings in the EVMS database. On all five of the scales, the Korean children's scores were significantly lower than those of the American children. The Korean children's HFDs were less colorful, less realistically colored, smaller, lower developmentally, and had fewer details than the HFDs drawn by American children in the database. Since both the Koreans and Americans who drew the HFDs were normal, typically developing, nonclinical children, how can we understand these differences?

Based on her knowledge of the literature and of her home culture, Tess (Lee 2011) offered some explanations regarding the impact of Korean social culture, educational practices, and artistic traditions upon children's drawings. Regarding the smaller size of the figures depicted in Korean children's HFDs compared to the American sample, instead of interpreting this difference negatively, as indicative of shyness associated with low self-esteem and feelings of inadequacy (Hammer 1980; Koppitz 1968), Tess explained that in Asian cultures shyness is a prized characteristic of children, indicative of fitting well within a society that values modesty and humility (Lee and Park 2011). As for the lack of environment depicted in most of the Korean children's HFDs as opposed to the full environments depicted in the American children's HFDs, Tess explained that Korean children's ingrained respect for those in authority (Yum 2000) likely resulted in their strict adherence to the directive to "draw a person from head to toe." They did just that: they drew only a person, with no surrounding environmental details. Finally, in attempting to understand the Korean children's lower scores on the developmental-level scale, Tess pointed to the differing artistic traditions of the United States and Korea. The Korean children's drawings frequently lacked the baselines and horizon lines that characterize the Western artistic construct of perspective, which was measured by the developmental-level scale of our scoring system. There were further differences between the two sets of HFDs that were also associated with cultural differences. For example, likely due to the greater exposure of Korean children to media including cartoons, the Korean children's HFDs were often drawn in a Manhwa animation style.

The most important implication of Tess's research (Lee 2011) is that, as art therapy spreads throughout Asia (Kalmanowitz, Potash, and Chan 2012), there is a need to establish normative samples of drawings by Asian children and adults. The scales that were used to rate the drawings in the EVMS HFD database were based on Western culture and constructs, and were not applicable when evaluating a small normative sample of Korean children's HFDs. If these scales were used for assessment with Asian children, and interpreted based on American and European norms, inferences would not be valid or useful. When establishing normative samples of Asian people's drawings, social, educational, and artistic traditions must be considered in developing valid art therapy assessment approaches.

The Diagnostic Drawing Series

Barry Cohen, MA, ATR-BC, Anne Mills, MA, ATR-BC, LPC, and Yuriko Yamashita Ichiki, PhD, address cross-cultural applications of the Diagnostic Drawing Series (DDS) (Cohen, Hammer, and Singer 1988), a standardized three-picture art interview.

The DDS is made with a 12-color pack of square, soft chalk pastels on 18" × 24" 60–70 lb. white drawing paper (Cohen 1985). Each of the three pictures in the series has its own piece of paper and specific directive and is rated using the DDS Rating Guide (Cohen 1986/1994/2012) for the presence of 23 descriptive, primarily structural criteria. They comprise a clearly defined common language for describing any therapeutic artwork. Using DDS rating criteria leads raters toward an empirical (rather than intuitive) understanding of the art.

Over the years, basic DDS directions have been translated into Arabic, Dutch, French, German, Japanese, Latvian, and Spanish. The DDS has been used clinically worldwide since the 1980s, and research studies have been conducted primarily in Japan, Canada, and the Netherlands. In the early to mid-1990s, Cohen collaborated with Dutch psychiatrist Olga Heitmajer on the use of the DDS with patients diagnosed with dissociative disorders. Central to their work was the controversy that multiple personality disorder (MPD; now Dissociative Identity Disorder, or DID) was an American diagnosis, induced by clinicians in highly suggestible female clients. When Heitmajer delivered her portfolio of DDSs by clients with MPD, supported by reliable Dissociative Experiences Scale (DES) scores, it became immediately apparent that not only did MPD exist in the Netherlands, but the art expressions of these people, as seen in the standardized examples of the DDS, were nearly identical to those by Americans diagnosed with DID. This concordance was due to *isomorphism*, which suggests that artwork is an external manifestation of an internal (psychological) state.

In 1994, Yuriko Yamashita Ichiki and Anne Mills compared the DDSs of 18 Japanese patients diagnosed with schizophrenia with American DDS schizophrenia research. The American research was based on DDSs from across the country; the Japanese sample was from one hospital that happened to offer Naikan therapy, an indigenous Japanese psychotherapy. Naikan therapy is characterized by isolating the patient in a dwelling or behind a screen for seven days. Food is brought to the patient without distraction or interaction. The patient is supposed to contemplate his or her conduct toward family members (especially parents), and to weigh his or her gratitude and responsibility. What is discovered through reflection can be written down or told to a guide who listens.

Mills reviewed the Japanese DDSs from slides, not the original art, and considered preexisting studies (Cohen et al. 1988, 1990; Kress 1992; Mills 1989; Ricca 1992; Sobol and Cox 1992). Based on this, Mills reported to Ichiki that the

DDSs of some people in the Japanese sample showed a graphic profile other than schizophrenia. Mills observed that the structural criteria of their DDSs resembled that of DDSs by people with trauma-related disorders (i.e., borderline personality disorder, post-traumatic stress disorder, DID).

At that time in Japan, many mental health professionals considered child sexual abuse to be relatively rare and so did not perceive its potential connection to symptoms in later life. Therefore, post-traumatic disorders, especially controversial diagnoses like dissociative disorders, were not recognized within the psychiatric population. (This has since changed.) Mills was proposing diagnoses that were not used much in Japan.

Mills pulled out the slides of the DDSs of patients she believed had post-traumatic disorders. Subsequently, it was noticed by Japanese colleagues that Mills-selected patients behaved differently from others in Naikan therapy. It was quite impressive to the Japanese that someone had predicted that just by reviewing slides of DDSs. Their point of view was that some patients with schizophrenia had done better than other patients with schizophrenia.

The alternate point of view, based on the DDS and its research, was that the Mills-selected patients performed differently because they did not have schizophrenia. The patients' responses, given the types of disorders more likely to benefit from the Naikan approach, supported the deduction that they had illnesses other than schizophrenia.

Do art therapists have the authority to make diagnostic decisions such as these that would change the lives of countless people in psychiatric treatment and impact health care budgets worldwide? In many cases, no. But do they have the capability? These cross-cultural vignettes show that art therapists familiar with DDS data were able to identify and distinguish among difficult-to-recognize psychiatric disorders using drawings (or slides) alone. Thanks to the universal language of art, combined with a structural approach to rating based on the principle of isomorphism, this three-picture art interview crafted from carefully selected art media and tasks, featuring a standardized collection protocol and research methodology, offers those trained in its use a uniquely valuable tool that can be administered for valid and reliable assessment, effective treatment planning, and paradigm-changing research with clients from any culture.

The Person Picking an Apple from a Tree

Janna Mulholland, MA, piloted an art therapy program at an English medium pre-nursery and elementary school in Southern India; this is a review of her experience.

The children with whom I worked spoke a variety of languages and came from mixed socioeconomic backgrounds. Teachers recommended students with behavioral difficulties to attend art therapy. Primarily, I worked with younger children around five years of age, with varying levels of English abilities. I began sessions with the "Person Picking an Apple from a Tree" (PPAT) assessment drawing to establish a clinical baseline (see Figure 3.3). However, I came to realize that I had no idea whether these PPATs were different from those of normative children in India. Thus, I collected drawings from other students not recommended for art therapy.

Figure 3.3 Clinical "Person Picking an Apple from a Tree" (PPAT)
by a five-year-old Asian Indian boy with possible ADHD
Illustrated in the color insert

The PPAT is a drawing created in response to the directive "draw a person picking an apple from a tree," on a 12" × 18" white drawing paper, using the 12-pack scented Sanford Mr. Sketch watercolor felt-tip markers. The drawing is rated with FEATS (FEATS; Gantt and Tabone 1998) and the Content Tally Sheet. The FEATS is a 14-item, 5-point rating scale and is used to measure formal elements such as line quality, logic, and realism. The Content Tally Sheet measures the presence or absence of certain details, such as colors used and extraneous details. The FEATS was created from clinical observations, literature review, and psychological symptoms from the *Diagnostic and Statistical Manual* (American Psychiatric Association 1994), with particular focus on major depression, bipolar disorder, schizophrenia, and organic mental disorders.

I chose to use the PPAT for multiple reasons. It has simple instructions that can be conducted in a short time frame, has versatility to different settings, can address a variety of issues with one assessment, and has been researched with adults and children from both client and normative samples. It also focuses on the formal elements of drawing (how the drawing is created) rather than the content (what is depicted in the drawing). This relieves some problems with cross-cultural studies where assessment is based solely on content by avoiding misinterpretation of culturally bound forms or symbols (Gantt and Tabone 2003), and with assessments that rely on interview techniques for rating and thus increase language barriers.

Language was the first difficulty I encountered. To be more culturally sensitive the directive was sometimes changed, substituting "fruit" for the word "apple," an appropriate modification noted by Gantt and Tabone (1998, p.16), and the directive was translated when possible. Administering an assessment with a simple specific directive differentiated between clients with limited English comprehension and those with behavioral issues who would not follow the directive. The lack of comprehension often went unnoticed in the classroom where the students picked up on cues from peers or received some explanations in their native language as well as English.

The second aspect I noticed when conducting this assessment within the South Indian culture was the standardized Mr. Sketch markers. From the children's excitement at the materials, it appeared that the majority of the children were rarely allowed to use markers. Materials in India are often rationed due to expense or scarcity, which may be the basis for the children's reactions. Mr. Sketch markers seem to have a higher liquid content than local varieties as children either commented that the markers to which they were accustomed were like paints or required heavy pressure. Some children asked if they might color in their forms, another sign of learned rationing of supplies, and demonstrating that how the children draw may be materially and culturally specific. It may also affect scores on the FEATS prominence of color scale. It is unknown whether the use of novel materials affected the drawings.

Art is taught in a more directive manner in South India and I found the children usually expected instructions and struggled with nondirected work. Challenges may have been encountered more frequently with open-ended art tasks, especially in the early stages of art therapy and because art in India is specifically defined. I noticed that most of the normative students in my sample asked if they could include content in addition to a person, apple, and tree. Conversely, the non-normative clients took the directive literally and did not include additional details.

Along with noting the English deficiencies and the differences in drawing content, the PPAT also revealed marked differences in drawing styles between my clients and the normative sample, which generally scored higher on the FEATS scale. This may indicate the appropriateness of this assessment in other cultures; however, further research and comparisons are necessary.

The Levick Emotional and Cognitive Art Therapy Assessment

Myra Levick, PhD, ATR-BC, HLM, creator of the LECATA (Levick 1983), summarizes her extensive research on the tool's multicultural implications.

The LECATA is administered on an individual basis only, to persons ages 3 and up. It is not recommended for use in a group setting but may be used with families. This assessment consists of five drawings: a free drawing and a story about the image (see Figure 3.4); a portrait of the self at present age; a scribble drawing with one color and development of the scribble using other colors; a drawing of a place that is important; and a drawing of the family.

*Figure 3.4 The first LECATA task, a free drawing and a story, created
by a first-grade Hispanic female aged 6 years, 11 months*

Illustrated in the color insert

*Her figures are grounded and her story is coherent, placing her at 7.5–8.5 years in the
cognitive domain. Her image indicates she is identifying with her mother (the larger figure),
placing her at 6.5–7.5 years in the emotional domain. Her overall average score for all five
tasks is 7.5 in the cognitive domain and 6.5 in the emotional domain. She is performing a year
above her chronological age cognitively and is age appropriate in the emotional domain.*

In the administrative manual, administration instructions are clearly defined (Levick 2009). It is important to use the standardized materials: 12" × 18" white drawing paper and a box of Craypas pastels with 16 sticks. A script for each task is provided and includes anticipated questions and suggested answers. The LECATA scores normal cognitive and emotional development, and a score sheet is provided for each task identifying age-appropriate developmental cognitive and emotional indicators. The performance age is noted on each score sheet and totaled and averaged on a work sheet included. The resulting averages of the two domains are compared to the chronological age of the subject.

Janet Bush, Founder and Director of the Clinical Art Therapy Program at the Miami-Dade County Public Schools, inspired the LECATA's development. In 1986, Bush, with school administration support, invited me to work with 11 art therapists and design a single art therapy assessment based on my work (Levick 1983). Miami has had a diverse population since the late 1900s, with Hispanics and African-Americans comprising the majority of inhabitants (see Table 3.1).

Table 3.1 The Levick Emotional and Cognitive Art Therapy
Assessment (LECATA): Demographic data of ethnic percentages

	Caucasian	African-American	Hispanic	Asian Pacific Islander	Native American
2000 National Census	60.4%	13.5%	16.8%	6.5%	2.8%
2000 Levick Study	66.6%	11.7%	14.16%	6.3%	0.6%
2012 Miami-Dade County Public Schools	8.3%	23.9%	65.9%	1.2%	0.6%

Sources: Internet publication by Miami-Dade County Public Schools; Levick (2009)

In 1998 I determined it timely to pursue normative research on the LECATA, given the skewed minority population in Miami-Dade County. I obtained permission to conduct this study in the Palm Beach County School District, considered to be more consistent with our national demographic percentages (Table 3.1). The LECATA was administered to 332 normal children, grades K through 6. Results are presented in Levick (2009).

The LECATA is the only art therapy assessment that scores developmental milestones manifested in graphic images in the cognitive and emotional domains. In over 20 years of use by many art therapists in the United States and abroad, there has been no evidence in cultural differences inhibiting the use or outcome of this assessment. The ability to provide age equivalency scores based on cognitive and emotional development allows art therapists to communicate across professional language barriers, which underscores the important contributions of art therapists in school settings (Levick and Siegel, in press).

In my experiences with the LECATA, neither I nor my assistants encountered any problems with students from an ethnic minority group. One principal had the LECATA consent forms printed in Creole, and one Haitian child I tested required an interpreter. She had no difficulty completing the five tasks in less than an hour. These examples highlight the applicability of the LECATA across multicultural contexts.

Children's Drawings

Simone Alter-Muri, Ed. D, ATR-BC, ATCS, LMHC, has conducted large-scale research to develop baselines on normative children's drawings across cultures, which she discusses below.

My study applies Lowenfeld's stages of art development to a global sample of children's drawings to determine whether or not these stages relate to chronological age (Alter-Muri 2012). The study also examines whether gender differences occur in the drawings of boys and girls ages 6 to 12. Art collected from the following countries was examined: Denmark, France, Germany, Italy, Korea, Lithuania, Malawi, Mexico, Nigeria, Somalia, Sweden, Switzerland, and the United States. The project is longitudinal and 715 drawings have been studied to date.

Participants were given a piece of white paper approximately 12" × 14" and a drawing instrument commonly used in the given cultural setting, such as crayons or colored pencils. Children were then asked to create one picture of a person or persons in an environment. A maximum of 20 minutes was allotted. Subjects were asked not to copy from other children.

The data collector then noted country of origin, age, and gender of the child. The sample was analyzed by determining the variables described in Lowenfeld's scale of artistic development as well as graphic indicators developed for the research project. The research chart designed for this study included symbols described as common images in gender studies as described in the literature. The chart looked at the variables of (1) gender and age of participants; (2) the stage of Lowenfeld artistic development to which the art corresponds; (3) whether the art contained over 50 percent of warm, cool, or both warm and cool colors; and (4) the inclusion or noninclusion of the following graphic indicators: a ground line, animals, weapons, vehicles of transportation, and sports. The collected data were then analyzed with the chi square statistic.

One data set was collected from children attending an after-school art class in Puerto Vallarta, Mexico. These children had some background in creating art as part of the school curriculum. The drawing assessment helped to develop an increased sense of community and dialogue among the children as they considered their own drawings as well as drawings done by their classmates and discussed how those images related to their lives.

Another collection of children's art was gathered at an elementary school in Vilnius, Lithuania, by a school teacher trained in the data collection procedure. After I analyzed the data, the teacher was able to use the analysis of the children's developmental stages reflected in their art in social, emotional, and academic realms. Not only did the data collection increase the depth of the study, but the test administrators also found the information to be a useful tool in the classroom.

This study contributes to the work of Betts (2006) and Deaver (2009) and to research I conducted (Alter-Muri 2002), addressing the need for normative assessment data. The present study expands on the current research, taking a new, international perspective and examining novel angles and variables in greater depth. Statistically significant findings indicated that differences exist between the drawings of boys and girls, such as that boys have a higher inclusion of weapons, vehicles, and sports in their art. Although not statistically significant, girls were found to have a greater inclusion of animals and insects. Thus, my current work adds unique data about gender and age (Alter-Muri 2012). This includes the creation of a new gender-based index for understanding differences in children's art. Furthermore, the data reveal that Lowenfeld's stages of art development correlated to chronological age are still relevant today. This information can aid in increasing art therapists' sensitivity to cultural similarities and differences in children's art.

Conclusion

Art therapists are employing a variety of tools and methods in cross-cultural and multicultural clinical and research contexts, with interesting findings and implications. While the anecdotes included in this chapter reflect the increasing importance of the need for culturally sensitive approaches in art therapy, they also reveal that this is just the beginning. With increased worldwide communication, art therapists should be able to improve their cultural competence with regard to assessment of clients. Internet-based resources can contribute to this process, such as the International Art Therapy Research Database (IATRD; www.arttherapyresearch. com). Further development of resources such as the IATRD, contributing to global information sharing among art therapists, should aid in facilitating the increasingly fair use of our tools and approaches with diverse peoples.

References

Alter-Muri, S. (2002) "Viktor Lowenfeld revisited: A review of Lowenfeld's preschematic, schematic and gang age stages." *American Journal of Art Therapy 40*, 3, 70–92.

Alter-Muri, S. (2012) *Children's art development and gender differences: An international study.* Manuscript in preparation.

American Psychiatric Association (1994) *Diagnostic and Statistical Manual of Mental Disorders, Fourth Edition.* Washington, DC: American Psychiatric Association.

Betts, D. J. (2003) "Developing a projective drawing test: Experiences with the Face Stimulus Assessment (FSA)." *Art Therapy: Journal of the American Art Therapy Association 20*, 2, 77–82.

Betts, D. J. (2006) "Art therapy assessments and rating instruments: Do they measure up?" *The Arts in Psychotherapy: An International Journal 33*, 5, 371–472.

Betts, D. J. (2012) "Positive Art Therapy Assessment: Looking towards Positive Psychology for New Directions in the Art Therapy Evaluation Process." In A. Gilroy, R. Tipple, and C. Brown (eds) *Assessment in Art Therapy*. New York: Routledge.

Betts, D. J. (in press) "A review of the principles for culturally appropriate art therapy assessment tools." *Art Therapy: Journal of the America Art Therapy Association.*

Cohen, B. M. (1985) *The Diagnostic Drawing Series Handbook.* Self-published handbook, Alexandria, VA.

Cohen, B. M. (1986/1994/2012) *The Diagnostic Drawing Series Rating Guide.* Self-published manual, Alexandria, VA.

Cohen, B. M., Cox, C. T., Mills, A., and Sobol, B. (Speakers) (1990) *Art by Abuse Survivors: A Lifecycle* (Cassette No. 569-05-90). Alexandria, VA: Audio Transcripts.

Cohen, B. M., Hammer, J. S., and Singer, S. (1988) "The Diagnostic Drawing Series: A systematic approach to art therapy evaluation and research." *The Arts in Psychotherapy 15*, 1, 11–21.

Deaver, S. (2009) "A normative study of children's drawings: Preliminary research findings." *Art Therapy: Journal of the American Art Therapy Association 26*, 1, 4–11.

Deaver, S. (in press) "The Need for Norms in Formal Art Therapy Assessment." In D. Gussak and M. Rosal (eds) *The Wiley-Blackwell Handbook of Art Therapy*. Hoboken, NJ: John Wiley and Sons.

Gantt, L. (2001) "The Formal Elements Art Therapy Scale: A measurement system for global variables in art." *Art Therapy: Journal of the American Art Therapy Association 18*, 1, 50–55.

Gantt, L. and Tabone, C. (1998) *The Formal Elements Art Therapy Scale: The Rating Manual.* Morgantown, WV: Gargoyle Press.

Gantt, L. and Tabone, C. (2003) "The Formal Elements Art Therapy Scale and 'Draw a Person Picking an Apple from a Tree.'" In C. A. Malchiodi (ed.) *Handbook of Art Therapy*. New York: The Guilford Press.

Hamilton, M. (2008) *Developing a standardized rating system for the Face Stimulus Assessment (FSA) using 12 scales adapted from the Formal Elements Art Therapy Scale (FEATS).* Unpublished master's thesis, Avila University, Kansas City, MO.

Hammer, E. (1980) *The Clinical Application of Projective Drawings.* Springfield, IL: Charles C. Thomas.

Kalmanowitz, D., Potash, J. S., and Chan, S. M. (eds) (2012) *Art Therapy in Asia: To the Bone or Wrapped in Silk*. London: Jessica Kingsley Publishers.

Kim, S. R. (2010) *A study on development of FSA evaluation standard and its validation.* Unpublished doctoral dissertation, Yeungnam University, Daegu, South Korea.

Koppitz, E. (1968) *Psychological Evaluation of Children's Human Figure Drawings.* New York: Grune and Stratton.

Kress, T. (Speaker) (1992) *The Diagnostic Drawing Series and Multiple Personality Disorder: A Validation Study* (Cassette No. 55). Denver, CO: National Audio Video.

Lee, H. E. and Park, H. S. (2011) "Why Koreans are more likely to favor 'apology,' while Americans are more likely to favor 'thank you.'" *Human Communication Research 37*, 1, 125–146.

Lee, T. S. (2011) *A cross-cultural study of Korean and American children's Human Figure Drawings.* Unpublished master's thesis, Eastern Virginia Medical School, Norfolk, VA.

Levick, M. (1983) *They Could Not Talk and So They Drew: Children's Styles of Coping and Thinking.* Springfield, IL: Charles C. Thomas.

Levick, M. (2009) *Levick Emotional and Cognitive Art Therapy Assessment: A Normative Study.* Bloomington, IN: AuthorHouse.

Levick, M. and Siegel, C. (in press) "Levick Assessment." In D. E. Gussak and M. L. Rosal (eds) *The Wiley-Blackwell Handbook of Art Therapy.* Hoboken, NJ: Wiley-Blackwell.

Lowenfeld, V. and Brittain, W. (1987) *Creative and Mental Growth, Eighth Edition.* New York: Macmillan.

Mattson, D. and Betts, D. (in press) "The Face Stimulus Assessment." In D. E. Gussak and M. L. Rosal (eds) *The Wiley-Blackwell Handbook of Art Therapy.* Hoboken, NJ: John Wiley and Sons.

Mills, A. (1989) *A statistical study of the formal aspects of the Diagnostic Drawing Series of borderline personality disordered patients, and its context in contemporary art therapy.* Unpublished master's thesis, Concordia University, Montreal.

Ricca, D. (1992) *Utilizing the Diagnostic Drawing Series as a tool in differentiating a diagnosis between multiple personality disorder and schizophrenia.* Unpublished master's thesis, Hahnemann University, Philadelphia, PA.

Sobol, B. and Cox, C. T. (Speakers) (1992) *Art and Childhood Dissociation: Research with Sexually Abused Children* (Cassette No. 59). Denver, CO: National Audio Video.

Yum, Y. (2000) *Cross-cultural Comparisons of Links among Relational Maintenance Behaviors, Exchange Factors, and Individual Characteristics in Close Relationships.* Pennsylvania State University, University Park, PA. (Unpublished doctoral dissertation.)

Chapter 4

Ethics in Art Therapy

Audrey Di Maria Nankervis

Introduction

Many years ago, there was an art therapist who wished to videotape the life of an art therapy group, in order to create a film to be used in training art therapy students. With that goal in mind, she asked the permission of the director of the agency at which she worked and, given the go-ahead, set about interviewing prospective members. She informed the candidates that each meeting of this particular art therapy group would be videotaped for the purpose of creating an educational film, but advised them that if they did not want to participate in a group that would be taped, they would be able to join another art therapy group. After much discussion with the interviewees, several of them decided to become members of the art therapy group whose sessions would be taped. Detailed consent forms were presented, discussed, and signed and the group began.

Upon termination of the group two years later, the art therapist began the process of editing the videotape. After months of editing, the film was completed. She decided to invite all the members of the group to view the film. After the film was shown, she produced a new set of consent forms and asked the members of the former group to sign them only if they felt comfortable with the way in which they were portrayed in the film. The original consent forms would be null and void. A few former group members decided not to sign the new consent forms and the art therapist spent the next few months editing their bodies, their voices, and their artwork out of the film.

This is ethical practice. Many of us would have clasped the clients' original signed release forms to our chests and been in a legally defensible position to produce the film. This art therapist went further—by not simply subscribing to the letter of the law (be it federal or state, licensing board, or credentialing body), but by conducting herself according to the spirit of the law. And what is the spirit, or intent, of the law? To put our clients' interest above our self-interest.

The art therapist, whose story has stayed with me since I heard it 30 years ago, is Judy Rubin, PhD, ATR-BC, who went on to become President and Honorary Life Member of the American Art Therapy Association (AATA), a psychoanalyst, and the author of some of the most influential books in our field.

Becoming an Ethical Art Therapist

I was pondering how best to convey the complex and ever-evolving concept of ethical practice in the field of mental health when I came across a drawing made by our four-year-old granddaughter Alannah to celebrate her Poppi Ken's 60th birthday (see Figure 4.1). It shows a smiling Alannah and her grandfather standing above a baseline of flowers (complete with bee) while the bands of a rainbow arch protectively over the pair. It brought to mind the components of the therapeutic alliance within which the work of therapy takes place: the foundation, the framework, and the relationship.

Figure 4.1 "Alannah and Poppi Ken in the garden…" (detail) by Alannah McLeod, aged 4

The Foundation

Whether the client is an individual or part of a couple, a family, or a group, the therapeutic relationship should be grounded in respect and empathy for the client and an appreciation of the dignity, the capability, and the autonomy of the client. With reference to the latter, regard for the right of a client (of whatever age) to make decisions for himself or herself can be seen in the encouragement of client involvement in all phases of treatment—from the initial therapeutic contact to the setting of goals and the provision of choices regarding media, subject matter, and the role of words in the sessions, through the termination phase of therapy.

The Framework

The overarching principles and standards that govern our work as art therapists form a supportive structure of protection for the client and direction for the therapist throughout the course of treatment. They stem from several sources, which might include (but are not limited to) the following.

Federal Laws

Health Insurance Portability and Accountability Act

An example of a federal law with which all health care providers in the United States who deal with governmental or commercial health insurance plans must comply is the Health Insurance Portability and Accountability Act (HIPAA; U.S. DoHHS 2004). Among other things, the provisions of this law ensure that protected health information (i.e., personally identifiable information related to an individual's past, present, or future physical or mental condition, provision of health care, or payment for health care) is kept private.

Since, as the saying goes, ignorance of the law is no excuse, it is the responsibility of the mental health professional to be aware of the parts of the law that affect his or her job and to practice them. For example, for art therapists, the duty to safeguard patient information might extend beyond taking care not to disclose (in person, over the phone, or by electronic means) identifying information without the necessary signed release forms, to altering the way in which they store and/or exhibit their clients' artwork in order to ensure confidentiality.

While, in most cases, parents or legal guardians have the right and responsibility to sign "permission to treat" forms or "release of information" forms for their minor children, it is important to be aware of exceptions.

Federal Substance Abuse Confidentiality Laws

Since federal regulations govern the confidentiality of alcohol and drug abuse patient records maintained in connection with the performance of any federally assisted alcohol and drug abuse program (U.S. DoHHS 1996), then:

> [i]f a minor patient acting alone has the legal capacity under the applicable State law to apply for and obtain alcohol or drug abuse treatment, any written consent for disclosure authorized under subpart C of these regulations [i.e., disclosures to prevent multiple enrollments in detoxification and maintenance treatment programs; disclosures to elements of the criminal justice system which have referred patients] may be given only by the minor patient. This restriction includes, but is not limited to, any disclosure of patient identifying information to the parent or guardian or a minor patient for the purpose of obtaining financial reimbursement. (U.S. GPO 2002, Title 42.I.A.2.14 (b))

In addition:

> Where state law requires parental consent to treatment the fact of a minor's application for treatment may be communicated to the minor's parent, guardian, or other person authorized under State law to act in the minor's behalf only if: (i) The minor has given written consent to the disclosure or (ii) The minor lacks the capacity to make a rational choice regarding such consent as judged by the program director. (U.S. GPO 2002, Title 42.I.A.2.14 (c))

State Laws

It is important that mental health professionals take the time needed to research the laws that govern practice in the states, provinces, or regions in which they reside (a situation that readily fluctuates). Although HIPAA focuses on ways in which to ensure the confidentiality of patient/therapist communications, other laws focus on exceptions to confidentiality.

In the Tarasoff case (1976), for example, the California Supreme Court ruled that:

> [w]hen a therapist determines or pursuant to the standards of his profession should have determined, that his patient poses a serious danger of violence to others, he incurs an obligation to use reasonable care to protect the intended against such danger. (Buckner and Firestone 2000, p.93)

Ten years ago, the laws of 27 states stated that therapists had a duty to warn the intended victim, 13 states had no laws pertaining to a therapist's duty to warn, nine states and the District of Columbia left it up to the therapist to decide, and the court in one state decided that the therapist did not have a duty to warn (Herbert and Young 2002). This disparity underlines the importance of mental health professionals making the effort to familiarize themselves with the relevant laws of the specific states, provinces, or regions in which they practice.

Licensing Board Requirements

Although many art therapists are not licensed, those who are must practice within the legal constraints of their state license or face sanctions. Licenses can be revoked for various reasons, such as revealing confidential information about a client without his or her consent or without having been court ordered to disclose that information, or performing, or attempting to perform, services beyond the scope of those authorized by the practitioner's license.

Ethical Codes of Credentialing Bodies and Professional Membership Associations

The mission of the Art Therapy Credentials Board (ATCB) is to protect the public. It does so by providing both a Code of Professional Practice and a means by which members of the public can recognize art therapists who have demonstrated accepted levels of experience, knowledge, and expertise in the profession (through its registration, Board certification, and clinical supervisor credential programs) (ATCB 2012).

The ATCB confers registration upon those graduates of programs approved by the AATA who have accumulated 1000 direct client contact art therapy hours after the completion of the Master's degree. A minimum of 50 hours of supervision must have been provided by a registered art therapist, while 50 hours may be may be provided by a Master's level licensed or credentialed professional with a Master's degree (or higher) in art therapy or a related mental health field. When an art therapist becomes registered, he or she is entitled to add "ATR" after his or her name (ATCB 2011a).

Registered art therapists may sit for a national certification examination administered by the ATCB. Those who pass the exam are entitled to add "-BC" to the ATR they earned when they became registered (i.e., ATR-BC, meaning Art Therapist, Registered, Board Certified) (ATCB 2011b).

Recertification requires art therapists to acquire 100 hours of additional qualifying continuing education credits every five years, in order to stay current with new developments in treatment and research. The ATCB joins other credentialing bodies in including an ethics requirement (of six continuing education credits) as part of this continuing education (ATCB 2011c).

The ATCB Code of Professional Practice provides art therapists with a set of Ethical Principles to guide them in the practice of art therapy, as well as Standards of Conduct, to which every credentialed art therapist must adhere. Among the provisions that relate specifically to the function of art therapists (rather than to mental health professionals in general) is Part I, Section 3.2, which addresses the Public Use and Reproduction of Client Art Expression and Therapy Sessions. The Code of Professional Practice also provides a mechanism whereby complaints against credentialed art therapists may be lodged, reviewed, and adjudicated (ATCB 2011d).

The American Art Therapy Association (AATA) is a membership organization that, among its many functions, sets standards for Master's degree programs providing art therapy education and provides art therapists with professional development opportunities through its annual conferences, its regional conferences, and its Institute for Continuing Education in Art Therapy (which provides online courses) (AATA 2012a).

The AATA's Ethical Principles for Art Therapists governs the conduct of its members (who may or may not be credentialed by the ATCB and, thereby, subject to the ATCB Code of Professional Practice) (AATA 2011).

Art Therapy Training Program Standards

Preparation for the practice of art therapy is achieved at the Master's degree level, which includes a minimum of 48 hours of coursework and 700 hours of supervised (practicum and internship) experience, at least half of which must consist of direct client contact. (Additional hours are required of those seeking licensure.) The AATA lists, among required content areas for programs meeting its approval, the proper application of ethical and legal principles of art therapy practice and a foundation of knowledge in cultural diversity theory and competency models applied to an understanding of diversity of art language and symbolic meaning in artwork and art making across cultures and within a diverse society. Of course, one would hope that the principles of ethical practice and multicultural work would be well integrated into every class offering (AATA 2012b).

Policies, Procedures, and Job Descriptions of Employing Agencies

Job descriptions should be checked to ensure that the employee is not expected to provide services outside or beyond his or her competence. Additional clinical or administrative responsibilities should be undertaken only given the appropriate education/training and supervised experience necessary to achieve competence.

The "Policy and Procedure (P & P) Manual" of public and private institutions can consist of volumes of regulations created for the purpose of ensuring the smooth operation of the agency, as well as minimizing lawsuits by ensuring consistency of practice among its employees. These P & P manuals set forth, among many other things, protocols for dealing with emergencies on the unit, requirements for documenting services, regulations regarding access to records, guidelines for conducting treatment planning conferences, and schedules governing the purging of charts. The P & P manual cannot override a state's statutes, so, again, it is essential that an art therapist know the laws governing the provision of mental health services in the state, province, or region where he or she practices.

Clinicians' Informed Consent

The informed consent document introduces the independent practitioner, advises the client as to what the practitioner intends to do, and establishes what is expected of the client. The ATCB, in its Code of Professional Practice (Part I, Section 3.1.11), states that the professional disclosure statement must include at least the following information: education, training, experience, professional affiliations, credentials, fee structure, payment schedule, session scheduling arrangements, and information pertaining to the limits of confidentiality and the duty to report. It specifies that the name, address, and telephone number of the ATCB be written in the document, along with the following statement: "The ATCB oversees the ethical practice of art therapists and may be contacted with client concerns" (ATCB 2011d, p.8).

Since the consent is informed only if the client understands the material, is competent to sign the document, and is willing to sign it (i.e., signs it of his or her own free will), it is imperative that the therapist spend time going over the provisions with the client, eliciting questions, and providing clarification.

Supervisory Guidance

Seeking culturally sensitive supervision with a credentialed professional who has clinical experience with the population with whom one works can not only enhance one's own clinical skills but also shine a light on one's blind spots, targeting areas in need of further attention. Since this important area is the focus of the next chapter by my colleague Lisa Garlock, I leave this topic in her capable hands.

The Relationship

The above is all well and good, but when we are facing an ethical dilemma, it all comes down to the individual, doesn't it? Because, even with a thorough knowledge of all the laws and policies, standards and procedures, the art therapist still has to work to interpret them, apply them, wrestle with their implications, and struggle to address the myriad situations for which codes and regulations provide no answer. Indeed, we may be most tested when there seems to be nothing to guide us but our desire to help and our sense of integrity.

How can we fulfil our role in an ethical manner? We can remember that learning does not stop with graduation but is a lifelong pursuit, we can keep abreast of ethical issues through continuing education, and we can obtain specialized training and supervision in areas in which we feel our skills are not sufficient. We can talk with peers about general clinical issues, bring up specifics with a culturally sensitive supervisor, and seek appropriate consultation on legal issues with an attorney who specializes in issues related to the treatment of people with mental illness. We can become aware of, reflect upon, and challenge our biases, preconceptions, and hidden agendas through creating artwork, journaling, and/or participating in our own therapy, and we can root out the ways in which they interfere with our intention to provide our clients with the best of care. We can advocate for the use of a strengths-based approach to therapy, rather than a problem- or deficit-oriented model, and we can assist clients in discovering, developing, and utilizing their strengths and resources in order to bring about the changes they want to make. Most importantly, we can remember that the decisions we make are not made within a vacuum, but within the context of a relationship—a relationship that is influenced by culture.

Cultural Considerations

If we think of the therapeutic relationship as a conversation between people of different cultural beliefs, values, traditions, and expectations, our job as therapists entails not only becoming familiar with our own patterns of communication, but also learning the language of our client's culture, as well as his or her particular dialect—because an individual is more than simply a representative of the culture of which he or she is a part. Perhaps it would be useful to think of differences not as polarities but as points on a continuum. Thus, cultural considerations can affect everything from what brings a client to therapy (the extent to which focus is placed upon physical ailments, emotional symptoms, and a holistic view of the self), to what role a client expects the therapist to play (that of a prescriber, a teacher, a listener, a judge), to the importance of time (how beginning and ending times are regarded, what is expected in terms of therapist availability outside of "the therapeutic hour"), and to what constitutes successful treatment (the absence of symptoms, a greater understanding of one's situation, the meeting of all goals, the learning of coping mechanisms, the need never to return to therapy). Other aspects of the relationship might include the role of gift giving and/or receiving, bartering, making artwork with (or in the presence of) the client, self-disclosing, nonsexual touching, and having unforeseen contact with clients outside of the therapeutic setting. The type of setting (e.g., medical, educational, psychiatric) and the particular needs of the client population (e.g., children, older adults) also have an influence. All of these factors have to be carefully considered in light of the cultural context in which the therapy is taking place. For more information on this and related topics, I heartily recommend reading *Ethical Issues in Art Therapy* by Bruce Moon (2006).

Role of Family, Friends, and Community

But what about all the other people in the client's life—specifically, those family members and friends who are just outside the scope of the therapeutic relationship? What roles do they play? In many Western modes of therapy, the focus is upon the individual. In many non-Western societies, however, the focus is upon the group of which one is a part and we might need to expand our view of therapy to encompass those on the periphery of the therapeutic relationship but integral to the client's life outside of therapy (see Figure 4.2).

Figure 4.2 "Alannah and Poppi Ken in the garden
with Nanna Audrey" by Alannah McLeod, aged 4

As therapists, we must always ask ourselves "Whose needs are being met by the decision I am making? Is this decision in my client's best interest? Am I benefiting from this decision in some (overt or covert) way and, if so, how? What are my motivations?" That is (some of) what we, as therapists, can do.

References

American Art Therapy Association (AATA) (2011) *Ethical Principles for Art Therapists.* Alexandria, VA: AATA.

American Art Therapy Association (AATA) (2012a) *Membership.* Alexandria, VA: AATA.

American Art Therapy Association (AATA) (2012b) *Educational Standards.* Alexandria, VA: AATA.

Art Therapy Credentials Board (ATCB) (2011a) *Registration.* Greensboro, NC: ATCB.

Art Therapy Credentials Board (ATCB) (2011b) *Examination.* Greensboro, NC: ATCB.

Art Therapy Credentials Board (ATCB) (2011c) *Maintaining Your Credentials.* Greensboro, NC: ATCB.

Art Therapy Credentials Board (ATCB) (2011d) *Code of Professional Practice.* Greensboro, NC: ATCB.

Art Therapy Credentials Board (ATCB) (2012) *Mission.* Greensboro, NC: ATCB.

Buckner, F. and Firestone, M. (2000) "Where the public peril begins: 25 Years after Tarasoff." *Journal of Legal Medicine 21*, 2, 187–222. (Reprinted by permission of Taylor & Francis Ltd, www.tandf.co.uk/journals.)

Herbert, P. and Young, K. (2002) "Tarasoff at twenty-five." *Journal of the American Academy of Psychiatry and the Law 30*, 2, 275–281.

Moon, B. (2006) *Ethical Issues in Art Therapy, Second Edition.* Springfield, IL: Charles C. Thomas.

U.S. Department of Health and Human Services (DoHHS) (1996) *The Health Insurance Portability and Accountability Act of 1996.* Washington, DC: U.S. DoHHS.

U.S. Department of Health and Human Services (DoHHS) (2004) *The Confidentiality of Alcohol and Drug Abuse Patient Records Regulation and the HIPAA Privacy Rule: Implications for Alcohol and Substance Abuse Programs.* Washington, DC: Department of Health and Human Services.

U.S. Government Printing Office (GPO) (2002) *Code of Federal Regulations.* Washington, DC: U.S. GPO.

Chapter 5

Walk Beside Me, Not Behind Me
Cultural Issues in Art Therapy Supervision

Lisa Raye Garlock

Background

Since 2003, I have worked as Clinical Placement Coordinator for the George Washington University Graduate Art Therapy Program. In that role, I participate in many aspects of supervision within an educational setting: placement site supervision, on-campus supervision, supervision of supervisors, evaluations from supervisors, and evaluations from students. I also supervise students when they don't have an art therapist supervisor on site, and support and advise supervisors in the field. We host supervisor workshops each semester, facilitated by master supervisors, where site supervisors and on-campus supervisors discuss and explore the many experiences they have had when training and supervising art therapy students. For several years I published an email newsletter highlighting relevant topics like diversity, models of supervision, working with difficult students, and best practices in art therapy supervision. In this chapter, I focus on the basics of supervision and culture.

What Is Clinical Art Therapy Supervision?

Clinical supervision is an integral part of the training and professional practice of all therapists. Clinical supervision has been defined in many therapy traditions and there are specific models of supervision based on various theories of therapy, psychology, and counseling (Campbell 2000). While clinical supervision has many layers of meaning, I focus specifically here on art therapy supervision and cultural issues. Essentially, art therapy supervision is a professional relationship between experienced art therapists and art therapy students or less experienced art therapists. Within this relationship, the responsibility of a supervisor is to guide, teach, mentor, and facilitate the development of the students'/therapists' professional skills and identity (Campbell 2000). Ideally, there is a co-creation of this relationship so that the supervisor and those under his/her supervision are comfortable enough to be able to discuss the full range of professional issues that arise during supervision (Williams 2010). Co-creation of the supervisory relationship puts the responsibility of the relationship on both participants and softens the power differential that can impede the flow of communication.

Clinical art therapy supervision can be facilitated individually or in a small group. According to the American Art Therapy Association's (AATA) educational guidelines, art therapy training in the United States requires that students have one hour of supervision at their internship site, plus at least 1.5 hours of group supervision on campus per week worked; the group size must be no more than eight students (AATA 2007). Art therapists must have 1000 hours of supervised art therapy employment after graduating from a Master's program in order to qualify for the professional credential of Art Therapist, Registered (ATR). After attaining their ATR, they may take the board certification exam (BC). Supervisors are usually registered, board-certified art therapists (ATR-BC), and some may also have their supervisor's credential, Art Therapy Certified Supervisor (ATCS). Supervisor's credentialing requires a combination of education in supervision and experience supervising students and/or professional art therapists (ATCB 2012).

As in therapy, trust must also be established in supervision; a supervisee must feel comfortable and empowered enough to be able to ask questions, explore different options, and try different approaches or directives, with the goal of becoming the best art therapist possible. In the art therapy supervisory relationship, art may be used to inform countertransference issues, struggles the supervisee may be having with a specific client or staff member, and other unspoken aspects of the supervisee's therapeutic process with clients. It is very important for a supervisor to be aware of how the line between supervision and therapy can sometimes become blurred; being able to identify when an issue needs to be addressed in supervision and when the supervisee needs to take the issue to his or her therapist is an important skill in a supervisor (Malchiodi and Riley 1996).

Cultural Issues in Art Therapy Supervision

Culture suffuses our lives on all levels. People who are not part of the dominant culture may often be more aware of cultural issues than those who are in the dominant culture. Being privileged and a member of the dominant culture can blind many people to what others' lives are like; often there are assumptions made that everyone lives as they do, when there are actually vast differences. Differences in power, gender, class, and skin color create hierarchies of various kinds, in the United States as well as in other countries. Ignorance of the possibility of different worldviews, values, and lifestyles can cause hurt and anger.

Culture plays an integral role in art therapy and art therapy supervision. According to the AATA ethical guidelines, "Art therapists obtain education about and seek to understand the nature of social diversity and oppression with respect to race, ethnicity, national origin, color, gender, sexual orientation, class, age, marital status, political belief, religion, and mental or physical disability" (AATA 2011). To work effectively with clients from different cultural and/or ethnic backgrounds, the art therapist must first understand and be comfortable with her or his own history, beliefs, attitudes, and culture (Cattaneo 1994; Dufrene and Coleman 1994; Golub 1989; Kramer and Gerity 2000; Walker 1994). In this chapter, I focus on power, as it is at the root of oppression and is a constant factor in therapy and supervision. I touch upon ethnicity and culture and conclude with the characteristics and skills of effective art therapy supervisors.

Power

The power differential within the supervisory relationship is perhaps most obvious when supervising students. The AATA ethical guidelines direct that "art therapists are aware of their influential position with respect to students and supervisees, and they avoid exploiting the trust and dependency of such persons. Art therapists, therefore, shall not engage in a therapeutic relationship with their students or supervisees" (AATA 2011). Supervisors are seen as the authority; they may be seen as judging, all-knowing, approving or disapproving, and someone to please or with whom to gain favor. At supervisor workshops held each semester, I hear supervisors say they are often "put on a pedestal" by their supervisees, especially in the beginning of the relationship; they may be seen as having all the power and knowing everything. If the supervisor must evaluate the supervisee, then the behavior of the supervisee may reflect a desire to do whatever the supervisee thinks will please the supervisor, in order to elicit a good evaluation. This desire to please can impede a supervisee's ability to learn, to challenge himself or herself to try new things, and to develop his or her own style of being an art therapist. If a supervisor is aware that a supervisee is thinking or acting in this manner, it is important that he/she look at what factors may be eliciting this behavior and bring it up in supervision.

An example of a cultural difference relating to power occurred when I was supervising an international student from Japan. In Japan, there is an extreme reverence for teachers, to an extent that is rarely seen in the United States. Here in the college, university, and other learning environments, we are much more informal than in many other countries. I had first-hand experience of this attitude toward teachers and other authority figures when living in Japan as a child. As a military dependent, I also observed the rigid hierarchy and power of rank that is a fact of military life, and which trickles down into family life. I developed a strong sensitivity to, and questioning of, power structures. In the case of my Japanese supervisee, she would noticeably walk behind me and defer to me in all situations. She never questioned me. Rather than asking questions and discussing issues as they came up, she mostly took notes, nodded, and smiled. This behavior made me very uncomfortable. Granted, she was a first-year student and most new students experience fear of making mistakes, nervousness about trying out the new things they're just learning, and navigating a new internship environment; my student had the added challenge of becoming familiar and comfortable with a completely different place and culture. Language may also have played a role, though this student spoke English very well; a common occurrence with international students is that they may speak English well, but comprehension may not be as strong. Different accents and speech patterns of Americans may also be a barrier to understanding for these students. In this situation, about midway through the semester, I sat down with my student to discuss how cultural expectations are different here from those in Japan. I expressed feeling very uncomfortable with the deference she showed me and told her that it was okay to question me about anything, that she could be informal, and that I didn't want her to walk behind me. She was very open to feedback, which may reflect the cultural deference to authority figures, but may also have reflected the trust that we had established. For the remainder of her internship, we worked together on developing our relationship with less of an overt power differential and more of an open curiosity and playfulness, and continued to have frank discussions about cultural expectations. I walked more slowly so that she wouldn't walk behind me and made it a point to model professional collegiality while keeping professional boundaries.

Another, more extreme example of dealing with a power differential was an experience two art therapy students had at an internship site in India during a Summer Abroad trip. The community sites where students were placed varied along a spectrum between wealthy sites and very poor, underfunded sites. Students worked with children and adults with physical and developmental disabilities, men with addictions, women with mental illness who were homeless, children with learning disabilities, and children living in severe poverty. One day, two students returned from their site with a disturbing report of patient abuse. At this site, physical discipline was used by the direct contact staff. According to the students, one of the aides beat a male teenager with a stick, explaining that that was what he needed in order to learn. Another time, a student observed a young man tied to a window latch with rope. This was a site that did not have adequate funding, took care of the most destitute and developmentally disabled from around the area, and could not hire educated staff. Though there were supporters and people trying to initiate change, clearly it was very slow to come at this facility.

The emotions that this treatment elicited were a huge issue in supervision. The two students at the site felt despair, helplessness, and anger, as did many in the whole group. This kind of treatment is not unique to India, of course: many states in the United States, for example, still have sanctioned corporal punishment in their schools (End Corporal Punishment 2012; Infoplease 2008) and there are regular news articles that uncover abuse in group homes for people with mental illness or developmental disabilities (Hakim 2012; Sun 2000). But when this type of treatment surfaces in facilities in the United States, it's clearly unacceptable and there are authorities who can be called upon to act. Here, however, the art therapy students and supervisors felt powerless because of language and cultural issues. The energy in the room during this supervision was heavy and charged at the same time. As empathetic people, we all felt outraged about the situation at this site. There was also a strong feeling of "Who are we to go into a site as visitors and tell them what or what not to do?" The students felt this even more acutely because they were students; we observed what seemed to be an even more distinct hierarchy and power structure within Indian culture than we see in the United States, particularly in the educational environment and between the wealthy and the poor. Because we were only there for two weeks, we felt that we were in no position to facilitate change. If any change happened at all it would most likely be minor and short-lived; it was also possible that the perpetrator of the harsh punishment would retaliate against the patients as soon as the students left.

Powerlessness is a very uncomfortable feeling. But it can help students to understand what many marginalized people feel, often on a daily basis, throughout their lives. It's impossible to have no power differential in the supervisory relationship, but supervisors must be aware of the power they hold and use it responsibly. An ideal supervisor does not try to mold a supervisee into a replica of himself or herself, but rather encourages the supervisee to develop his/her own natural style, theory base, and way of working.

Ethnicity and Culture

According to the AATA ethical principles, art therapists are responsible for developing multicultural competence (AATA 2011). This includes awareness of self and others, knowledge about other cultures and differences between cultures, and skills in providing culturally sensitive and responsive art therapy. When the supervisor and supervisee are from different countries, cultures, or ethnicities, many of the differences are obvious. In a pluralistic culture like the United States, the combination of ethnicities and culture that I've seen in art therapy supervision is broad: Anglo-American and African-American, African-American and Vietnamese, Japanese and Latino, Nigerian and Italian American, and Anglo-American and Puerto Rican. On top of infinite variations of culture and ethnicities, add religion, gender, age, sexual orientation, and any number of other differences in the culture of the workplace. The complexity of supervision is multidimensional. It is the responsibility of the supervisor to make an effort to learn about and understand the supervisee's culture, and to bring up cultural topics in supervision in a way that does not assume or stereotype. Of course, it is useful if the supervisee also learns about the supervisor's culture and asks questions that help increase his or her knowledge about that culture.

I've seen misunderstandings that can come from not acknowledging or discussing cultural issues, which then grow into attitudes of defensiveness, mistrust, impatience, intolerance, and stagnation, in both the supervisor and supervisee. Some of the areas that may be different between cultures include how human relationships are experienced, how time is viewed, spirituality and religion, and the types and roles of art within cultures.

Examples of how time is viewed can be seen in cultures that place a high value on being punctual, juxtaposed with cultures where the pace is slower and time is not as important, so people may not be "on time" for appointments. There are people, as well as cultures, that live in the present moment, and for whom the past and future are irrelevant. In other cultures, a future focus is the norm (Locke 1992). It is important, then, to be aware of differences in time values; otherwise, constant lateness may be perceived as disorganization, apathy, or poor planning. If time values are different between supervisor and supervisee, this may be a topic for supervision.

When it comes to art, people obviously differ in terms of their familiarity with materials, skills, and training, and other factors that affect art-making. Some cultures have deep artistic traditions in weaving, sculpture, and painting (Atkinson, Casas, and Abreu 1971; Farley 1993; Locke 1992); other people may have experienced oppression of their culture which resulted in the loss of their artistic traditions (Anderson and Garlock 1988). Art therapists are constantly educating others about the benefits of creating art, regardless of what the finished product looks like. However, the concept and importance of beautiful art may be a strong feature in some cultures: if a person is making art, then it must be "good." There can be much pressure placed on conforming to what is considered beautiful or proper art. For instance, India has a long, rich tradition of incredibly intricate, decorative, and beautiful art and it infuses their daily lives, culture, and history. Bridging the divide about what art should be and what it can be was a challenge we experienced at all the internship sites in India during Study Abroad. One particular site prided itself on the art that clients made, though it was the aides who were actually making the art: an aide would hold a client's hand to place collage pieces where the aide wanted them to go. This is partly an example of how important "pretty" art is, and also how important it is to make sure the expectations of the aide's job were met. Our perspective, and a tenet of art therapy, is to support independence by letting clients try things on their own and make mistakes; in this way they learn new skills, thereby building self-confidence and strengthening their own voice in the process. As an art therapist and art therapy supervisor, it is important to be knowledgeable about history and art from different cultures. Images, patterns, symbols, media, and styles vary widely across cultures, and individuals from within a culture add another layer by having their own unique symbolic language. While it is unrealistic to be well versed in art of all the different cultures, each time we meet with a new client or supervisee we have the opportunity to learn more about aspects of his or her culture. Art therapy supervisors understand that each supervisee is a unique individual. Even if the supervisor and supervisee appear to come from the same or similar backgrounds, there are still many ways in which they may differ. Part of the supervision experience, for both parties, is the continuation of developing self-awareness and understanding of self and others;

curiosity is the operative word in this process, and art-making can be an integral part of the growing process.

Characteristics and Skills of Effective Art Therapy Supervisors

As art therapy supervisors, we try to encourage students and supervisees to be open to whatever clients bring to a session; likewise, supervisors must be prepared for whatever the supervisee brings to supervision—or to bring up what the supervisee may be afraid to say. Supervisees may plan directives or art experientials, but ultimately they need to be flexible, really listen, and be in tune with the client, and accept that this may make them feel vulnerable or uncomfortable. To be attuned and open to clients requires self-awareness and self-confidence; immersion into another culture often intensifies self-awareness and reduces self-confidence, whether it's working with clients from very different backgrounds in the United States or traveling abroad to work with people in a different country. Supervisors must be able to see when cultural issues are at play, whether within the supervisory relationship or between the supervisee and clients, and bring them up for discussion during supervision. Supervisees need to understand and accept that they aren't expected to know everything; this is key to developing effective therapeutic and supervisory relationships.

Several years ago, I surveyed placement site supervisors and student supervisees to see what specific characteristics and behaviors they thought made for an effective supervisor (Campbell 2000). The supervisors felt that the most important characteristics of a supervisor were being respectful, competent, encouraging, genuine, and supportive. The students felt that the most important supervisor characteristics were being supportive, open, flexible, encouraging, competent, and respectful. The supervisors and supervisees all agreed that being supportive, showing respect, offering encouragement, and being competent were necessary characteristics in a supervisor, ensuring a rewarding supervisory relationship. When sampling the students' evaluations of their sites, most of the evaluations that recommended the placement to future students also described the supervisors as competent, encouraging, supportive, and respectful.

Supervisors rated the following supervisory behaviors as most important:

- providing constructive criticism and positive reinforcement

- having the courage to expose vulnerabilities, make mistakes, and take risks

- being accessible and available

- caring about the well-being of others

- encouraging the exploration of new ideas and techniques.

Students felt that the following were the most important supervisory behaviors:

- ability to assess the learning needs of the supervisee

- being invested in the supervisee's development

- encouraging the exploration of new ideas and techniques

- providing constructive criticism and positive reinforcement

- having the courage to expose vulnerabilities, make mistakes, and take risks.

(Campbell 2000)

Both supervisors and students agreed that providing constructive criticism and positive reinforcement, being encouraging of the exploration of new ideas and techniques, and having the courage to expose their own vulnerabilities, making mistakes, and taking risks were effective supervisory behaviors.

Another important consideration for effective supervision includes having uninterrupted time. If an art therapy supervisee is paying for supervision, then scheduled time is not usually a problem. Art therapy interns, however, must advocate for a scheduled hour a week with a supervisor who is often extremely busy, and this can be challenging. When training art therapy students, supervision needs to be a priority; the physical and emotional supervision space must be respected, and if a supervision session is missed, it must be made up for at another time. Clear expectations of supervision are necessary for both supervisor and supervisee, so outlining those expectations together goes along with co-creating the relationship. In art therapy supervision, bringing in client art or photographs of client art is an integral part of art therapy supervision, and an important area of learning for the supervisee. Making art in supervision is also common in art therapy supervision, but the art-making needs to be focused on specific supervision issues (Case 2007; Malchiodi and Riley 1996).

Conclusion

When it comes to working with diverse populations, we must first know ourselves. Sue and Sue (2008) lay out three main areas on which to work in order to become culturally competent: self-awareness, knowledge, and skills. McPhatter (2004), in her cultural competence attainment model within organizations, uses similar terms to discuss the importance of these basics. Regardless of terminology, we must understand our past, individually and collectively, learn about the people we work with and the cultures they come from, and continually sharpen our therapeutic skills.

There is necessarily much struggle in supervision, but that is what we need to do in order to learn and grow. Likewise, learning to be culturally competent is an ongoing challenge. Internally, we must learn to continually assess our own assumptions, expectations, and behavior toward others. Externally, it is critical to be open to learning about other cultures and countries and keep current about events that affect us all in a global world. When working within a different culture or with someone from a different place, differences are obvious and it may be easier to talk about and celebrate them, since there is so much that is new and interesting. Culture within the United States is rich and continually evolving, and reflects the need for art therapist supervisors to also continually learn, grow, and evolve. Our task as supervisors is to ensure that the next generation of art therapists has the necessary tools to build on what they learn from us.

References

American Art Therapy Association (AATA) (2007) *Masters Education Standards.* Available at www. americanarttherapyassociation.org/upload/masterseducationstandards.pdf, accessed on June 17, 2013.

American Art Therapy Association (AATA) (2011) *Ethical Principles for Art Therapists.* Available at www.americanarttherapyassociation.org/upload/ethicalprinciples.pdf, accessed on June 17, 2013.

Anderson, M. and Garlock, J. (1988) *Granddaughters of Corn: Portraits of Guatemalan Women.* Willimantic, CT: Curbstone Press.

Art Therapy Credentials Board (ATCB) (2012) *Certified Supervisor Credentials.* Available at www.atcb. org/home/certifiedcredential, accessed on June 17, 2013.

Atkinson, D., Casas, A., and Abreu, J. (1992) "Mexican-American acculturation, counselor ethnicity and cultural sensitivity, and perceived counselor competence." *Journal of Counseling Psychology 39,* 4, 515–520.

Campbell, J. (2000) *Becoming an Effective Supervisor: A Workbook for Counselors and Psychotherapists.* Philadelphia: Taylor and Francis.

Case, C. (2007) "Imagery in Supervision: The Non-Verbal Narrative of Knowing." In J. Schaverien and C. Case (eds) *Supervision of Art Psychotherapy: A Theoretical and Practical Handbook.* New York: Routledge.

Cattaneo, M. (1994) "Addressing culture and values in the training of art therapists." *Art Therapy: Journal of the American Art Therapy Association 11,* 3, 184–186.

Dufrene, P. and Coleman, V. (1994) "Art therapy with Native American clients: Ethical and professional issues." *Art Therapy: Journal of the American Art Therapy Association 11,* 3, 191–193.

End Corporal Punishment (2012) *International, Regional, and National Campaigns for Law Reform to Prohibit All Corporal Punishment of Children.* Available at www.endcorporalpunishment.org/pages/frame.html, accessed on June 17, 2013.

Farley, C. (1993) "The art of diversity: Hyphenated Americans can be found at the cutting edge of all the arts." *Time Magazine 142,* 20, 20–24.

Golub, D. (1989) "Cross-Cultural Dimensions of Art Psychotherapy." In H. Wadeson, J. Durkin, and D. Perach (eds) *Advances in Art Therapy.* New York: John Wiley and Sons.

Hakim, D. (2012) "Lawmaker to file suit charging abuse of his disabled son." *The New York Times, September 30.*

Infoplease (2008) *Corporal Punishment in Public Schools, by State*. Available at www.infoplease.com/ipa/A0934191.html, accessed on June 17, 2013.

Kramer, E. and Gerity, L. A. (2000) *Art as Therapy: Collected Papers*. London: Jessica Kingsley Publishers.

Locke, D. (1992) *Increasing Multicultural Understanding: A Comprehensive Model*. Thousand Oaks, CA: Sage Publications.

Malchiodi, C. and Riley, S. (1996) *Supervision and Related Issues: A Handbook for Professionals*. Chicago: Magnolia Street Publishers.

McPhatter, A. R. (2004) "Culturally Competent Practice." In M. J. Austin and K. M. Hopkins (eds) *Supervision as Collaboration in the Human Services: Building a Learning Culture*. Thousand Oaks, CA: Sage Publications.

Sue, D. W. and Sue, D. (2008) *Counseling the Culturally Diverse: Theory and Practice, Fifth Edition*. Hoboken, NJ: John Wiley and Sons.

Sun, L. H. (2000) "Retarded man left stranded, in restraints; DC agency keeps 30-year-old in hospital for 8 months, citing lack of space, legal guardian." *The Washington Post, July 13*.

Walker, S. (1994) "The artist in search of self: Howardena Pindell." *School Arts 94*, 1, 29–33.

Williams, K. (2010) *Mastering Supervision: Creating a Learning Environment for Both Supervisor and Supervisee*. Workshop conducted at the George Washington University Art Therapy Program, Alexandria, VA, October.

Part II

The Culturally Sensitive Art Therapist

Chapter 6

The Impact of Culture and the Setting on the Use and Choice of Materials

Sangeeta Prasad

It was a sultry day in Chennai, India, where I was conducting an art therapy group with children at a school. My challenges were to work with a limited number of art supplies and space and to make sure that the paper was not flying under the fan, that the children's painting water was full, and that my voice could be heard over the chatter of excited children and the noise on the street. I also had to speak in two languages, English and Tamil. Such experiences, while working as an art therapist in different environments, have made me realize that culture and setting have an impact on my work. This chapter addresses some issues that an art therapist will have to pay attention to when transferring her practice from one culture to another.

When we begin our work in any setting, the most important aspects to consider are space, choice of materials, language, and the process of art making. We also have to be aware that when we are working in cultures that we may not be familiar with, we need to understand the role and goals of art therapy within this new setting (Wadeson 2000). The art therapist will have to become informed about the community's exposure to art, therapy, and art therapy (Cattaneo 1994). Once we have an understanding and awareness of these factors, it is possible to set up a therapeutic and healing environment. It is finding a way to develop art therapy in a new culture that can be challenging. In addressing the cross-cultural issues that affect the therapeutic relationship, Westrich states: "Art Therapists should identify materials, processes, and the use of structure that will lead to a constructive therapeutic art session" (Westrich 1994, p.189).

If the concept of art therapy is new to the setting, institutions often do not feel the need to create a special space for the therapist to work or store art supplies. For example, when an art therapist from the United States began working in the pediatric oncology unit of a hospital in Chennai, India, she was given no space to store her art supplies. This limited her choice of materials to what she could physically carry using public transportation. She had to make sure that she did not run out of supplies like paper, and come up with things for the kids to do within these limitations.

The lack of space also impacted her privacy with her patients. Hospitals in India tend to have a companion known to the patient sitting by the bedside. In the case of children this is usually the mother. Without a separate room in which to interact with the child, the therapist had to devise ways to either occupy the parent or keep her from being overly involved with the child's expression in art. Sometimes she even provided art materials when the mother seemed overwhelmed with what was going on with the child. She had to create a safe environment within a community space to foster self-expression.

Another aspect is that the sense of physical space for art making can be very different depending upon the socioeconomic level of the population one is working with in a given country. While in some places one may have tables and chairs, in other places the floor is your working surface (Figure 6.1). People in Asia and Africa are used to working on the floor and the art therapist will have to get used to sitting down with them. This not only changes the physical ability to move around the room, but also changes the dynamic between the therapist and student. It is important to plan the art activity in such a way as to have the materials accessible without the kids having to get up and retrieve them. It is also difficult for the art therapist to constantly get up from the floor or walk around as she may be used to doing when she is working with children at tables.

Figure 6.1 Picture of a child working on the floor

In many cultures, space for art making could be in a public area. Therefore the goals of art therapy like maintaining confidentiality may have to be modified accordingly. In altering the goals the therapist must be very careful not to resort to simple art projects, like painting a pot or a landscape as one would do in an art class, which are only product oriented. While these projects are wonderful art activities, they do not foster the basic goals of art therapy: to promote self-expression, provide choices, and encourage children to use creativity to bring about change (Rubin 2010).

The ideas of therapy and confidentiality are different in each culture; sometimes space is more communal and open (Chilote 2007). When an art therapist was working in a school in India, she was given a multipurpose room that was near a kitchen. At times she shared the room with other teachers, while staff walked in and out of the kitchen. She had to learn that space is dynamic and, in a country where space is at a premium, it is used for a lot of different things. A house may be a single room and therefore it is your dining room, sitting room, and bedroom. The sense of boundaries or privacy is also different. People do not feel that a space must be used for a particular purpose or that when a therapist is working with a child one cannot interrupt. Either the therapist must educate the population or the setting one is working with as to the requirements of art therapy or she or he must adapt to the new laws of the land.

The art room is usually a space with various art supplies to inspire people with diverse needs and abilities (Moon 2010). A wide range of art supplies provides the person with choices about how to express what they may be going through. These choices can vary according to the culture one is working in. In some places it becomes impossible to provide choices due to the large numbers of people or the space that one is working with. Another factor is the perception of the materials presented. For example, when working in India, we found that children who had not been exposed to art or art materials did not want to share the materials with other group members. Children who had had exposure to art seem to have no difficulty in sharing art supplies. While in one group it was important to provide familiar art supplies that they knew they would continue to get, in the other group it was fine to have a limited amount of art supplies and have the children share. As Moon (2010) states: "Awareness of these internalized biases, coupled with ongoing self-education about the multiplicity of ways that art is construed and constructed in various contexts, can help art therapists be open to the diverse language of expression through media and materials" (p.12).

Another important aspect of working in a culture different from that of the art therapist is language and verbal communication (Wadeson 2000). Often there is a need for a translator. This translator may be a staff or a volunteer at the setting. Since these people may be familiar with the group and have a different relationship with the participants it is important to define the role of the art therapist and the translator within the group (Kalmanowitz, Potash, and Chan 2012). Often the translator may go beyond his/her role and become a co-leader without understanding the implications of his/her actions. In one such instance, when a translator was asked to translate "draw a picture of a day you will never forget," she added that the children could draw about a birthday party or other things they could remember. While in an art class this would have been fine, in an art therapy session the goal is to find out what the students' reaction is to the topic presented. In suggesting a happy occasion the translator ruled out the possibility that a student might have wanted to share a sad or traumatic event. It is very important to discuss what went on in the group after each session with the translator because she may be unaware of the impact of her words and how to react to the images or content in the artwork (Hiscox and Calisch 1998).

Another way of bridging the language barrier is by creating a sample book of art ideas. This can help the person look at the choices they have. While working in India within a setting where the children spoke many different languages and no English, an art therapist created many samples with open-ended themes that helped the children choose what they would like to work on. Predrawn mandalas (patterns drawn within a circle—see Figure 6.2) became one of the favorites among the children. The choices in art gave the children a sense of control, something they might not have had as they underwent cancer treatment. The attraction to mandalas also may have been related to the kolams and rangolis (floor drawings) that they were comfortable with and provided them with an opportunity to create something that was familiar and safe. While there may not have been verbal communication, through the increased involvement in the time spent on each artwork as well as the number of children wanting to participate in art therapy it was apparent that the children were beginning to find value in this form of expression.

Figure 6.2 Predrawn mandala
Illustrated in the color insert

In order to understand the influence of culture on the use of material and space, I decided to interview art therapists who have conducted art therapy in various cultural settings across Europe, Asia, South America, and Africa. Most of the art therapists who were interviewed stated that they initially took art supplies with them from the United States. However, they soon found that this method was neither sustainable nor effective, due to the large numbers of participants in some countries, as well as uncertainty of continued supply of such materials. Art therapist Cathy Moon shared in her interview questionnaire:

> My colleagues and I also learned by making mistakes, in particular, by bringing to Africa whatever materials people in the United States wanted to donate. We now only bring with us materials that are available locally, and are sensitive to the issues raised by introducing materials into a culture. We also rely heavily on materials that are readily available—found objects, materials from nature, and our own bodies (for performance or performing arts).

The other reason for not bringing in art supplies is that the group may not be familiar with the materials provided and this can lead to hoarding or misuse. When conducting an art therapy session with third-graders in India, I was unaware that children in a particular school had not used scissors. When I offered these to the children, I observed that they were excited and surprised. Soon, however, I found that a girl who was enjoying the freedom to cut had also taken the liberty of cutting a bit of her hair. It may have been helpful for me to provide some guidance on the appropriate use of the scissors.

It is important to provide materials that can be replaced or acquired locally by the person receiving art therapy if he/she wishes to continue the process outside of the sessions (Moon 2010). I have also adapted local material quite often to fill the role of traditional Western supplies. For instance, when visiting a clay studio, I found large pieces of discarded plaster molds and used these as chalk to draw on the concrete floors, since large chalk was not available. The kids, who were two to three years old, enjoyed using the large pieces and freely drew on the bare floor. In another instance, at a school for mentally and/or physically disabled children, where there were very few art materials, I had the children draw on the floor with chalk. The staff was amazed to see how the children enjoyed the process of drawing with chalk, which is an inexpensive and common material.

The way in which the particular population with which one is working views or understands art has an impact on how one uses art in therapy (Dissanayake 1992). The culture of the institution or the people themselves may hold a more traditional view of art—that is, to create a product. But in art therapy it is the process of art making itself that helps individuals work through their thoughts and feelings. In the earlier example, when I demonstrated the use of chalk to draw, the teachers were able to observe how the process of working together, expressing thoughts and observations, and communicating through the visual media were important aspects of art therapy. The teachers then realized that art does not have to be a finished product that looks beautiful or useful; rather, the act of visual expression could be used to bring out the thoughts and feelings of the children and therefore used therapeutically. This was a very different concept for the staff who usually taught children to achieve a finished product by holding the hand of the child and helping them to paste or draw. Here, I found myself introducing a very different concept of art to the culture of the school: the idea of process over product.

At times it is challenging to find art materials in the same form as we may have worked with. Clay is not always available in the processed form as it is in the West. Therefore, in India I acquired clay from construction sites or from local potters. Paper is expensive in most countries, and I seldom use large sheets of paper (18" × 24"). The expense is not the only reason; I found that when people are accustomed to smaller spaces, large paper is overwhelming and feels wasteful and hence intimidating. The smaller paper is in proportion to the physical space usually available for art making and fits with the concept of space people have when living in crowded environments. Many times I have used old newspaper as a surface for art making and painting.

An art therapist may have to adapt a particular theme to the culture that one is working with (Gil and Drewes 2005). In a mandala drawing, I asked children to incorporate found materials into the art process. The children used crayons and added the found objects to create a three-dimensional mandala (Figure 6.3). The process was exciting and dynamic as it gave the children an opportunity to be creative within the given space and time. It also helped the children bring their environment into their art expression. I have also used mangoes or other fruits to replace apples for the theme of "draw a person picking apples from an apple tree." I make sure it is a similar-looking tree.

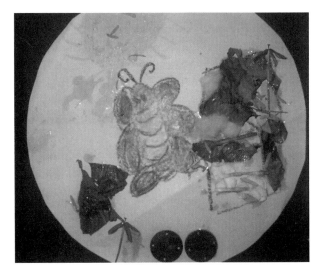

Figure 6.3 Picture of mandala with found material

Illustrated in the color insert

A challenge when visiting other countries is the expectation of what may be provided. Flexibility seems to be the key to making do with what one has and is given. As Cathy Moon, an art therapist who has worked in Africa, states:

> You have to be ready for anything, to be flexible and make do. These are some of the things I have experienced: throngs of children who overwhelm the available space; locked spaces and the person with the keys is gone; no tables or one table for 150 kids; having to keep kids busy and engaged while waiting two hours for their lunch to arrive (and sending them home without lunch would be unthinkable because they will get no lunch at home and they probably didn't have any breakfast either); general lack of even basic materials (e.g., a pair of scissors); etc. So being flexible and making do might mean working on a dirt floor or on mats laid on the grass. It means working with the materials around you: sand, dirt, leaves, seeds, etc. It means not having the luxury of sticking to visual art; sometimes song, dance, and games are just what are needed.

In one instance, I had arranged for graduate-level art therapy students to work at a particular school in India. They were excited, but when they arrived the principal was nowhere to be found. The students found that they had not been assigned a class to work with and later were told to go work in any class. They decided to create a mural so that they could accommodate as many children as possible. The children were asked to draw an animal they thought represented them and these animal drawings were then incorporated into the mural. The staff and children were delighted to see how their individual creations made up a mural.

Traditional art techniques and materials can be made to go beyond their customary use for religious and decorative purposes and integrated into art therapy. In order to find a way for graduate-level art therapy students from the United States on a study abroad program to interact with the local women through art, I decided to ask the staff of a school in Chennai to create a rangoli, an Indian floor design. The staff was very happy to demonstrate the art they used mostly during festivals and religious holidays. I incorporated mandalas around the rangoli that the students created with the same materials used by the staff in this case—rock salt. This turned out to be a unique experience for both the school staff and the art therapy students. The staff was happy to show the students how to use the materials and see how their artwork was integrated into the colorful renderings. This resulted in a cross-cultural art exchange where people from very different backgrounds sat on the floor and created art together. The school staff was delighted that the students from America participated in their art making and the students seemed to feel a sense of oneness with the culture by participating in this traditional form of art. Amazingly, the school staff saw that the students had created varied designs in their mandalas, something the staff had not seen in their traditional art form. The two groups had used a traditional art form to connect and communicate in a nontraditional manner (Figure 6.4). The next day the designs were shown to the school's pupils and their parents, as well as other school staff members, and all were in awe of what had been created. "Art making and art viewing can stimulate empathy by activating the imagination and fostering genuine relationships" (Potash and Ho 2011, p.74). This relationship has continued with each new group of students and the staff of this school.

Flexibility, adaptation, and innovation are the key to working in different cultures with varied traditions and environments (McNiff and Barlow 2011). It is important for an art therapist to know that her tools are not her only contribution to bringing the art process to individuals but that her creativity is an important part as well. The art therapist creates an environment of healing with cultural awareness and sensitivity (Gil and Drewes 2005). It is important that art therapists do not bring their knowledge in a set frame; instead, they must be dynamic, adapting, and accommodating so as to not lose the essence of art therapy. The process must not be lost (McNiff 1988). With all the accommodations and adjustments, the essence of art therapy principles must remain. As a little kid once told me in India, "I like coming to art therapy because this is different from art class."

Figure 6.4 Rangoli

References

Cattaneo, M. (1994) "Addressing culture and values in the training of art therapists." *Art Therapy: Journal of the American Art Therapy Association 11*, 3, 184–186.

Chilote, R. (2007) "Art therapy with child tsunami survivors in Sri Lanka." *Art Therapy: Journal of the American Art Therapy Association 24*, 4, 156–162.

Dissanayake, E. (1992) *Homo Aestheticus: Where Art Comes From and Why*. New York: Free Press.

Gil, E. and Drewes, A. A. (2005) *Cultural Issues in Play Therapy*. New York: Guilford Press.

Hiscox, A. R. and Calisch, A. C. (1998) *Tapestry of Cultural Issues in Art Therapy*. London: Jessica Kingsley Publishers.

Kalmanowitz, D., Potash, J. S., and Chan, S. M. (2012) *Art Therapy in Asia: To the Bone or Wrapped in Silk*. London: Jessica Kingsley Publishers.

McNiff, S. (1988) *Fundamentals of Art Therapy*. Springfield, IL: Charles C. Thomas.

McNiff, S. and Barlow, G. (2011) "Cross-cultural psychotherapy and art." *Art Therapy: Journal of the American Art Therapy Association 26*, 3, 100–106.

Moon, C. H. (2010) *Materials and Media in Art Therapy: Critical Understandings of Diverse Artistic Vocabularies*. London: Routledge.

Potash, J. and Ho, R. T. H. (2011) "Drawing involves caring: Fostering relationship building through art therapy for social change." *Art Therapy: Journal of the American Art Therapy Association 28*, 2, 74–81.

Rubin, J. A. (2010) *Introduction to Art Therapy: Sources and Resources*. New York: Routledge.

Wadeson, H. (2000) *Art Therapy Practice: Innovative Approaches with Diverse Populations*. New York: Wiley.

Westrich, C. (1994) "Art therapy with culturally different clients." *Art Therapy: Journal of the American Art Therapy Association 11*, 3, 187–190.

Chapter 7

The Process of Attunement between Therapist and Client

Jennie Kristel

In this chapter, the impact of culture on the therapist–client relationship is explored. One does not need to leave home to experience the deep richness of cross-cultural interaction. The cultural diversity of our rapidly changing world is seen increasingly in our home communities, and our clinical practices are becoming more defined by that cultural mosaic. At the same time, all too often cultural norms are defined by the cultures dominant in a geographical region. This domination rests on a series of cultural assumptions that tend to diminish or ignore the experiences and concerns of people of minority cultures (Sue 1998). This microaggression can often be very subtle. For example, in speaking with an African-American colleague, she gave examples of experiences that are common for people of color. She discussed being in a restaurant with others who were white and the white waiter taking orders from all at the table except for her. She also spoke of being in meetings in which she was racially a minority in which others were asked questions and she was overlooked. The same thing often happens in terms of gender issues between men and women. "In restaurants, for instance, men are often given the check, even if it's the woman paying!" (Freeman, personal communication, 2012).

Understanding Cultural Difference

Since 2003, I have had the opportunity to work in several countries in South Asia. During that time I have taught and practiced Playback Theatre and expressive therapy at the behest of local non-government organizations (NGOs) and universities. My introduction to Asia was a teaching trip to Bangladesh—a deep immersion in experiences of people and cultures vastly different from my own. As a white Jewish American woman, I have experienced situations in Asia similar to those in my colleague's discussion in the introductory paragraph. Being overlooked, or not taken seriously, were issues I had in particular working with my male colleagues. Bangladesh is a beautiful country, beset by severe poverty, with a rich and complex history. The people I work with are sincerely committed to righting the wrongs in their country and building social, economic, and environmental justice. Quickly realizing that any ideas I might have about the culture of Bangladesh might not be accurate, I began to look carefully at my own background, expectations, and biases. I believe, had I not done so, that I would have been unable to truly understand those with whom I was working. Introspection, careful consideration of cultural similarities and differences, and maintaining awareness of boundaries that exist between myself and others are all part of the attunement process (Erskine 1998). To begin, I approach my work with the concept of "stepping into the shoes" of those with whom I will be working. By doing so I try to understand and appreciate their hurts, perspectives, and desires. I know that I cannot possibly know everything nor should I expect this. To do this, to truly understand the mindset and worldviews of persons whose cultural beliefs and experiences may be very different from my own, I first need to look at what is in my worldview in order to be aware of my own cultural process. Tervalon and Murray-Garcia (1998) call this "Cultural Humility," which incorporates a commitment to self-evaluation and critique and to "redressing power imbalances" between the client and therapist (p.17). Culture is deeply embedded in all of us, and an understanding of cultural differences is as essential to the practice of therapy as it is to teaching. As clinicians, we seek to truly meet our clients, to become attuned to their lives and needs. This can only occur when one has addressed one's own cultural identity as well as that of one's clients. Many psychological boards around the globe, such as the as the American Art Therapy Association (AATA) and the British Association of Art Therapists (BAAT; see BAAT 2005), now believe strongly that therapists must acknowledge cultural differences and address oppressive and discriminatory practices, beliefs, values, and attitudes within therapy that would be inconsistent with counseling goals. Such practices support us in demonstrating essential cultural competences and, just as important, respect for the diversity of the community we are working in (ACA 2005, p.4).

It is my experience that one may discover much about another person by asking about their cultural history. In many countries, people living in cities will hold a dramatically different set of cultural expectations and norms than their counterparts in the countryside, even though each person defines him or herself as a citizen of the same country and as sharing a common background. The United States may well be unique in the sheer diversity of the cultures represented within its borders. Being American has many possible meanings, as we come from a wide variety of socioeconomic backgrounds, ethnicities, and cultural histories. Thus, it is naive for clinicians to assume we have an understanding of all of the cultural norms shaping our clients (Vontress, Johnson, and Epp 1999). Rather, we, and they, benefit from our efforts to understand the world from other cultural perspectives. Additionally, looking at our own cultural backgrounds and biases supports us in analyzing the beliefs, biases, and attitudes that may have been passed down through many generations to our clients (Singer 2006). It is crucial that we remember that the way each client relates to the world is shaped by cultural norms that may not be obvious to us as clinicians. In thinking about this, shaping the way in which we use art therapy directives and materials is important to keep in mind (Malchiodi 1998, 2012).

At the heart of the art therapist's work is an intense desire to help relieve the suffering of others. In arts-based therapy, both client and therapist explore a variety of creative ways of thinking about and processing life events.

In observing changes that occur as a result of therapy with this deepening attention to attunement, the results are wide ranging, transpersonal, and profoundly emotionally complex. When we ourselves are unable to attune to our clients' emotional and cultural perspectives, cues that stem from deep generational and collective coercions that contribute to their pain might be missed in the process (Faris and van Ooijen 2012).

The Role of Intersubjectivity and Attunement

Intersubjective: Existing between conscious minds; shared by more than one conscious mind. (*Shorter Oxford English Dictionary* 2002)

Intersubjectivity represents a comprehensive emotional, intentional/ motivational, attentional, reflective, and behavioral experience of the other. It emerges from shared emotions (attunement), joint attention and awareness, and congruent intentions. (Becker-Weidman 2012)

The deep work of therapy comes from a place of knowing the other—that is, of attunement that transcends textbook knowledge. The centrality of this attunement is an unbroken feeling of connection between clinician and client. This level of resonance has been increasingly documented in recent years and is now considered key in the therapeutic process (Erskine 1998). Attunement may be understood as an *intersubjective* process. That is, it is a psychological process that occurs between two or more persons engaged in an emotionally and cognitively rich relationship. The concept of intersubjectivity is a powerful tool for understanding interactions and emotional states within relationships. *Attunement*, an interpersonal process of sharing emotions, can be perceived as either positive or negative by those in the relationship and is reflected in experiences of being in or out of attunement in relationships.

Becker-Weidman observes that while attunement is a necessary condition for therapeutic work, it does not constitute all of the process: "One may have a high degree of attunement with another and still have a discordant relationship fraught with tension and miscues" (Becker-Weidman 2012).

Often in my work with clients who have strong emotions, such as anger, sadness, or fear, the act of attuning—of understanding on a deeper, more psychic level—is the process of my being aware of my own issues around emotions in order to understand the depth of the client's emotions such as suffering. It is important to witness anger to support clients in becoming fully conscious of what the anger is and where it comes from; it is also important for me as their therapist to understand in what ways their anger may trigger miscommunications between us. The process of attunement, then, is to become aware of and to jointly witness pain, both old and current, and support clients in making deeper connections about themselves. The process of attuning does not, however, stop the emotions from arising within the client. It simply allows it to be present.

Attunement engages both the therapist and the client emotionally, kinesthetically, and psychologically, encouraging the development of vulnerability. By attuning, one is able to create a more resilient bond that supports the client in feeling valued and listened to (Beihl 2012; Erskine 1998).

Attunement and other forms of intersubjectivity also alter brain structures and patterning. A highly attuned relationship with another person is important in developing new neural pathways, a vital process when working with traumatized individuals (Schore 2011). Central processes within psychotherapy, attunement, and other forms of intersubjectivity allow the client to link emotion and cognition. Shared, reciprocal experiences between the therapist and client, representing a comprehensive emotional, intentional/motivational, attentional, reflective, and behavioral experience of the other, are then experienced (Schore 2003).

Erskine suggests that there are certain critical aspects of attunement: the meeting of relational needs and security (basic needs such as food, shelter, and safety), experiences of being validated, and the affirmation of one's significance within a relationship. The therapist's interest must be genuine, dependable, safe, and largely transparent. The clinician must interact with the client in a non-shaming, nonjudgmental manner. When these conditions are met, the client is likely to experience deep validation (Erskine 1998).

The process of intersubjectivity is bidirectional. In such moments of deep connection and shared attunement, both client and therapist are acutely aware of the deep emotional experiences residing between and inside of each other. Intersubjectivity is also in operation when there is a negative potential countertransference interaction between therapist and client. (The psychoanalytic concepts of transference and countertransference refer to the tendency for old, often unhealthy, relationship patterns to be played out in therapy as part of the trust-building process.) For instance, a client who may be experiencing pain or anger may evoke a memory of something that the therapist has experienced. This may result in a discord between the therapist and client that would need to be attended to in order for the therapy to go forward. This is an appropriate time for the therapist to pose a question about the therapeutic process itself, such as "Is this working right now?"

Misunderstandings and hidden resentments are inevitable in the therapeutic relationship. Memories of past wounding, and the accompanying feelings of shame and pain, are likely to be difficult for the client; for a variety of reasons it may be challenging for the individual to talk about this if these memories come up in the context of the therapeutic relationship through transference. If the clinician is unaware that his/her responses to the client are reopening or feeding into the client's pain, due to being unaware of cultural misunderstandings or other issues such as countertransference, then it may be appropriate for the clinician to become aware of issues that stand in the way of clear relationship and understanding. Training is the key. In order for the therapist to offer a positive, concordant relationship to the client, the resolution of disturbances must be part of the relationship. It opens an important door, welcoming feedback from the client and allowing basic trust to be regained within the therapeutic relationship (Becker-Weidman 2010).

Individuals and communities need to be able to feel a sense of closeness, to experience positive attachments, in order to grow strong interpersonal relationships. When people do not feel this sense of attachment, it is hard to form positive relationships which are the foundation for healthy and active lives, both within the family and in the community at large. Often, it is not until people arrive in therapy that they become aware of their difficulties in forming positive attachments in my private practice; new clients frequently report that their relationships are stressed. Inherent within therapy is the movement of the client–therapist relationship from this deeply stressful place to a connection based on trust and comfort. One needs to look at the role of attachment and identity in this process. Erickson, Maslow, and Stern looked at the human life cycle, creating a set of theoretical developmental stages covering the entire lifespan. "These stages describe a series of developmental tasks, broadly linked to brain development, that govern the formation of identity as an outgrowth of interpersonal relations (such as trust vs. mistrust, autonomy vs. shame and doubt)" (Stern 1985, as cited in Erskine 1998). In other words, self-esteem arises from a direct relationship.

While attunement begins with the process of being empathic to a client, it goes well beyond this. Attunement is a deep kinesthetic response to affect and allows for the profound reparation of old wounds. Attunement includes not only what the therapist says but also how he or she moves and responds physically to a client. "It is a complex, emotional exchange between client and therapist in which the client is actively participating, engaged and responded to" (Levenson 1982, as cited in Beihl 2012, p.20). Healing rests on the therapist's capacity to see beyond the words spoken to acknowledge the deeper relational responses that might be seen and not heard. To be attuned effectively to the needs of clients who are often going through emotionally challenging times, the clinician must understand his or her own behavior and how that might impact the therapeutic alliance. If not, "ruptures" (Beihl 2012; Erskine 1998) in the attunement process can occur, in which there is failure to connect either verbally or nonverbally to the inter- or intrapsychic needs of the client. This could be as simple as a comment that might make sense in terms of the therapist's own cultural reality, but could feel insulting to the client (Beihl 2012).

Making change is not just about changing our thoughts or actions. It is often a process of becoming aware of lifelong assumptions about ourselves and the world around us, of ideas shaped and framed by those who are closest to us. Only after becoming aware of these limiting concepts is the client able to make room for change, to loosen the walls of resistances built in order to protect them from the effect of negative attachments.

Cognitive development research has been supported by neurological research. Neurological research is also demonstrating that using the arts to aid clients to better understand and manage attachment anxiety changes the neural pathways in the brain significantly (Malchiodi 2012). According to recent research in neuroscience, our brains are formed and shaped by our early parent–child attachments. These very same attachments influence, play out, and are hopefully resolved in the therapeutic alliance (Siegel 1999).

Memory is a psycho-physiological phenomenon. From birth onward, children attune to the world around them and form attachments to caregivers and objects. We experience our memories (both positive and negative) somatically and cognitively (Schore 1996). As children, we begin kinesthetically by making marks, using our whole bodies. Our physical and cognitive memories are created and encoded on the brain at an early age as part of the attachment process. A powerful therapeutic alliance has the opportunity to recode the synaptic connections of the memory system (Schore 2003). Literally, new pathways are created to improve brain function.

Looking at Our Cultural Relationships

A central tenet in psychotherapy is that clinicians must look at, and be aware of, their own biases, judgments, and prejudices. One of the ways that therapists attune is to become deeply aware of the ways their personal biases and life stories may enter into the therapeutic relationship, either negatively or positively. Nowhere is self-assessment more crucial than in cross-cultural work. When working with culturally different clients one needs to do a self-assessment to uncover the prejudices and beliefs one has developed about other cultures over the course of one's lifetime. In supervision we may ask the clinician to speak about the ways he or she has been influenced to think about people of differing ethnic and/or cultural backgrounds. How has she/he been taught to think about her/his own background in relationship to cultural and ethnic others?

Cultural Competence?

When I went to Bangladesh the first time, I carried a set of assumptions about the people who live there, what they eat, how they behave, and how they dress. I was ignorant about their relationship to art and the world of art. I soon found that many of my assumptions were faulty, and that reading the guide books didn't necessarily help me. I had to reassess my level of cultural awareness, my assumptions about the people of Bangladesh, and the biases and assumptions I had formed based on these beliefs. The idea of people using art in their everyday lives is new and evolving.

In developing a way to frame our work with cultural competence, we need to ask ourselves as clinicians some questions. These include:

- Who am I as a cultural being?

- How am I prejudiced?

- Am I being racist?

- What privilege, power, or control do I hold due to my ethnicity?

- How do I hold myself responsible for myself and others?

(Farrell, as cited in Ellis and Carlson 2007, p.58)

Other questions could be "How do I perceive the role of disability as a cultural identity? In what way does this impact how I am with my clients? How do I conceptualize my role as an arts therapist, and the ideas of art therapy, when working with other ethnic populations?" Beginning to ask these questions of ourselves is a basic way to begin the process of culturally attuning ourselves to our clients. It is easy to make assumptions that are based on our own histories, or on what we see, hear, or read in the media, rather than looking at what is happening for our client from their perspective. Most clinicians want to help their clients. Most of us enter this profession from a place of wanting to have meaningful work that is empathic and connective. Developing skills for establishing a connection with those from a very different background can be challenging if one does not have the ability to understand the cultural backgrounds of their clients and situations they have endured.

For instance, it was important that I had a deep understanding of the Bangladeshi perception of art and creating art. Art and art making is not thought of or done in the same way as in other countries. In Bangladesh, one will see art on rickshaws and trucks, often beautifully constructed posters and themes of the lives of Bangladeshis (see Figure 7.1).

Figure 7.1 Rickshaw with folk painting, Bangladesh

Therefore, in order to understand the cultural relevance around art and art making, I needed to deeply understand their cultural and ethnic beliefs. There will come moments when we fail to meet the client's needs and anxieties, or to address their negative reactions to our verbal/nonverbal behaviors (Beihl 2012). We are, like our clients, human, and we will inevitably miss key references when we ourselves become caught up in whatever emotion we are experiencing. The more aware of our own issues, beliefs, and prejudices we become, the more we can align ourselves with our clients who are struggling with similar dark spaces. There is a certain letting go required on the part of the therapist: acknowledging that they may not have handled a session well, or that they did not respond to the client in a way that the person was able to hear. Such moments invite us to seek reattunement, to bring the process back to the self in order to reshape and repair our patterned responses to the other.

It is imperative that the art therapist acknowledge and understand not only the personal symbols and metaphors clients use, but their cultural symbols as well. Attuning through art is critical to the art therapy process. Images can be both an anchor and signpost for expressing emotions (Davis 2010). Deeply attuning to images from a cultural perspective strengthens the relationship between therapist and client. Attunement can be facilitated through art when the client and therapist work together on an art piece. A conversation on paper using line, form, and symbol can be very instructive in understanding the underlying dynamics between the therapist and client, as well as cultural ideas and concerns regarding the sharing of space. In many Asian cultures nature is a predominant theme, with natural objects and processes used as a way of expressing the emotional nature of human experience. For instance, in a village in Bangladesh I worked with a group of women who had experienced the deaths of their children in a major accident a number of months earlier. At one point, to prepare for an art directive for creating a supportive community, I suggested a visualization that included walking down a garden path. During the exercise many of the women began to cry, and I discovered that in that community the symbol for family is a garden, and that children are represented by flowers. The visualization that was intended to help participants relax and experience support in finding a sense of peace had in fact done the complete opposite. Understanding this and aligning with their symbols allowed us to explore within the metaphorical field, and to find a culturally appropriate symbol, a symbol that supported their need to experience a sense of rest.

Conclusion

In the end, cultural sensitivity is a reflection of our ability to attune and respond to those who seek our aid. Art therapists need to adhere to the same principles and practices used by therapists from all mental health disciplines when exploring issues of attunement and cultural competency. Cultural sensitivity is being addressed in a number of different populations by art therapists. This is stressed in much of the current writing about art therapy, as many art therapists are now working with cultural populations, including refugees, in their home countries or abroad. This expanding role for art therapy has made the need for cultural attunement ever more apparent. Part of the process of attunement, from a cultural perspective, is simply asking questions of your client. Expressing a clear desire for cultural understanding between you and your client encourages the formation of a concordant relationship, one that deepens trust between the therapist and client. Asking clients a question regarding the meaning of metaphors and symbols from a cultural perspective also opens the door for the clients to understand that their beliefs and values are based on culture, and that culture and ethnicity have value and meaning. In the end, being as curious, accepting, and aware of your own self as you are asking your client to be, and being willing to test the emotional waters when things get challenging between you and your client, are the markings of a deep and growing therapeutic relationship.

References

American Counseling Association (2005) *ACA Code of Ethics*. Alexandria, VA: Author.

Becker-Weidman, A. (2010) *Didactic Developmental Psychotherapy: Central Practices and Methods*. Lanham, MD: Jason Aronson Publishers.

Becker-Weidman, A. (2012) *Intersubjectivity: The Core of Effective Therapeutic Parenting and Therapy*. Available at www.center4familydevelop.com/Intersubjectivity.pdf, accessed June 17, 2013.

Beihl, H. (2012) "Healthy human attachment and the client–therapist relationship: Attunement, resistances and ruptures." *BC Psychologist*, Oct.–Nov., 18–21.

Davis, B. (2010) "Hermeneutic methods in art therapy research with international students." *Arts in Psychotherapy 37*, 3, 179–189.

Ellis, C. M. and Carlson, J. (2007) *Cross Cultural Awareness and Social Justice in Counseling*. London: Routledge.

Erskine, R. (1998) "Attunement and involvement: Therapeutic responses to relational needs." Available at www.integrativetherapy.com/en/articles.php?id=31, accessed on July 23, 2013.

Faris, A. and van Ooijen, E. (2012) *Integrative Counselling and Psychotherapy: A Relational Approach*. Thousand Oaks, CA: Sage Publications.

Malchiodi, C. A. (1998) *The Art Therapy Sourcebook*. Los Angeles: Lowell House.

Malchiodi, C. A. (2012) *Handbook of Art Therapy*. New York: Guilford Press.

Schore, A. (1996) "The experience dependent maturation of a regulatory system in the orbital prefrontal cortex and the origin of developmental psychopathology." *Development and Psychopathology 8*, 59–87.

Schore, A. (2003) *Affect Dysregulation and Disorders of the Self/Affect Regulation and the Repair of the Self*. New York: W. W. Norton Publishing.

Schore, A. (2011) "The right brain implicit self lies at the core of psychoanalysis." *Psychoanalytic Dialogues 21*, 1, 75–100.

Shorter Oxford English Dictionary (2002) Fifth Edition. New York: Oxford University Press.

Siegel, D. J. (1999) *The Developing Mind: How Relationships and the Brain Interact to Shape Who We Are*. New York: Guilford Press.

Siegel, D. J. (2010) *Mindsight: The New Science of Personal Transformation*. New York: Bantam Books.

Singer, R. (2006) *The Therapeutic Relationship Is the Most Important Ingredient in Successful Therapy*. Available at http://EzineArticles.com/216007, accessed June 17, 2013.

Stern, D. (1985) *The Interpersonal World of the Infant: A View from Psychoanalysis and Developmental Psychology*. New York: Basic Books.

Sue, S. (1998) "In search of cultural competence in psychotherapy and counseling." *American Psychologist 53*, 4, 440–448.

Tervalon, M. and Murray-García, J. (1998) "Cultural humility versus cultural competence: A critical distinction in defining physician training outcomes in multicultural education." *Journal of Health Care for the Poor and Underserved 9*, 2, 117–125.

Vontress, C. E., Johnson, J. A., and Epp, L. R. (1999) *Cross-Cultural Counseling: A Case Book*. Alexandria, VA: American Counseling Association.

Chapter 8

On Being Human
Color and Culture
Paula Howie

Learning about Color

Just as it is impossible to determine the exact boundary when a hue moves from blue-green to green-blue, so it is impossible to demarcate culture and color. Indeed, culture and the way we see colors in our environment are inextricably intertwined.

As a child growing up in the 1950s, a box of 64 Crayola crayons was one of the pleasures and wonders of my young life. As a middle-class child living in the United States, I was taught primary and secondary colors and how to mix them in grade school. I was also exposed to beautiful and varied colors on television, in clothes, in food, and in print media such as comics and magazines. My color education was culturally bound and unique to that place and time. My counterparts in other countries had their own unique experiences with color, their environment, and their education.

Currently, my shared identities are that of artist and art therapist. I have been interested in the way color is used and perceived in my own artwork and that of my clients. My interest in clients' drawings and paintings evolved over time as a part of my practice, which began in the mid-1970s, and continues into the present. There seems to be a correlation between the amount of color and the colors most frequently used by clients whose diagnoses are similar. Linda Gantt and I presented a paper on diagnosis and art at an AATA conference (Gantt and Howie 1979); this was, to my knowledge, the earliest classification of pictorial markers, including color, in client art. Part of this work was informed by a particular interest in the use of color. Based on clinical impressions rather than on research, this paper sparked a great deal of interest and continues to generate research in our field (Gantt and Tabone 2003).

In the early 1980s, under the direction of Dr. Bernard Levy and with the assistance of several George Washington University interns, I studied the psychological literature that pertains to the meaning of color. A small portion of this work is reported later in this chapter, since the work is limited by timeworn material and by the fact that it did not include the cultural underpinnings of color.

My identity as a watercolor artist has solidified an interest in grasping and appreciating one's emotional connection to colors. As you might expect, mixing and experimenting with colors holds endless fascination for me (Figure 8.1).

Figure 8.1 Watercolor palette

Illustrated in the color insert

Through a Cultural Lens

Clearly, my heritage has influenced my way of observing my surroundings and how I understand color. But how has this happened and how pervasive is this influence? Oliver Sacks (1995) states that:

> color vision in real life is part and parcel of our total experience, is linked to our categorizations and values, becomes for each of us a part of our life-world, of us... It is at higher levels (of brain/mind) that integration occurs, that color fuses with memories, expectations, associations, and desires to make a world with resonance and meaning for each of us. (pp.28–29)

Colors affect us in different ways because we are looking through a cultural and experiential lens that is uniquely our own. However, the influence of culture on perception is a hotly debated topic and varies with one's philosophical underpinnings.

For instance, the linguistic relativity principle, which was popular in the 1950s, holds that differences in the way languages encode cultural and cognitive categories affect the way people think, such that speakers of different languages think and behave differently (King 2005). From the late 1980s, scholars of linguistic relativity agreed upon cultural effects in the domain of spatial cognition, in the social use of language, and in the field of color perception. Certain kinds of cognitive processes are affected but other processes are better seen as subject to universal factors. Berlin and Kay's color study (1999) found that, regardless of language or culture, there are 11 basic colors that all humans see. An astounding finding from their work was that speakers of languages that do not discriminate

11 basic colors can nonetheless sort them, leading to the postulation of the universality or innate ability to perceive these colors. Colors may be called different names but the perceptions of them are similar.

Visual Components of Color

Recent evidence suggests that the development for color vision in humans may have occurred 500 to 800 million years ago (King 2005). The earliest examples of human art use color as a channel for communication. Comparisons of human languages demonstrate that we do not necessarily all make the same distinctions among colors, nor are all of these distinctions necessary for our survival. However, distinguishing red from other colors is second only to a fundamental division between black and white (King 2005).

Color vision involves physical, chemical, physiological, psychological, and cultural components. "This process begins with the generation of signals in retinal receptors, involves comparisons and evaluations of the information that is transmitted to the brain and terminates with the declaration of particular hues in order to describe a scene" (Arnold 2001, p.383).

Sir Isaac Newton, writing in his book called *Opticks*, was the first person to show, by using a prism, that white light was actually all colors of the spectrum (Sacks 1995). Light could be split into component colors and it could also be reconstructed from those component colors by using a prism. Newton's color circle, which was made of red, orange, yellow, green, blue, indigo, and violet sections, looks white when spun on a top. This was the kind of evidence that led Thomas Young to his theory that there are three color receptors—red, green, and blue—in the retina. Fifty years later, Helmholtz rediscovered Young's work that color was a direct expression of the wavelengths of light absorbed by the three reflectors of the eye with the nervous system. This became known as the Young–Helmholtz hypothesis (Arnold 2001; Sacks 1995).

Johann Wolfgang von Goethe was a great poet, playwright, and novelist in the German language. In 1810, he published his *Theory of Colours*, which he considered his most important work (Sacks 1995). Goethe reformulated the topic of color in an entirely new way. Newton had viewed color as a physical problem, involving light striking objects and entering our eyes. Goethe realized that the sensations of color reaching our brain are also shaped by our perception, by the mechanics of human vision, and by the way our brains process information. Therefore, according to Goethe, what we see of an object depends upon the object, the lighting, the background, and our perception. Goethe took issue with "Newton's notion of an invariant relationship between wavelength and color," saying that this could hardly account for the complexity of color perception in real life. In other words, due to his personal experiences, Goethe formulated his own theory of color (Sacks 1995, p.21). Later researchers proved that the brain does indeed form colors and that colors occur not only in the world but are also constructed and interpreted by the complex workings of the brain.

Through the Looking Glass

Color is described in terms of hue or *chroma*, which is the name for the color (i.e., red, yellow, blue, etc.). Saturation is the degree of purity of the color, and intensity refers to the relative lightness or darkness of the color (Stone 2002).

In order to highlight how color perceptions vary among cultures, linguists look at how we categorize certain colors. For instance, in Russian there are two words for what most English-speakers call the color blue. Dark blue, "siniy," is a distinct color from light blue, "goluboy" (Shaughnessey 2010, p.2). These color categories are unique to speakers of the Russian language. Similarly, in Hungarian there are two terms for what we normally include in "red"; in Japanese one word covers green, blue, or all dark stimuli; Welsh has one word that means green, blue, gray, or brown. There is a similar example in Chinese. Red is "hóng" and pink is "n hóng" or literally "powder red," a linguistic derivation similar to "light blue" in English (Shaughnessey 2010, p.2).

In addition, researchers have also included age, gender, geography, economic class, education, technology, personal experience, and ethnicity in the mix of variables affecting color perception (Shaughnessey 2010).

A Personal Search for the Meaning of Color

In my first attempt to learn something about the use of color in drawings and paintings, I ran across a wealth of information concerning the relation of color and emotional states. I was somewhat taken aback to learn that there was little experimental evidence to support much of this material. Not surprisingly, I was also struck by the contradictions found in these writings. Despite these contradictions, I began to do a comprehensive review, giving special weight to those writings that included more clinical or research data.

I categorized more than 150 sources out of 400 sources identified. For clarity, the color literature has been divided into four major categories. They are as follows: *color meaning* includes the affective impact of color in studies where the actual colors are used; *color preference* includes individual or ethnic group preferences for certain colors; *reaction to color* concentrates on color tests, which make interpretations from an individual's manipulation of color (e.g., Max Phister Color Pyramid Test [in Schaie 1963]; Mosiac Test by Lowenfeld (2005); Rorschach Ink Blot Test [1949]; Luscher Color Test [1990]); and *color use*, which concentrates on studies showing the use of color in free productions of patients and normal groups. These categories were the most expeditious delineations given the massive amount of writing on the subject of color.

In this chapter, I look primarily at the meaning of color, as the literature on this subject is extensive. I have focused on adults, as the literature on the use and color preference of children is too general to include.

Theories on the Meaning of Color

Most of the studies on the meaning of color refer to color in relation to affect and personality characteristics and the correlation between these aspects of the human psyche. Webster defines affect as "the conscious subjective aspect of an emotion considered apart from bodily changes." In most work on the meaning of color, there is some attempt to show that color is linked with affect and that this can be proved. This is also a basic art therapy principle—with the caveat that one must always be cognizant of the personal and cultural meaning of a particular color for the client. For instance, I once presented the artwork of a Latino client in a team meeting at my place of work. The client had used black and the team was wondering about his depression. One of the Latino physicians explained that, in his culture, black was related to strength. This opened up a discussion about following up to find out how the client saw his color choice. Color and affect were shown to be significantly correlated in some studies (Crane 1962), but were not proved to be substantial in others (Choungourian 1967; Schwartz and Shagassi 1960).

Studies that concern color preference give no clearer account of the matter. Some writers claim that color preference is a matter of individual taste, while others maintain there exists an overall color preference scheme. Bjerstedt (1960) states that warm–cool color preferences are indicators of personality. Choungourian (1967) showed in his study that it is doubtful there is any correlation between warm–cool color preference and introversion–extroversion as Bjerstedt had asserted. As stated above, most authors maintain that there exists a connection between color and affect, but what exactly this connection is and how it fits in with color preference, color meaning, reaction to color, and color use is a matter of individual judgment.

Even the enormous amount of research carried out by the proponents of Rorschach's test shows some contradictions. There are those who believe in a phenomenon known as "color shock." This is seen on the color plates of the Rorschach and is linked to a subject's increased response time on these cards. For all the evidence supporting the theory of color shock, there is as much evidence that it does not exist (Keehn 1953a, 1953b).

Current Reflections on the Meaning of Color

Although, as noted above, there are cultural meanings to color, colors also have meaning across cultures and are a reflection of a particular time and place in history. In our dynamic world, views about colors are constantly changing or being modified by personal experiences. This was as true when Aristotle experimented with mixing colors and sounds (Gage 1999) as it is today. Colors define, differentiate, and modify our world in a way that form and volume cannot.

The following is a breakdown of the current views of our primary and secondary colors including black and white. Each color often has divergent and conflicting associations which no doubt reflect our human experience.

Red

Red is the color of life and blood but it can transform into cruelty and conflict. In Roman times, red meant war. Debra Amos (2013), when discussing the civil war in Syria, stated: "[O]ne teacher told me that kids only paint in red, and it's almost impossible for them to draw human beings without blood coming out of them." These children were reacting to the trauma they had witnessed in a way unique to their humanity, individual experiences, and culture.

In African symbolism red is the color of *nyama*, the potential force in all things and the blood of all beings (Ronnberg and Martin 2010). In African art, the warrior had red eyes, as did the vengeance-seeking Greeks. In China, as well as in Stone Age Europe, red pigment was buried with the bones of the dead to symbolize renewal of life (Benz and Portman 1972).

Today red is used in publications and media to get attention. Rooms painted totally red make people anxious, but rooms with a red accent can cause people to lose track of time, and can stimulate appetite (Stone 2002, p.34).

Orange

Orange is a secondary color made by mixing red and yellow. It is seen as both vigorous (red) and ethereal and everlasting (yellow). In the Buddha's time, prisoners wore orange, and today Buddhist monks wear bright orange robes to signify compassion for the dispossessed and condemned (Ronnberg and Martin 2010).

The vivid orange and black markings of the monarch butterfly warn off potential predators; its milkweed diet makes it toxic to eat. Roman brides wore a flame-like veil signifying Aurora or goddess of the dawn. In Roman mythology, Jupiter was purported to have presented an orange to Juno on their wedding day (Ronnberg and Martin 2010).

Today orange is associated with happiness, contentment, and fertility. In current marketing strategy, since it symbolizes appetite, it can be used to indicate that a product is suitable for everyone, and can make an expensive product have mass appeal (Stone 2002).

Yellow

Pure yellow is the most cheerful color, symbolic of the sun, brightness, and warmth. It is the symbol of the deity in many cultures. Dark yellow represents caution, decay, illness, and deceit (Stone 2002).

In traditional Chinese belief, yellow was linked with the sun and the emperor, who, during the Ch'ing dynasty, was the only person allowed to wear it (Theroux 1994). *Huang*, the Chinese word for yellow, also means radiant. The ancient Mayans of Mexico used *Kan* or yellow for the god who held up the sky (Ronnberg and Martin 2010).

Golden yellow in Islamic cultures stood for wise counsel, while pale yellow stood for betrayal and deceit. In Western cultures, yellow can be associated with cowardice or the informer (canary) (Ronnberg and Martin 2010).

Today it is noted that yellow is most stimulating to the eye and that it speeds up metabolism. Therefore, it is not used on notepads or monitor backgrounds due to its fatiguing effects on the eye. In advertising and media, it is usually a softer tint (Stone 2002).

Green

Green is the color of life and growth but it can also symbolize immaturity and inexperience. The ancient Egyptian god Osiris, who returned to life bringing the spring, was depicted as green (Ronnberg and Martin 2010).

The Christian crucifix, representing death and resurrection, was pictured as green (Ronnberg and Martin 2010). Sacred to Islam, green is the color of Mohammad's flag, of the dome and interior of his tomb, and of the green and white flags of his descendants (Theroux 1996).

The more negative aspects of green are those of illness, death, poison, slime, mold, pus, and nausea. "In the psyche, too, there is the green-eyed monster of jealousy, and being 'green with envy'" (Ronnberg and Martin 2010, p.646).

In current usage, green implies nature as well as caring for the planet and being ecologically aware and all that goes with this—hope, life, youth, renewal, and vigor. Green rooms help people to unwind, and green is a popular color in hospitals because it relaxes patients (Stone 2002).

Blue

Blue represents sadness and depression as well as wisdom, trust, and loyalty. Jupiter, Krishna, Vishnu, Odin, and the Virgin Mary's cape were depicted in shades of blue (Ronnberg and Martin 2010). Homer, the Greek poet, had no word for blue, referring to the sea as dark red (Gage 2000). In a majority of the world's languages the same word means both blue and green (Theroux 1994, p.56).

Blue pigment was difficult to make, and therefore early man did not have it (Figure 8.2). In current times, it is used in bedrooms because it causes the body to produce calming chemicals (Stone 2002). In addition, studies show that students score higher and that weightlifters lift heavier weights in blue rooms. People retain more when reading information written in blue text (Stone 2002).

Figure 8.2 "Oceania" by the author depicts the availability
of the color blue to modern painters

Illustrated in the color insert

Purple

A mixture of red and blue, purple brings together opposites such as the red of passion and the blue of reason, the real and the ideal, love and wisdom, heaven and earth, or, psychologically, the union of opposing energies within an individual (Ronnberg and Martin 2010). Purple is also a difficult color to make and, therefore, was rare in ancient cultures.

In Chinese Taoism, purple presents a transition between yang and yin, active and passive. Shinto priests in Japan use purple for their robes along with natives in the Tehuantepec area of southern Mexico. The Aztecs and Incas considered purple a royal color. In Christian symbolism it connotes spiritual growth and the union in Christ of what is divine and what is human (Ronnberg and Martin 2010).

Black

Black can connote reliability, strength, or steadfastness, as well as rot, decay, or dirt. Dirt holds the promise of life, as did the flooding of the Nile, with its fertile, black soil. The silt deposited each year contributed to the development of civilization in Egypt. Black deities such as the Hindu goddess Kali, the Christian Black Mary, the

Egyptian goddess Isis, and the Greek goddesses Persephone, Artemis, and Hecate all possess the black womb of death and the promise of the new life (Ronnberg and Martin 2010). In Navajo tradition, black is sinister but can also conceal and protect. In parts of Africa, black is the color of the north from which the rains of renewal come. Black signifies an inner journey of transformation and eventual self-awareness of the soul. The Sufi mystic poet Rumi described black as "the consummation of all colors" (Ronnberg and Martin 2010, p.658).

In current times, black is a popular color for clothing because it is visually slimming and denotes power, stylishness, and sophistication. Priests wear black to signify submission to God (Stone 2002).

White

White symbolizes new beginnings, the ethereal, and spring time, as well as infirmity, disembodiment, and the pale horseman of death. In Hindu mythology, it is the maternal ocean and source of the nectar of immortal life. From its waters emerge saps and elixirs, the white cow of all desires, and the moon-white elephant which symbolizes the Vishuddha chakra (the chakra is the throat or "void" in which all the elements intermingle) (Ronnberg and Martin 2010, p.660). White Buffalo Woman in Sioux legend gives the sacred pipe and all the holy rituals honoring Grandmother and Mother Earth. White also represents the ash of bitter suffering and hard-won wisdom, and the white hair of the knowing old man or crone (Ronnberg and Martin 2010).

Conclusion

The mysteries of color and culture may never be fully resolved. Color continues to be one of mankind's richest and most unique gifts. It provides a means of expression for the artist and the poet, who create colors aesthetically, "bringing us the pigments of sensate reality as well as the tones of invisible dimensions" (Ronnberg and Martin 2010, p.636).

Color does so much for us, signaling the changing of the seasons in the alizarin and gold leaves of fall, telling us of the warming of the spring with its sap green, allowing us to see the blue, repulsive tint of spoiled food, signaling when the vermillion tomato or raspberry is ready to eat, and giving us the titanium starkness of winter. Most mammals are colorblind, but due to our color sight we have an advantage in discerning predators, fleeing from danger, and identifying friends.

Even though there is no single theory that summarizes the meaning of color in all cultures, there is a general understanding that certain colors can be attributed to individual personality traits, cultural norms, and human perception. The color we perceive, no matter what it is called, is one of the most fundamental aspects of our physicality and humanity. If eyes are considered to be windows to the soul, then color, one of our special gifts from the universe, is its illumination.

References

Amos, D. (2013) "In War-Torn Northern Syria, Children 'Only Paint in Red'." *NPR Morning Edition*, January 4.

Arnold, W. N. (2001) "Color and meaning: Art, science, and symbolism." *Leonardo 34*, 4, 383–384.

Benz, E. and Portman, A. (1972) *Color Symbolism: Six Excerpts for the Eramos Yearbook.* Dallas: Spring Publications.

Berlin, B. and Kay, P. (1999) *Basic Color Terms: Their Universality and Evolution.* Stanford: CSLI Publications.

Bjerstedt, A. (1960) "Warm–cool color preferences as potential personality indicators: A preliminary note." *Perceptual and Motor Skills 10*, 31–34.

Choungourian, A. (1967) "Introversion–extroversion and color preferences." *Journal of Projective Techniques 31*, 92–94.

Crane, R. (1962) "An experiment dealing with color and emotion." *Bulletin of Art Therapy 1*, 3, 25–28.

Gage, J. (1999) *Color and Culture.* Berkeley: University of California Press.

Gage, J. (2000) *Color and Meaning: Art, Science, and Symbolism.* Berkeley, CA: University of California Press.

Gantt, L. and Howie, P. (1979) "Diagnostic categories and pictorial characteristics." *Proceedings: American Art Therapy Association Conference.* Mundelein: American Art Therapy Association.

Gantt, L. and Tabone, C. (2003) "The Formal Elements Art Therapy Scale and Draw a Person Picking an Apple from a Tree." In C. Malchiodi (ed.) *Handbook of Art Therapy.* New York: Guilford Press.

Keehn, J. D. (1953a) "Rorschach validation II: The validity of colour shock in the diagnosis of neuroticism." *Journal of Mental Science 99*, 224–234.

Keehn, J. D. (1953b) "Rorschach validation III: An examination of the role of colour as a determinant in the Rorschach test." *Journal of Mental Science 99*, 410–438.

King, T. (2005) "Human color perception, cognition, and culture: Why 'red' is always red." *IS&T Reporter 20*, 1, 1–8.

Lowenfeld, M. (2005) *The Mosaic Test.* East Sussex: Academic Press.

Luscher, M. (1990) *Luscher Color Test.* New York: Pocket Books.

Ronnberg, A. and Martin, K. (2010) *The Book of Symbols.* Cologne: TASCHEN.

Rorschach, H. (1949) *Psychodiagnostics: A Diagnostic Test Based on Perception.* New York: Grune and Stratton.

Sacks, O. (1995) *An Anthropologist on Mars.* New York: Vintage Books.

Schaie, K. W. (1963) "The colour pyramid test: A nonverbal technique for personality assessment." *Psychological Bulletin 60*, 530–547.

Schwartz, M. and Shagassi, C. (1960) "Responses to color and conflict-inducing stimuli in a psychiatric population." *Perceptual and Motor Skills 11*, 245–252.

Shaughnessy, M. (2010) *Seeing Languages Differently.* Available at http://boingboing.net/2010/06/27/seeing-languages-dif.html, accessed on June 17, 2013.

Stone, V. (2002) *Colours: The Formula of Light.* Available at www.scribd.com/doc/11272712/ColoursThe-Formula-of-Light, accessed July 23, 2013.

Theroux, A. (1994) *The Primary Colors.* New York: Warner Books.

Theroux, A. (1996) *The Secondary Colors: Three Essays.* New York: Warner Books.

Chapter 9

How Spirituality Impacts
Art Therapy

Mimi Farrelly-Hansen

My Therapeutic Approach

When a client arrives, I invite them to settle into their chair and consciously attend to their breathing. Joining them in the silence, I affirm their intrinsic health and inwardly renew my intention to meet them open-heartedly and be of service. Because I want people to appreciate that I value them as more than a tangle of problems to solve, my intake questionnaire asks questions like "What sustains you and gives you hope?" as well as "How's your nutrition? Exercise and self-care? Hobbies and interests? Religious and/or spiritual resources?" During our first few sessions I often assess a client through an art assessment adapted from Roberta Shoemaker-Beal's WhATS?, the Wholistic Art Therapy Series (2011). Here simple art materials (colored pencil, oil pastels, or markers) and four 10-inch paper plates are given with the invitation to express the four main aspects of one's being: body, mind, emotions, and spirit. If a person prefers working three-dimensionally, I offer clay or assemblages of found objects gathered from a visit outdoors. Most people find this exercise both safe and informative. Just noting the similarities and differences in their four pieces, as well as what sort of an impact each one makes alone or in various pairings, often suggests new possibilities for handling the issue that brought them to therapy in the first place. With new resources at hand, their presenting difficulties can be located within a larger context, allowing for a treatment plan that honors strengths as well as vulnerabilities.

The scenario just described takes place in a comfortable home studio with a separate entrance, on the western edge of the Great Plains, near a medium-sized city in northern Colorado. Gardens, fruit trees, and views of the Rocky Mountains abound, along with a collection of perennial plants tough enough to flourish in this hot, dry, windy climate. Thanks to designated "open space" nearby, nature with its faithful cycles of death and rebirth is reassuringly close at hand. The drop-in center, discussed later, is a few miles away. The overarching umbrella for my work is transpersonal psychology, meaning that I include spirituality in the scope of assessment and treatment, seeking to blend the wisdom of the world's spiritual traditions with the wisdom of modern psychology (Cortright 1997; Farrelly-Hansen 2001). The above description from my private practice shows my allegiance to both transpersonal *perspective* (understanding the client as a psychological and a spiritual being) and *path* (the personal disciplines I undertake and ask my clients to take in their journey to greater wholeness). For me, Buddhist psychology is a strong influence (Kornfield 2010). I believe in people's basic goodness, that they are doing the best they can with the skills they have to cope with the hand they've been dealt. Inspired by the Dalai Lama's naming of kindness as the prime content of his religion, I use, and often discuss with clients, the benefits of practicing sitting meditation as a tool for learning to observe one's thoughts and feelings without judging them and without running away. I work at replacing judgment toward a client or toward myself with an attitude of openness and curiosity. I also rely on regular time in my studio to remind me of what it feels like to negotiate the disciplines (spiritual as well as artistic) of surrendering control, navigating chaos, and tolerating ambiguity as a response to everything from joy to pain to bewilderment over life's big questions. Finally, I continue to befriend my own personal rough edges through supervision and, as needed, psychotherapy. Thirty years of providing art therapy to others has taught me that I can only accompany my clients as far into their own depths as I have ventured into mine.

Feminist relational-cultural therapy also informs my work. Developed at the Stone Center of Wellesley College, this model, according to Jordan, sees "the yearning for and movement toward connection as central organizing factors in people's lives and the experience of chronic disconnection or isolation as a primary source of suffering" (Jordan 2004, p.11). In addition, unlike Western society's cultural bias toward individualism, competition, self-sufficiency, and hierarchical power, proponents of this theory believe in mutuality and mutual empathy, allowing me as therapist and my client as fellow human being to be vulnerable to each other and to collaborate in the healing process (Jordan 2004). Both Buddhist and feminist psychologies are part of a transpersonal *context*—in other words, one's beliefs, values, and intentions as a therapist (Vaughan 1979). Within that framework, my primary technique is always art therapy, with occasional help from the art therapy focusing technique (Rappaport 2009), the body-centered practices of Hakomi (Kurtz 2007), and using nature as a resource (Farrelly-Hansen 2001).

Spirituality and Religion: Definitions

Nowadays it seems that every branch of mental health has its own subgroup dedicated to these two topics and has produced a set of guidelines for how to assess them (Culliford 2011). A leaflet from the Royal College of Psychiatrists in England likens spirituality to "experiencing a deep-seated sense of meaning and purpose in life, along with a sense of belonging…acceptance, integration, and wholeness…especially important in times of emotional stress, physical and mental illness, loss, bereavement, and death" (Culliford 2011, pp.37–38).

Spiritual comes from the Latin root *spiritus*, meaning "breath, courage, vigor, and soul" (Webster 1973, p.1373). As a hatha yoga practitioner of many years, I find comfort in remembering that my connection with that deeper level of knowing and meaning called by many names (God, Goddess, Krishna, Allah, Brahman, the Tao, the One, et al.) is as close to me as my breath. When I breathe slowly and deliberately, I feel invigorated, more receptive to what the Bible calls "the still small voice" (1 Kings 19:12) guiding me toward attitudes and behaviors more aligned with my true self than with my everyday ego. Noticing my breath becomes a source of gratitude, a connection to the more than seven billion co-inhabitants of the planet who depend on the same air that I do.

The word *religion* is another matter. From the Latin root *religio*, meaning reverence for the gods, religion is generally understood as "any specific system of belief, worship, conduct, etc., often involving a code of ethics and a philosophy" (Webster 1978, p.1200). Put differently by Cortright, "religion is the organized established structures," whereas "spirituality is the soul's free quest for the divine" (Cortright 1997, p.13).

Some art therapists may not bring their own religious beliefs or spiritual orientation into the therapeutic arena, while for others these may serve as a background to the theoretical practices they identify with. In my own case, belonging for over 30 years to a Mainline Protestant church with a strong peace and justice orientation has been important. Its study groups, workshops, and retreats have exposed me to stimulating material and new relationships. Within that loving fellowship I have grown by offering art therapy opportunities on a broad range of topics such as working with dreams, praying through liturgical dance, or gaining inspiration from the life and art of the twelfth-century visionary writer and composer, Hildegard of Bingen. My late colleague, Dr. Clyde Reid, used to remind me of how, historically, our church has provided ways for us to respond effectively to the world's tragedies, from terrorist attacks to hurricanes, to forest fires, droughts, and floods. The church's record on civil rights, education, and serving the destitute has been amazing. In his view, "Modern religion without spirituality is bone dry and perilously empty. And spirituality needs some structure, some context to help it fulfill its promises" (Reid 2001, p.5).

When at work, I reference my own religious or spiritual perspectives judiciously, remembering that their usefulness may be mostly for me in terms of life-enhancing rituals and inspiration. I am aware of what I don't know, aware of my own biases and blind spots. I am also aware that religious affiliation in the United States is definitely on the decline, with 20 percent of 46 million respondents to a 2012 PEW poll declaring no religious affiliation, even though, paradoxically, many of those same "nones" (i.e., having no religious affiliation) self-identify as religious and have a daily practice of prayer (Glenn 2013). I also know that for individuals of a fundamentalist persuasion I may not be the therapist of choice. Still, for most of my private clients, my transpersonal orientation is an asset. The majority are older adults dealing with questions about ultimate meaning, death, and the isolation and grief accompanying the accelerated losses of loved ones as well as issues related to retirement, declining health, and other end-of-life transitions. Many of these individuals openly express their hunger for spiritual nourishment and community. In the studio, their artistic explorations tend toward free choice paintings, drawings, or collage. Practices like shrine making or creating labyrinths or illustrating a favorite prayer or poem from a wide range of wisdom traditions are appealing, often leading to honest conversation about faith and its expression in today's world.

Soft Voices Drop-In Center

Spirituality has a different face at a community drop-in center for persons with mental illness. Here spirituality is expressed as radical hospitality, an open-hearted warmth toward all who enter. Founded in 2003 as a collaboration between Longmont's First Congregational Church, the county Mental Health Partners, and the Outreach United Resources (OUR) agency, the center's mission is to establish "a safe haven for people with mental illness and their friends to socialize, to empower themselves, to express creativity, and to build community" (see www.softvoices.org). Fueling the initial impetus for the center were three factors: the unmet needs and isolation of several church families supporting someone with a persistent mental disorder; the church Mental Health Ministry's desire to combat stigma through education; and the reality of huge and ongoing funding cuts for the county's Mental Health Partners. Interest in moving forward was high; a centrally located, nearly free space quickly became available; a handful of church members (myself included) signed up to be trained for hosting three two-hour weekly sessions. A director, a person in recovery from mental illness, was named and offered a modest salary by Mental Health Partners. All other roles were filled by volunteers and members of an advisory board who represented the three founding organizations as well as several mental health consumers.

Today Soft Voices extends hospitality to anywhere from 6 to 26 visitors (a.k.a. members) per session. These individuals suffer from schizophrenia, bipolar disorder, depression, anxiety, and other disorders, and are among the most invisible, overlooked, and impoverished residents in our city. Many struggle to find food and shelter; many lack both the concentration skills and the social skills to qualify for steady employment. For people like this, Soft Voices is a true haven. Some attend all four weekly sessions, share meals, go for daily walks together, and often gain the necessary confidence and capacity to find paid or volunteer work in the community.

Early on I established Friday as "art day," and instantly ran up against the reality that Soft Voices was first and foremost a drop-in center, not a community art studio! Some people loved art, had prior training, and couldn't wait to get their hands on materials they couldn't afford otherwise. Some were curious but afraid. Another group came exclusively for food and fellowship. Negotiating these three sets of needs in a fairly tight space became an ongoing dance. Each week I would arrive with a warm-up activity or skill-building idea. Pass-around drawings or sculptures were a big hit! People had such a need to relax, socialize, make up outrageous stories, and laugh. I felt like the court jester, bringing in anything that might engage them: art books, magazines, films, fresh flowers, bird skeletons. Eventually the program began to take on a life of its own, with many folks making art throughout the week, using a wide array of traditional art media along with found objects scrounged from dumpsters. Recognized member artists were sought out for help by beginners wanting to join in the fun. A craft program with a volunteer leader added more creative outlets.

Crowded and cramped as this space is, here I and the other art volunteers function like the art mentors who staff community art studios across the country (Franklin, Rothus, and Schpok 2007; Timm-Bottos 2001; Vick and Sexton-Radek 2008). We work alongside our members, often revealing aspects of our own life stories. We teach and are taught. Sometimes there is contact outside of the center—at a coffee shop, a gallery, the public library. We influence one another and are the better for it.

I see that art making done in this setting supports experimentation, risk taking, problem solving, social contact, interdependence, and self-esteem. Over time some members trade in their "mentally ill" identity for an artist's identity. I bring in my own work and discuss it, both process and product, with others. Art volunteers and members do the same. Our collective trust deepens. Many get hooked on learning new skills or risk sharing their own talents by leading a mini workshop. Community artists inspire us. We all grow through opportunities to exhibit and sell finished work at local venues as well as through the online Etsy website. Additionally, we share our love of poetry at community readings, enjoy outings to museums and recreation areas, and applaud the offerings of the monthly music program.

Thanks to the safety of the drop-in center, hard truths can be shared. While open dialogue about religion has been banned from the premises because of the emotional heat it generates, spirituality in the form of compassion is practiced daily. Community members struggle with compromised health, limited income, the realities of stigma, and the losses of childhood dreams once within reach. Volunteers are challenged to stay present to whatever is happening and to practice empathy too.

Member Profile: Meet Bruce David

One of our longest-attending members is Bruce David (name changed for privacy issues), a humble, hospitable man of great faith and one of our most disciplined, dedicated artists and poets. Let me describe him briefly before you read his own words about art making.

Bruce is a fiftyish man with bushy gray Albert Einstein hair held in place by a well-loved baseball cap. He walks slowly, often with a cane. Always he carries a cloth bag with a sketchbook and a gallon Ziploc bag full of colored pencils. Soft spoken and shy, Bruce feels things deeply and is often moved to tears by an event in his own life or that of a friend. Here's how he described himself in a poetry chapbook (a small collection of poems centered on a specific theme) that we helped him produce to give away or sell recently:

> For me, art is something recent. I started coming to Soft Voices in 2003 after getting diagnosed with a rare neurological condition called CADASIL [syndrome] that had already caused me to have several strokes. I had to stop my long-time job as a surgical assistant. My left side was partially paralyzed so I couldn't draw or paint. Mimi got me started writing poetry, which saved my life! She really helped me to come out of my shell. My wife and son encouraged me a lot too. So far I've written over 2000 poems and have read some of them at local coffee shops. I write about my feelings and my faith. I guess my writing's pretty honest because sometimes it makes people cry, and they thank me for telling the truth.
>
> These days I draw a lot too. My left hand can work again, so I've filled three sketchbooks with colored pencil and watercolor pencil drawings that take two to four days to complete and are inspired by a picture in a magazine or book.
>
> Why do I do art? Because it frees me from physical and mental boundaries. It lets me explore. It's a way to escape and stay on the positive side. (Bruce David, personal communication, 2011)

See Figures 9.1 and 9.2 for examples of his work.

Bruce David's Poem: Stay with Me Until...

Thoughts and memories are slowly starting to fade away.
I know because I can personally feel it.
It's kind of like water,
Slowly drying up in the desert sands.

Figure 9.1 "Spirit Nation," colored pencil, 4½" × 6½" paper

Illustrated in the color insert

Figure 9.2 "Crossing Waterfalls," colored pencil, 4½" × 6½" paper

Illustrated in the color insert

Conclusion

The spirituality embodied in transpersonal psychology has provided me with a broad and trustworthy umbrella for what goes on in an hour of individual art therapy or a two-hour art session at a drop-in center. My work is enriched by both the perspective and the path that including spirituality provides. In private practice I help my clients probe troublesome issues and create ways of softening their impact. There, change is a real possibility. People "graduate" and move on, often having reclaimed spiritual resources and renegotiated religious woundings. At Soft Voices, where the chronicity of suffering is real, members initially find spiritual support in the hospitality and empathy of the staff and other members. Making art and daring to show it at local venues, alongside the art made by Soft Voices volunteers, helps build self-esteem and reinforces a sense of belonging to a wider community. Outside of Soft Voices, participation in 12-step programs offers additional options for fellowship and service. Over time a handful of members achieve enough recovery from their mental handicaps to enjoy church membership and other community involvements (Leff and Warner 2006).

Overall I have found that reaching into the spiritual domain with clients supports positive change in much the same way that art making can, through experiences of relaxation, present centeredness, mystery, expanded view, gratitude, and awe. Additionally, helping clients believe in their essential goodness reduces shame and violence toward themselves and others, increases empathy, and deepens the experience of being fundamentally lovable and deeply connected. Perhaps the thirteenth-century poet and mystic Rumi, who consistently allied himself with the impulse to praise and recognize every person and every moment as sacred, said it best:

> There is a community of the spirit.
> Join it and feel the delight
> of walking in the noisy street
> and *being* the noise.
>
> *(Barks 2004, p.3)*

References

Barks, C. (2004) *The Essential Rumi*. New York: HarperCollins.

Cortright, B. (1997) *Psychotherapy and Spirit: Theory and Practice in Transpersonal Psychotherapy*. Albany: State University of New York Press.

Culliford, L. (2011) *The Psychology of Spirituality*. London: Jessica Kingsley Publishers.

Farrelly-Hansen, M. (ed.) (2001) "Nature: Art Therapy in Partnership with the Earth." In *Spirituality and Art Therapy: Living the Connection*. London: Jessica Kingsley Publishers.

Franklin, M., Rothus, M., and Schpok, K. (2007) "Unity in Diversity: Communal Pluralism in the Art Studio and the Classroom." In F. Kaplan (ed.) *Art Therapy and Social Action*. London: Jessica Kingsley Publishers.

Glenn, H. (2013) *Losing Our Religion: The Growth of the Nones.* Washington: NPR.

Jordan, J. (2004) "Towards Competence and Connection." In J. Jordan, M. Walker, and L. Hartling (eds) *The Complexity of Connection.* New York: The Guilford Press.

Kornfield, J. (2010) "All Day with Jack Kornfield." Unpublished manuscript from Buddhism and Psychology, FACES Conference, Boulder, CO.

Kurtz, R. (2007) *Body-Centered Psychotherapy.* Mendocino, CA: LifeRhythm.

Leff, J. and Warner, R. (2006) *Social Inclusion of People with Mental Illness.* Cambridge: Cambridge University Press.

Rappaport, L. (2009) *Focusing-Oriented Art Therapy: Accessing the Body's Wisdom and Creative Intelligence.* London: Jessica Kingsley Publishers.

Reid, C. (2001) "Spirituality vs. Religion." Unpublished manuscript, Boulder, CO.

Shoemaker-Beal, R. (2011) *The WhATS: The Wholistic Art Therapy Series.* Wimberley, TX: Author.

The Holy Bible, Revised Standard Version (1962; original publication date 1611). San Francisco, CA: The World Publishing Company for Cokesbury.

Timm-Bottos, J. (2001) "The Heart of the Lion: Joining Community through Art Making." In M. Farrelly-Hansen (ed.) *Spirituality and Art Therapy: Living the Connection.* London: Jessica Kingsley Publishers.

Vaughan, F. (1979) "Transpersonal psychotherapy: Context, content, and process." *The Journal of Transpersonal Psychology 11,* 2, 101–110.

Vick, R. and Sexton-Radek, K. (2008) "Community-based art studios in Europe and the United States: A comparative study." *Art Therapy: Journal of the American Art Therapy Association 25,* 1, 4–10.

Webster, M. (1973) *Webster's New Collegiate Dictionary.* New York: G & C Merriam Co.

Webster, M. (1978) *New World Dictionary.* New York: William Collins and World Publishing.

Chapter 10

Practicing Multiculturally Competent Art Therapy

Cheryl Doby-Copeland

Becoming a multiculturally competent practitioner, educator, administrator, or member of society requires a continuous commitment to acquire multicultural self-awareness, multicultural knowledge, and the skills to provide multiculturally relevant services (Sue, Arrendondo, and McDavis 1992), and is an indispensable foundation for clinical expertise (Constantine 2002; Fuertes and Brobst 2002). With that statement in mind, I realize I was thrust into making this commitment many years before I decided to become an art therapist or understood the meaning of cultural competence. In this chapter, I describe several personal experiences and strategies that fostered my commitment to develop multicultural competence.

Introduction

My earliest memories as an African-American girl growing up in Washington, DC during the Civil Rights Movement forged my burgeoning respect for racial cultural difference. I had just turned ten years old when the Reverend Dr. Martin Luther King, Jr. made his iconic "I Have a Dream" speech on the steps of the Lincoln Memorial. Three months later I was rushed home from elementary school after the assassination of President John F. Kennedy. The historical significance of these events notwithstanding, my exposure to them initiated my racial cultural identity awareness. Living in Washington, DC in 1968 after the assassination of Dr. King, I witnessed the riots in the nation's capital and watched on television the civil unrest occurring in major cities across America. These were years of immense racial polarization in the United States (Doby-Copeland 2006a).

Eventually my artistic pursuits required riding the bus past Vietnam War protesters near the White House to Saturday art classes at the Corcoran Gallery of Art. One of our first tasks was to create a self-portrait using colored mosaics. My first exposure to racial prejudice came when a Caucasian boy used an unmistakably prejudicial remark to admonish me to use the correct shade of brown mosaics for my skin tone (Doby-Copeland 2006a). This experience remained with me for many years and represents my initial contact with racial bias and prejudice. Consequently, these cultural and contextual factors became the motivation for my commitment to effective art therapy practice and multicultural competence.

Multicultural Competence Awareness

We as art therapists must be mindful of our social responsibility to become change agents and inoculate our clients against racial injustice, oppression, discrimination, and stereotypes that affect them personally (Junge et al. 1993). Racial, ethnic, and cultural prejudice arises in the form of preconceived judgments about individuals from selected groups. Developing multicultural competence requires an understanding of the interplay between privilege and oppression in order to increase minority clients' satisfaction with therapy (Hays 2008). A minority client's history of prejudice and oppression affects the amount of social support he/she receives, as well as his/her employment and socioeconomic status, while encouraging maladaptive coping responses including anxiety disorders, depression, suicide, substance abuse, violence, and physical illnesses such as hypertension and heart disease (Ancis 2004).

Racial/Cultural Identity Development

Racial/cultural identity development (R/CID) has emerged as a major theoretical paradigm for conceptualizing, diagnosing, and acknowledging sociopolitical influences within group differences (Sue and Sue 2013). The R/CID model explores the idea that racial group membership dictates the individual client's preferences for the therapist's culture and the client's responses to therapeutic interventions. The R/CID model includes attitudes toward one's self, attitudes toward others of the same minority, attitudes toward others of a different minority, and attitudes toward the dominant group at each stage (Sue and Sue 2013). Several different multicultural R/CID models have been researched (see Appendix A).

> The R/CID model defines five stages of development that oppressed people experience as they struggle to understand themselves in terms of their own culture, the dominant culture, and the oppressive relationship between the two cultures: conformity, dissonance, resistance and immersion, introspection, and integrative awareness. (Sue and Sue 2013, p.296)

My personal R/CID involved a progression from the *Conformity* ego status, in which I identified with White standards of self-definition, to the *Dissonance* ego status, where I began to question my lack of fit in the White world. As a girl, my mother straightened my kinky hair, which was the accepted standard, and placed me in the *Conformity* status. The Black Pride movement in the United States ignited my personal feelings of *Dissonance*. Attending college during the years when students were protesting the lack of African-American studies in college curricula became the contextual influence that moved me from the *Dissonance* racial identity ego status to the *Immersion* status. My progression to the *Immersion* status, in which I idealized my racial group by wearing dashikis and having an Afro hairstyle, was most evident during my early college experiences. During my

self-awareness development, I explored the concept of White privilege and R/
CID. McIntosh (1988) delineated a list of the daily effects of White privilege
in her life. Examples from her list include "I can, if I wish, arrange to be in the
company of my race most of the time" and "I can go shopping alone most of the
time, fairly well assured that I will not be followed or harassed by store detectives"
(McIntosh 1988, p.79).

My graduate training, and eventual service on the American Art Therapy
Association's (AATA) Multicultural Committee, propelled me through the
Internalization status, in which I developed the capacity to objectively assess and
respond differentially to qualities and viewpoints of my own racial group and
the dominant racial group (Helms 1994). My early AATA service focused on
encouraging individuals from minority groups to enter and study in the field of art
therapy, and topical presentations made at the AATA annual conference promoted
strategies for developing multicultural competence. An *Integrative Awareness*
status is my priority and necessitates maintaining a positive racial identity while
empathizing and collaborating with members of other oppressed groups in order
to manifest holistic self-exploration through the use of culturally competent art
therapy interventions.

Culturally Biased Assumptions

> From my mind's eye, I see the woman hesitate. She is volunteering in an
> inner-city shelter and comes very close to handing the black boy a flesh-toned
> crayon to color the arms of a figure in his coloring book. She halts when she
> realizes that the crayon is the shade of her skin, not his. (Hoare 1994, p.24)

Hoare (1994) illustrates the volunteer's potentially culturally biased assumption
using art materials. Providing effective art therapy to diverse clients requires
acceptance that every individual involved in the therapy encounter, both therapist
and client, comes to that moment with a set of cultural assumptions. Pedersen
(1994) describes several of the most frequent examples of culturally biased
assumptions: assumptions of what constitutes normal behavior, dependence on
professional jargon, overemphasis on individual instead of collectivist viewpoints,
neglect of historical influences on contemporary treatment problems, and cultural
encapsulation (ethnocentric perspective). Accordingly, differences in the therapist's
and client's belief systems have far-reaching implications for diagnosis, clinical
case conceptualization, and identification of treatment interventions, compliance,
and treatment recommendations.

Multicultural Competence Knowledge

Culture-specific information in art making is particularly important for art therapists, and involves developing an understanding of the affective meaning of symbols and color usage (Alter-Muri 2002; Chebaro 1998; Kellogg et al. 1977; Mangan 1978; Mooney 1891). Multicultural knowledge acquisition begins with an exploration of the research on the specific culture in an effort to understand the worldview of an individual from another culture in a nonjudgmental manner (Cattaneo 1994; Sue and Sue 1999). Sue and Sue (1990) define worldview as the attitudes, values, opinions, and concepts that inform decision making and behavior.

Cognitive empathy is demonstrated when the therapist examines the cultural and contextual nature of the client's worldview, which includes the influences of family values and possible experiences with discrimination, racism, and heterosexism (Sue and Sue 2013). My graduate art therapy training did not include an emphasis on racial cultural differences in artistic expression or the use of symbols/imagery or color. While in training at a large psychiatric hospital, I witnessed the culturally biased assumptions of an Asian psychiatrist's interpretation of the artwork of a Puerto Rican client. The Asian psychiatrist considered the Puerto Rican client's depiction of his house on stilts as evidence of an unsteady personality rather than an accurate representation of the structure of his native home (Doby-Copeland 2006a). I realized my culture-specific knowledge gave me a greater understanding of the Puerto Rican client's imagery. This experience convinced me of the importance of gaining specific multicultural knowledge to provide effective multicultural art therapy.

Vontress, Johnson, and Epp (1999) recommend conducting a cultural inventory (cultural biography) to obtain culture-specific client information. For example, many world cultures have a collectivistic and interdependent orientation, and the structure of many families is hierarchical in nature (Sue and Sue 2013). Therapists are encouraged to experience diverse cultures by attending community-based events, cultural art exhibits, and rituals celebrating food, music, and dance (Doby-Copeland 2006b). When planning art therapy interventions, culture-specific knowledge will inform your decisions on whether to use an *emic* perspective (culture-specific behaviors, terms, and ideas) or an *etic* perspective (culture-universal behaviors, terms, and ideas).

A thorough discussion of the culture-specific characteristics of individual racial cultural groups is beyond the scope of this chapter. Sue and Sue (2013, p.351), however, offer the following information relative to certain culturally diverse groups:

- African-Americans prefer an egalitarian therapeutic relationship.

- Asian Americans prefer a more formal relationship and concrete suggestions from the counselor.

- Latino Americans do better with a more personal relationship with the counselor.

- American Indians/Alaska Natives prefer a relaxed, client-centered listening style.

However, culture-specific information cannot be applied rigidly, as this knowledge has the potential to foster stereotypes. Therefore, an appreciation of within-group differences is required, which considers such issues as acculturation, the identification of cultural beliefs related to the therapy/mental health, and unique subjective experiences (Sue and Sue 2013).

Multicultural Competence Skill

Racial Microaggressions

Overt acts of racism (i.e., cross-burnings and racial segregation) have evolved into often unrecognizable/unintentional behaviors in the therapeutic process (Ridley 2005). Racial microaggressions, a form of aversive racism (Constantine 2007), are the subtle and commonplace exchanges that convey denigrating messages to a target group—for example, people of visible racial ethnic groups, religious minorities, women, people with disabilities, and gay, lesbian, bisexual, and transgendered individuals (Pierce et al. 1978; Sue et al. 2007). Sue and Sue (2013, pp.154–155) posit three types of microaggressions: *microassault* (blatant, verbal, nonverbal, discriminatory, and biased sentiments—for example, using labels such as *rag head, faggot,* or *nigger*); *microinsult* (unintentional behaviors or verbal comments, which are rude, demeaning, or insensitive—for example, describing an African-American's speech as articulate, or stating they are a credit to their race, which implies African-Americans are less intelligent than Whites; or conveying surprise when a female is good in math); and *microinvalidation* (behaviors or verbal comments that exclude, negate, or psychologically dismiss the target group—for example, color blindness [denying an individual as a member of a race or culture], or when a therapist negates the client's experience of racial prejudice/oppression as a stressor by attributing the client's feelings to paranoia).

Multicultural treatment skills require the intentional application of therapeutic interventions with diverse populations. Pederson (1994, p.240) offered a "Triad Training Model" to measure effective multicultural skill development that includes articulating the therapy concerns from the client's perspective, recognizing resistance from a culturally diverse client in specific rather than general terms, diminishing therapist defensiveness in a culturally ambiguous relationship, and learning recovery skills for getting out of trouble when mistakes are made in therapy.

Multicultural and International Clinical Case Conceptualization

Heppner, Leong, and Gerstein (2008) reference a conceptual framework for international competency in psychotherapy that draws from Bronfenbrenner's (1979) ecological model. Bronfenbrenner's model describes five distinct systems and the interactions among them: microsystem, mesosystem, exosystem, macrosystem, and chronosystem. Although Bronfenbrenner's theory was originated as a process to understand child development, his recommendation of observing the interactions of individuals in their natural environment is applicable to art therapists providing psychotherapy in international settings. The microsystem denotes those relationships and interactions that are closest to the child—that is, family, peers, and school. The mesosystem represents the influences closest to the child—that is, relationships with parents or between parents and school. The exosystem is the larger social context—that is, the community that surrounds children indirectly by way of their parents. The macrosystem is farthest from the child and represents the cultural values, economic conditions, political systems, and laws that influence the child's development. Lastly, the chronosystem integrates the unique effect of a child's personal history. Heppner et al. (2008) recommend, when providing psychotherapy in international settings, that therapists consider international clients in the context of the systems that influence their life, values, beliefs, personality, and behavior.

Practicing Multicultural Awareness

The application of Bronfenbrenner's clinical case conceptualization approach to international clients can be very challenging, given a potential new language; unfamiliar social, cultural, political, religious, and economic systems; and unaccustomed norms, values, and behaviors (Ægisdóttir and Gerstein 2010). An initial step in understanding how international clients are influenced by their cultural context is developing an awareness of the microsystem and macrosystem influences.

When the therapist determines his/her current stage of R/CID in terms of values, beliefs, race, culture, class, and power determinants, that awareness will assist in conceptualizing the influence of the therapist's racial cultural identity on therapeutic interactions with clients of different racial and/or cultural backgrounds. For example, if an African-American client in the Immersion ego status (preference to identify primarily with African-American culture) engages in art therapy with a White therapist in the Contact ego status (oblivious to racism and its role in the client's world), the therapist's acquired multicultural self-awareness increases the likelihood of culturally sensitive treatment interventions. Art therapists are encouraged to maintain an active awareness of the racial and cultural assumptions that influence their conceptualization of the therapy process, and to maintain an open mind to truly understand the worldview of his/her culturally different client (Sue and Sue 1990).

Practicing Multicultural Knowledge

Multicultural knowledge requires developing an understanding of the therapist's own cultural heritage and customs, and the impact such knowledge has on the therapist's conceptualization of normal and abnormal behavior. Moreover, therapists are encouraged to develop an understanding of *culture-bound values* (individually centered, verbal/emotional/behavioral expressiveness, communication patterns from therapist to client, openness and intimacy, cause and effect linear approach, and distinctions between mental and physical health); *class-bound values* (strict adherence to 50-minute therapy time frame, ambiguous or unstructured approach to problems, and seeking long-range goals); and *language variables* (using standard English and emphasizing verbal communication) (Sue and Sue 1990, p.34).

An important component of multicultural knowledge competence is an understanding of how the therapist's theoretical orientation shapes his/her conceptualization of the therapy process and the client's dynamics. The therapist's theoretical orientation determines the assessment/diagnostic decisions and procedures, selection of interventions, and therapeutic outcomes/recommendations. It is possible to use any of the contemporary theoretical perspectives (e.g., psychodynamic, person-centered, cognitive-behavioral) to provide therapy to culturally diverse clients, while being mindful to compensate for these and many other theoretical approaches' lack of inclusion of cultural or racial dynamics as components of the therapy process (Helms and Cook 1999).

Art therapists using a psychodynamic approach to therapy are reminded, when interpreting the client's past as a critical source of information, to avoid overlaying their own cultural, racial, and socioeconomic biases on their interpretations. Client experiences that may seem aberrant to the art therapist may be normal for the client in the context of his/her racial/cultural social environment (Helms and Cook 1999). International clients' exposure to racism, ethnocentrism, sexism, and classism contribute to their presenting problems. Psychodynamic theory credits considerable responsibility to the parents (primarily the mother) for the client's maladaptive personality development. Parenting styles, family roles, and systems are different in collectivistic societies. Using Bronfenbrenner's theory and being aware of the various types of families that exist in international society will increase the therapist's multicultural knowledge and the likelihood of framing appropriate questions. The goal of developing an autonomous/individualistic personality, another aspect of psychodynamic theory, may not be congruent for all multicultural/international clients. Art therapists are advised to make collaborative decisions regarding the client's treatment goals to ensure cultural relevance.

Many international clients may not use equivalent defense mechanisms to manage anxiety. Gaining an understanding of the purpose served by the defenses in the client's early development may provide a basis for assessing normal and abnormal personality development in the context of the client's culture. It is also important to consider that defenses, which are characterized as internal strategies used to address self-induced anxiety, may be necessary for the international/ multicultural client's psychological and physical survival (Helms and Cook 1999).

In client-centered or person-centered approaches to therapy the therapist exhibits genuineness, unconditional positive regard, and empathic understanding, while placing emphasis on self-actualization (Rogers 1980). A challenge for art therapists using this approach with multicultural/international clients is its emphasis on verbal communication. Although art therapy interventions can minimize verbal interactions, an over-emphasis on verbal communication may pose a problem for clients who are hesitant to discuss their feelings related to race and culture. Many clients from collectivistic cultures may express these feelings nonverbally. The goal of self-actualization may be challenging for multicultural/ international clients given societal barriers. Frequently multicultural/international clients have to manage an identity to be used in the marketplace that is very different from the identity they use to remain a member of their home culture. Therefore, the art therapist may have to support the client in recognizing the interface and conflict between the client's need to manage multiple identities.

Art therapists who use a cognitive-behavioral approach to treatment blend behavioral approaches for externalizing behaviors with cognitive approaches for internal behaviors (e.g., irrational thoughts). Cognitive-behavioral therapists believe a client's behaviors are determined by the manner in which he/she thinks about the world, and they assist the client in identifying and reframing cognitions that contribute to self-defeating behaviors. When working with multicultural clients using a cognitive-behavioral approach, art therapists should be mindful that these clients might not perceive a separation of mind (cognition) and body (emotions). Many multicultural clients believe the mind, body, and spirit are inseparable. That said, cognitive-behavioral approaches can allow for a focus on external or cultural factors that contribute to the client's self-defeating cognitions (Helms and Cook 1999).

Current emphasis on evidence-based practices is providing optimism that research evidence begins with a comprehensive understanding of the client's cultural background and treatment concerns, while considering which therapeutic approach is most likely to provide the best outcome. Empirically supported treatments like evidence-based practices are primarily derived from qualitative studies, clinical observations, methodical case studies, and interventions provided in the client's natural setting (Sue and Sue 2013). Multicultural competence within the evidence-based practice framework focuses on the quality of the therapeutic alliance and the necessary skills therapists need to assess the client's strengths and weaknesses.

Practicing Multicultural Skill

Art therapists use their knowledge base to develop appropriate, sensitive, and effective interventions to work with multicultural and international clients. Assessment tools are adapted to meet the needs of racially and/or culturally different clients. Interventions are generated based upon a wide variety of verbal and nonverbal responses. Art therapists understand that skill is required to send and receive communication effectively—for example, to determine when to use directness and confrontation. Accuracy of communication requires an understanding of cultural cues, subtlety, and indirectness of communication (Sue and Sue 1990). The multiculturally skilled therapist may have to include nontraditional resources, including indigenous healers, culture brokers (community representatives/mediators), and community-based strategies, which are outside of the intrapsychic counseling model (Sue and Sue 1999).

Practicing multiculturally skilled art therapy allows for admitting the limitations of your knowledge, while communicating a genuine willingness to understand the client's worldview. Although multicultural competence focuses on the differences between client and therapist, these differences should not be perceived as problems. When art therapists view cultural differences as positive attributes, they allow for resolving the challenges that arise in the cross-cultural therapeutic relationship, and display the characteristics of multiculturally competent therapists (Sue and Sue 1990).

Conclusion

Multiculturally competent art therapists have the ability to work effectively with culturally diverse individuals, have developed an understanding of their own worldview, are continuously increasing their knowledge of other culturally diverse groups' worldviews, and have acquired the skills to intentionally implement culture-based interventions/treatment strategies. Multiculturally proficient art therapists value diversity and consistently provide therapy services that are sensitive and responsive to multicultural issues. My effort to achieve multicultural proficiency is an ongoing process. In this chapter I have attempted to provide cultural competence strategies that foster the therapist's self-awareness and promote self-expression when providing art therapy to multicultural and international clients.

References

Ægisdóttir, S. and Gerstein, L. H. (2010) "International Counseling Competencies: A New Frontier in Multicultural Training." In J. G. Ponterotto, J. M. Casas, L. A. Suzuki, and C. M. Alexander (eds) *Handbook of Multicultural Counseling, Third Edition.* Thousand Oaks, CA: Sage.

Alter-Muri, S. B. (2002) "Viktor Lowenfeld revisited: A review of Lowenfeld's preschematic, schematic and gang age stages." *American Journal of Art Therapy 40*, 170–192.

Ancis, J. R. (2004) "Culturally Responsive Practice." In J. R. Ancis (ed.) *Culturally Responsive Interventions: Innovative Approaches to Working with Diverse Populations.* Philadelphia: Brunner-Routledge.

Bronfenbrenner, U. (1979) *The Ecology of Human Development: Experiments by Nature and Design.* Cambridge, MA: Harvard University Press.

Cattaneo, M. (1994) "Addressing culture and values in the training of art therapists." *Art Therapy: Journal of the American Art Therapy Association 11*, 3, 184–186.

Chebaro, M. (1998) "Cross Cultural Inquiry in Art and Therapy." In A. R. Hiscox and C. A. Calisch (eds) *Tapestry of Cultural Issues in Art Therapy.* Philadelphia: Jessica Kingsley Publishers.

Constantine, M. G. (2002) "Predictors of satisfaction with counseling: Racial and ethnic minority clients' attitudes toward counseling and their ratings of their counselors' general and multicultural counseling competence." *Journal of Counseling Psychology 49*, 255–263.

Constantine, M. G. (2007) "Racial microaggressions against African American clients in cross-racial counseling relationships." *Journal of Counseling Psychology 54*, 1–16.

Doby-Copeland, C. (2006a) "Things come to me: Reflections from an art therapist of color." *Art Therapy: Journal of the American Art Therapy Association 23*, 2, 81–85.

Doby-Copeland, C. (2006b) "Cultural diversity curriculum design: An art therapist's perspective." *Art Therapy: Journal of the American Art Therapy Association 23*, 4, 172–180.

Fuertes, J. N. and Brobst, K. (2002) "Clients' ratings of counselor multicultural competency." *Cultural Diversity and Ethnic Diversity Psychology 8*, 214–233.

Hays, D. G. (2008) "Assessing multicultural competence in counselor trainees: A review of instrumentation and future directions." *Journal of Counseling Development 86*, 95–101.

Helms, J. E. (1994) "How multiculturalism obscures racial factors in the therapy process: Comment on Ridley et al. (1994), Sodowsky et al. (1994), Ottavi et al. (1994), and Thompson et al. (1994)." *Journal of Counseling Psychology 41*, 62–165.

Helms, J. E. and Cook, D. A. (1999) *Using Race and Culture in Counseling and Psychotherapy: Theory and Process.* Boston: Allyn and Bacon.

Heppner, P. P., Leong, F. T. L., and Gerstein, L. H. (2008) "Counseling within a Changing World: Meeting the Psychological Needs of Societies in the World." In W. B. Walsh (ed.) *Biennial Review of Counseling Psychology.* New York: Taylor and Francis.

Hoare, C. H. (1994) "Psychosocial Identity Development in United States Society: Its Role in Fostering Exclusion of Cultural Others." In E. P. Salett and D. R. Koslow (eds) *Race, Ethnicity and Self: Identity in Multicultural Perspective.* Washington, DC: National MultiCultural Institute.

Junge, M. B., Alvarez, J. F., Kellogg, A., and Volker, C. (1993) "The art therapist as social activist: Reflections and visions." *Art Therapy: Journal of the American Art Therapy Association 10*, 148–155.

Kellogg, J., MacRae, M., Bonny, H. L., and DiLeo, F. (1977) "The use of the mandala in psychological evaluation and treatment." *American Journal of Art Therapy 16*, 123–126.

Mangan, J. (1978) "Cultural conventions of pictorial representation: Iconic literacy and education." *Education Communication and Technology 26*, 245–267.

McIntosh, P. (1988) *White Privilege and Male Privilege: A Personal Account of Coming to See Correspondences Through Work in Women's Studies.* Working Paper No.189, Wellesley College Center for Research on Women, Wellesley, MA.

Mooney, J. (1891) "The Sacred Formula of Cherokees: Color Symbolism." In *Internet Sacred Text Archive.* Available at www.sacred-texts.com/nam/cher/sfoc/sfoc24.htm, accessed on June 17, 2013.

Pederson, P. B. (1994) *A Handbook for Developing Multicultural Awareness, Second Edition.* Alexandria, VA: American Counseling Association.

Pierce, C., Carew, J., Pierce-Gonzalez, D., and Willis, D. (1978) "An Experiment in Racism: TV Commercials." In C. Pierce (ed.) *Television and Education.* Beverly Hills, CA: Sage.

Ridley, C. R. (2005) *Overcoming Unintentional Racism in Counseling and Therapy, Second Edition.* Thousand Oaks, CA: Sage.

Rogers, C. R. (1980) *A Way of Being.* Boston: Houghton Mifflin Company.

Sue, D. W. and Sue, D. (1990) *Counseling the Culturally Different: Theory and Practice.* New York: Wiley.

Sue, D. W. and Sue, D. (1999) *Counseling the Culturally Different: Theory and Practice, Third Edition.* New York: Wiley.

Sue, D. W. and Sue, D. (2013) *Counseling the Culturally Diverse: Theory and Practice, Sixth Edition.* Hoboken, NJ: Wiley.

Sue, D. W., Arrendondo, P., and McDavis, R. J. (1992) "Multicultural Competence Standards: A call to the profession." *Journal of Counseling and Development 70,* 477–486.

Sue, D. W., Capodilupo, C. M., Torino, G. C., Bucceri, J. M. et al. (2007) "Racial microaggressions in everyday life: Implications for clinical practice." *American Psychologist 62,* 271–286.

Vontress, C. E., Johnson, J. A., and Epp, L. R. (1999) *Cross-Cultural Counseling: A Casebook.* Alexandria, VA: American Counseling Association.

Resources
Further Reading

Bowers, E. M. (1996) *Directory of Culturally Diverse Art and Play Therapy Materials for Children and Adolescents.* Orangevale, CA: Author.

Pederson, P. B. (2004) *110 Experiences for Multicultural Learning.* Washington, DC: American Psychological Association.

Pope, M., Panglinan, J. S., and Coker, A. D. (2011) *Experiential Activities for Teaching Multicultural Competence in Counseling.* Alexandria, VA: American Counseling Association.

Online

American Art Therapy Association Multicultural Committee Selected Bibliography and Resource List (November 2005). American Art Therapy Association Inc. Available at www.arttherapy.org/upload/multiculturalbibliography.pdf.

Art Therapy Multicultural/Diversity Competencies (December 2011). American Art Therapy Association Inc. Available at www.arttherapy.org/aata-multicultural.html.

Part III

The Practice of Culturally Based Art Therapy in Educational Settings

Chapter 11

Art Therapy in Schools
Its Variety and Benefits

Emmy Lou Glassman and Sangeeta Prasad

Why Use Art Therapy in Schools?

Oftentimes, academically strong schools or education programs around the world find that some students enrolled are not able to successfully engage in the learning process for one or more reasons. It would be ideal if, despite the challenging personal circumstances that some face, those students could learn just as easily as others. The school, sometimes a second home to students, is thus challenged with having not only to educate the student, but also to provide supports that overcome obstacles, foster learning, and address the needs of the whole child.

Perhaps a child is living with a terminally ill parent at home. He may become anxious, fearful, or depressed thinking about what will become of that parent and himself. Focusing on school lessons is more of a struggle due to his emotional response to this traumatic life situation. Perhaps a teenager suffers from low self-esteem and avoids attending school on a regular basis. Or perhaps another student's learning differences have resulted in an accumulation of frustrated school experiences. These built-up feelings and attitudes may cause him/her to give up on his/her academic performance. Each of these situations could result in a student's negative frame of mind regarding learning and his/her own ability to do so.

In an attempt to meet the educational demands of diverse populations, schools all over the world continue to create unique programs that attempt to satisfy these varied needs. Addressing a student's education obstacles, whether they are social, intellectual, physical, or emotional, is often the first step. In this chapter, we share how a number of schools and education programs have incorporated the useful, natural, and productive tool of art therapy in order to individualize and aid the learning process. We also address some cultural adaptations that art therapists have made to bring art therapy to their particular school settings.

Successful International School Art Therapy Programs

Art therapists have sensed the importance of and need for art therapy in schools, and have thus created a significant presence there. In the United States, where art therapy services vary, some school districts have numerous art therapists, while others have a few or just one. In the American Art Therapy Association's (AATA) *Toolkit for Art Therapy in Schools* (AATA 2011), which focuses on kindergarten through grade 12, eight different kinds of art therapy programs have been highlighted. The toolkit provides a brief overview of the innovative ways that art therapists have integrated art therapy into schools for children who have a wide variety of needs. According to this toolkit, while some of the schools provide art therapy as part of the Individual Educational Plan (IEP)—a government-mandated plan for all students with special learning needs—other schools provide art therapy as enrichment or as an after-school program. In one model, the Miami-Dade County Public School Board has established an art therapy program with approximately 20 art therapists who use a structured program with well-established guidelines that focuses on meeting IEP goals. Another model exists in the Mt. Lebanon School District in Pennsylvania where an after-school art expression program has been created as a nonprofit model. Here, art therapists conduct art expression groups for mainstream and special-needs students to provide opportunities for increased socialization, self-esteem, and communication skills. Many of the art therapy programs mentioned in the toolkit illuminate a wide variety of approaches being used in other school systems within the United States.

Globally, we have found that there are many different and innovative ways in which art therapists work within their school districts. Influenced by the kind of educational system present in each country, the art therapist may work under the local education department or privately with for-profit or nonprofit institutions. Awareness of and cultural views about the field of art and its role in education seem to influence how art therapy is being introduced. Following are a few ways in which art therapy is being established in various parts of the world.

In Israel, most art therapists are trained in the United States or Europe and placed in schools by the Ministry of Education. The art therapist may work with a population of varied needs. In her book *Art Therapy in Schools: Effective Integration of Art Therapists in Schools*, Dafna Moriya discusses the role of art therapy in Israeli schools and the structure needed to integrate it within a school system, going on to outline challenges faced and strategies that may help (Moriya 2000).

According to Unnur Ottarsdottir in Iceland, special education services, including art therapy, are provided within the mainstream schools. Art therapists work with individuals and groups by incorporating elements from student coursework, such as letters, words, numbers, spelling, etc., into the art making. The art therapist works as both a special educator and an art therapist (Ottarsdottir 2010).

In the United Kingdom, as in the United States, art therapy is well established in several school systems, with a wide range of programs. According to Fuyuko Takeda in *Arts Therapies in Schools: Research and Practice*, "with the introduction of the National Service Frameworks (NSF) by the Department of Health in 2004, the school has extended its role as a place for teaching and learning, and has provided a wide range of services including therapeutic support" (Takeda in Karkou 2010, p.217). This act created numerous staff positions for art therapists within schools in the United Kingdom. Art therapy in other European countries is varied and there is little information published on art therapy in schools there. It should be noted, too, that most of the art therapists in Europe are educated in the United States and United Kingdom.

Art therapy is in its infancy in Asian and African schools, despite the great need in those regions. In India, for example, due to the varied school systems and socioeconomic levels, different kinds of art therapy approaches are needed. While one school may be able to afford an art therapist, another school may struggle to provide the basic infrastructure for learning. Space and materials are the biggest challenges when working in Africa or Asia (Prasad 2008). India is a country that is rich in traditional art, with higher education available in the fine arts, visual communication, and graphic design. However, the fields of art education and art therapy have not yet become part of the curricula for undergraduate or graduate-level studies. There is a need for trained professionals in this area.

According to statements from our interview with Hing-Chung Chow, an art therapist who works in Hong Kong, "Art therapy is still not a recognized discipline…and not an established post in schools." Chow points out, however, that if a school finds a need and has the funds, it might employ a short-term resident art therapist for 6 to 12 months. If a school is in need of facilitating a project of six to ten sessions, it might also investigate hiring an art therapist.

In Korea, there is an increasing awareness of the role of art in healing. Many hospitals and educational settings are beginning to integrate art therapy into their therapeutic services. In special education settings, art therapy is blended into art education to provide therapeutic benefits to art making. According to Lee Min Jung, Korean culture, family values, and Confucian ideas have historically influenced the role of therapy in treatment. Now there is a change taking place from the family- and community-centered support and way of life to a more individualist way of thinking. These changes have ushered in a need and appreciation for different forms of self-expression (Kalmanowitz, Potash, and Chan 2012).

In looking at the art therapy programs in schools around the world, it is evident that art therapists are challenged to meet the needs of children within the family structure, to understand the larger cultural philosophy, and to respect the role of the individual within the community. Reflecting on his work in Hong Kong, art therapist Jordan Potash states: "Among the other struggles associated with the governance and maintaining citizen well being, politicians, educators, entrepreneurs and practitioners in Asia often need to negotiate the lines between adhering to, adapting or relinquishing cultural values in the face of contemporary needs" (Kalmanowitz et al. 2012, p.48). These challenges to the establishment of art therapy in settings around the world appear to be universal.

Roles of the Art Therapist in Schools

In her book *The Handbook of School Art Therapy*, Janet Bush (1997) outlines the various roles of school art therapists in the Miami-Dade counties in Florida. These roles, or ones similar to what she describes, may be found in many school art therapy programs. Bush discusses the *Art Education Therapist* as someone who combines a background in art education with art therapy. Someone in this role would be able to implement art lessons while at the same time having the skill to identify pathologies seen in student artwork and treat those pathologies. Students with handicaps such as autism, emotional disabilities, or cognitive challenges would require an unconventional art curriculum and depend on adaptive teaching approaches. Most regular education art teachers are not equipped to teach art to students with disabilities such as these (Bush 1997).

Illustrating this point is the case of an art teacher who had sincere intentions of helping children with severe developmental delays. She loved art and felt she was capable of teaching these children. However, the teacher had no training in special education or art therapy. She struggled to find ways to teach those who could not communicate verbally or draw in the traditional manner beyond a scribble. Eventually, it became evident that the teacher's lack of training and understanding of the population was frustrating her ability to teach. When she observed an art therapist working with the children, she was amazed at how various therapeutic approaches and processing techniques promoted successful work with this challenging group. The teacher was able to recognize that it was not enough to know how to draw and teach another person those skills. She saw that art therapy used the innate abilities of a person to find expression through the visual and creative process and that a scribble was not a mere scribble, but rather a reflection of the feelings and ideas of the individual child.

Bush goes on to describe the *Clinical Art Therapist* as a school art therapist who is not a certified art teacher. In the Miami-Dade setting, clinical art therapists do not teach, although studio art training is part of their requisite knowledge. The emphasis in this role is not only on the art itself, but also on the use of art psychotherapy—therapeutic and diagnostic practices with children who have myriad challenges. These clinical art therapists may serve both exceptional and regular education students in an assigned caseload on a continuing basis. An art therapist *consultant* also performs the duties of a clinical art therapist but on an individual referral basis.

Finally, Bush discusses art therapists who concentrate on the staff development of school personnel and who are called *Trainers*. Their task is to serve the school's counselors, psychologists, and classroom teachers by expanding their knowledge of child development and art. Designed as a preventive measure, this training enables school personnel to informally assess student artwork and be able to spot the early stages of cognitive and/or emotional issues in children (Bush 1997).

The art therapist may take on these different roles in a school with more emphasis on one or another. School art therapists hold an unusual position as staff/faculty. Unlike the principal, school psychologist, school social worker, or school counselor, the art therapist often works more frequently with students, sometimes seeing them every day. Throughout the school year, the art therapist may identify learning and emotional needs, growing academic capabilities, shifts in personality, changes in home circumstances, or stresses that students are facing. Often, because of what he or she sees in the art studio and in the art itself, it is the art therapist who is the first to be aware of these changes. Holding a key role within the education framework, the art therapist consults regularly with the clinical and/or administrative staff to relay updates and to provide insight about each student and his/her progress.

Becoming a School Art Therapist in the United States

There is a clear distinction between the training of an art therapist and that of an art educator. Most art therapists in schools hold a Master's degree in art therapy which focuses on both art and psychology. Each accrues over 1000 hours in the field as a student intern. Art therapists are trained to understand a student's verbal and nonverbal messages as well as to interpret both their art process and the final art product beyond its aesthetic value. Art therapists also observe and understand the student's behaviors, prepare to assess the student, and then create goals or a treatment plan for the individual in a way that complements the education system in place.

Many art therapists who work in schools may be required to hold a degree in teaching and a license to do so. Such training can offer further skills to the individual working in this unique situation. Classroom management, coupled with group art therapy techniques, can aid in focusing a group to appropriately and enthusiastically engage in art making.

An undergraduate degree or concentration in art education would also add richness to an art therapist's repertoire. He/she would have a deeper understanding of what each medium or technique could offer a student, what each may elicit from the student, and the degree of skill needed in using that medium or technique. When necessary, lessons on mastery can help a student more richly interpret his/her thoughts and feelings through his/her artwork.

The Value of Having Art Therapy in Schools

The integration of art therapy with education enhances the possibility of reaching an abundance of children with learning challenges. Schools that include art therapy as an integral part of their program are not only offering additional services to their students for the purpose of better educating them, but are also helping the students to know themselves better. While the focus is on working through obstacles in order to have educational success, what may result are healthier and more socially acceptable behaviors, raised self-esteem, and a more positive attitude about school and learning.

One of the most valuable aspects of using either individual or group art therapy in a school setting is its flexibility in serving students in a short- or long-term capacity. Short-term art therapy interventions, with a particular focus, are often successfully adopted in schools. In one such case, a four-year-old boy in India, referred for art therapy because of his distracting and disruptive behaviors, was eventually found to have had difficulty understanding the English language in class. A speaker of the Tamil language, he had found ways of gaining attention through his noncompliance. In art therapy, the boy learned that he could "converse" creatively. The art therapist was able to understand his artistic communications, a language that they both understood. He began to trust the art therapist, gain self-esteem, and settle down in class. He overcame his resistance to learning and changed the perception of his being a "bad kid" during the three months of art therapy intervention, the only psychological service he received during this time period.

Art therapy services may also be provided to a student over the span of several years while attending a school. Illustrating this is the case of an emotionally disabled high school student who had been adopted as an infant. Never able to reconcile to the fact that his birth mother had "given him up," the boy was angry. None of his relationships was healthy. Most of his anger was with his adoptive mother, but that anger spilled over to the rest of his life. The artwork he created during his four years in the art-as-therapy classroom revolved around a repeated theme—a large wooden sailing ship, sometimes in rough seas, sometimes on fire, often in battle with other ships. With sensitivity and guidance from the school art therapist, the student was given the opportunity to metaphorically work on his issues, make empowering media choices, and discuss the progressive images with her. Finally, as graduation approached, the ship was seen sailing smoothly on still waters, heading toward a new destination in the distance. His relationship with his mother improved greatly, he enjoyed a growing circle of new friends, and a vocational school program waited for him after graduation. Artistically working through emotional obstacles, this student was eventually able to integrate newly formulated creative solutions into his life. Rather than a "quick fix," students like this have been left with long-term ingrained experiences that have acted as tools which strengthened their problem-solving abilities.

Art therapy programs exist in a wide assortment of school settings, from residential treatment facilities, to detention/jail centers, to public or private schools that serve mainstream students or those identified as having emotional, intellectual, or physical disabilities. All of these programs exist for the same reason—to help children access their education and overcome learning obstacles to do so.

Overall Benefits of Art Therapy in Schools

As a result of art therapy interventions in their schools, students around the world may emerge stronger from their programs in the following ways. Typically they:

- are more adjusted to their world

- feel less depressed, anxious, angry, or violent

- are more independent and better able to self-advocate

- possess better social skills, raised self-esteem, and a more defined self-concept

- possess increased tolerance for frustration

- develop a better problem-solving capacity

- display a sounder academic performance

- possess improved sensory or motor skill adaptation

- develop conflict resolution skills

- establish better attendance at school due to more involvement with their work

- hold a healthier, more positive attitude about learning and school.

With growing evidence such as this, ideally any student with a need should be able to receive art therapy services in school. Although not universal as yet, school art therapy, in its various stages of development, has clearly made a difference in the lives of many students around the world. As a parent once said, "After starting art therapy, my child seems to love life more."

References

American Art Therapy Association (AATA) (2011) Art Therapy Tool Kit. Gain Important Education Outcomes: Implement a Successful Art Therapy Program within K–12 Schools. *The American Art Therapy Association*. Available at www.americanarttherapyassociation.org/upload/toolkitarttherapyinschools.pdf, accessed on June 17, 2013.

Bush, J. (1997) *The Handbook of School Art Therapy: Introducing Art Therapy into a School System.* Springfield, IL: Charles C. Thomas Publisher.

Kalmanowitz, D., Potash, J. S., and Chan, S. M. (2012) *Art Therapy in Asia: To the Bone or Wrapped in Silk.* London: Jessica Kingsley Publishers.

Karkou, V. (2010) *Arts Therapies in Schools: Research and Practice.* London: Jessica Kingsley Publishers.

Moriya, D. (2000) *Art Therapy in Schools: Effective Integration of Art Therapists in Schools. Strategies for Dealing with the Challenges Facing the Art Therapist in the School System.* Ramat Hasharon: Author.

Ottarsdottir, U. (2010) "Writing-Images." *Art Therapy: Journal of the American Art Therapy Association* 27, 1, 32–39.

Prasad, S. (2008) *Creative Expression: Say It with Art.* Chennai, India: Author.

Resources
Further Reading

Frostig, K., Essex, M., and Hertz, J. (1998) *Expressive Arts Therapies in Schools: A Supervision and Program Development Guide.* Springfield, IL: Charles C. Thomas Publisher.

Kearns, D. (2004) "Art therapy with a child experiencing sensory integration difficulty." *Art Therapy: Journal of the American Art Therapy Association 21*, 2, 95–101.

Malchiodi, C. (1998) *Understanding Children's Drawings.* New York: Guilford.

Pleasant-Metcalf, A. and Rosal, M. (1997) "The use of art therapy to improve academic performance." *Art Therapy: Journal of the American Art Therapy Association 14*, 1, 23–29.

Safran, D. (2002) *Art Therapy and ADHD: Diagnostic and Therapeutic Approaches.* London: Jessica Kingsley Publishers.

Silver, R. (1999) *Contemporary Art Therapy Approaches with Adolescents.* London: Jessica Kingsley Publishers.

Silver, R. (2000) *Developing Cognitive and Creative Skills Through Art: Programs for Children with Communication Disorders or Learning Disabilities, Third Edition.* New York: Albin Press.

Williams, K. and Thayer, C. (1999) "Postscript to the American Art Therapy Association's 1996–1997 Membership Survey." *Art Therapy: Journal of the American Art Therapy Association 16*, 2, 87–88.

Online

Art Therapy Connection. Available at www.arttherapyconnection.net, accessed on June 17, 2013.

Art Therapy in Schools—International Art Therapy Organization. Available at www.internationalarttherapy. org/SchoolArtTherapy.pdf, accessed on June 17, 2013.

British Association of Art Therapists (BAAT). Available at www.baat.org/index.html, accessed on June 17, 2013.

Conditions for the receipt of Professional Standing Certificate from the Ministry of Health. YAHAT—The Israeli Association of Creative and Expressive Therapies. Available at www.yahat.org/english/ diploma.asp, accessed on June 17, 2013.

Chapter 12

Working Cross-Culturally with Children at Risk

Audrey Di Maria Nankervis

One of the five-year-olds with whom I worked always called art therapy "art thirsty" and, indeed, the inner-city youth who bounded, trudged, raced, stomped, or eased their way into my office every school day for nearly 30 years were thirsty—thirsty for opportunities to express themselves. Art therapy offered these emotionally disturbed, latency-aged children a chance to communicate their feelings, their worries, and their hopes in symbolic form and, in the process, to gain a sense of accomplishment and confidence. The array of artwork that they produced provides a durable record of challenges faced, problems solved, and goals met.

Lessons to Be Learned

When I moved to Washington, DC in the early 1970s, I lugged along my cultural baggage, derived, in part, from growing up in a small rural area in the White Mountains of northern New Hampshire. These were very white mountains indeed, populated by White Anglo-Saxon Protestants and a few Catholics, fewer Jews, no Hispanics or Asians, and only one African-American family.

In those days, Washington, DC was known as Chocolate City since African-American residents made up 70 per cent of the population. Despite thousands of Caucasians flooding into the district during morning rush hour to work in government or other jobs, evening rush hour would carry most of them back to Maryland or Virginia. At the time, art therapy programs offered no multicultural or ethics courses and all faculty members and students in our program were white. When, shortly after completing the art therapy program, I was hired as an art therapist at a public, community-based psycho-educational program, I was one of only two white staff members.

With the enthusiasm of one who doesn't even know that she doesn't know, I set about my job, which was to provide 32 children, who had diagnoses such as Attention Deficit Hyperactivity Disorder, Oppositional Defiant Disorder, and Conduct Disorder, with individual art therapy as their primary therapeutic modality and to conduct any art therapy groups needed. No problem. Did I mention that all the children were African-American? (In fact, during the next three decades, only one white child and three Hispanic children would enroll in our program; for most of those years, I would be the only full-time staff member who was white.)

As we were processing our first art therapy group session not long after I had arrived, my co-leader (who was African-American) asked me what I thought of being the only white person in the room. "I don't see the children as black," I said. "I don't see them as being any particular color at all." My naivete—and my arrogance—was dashed when he quickly responded, "Well, you can be damn sure that they won't be seeing you as anything other than white." I learned very quickly that the color blindness of the self-professed liberal was just another form of racism and that applying, generically, to minority clients the art therapy training I had received might be neither effective nor beneficial.

Over the years, the process of looking in the mirror that was held up to me by my co-leader that day (exposing the bias and preconceptions that reside beneath denial and defensiveness) continued—thanks to the willingness of the staff to challenge racism whenever it occurred; to the availability of weekly individual supervision sessions with Frances Cress Welsing, MD, renowned for her lectures and publications on racism; to the wealth of training in cross-cultural and cross-racial counseling provided by our city government; and to the psychoanalysis that provided me with a place to begin to recognize, acknowledge, name, and confront what I saw in that mirror. It wasn't comfortable; it wasn't meant to be. The sedimentary layers of cultural bias, laid down since childhood, can feel so familiar that it often takes a jolt to see that what we are standing on is a slippery slope, indeed—and that the position of white privilege rests on the hearts and minds, hopes and dreams of those who are less privileged but no less worthy.

As clinicians, we cannot be free of cultural bias, but we can aim to be, so that our expectations of, speculations about, and interactions with our clients are not unduly colored by our own assumptions. We can refrain from using language that uses skin color in a negative way (e.g., referring to a black mood) and can refuse to assume that the use of black in a drawing denotes depression. Needless to say, this is a continuing task, not unlike attending to countertransference as it arises. We can also strive to become attuned to the cultural values and beliefs that our clients bring to the therapeutic relationship, while remaining keenly aware of their uniqueness as individuals. Although nothing can replace well-supervised experience, books that I found particularly helpful were Nancy Boyd-Franklin's *Black Families in Therapy* (2003; first published in 1989) and Charles Ridley's *Overcoming Unintentional Racism in Counseling and Therapy: A Practitioner's Guide to Intentional Intervention* (1995).

Setting the Stage

How can we connect with clients of a culture and/or race other than our own?

Being Accessible

Located in the inner city, near bus and subway stops, the facility itself was readily accessible to those with very limited resources. The culture of our program was an inclusive one. Both child centered and family focused, our multidisciplinary staff went to great lengths to make everyone feel welcomed. Doors were thrown open to parents, caregivers, and families not only for intake conferences and IEP meetings, but also for children's programs, holiday celebrations, luncheons, awards ceremonies, and PTA meetings. Teachers met with parents outside of school hours; social workers traveled to homes.

Working with African-American youth necessitates understanding the importance of extended family members (where family friends become "Aunties" and a favored neighbor might accompany a parent to treatment team meetings). The family art evaluations that I conducted for many years at our school's sister residential treatment program at times included extended family members. Key, too, is an appreciation of the role played by older adults in the African-American family. At his initial visit to the school, a six-year-old child with whom I was to work was accompanied by his mother, his grandmother, and his great-grandmother.

The fear or horror of relinquishing one's child to foster care (which, on a subliminal level, harkens back to the time of slavery when owners could wrest a child from a parent's arms and ferry him or her away at will) would, at times, lead relatives or friends to assume responsibility for raising children when a parent was unable to do so (what Boyd-Franklin has called "informal adoption"). For one year in particular, when 60 percent of our students were living with people to whom they were not related, it was essential to understand the roiling mixture of feelings this might engender in a child, as well as to be utterly consistent in the provision of clinical services for that child. For this reason, I provided intensive, long-term individual art therapy (one to three times per week for the length of their stay, which could range from one to four years) and my art therapy interns were asked to commit themselves to working with their child clients for the entire school year.

Religion played a significant role in the lives of our families, and our communal luncheons, children's presentations, and plays were always introduced with prayer. Children would often bring up in therapy religious practices which, in some instances, consisted of daily church attendance. Since, at times, staff members were treated as members of the students' extended family, they would be invited to the funerals of the students' parents and siblings and would go together to these services to provide comfort and support. I recall one six-year-old child leaving his mother's open coffin to nestle in between his teacher and his therapist in the pew in which they were seated.

My interns and I got to know each of the parents, showed them our offices, and encouraged them to stop by should they have any questions at all or want to talk about how their children were doing. We participated in all treatment team meetings, IEP development meetings, and staff meetings. Outside of individual or group art therapy time, we worked with the children on scenery and props for Kwanzaa celebrations, Christmas plays, Black History Month festivities, graduation, and summer programs, clarifying to children and staff the difference in purpose and structure of these auxiliary arts activities.

Providing Materials that Invite, Encourage, and Support

Children often come into their first art therapy sessions expecting to fail. They are afraid that they are going to "mess up" or that their art is going to be compared unfavorably with that of other children. As one seven-year-old angrily demanded, "Why do you let all the other kids make good things and you only let me make crappy things?" Since the arts tap creative resources of which the children are not even aware—and since the goal is not to produce uniform work but to celebrate the diversity of each child's unique creation—engaging in the therapeutic use of art can help the child to learn to value those qualities about himself or herself that are special and different, thus raising the child's sense of self-esteem.

Welcoming a child new to art therapy, I would ask, "If you had a magic power and could change anything in your life, what would it be?" The children's goals were, invariably, different from those of their parents or teachers: wanting to have a friend or needing help with homework, rather than seeking decreased impulsivity or increased attention span. The child's answers—as well as material gleaned from both the nondirective, open-ended assessment procedure developed by Edith Kramer (in which the child would be asked to complete a drawing and a painting, and to model clay) and the child's chart—were used to set goals toward which we would work. Strengths and resources which would enable changes to be made could be discovered through the art process itself.

Problems encountered in making art often parallel problems encountered in life. Addressing them as they arise in the art and working them through within the context of the creative process can help the child to learn that areas in need of change can be targeted, that apparent "mistakes" can be salvaged, that resources can be identified, that problem-solving skills can be developed, and that feelings of pride can be derived from successfully meeting the goals that one has set for himself or herself. The process can help the child to increase the ability to control impulses, to increase the level of frustration tolerance, and to increase the capacity to delay gratification. It can also help the child to perceive himself or herself as someone who is capable.

A ten-year-old child who tended to focus upon his mistakes was encouraged to think of all the things we wouldn't have if people did things right all the time. I began the list with erasers, whereupon he added paper towels, soap, and new clothes. When, a short while later, he inadvertently spilled the paint he was using, he looked up at me and, smiling shyly, said, "Good thing we have paper towels, eh?" Yes, indeed.

Multicultural Media

As art therapists, the tools of our trade usher in countless opportunities to encourage a strong sense of racial identity. "Multicultural" crayons, markers, colored pencils, and paints (such as those made by Crayola)—in a variety of skin tones such as cinnamon, ebony, peach, copper, and bronze—support this. An African-American child who might grab the first brown he saw with which to draw a self-portrait— or might refrain from coloring it in—might be invited to inspect the variety of brown shades available. I remember a seven-year-old child who got so excited about the idea of finding "his" brown that he tried out 27 different kinds of brown media (chalks, pastels, pencils, crayons, markers, and oil pastels of various brands), carefully drawing a thick line of each before placing his hand beside it and checking it against the color of his skin. Not finding the exact shade, he was encouraged to try mixing paints. He went on to create a wide array of brown hues, carefully checking each one in turn before exclaiming with delight, "I found it!" He used his color to paint a life-sized self-portrait that hung in the art therapy room until he proudly rolled it up to take with him at the end of the school year. An array of children's books support this theme. Two of the children's favorites were Vivian Church's *Colors Around Me* (1971) and Wilesse Commissiong's *The BEST Face of All* (1991). Folders of collage materials and magazines that feature photographs of African-Americans were given a prominent place on the shelves too.

Multicultural Finger Puppets

When children entered the art therapy room, one of the first things they spotted were sets of finger puppets in a wide variety of ages and skin tones, knitted by my mother. Displayed on pairs of cardboard hands with fingers splayed, the 1.5- to 3-inch-high children, mothers, fathers, grandmothers, teenage boys and girls, and babies (even a little pair of twins) were painstakingly garbed and coiffed. Grandmothers wore gray or white hair in buns or curls, pearl earrings, hats, and shawls, teenage boys sported Jheri curls, Afros, or dreadlocks, while girls displayed beaded cornrows or tiny braids capped by multicolored barrettes. Although my mother still lived in those white mountains, she would watch *Oprah*, knitting needles in hand, to come up with styles that were up to date. Children who were not ready to put pencil or paint to paper would slip their fingers into the puppets and begin a conversation.

Multicultural Dolls and Doll-Making Materials

My mother went on to make soft two-foot-tall dolls in different shades of brown and black, which the children would cuddle and talk to. The dolls inspired many children to make their own, and a bin in the art therapy room was always stocked with a range of socks and gloves in shades from black to beige that could be turned into dolls. Many boys and girls terminated from art therapy knowing how to sew by machine and by hand.

Use of the Self

At times, I found that more self-disclosure was called for than I would usually use as a psychodynamically trained therapist. During another session of the early art therapy group mentioned above, the children were talking about things that black people do and things that white people do. Directing their comments to the co-leader, who was African-American, they said, "Mr. Johnson, white people don't play pinball, do they? And they don't know how to do karate, do they? And they all live in Maryland and Virginia, don't they?" Mr. Johnson paused for a moment and then said, "Why don't you ask Ms. Evans [as I was called then]?" "Ms. Evans, you don't ever play pinball, do you?" I answered that, yes, I had played pinball. "Ms. Evans, you don't do karate, do you?" As I was spending two evenings a week at a dojo, I answered that, in fact, I did know karate. "Ms. Evans, where do you live? Maryland or Virginia?" I answered that I lived in DC. "Mr. Johnson, Ms. Evans doesn't live in DC, does she?" "I don't know," he replied. "I live in Maryland."

Many of the children referred to me as light-skinned (and, given the preponderance of African-American residents in the city, one of the social workers said that some of the children had never had occasion to meet a white person). Referring to me in this way (rather than as white) gave me the opportunity to observe (aloud) that they seemed to feel that I, like them, was African-American. When they nodded (as they usually did), we would explore what that meant to them. Then, I would ask what it would be like if I were white. Often this would bring agitation or protestation, occasionally even a shudder. Encouraged to elaborate, the children would begin to talk about how white people treated black people, behavior they had heard about from family members or read about in school or seen on television. A ten-year-old spoke of how it felt to board a city bus and have a white lady move her purse from the aisle side of the seat to the window side—and his desire to shout, "Hey, I don't want your purse, lady!" Other children would talk about black people having to be "twice as good as whites" just to get the same job (sentiments their parents might have voiced and experienced). Acknowledgment of the distress of dealing with this grim reality gradually led to discussions of what might be done about it.

Art Therapy Interventions

Besides endeavoring to bring cultural awareness and sensitivity to whatever issues the children brought to their sessions, the art therapy interns and I used our skills to address, pro-actively, cultural issues in visual ways, through projects such as the following.

"I Can Achieve Anything!": A Vocational Mural

When we cannot visualize our goals, we cannot hope to attain them. The arts can help children to give their dreams concrete form, turning wishes into pictures that map out avenues by which they might seek to achieve them.

Since so many of the male children, asked what they might like to be when they grew up, said that they would like to be professional football players—and knowing that only a tiny percentage of those who want to do so will actually end up playing in the major leagues—art therapy interns Leslie Milofsky and Andrea Poggi and I decided to cover a large (12' × 15') wall in the building with a vocational mural that would expand the children's vision of both the range of vocational paths available and the variety of occupations within those paths.

Entitled "I Can Achieve Anything!", the mural pictures children "On the Road to Success," a road that begins with "Family Love" and ends with a large rising sun (labeled "My Bright Future"). The sun's 17 rays represent careers in fields such as Sports, Technology, Business, Entertainment, and Education. Along each ray seven professions are listed; so, for example, the ray that represents Sports includes, besides professional athletes, physical education teachers, exercise instructors, equipment sales people, and coaches. The children became very familiar with the mural and, as they became more conversant with the variety of fields and jobs available, their interests expanded.

"Steps to Success": A Tool to Help Children Track Their Progress

The school's behavior management-level system was given visual form by means of a mural that illustrated a series of stair steps that led from the lowest level (painted blue) to the highest (painted black). At the beginning of each school year, the children's photographs were hung on hooks on the blue level and, as they earned points for classroom behavior, they would shift their photos to hooks on the next highest level during an awards ceremony. Reaching the black level meant that they were ready to graduate from our program and return to their neighborhood school.

"Growing Up Healthy in the Nation's Capital": A Diorama

In an effort to highlight all that was happening in the children's lives that was positive amidst the crime statistics that filled city news reports, art therapy interns Berre Burch and Jennifer Dipasupil and I assisted the children in creating a diorama composed of 45 clay figures, shown jogging, playing football, jumping rope, flying kites, playing soccer, walking dogs, planting flowers, reading, and picnicking. The figures were placed among clay trees, park benches, and recycling bins within an eight-foot-wide space that represented the National Mall, from the cardboard Capitol building on the left to the paper Washington monument on the right, with Smithsonian Institution museums in between. The diorama was exhibited in the office of the Secretary of the US Department of Health and Human Services from mid-2001 to early 2003.

"Art Therapy/Photography Group": Promoting Self-Expression via Photos and Words

After being trained in Wendy Ewald's "Literacy Through Photography" approach (2001), art therapy interns Amy Babish and Tori Kelly and I led an art therapy/ photography group designed to help children build problem-solving skills and increase their sense of creativity and competence while exploring their worlds. The children were provided with simple cameras, ground rules, and encouragement; each took pictures and wrote poems or stories about aspects of their lives that were important to them, such as their families, their neighborhoods, their dreams, and what each of them regarded as "the best part of me."

"It Takes All Colors!": A Schoolwide Group Session Addressing Color

Following incidents of teasing of very light-skinned and very dark-skinned children in the school, art therapy interns Katie Kronmiller and Denise Padilla and I came up with a way of addressing the issue during a group session that would involve all the staff and all the children of the school (which, on that day, would number 50). In preparation for the session, we rolled out a 20-foot-long paper, folded it in half, and traced the outline of a person who was ten feet tall. We cut the top humanoid form into 50 "jigsaw puzzle" pieces and, using black marker, traced each piece onto the bottom form in its appropriate place. Then we mixed 50 shades of paint, from beige to black, and painted each piece a different shade. The next day, each group member picked a puzzle piece out of a large basket, went to the center of the circle, and, with the help of the other group members, placed it on the appropriate spot.

When completed, the group members could see what was written across the figure: "It Takes All Colors!" This led to a discussion of the connection between bias regarding skin tone and the attitude and behavior of slave owners—and the importance of celebrating differences.

"Summers: Past and Present": An Intergenerational Art Therapy Quilting Project

During the summer of 2004, drawing on the importance of elders to African-American children, art therapy intern Kathleen Barron and I brought together children from our school and elders from the First Baptist Senior Center up the street to create a memory quilt, a project that was supported in part by the American Art Therapy Association. The participants, who ranged in age from 5 to 91, worked in pairs during a series of meetings, each sharing in words and in drawings memories of favorite summer activities. The appliquéd quilt, depicting subjects as diverse as horseshoe pitching, firefly collecting, and ice cream making, was installed in the office of the Secretary of the US Department of Health and Human Services during a reception that honored both the older adults and the children, at which time the pairs of elders and children who had worked together spoke about what their relationships meant to them. It is now housed in the Ronald McDonald House, which provides accommodations to family members of children receiving treatment at the National Institutes of Health.

Postscript

In 2006, our public psycho-educational facility closed its doors for the last time, due to shifting priorities on the part of the government that funded it. The walls containing the vocational mural and the "Steps to Success" mural were whitewashed and the building was readied to serve another function. What happened to our school is a painful but important reminder that sometimes it is not enough to do a good job; we must work to ensure that the policy-makers are allocating sufficient resources for special education and mental health services. The legacy of our school lies in the enduring friendships forged by its amazingly dedicated and creative staff and in the lives of the children with whom we had the privilege to work.

References

Boyd-Franklin, N. (2003) *Black Families in Therapy: Understanding the African American Experience, Second Edition.* New York: The Guilford Press.

Church, V. (1971) *Colors Around Me.* Chicago, IL: African American Images.

Commissiong, W. (1991) *The BEST Face of All.* Chicago, IL: African American Images.

Ewald, W. (2001) *I Wanna Take Me a Picture: Teaching Photography and Writing to Children.* Boston, MA: Beacon Press.

Ridley, C. (1995) *Overcoming Unintentional Racism in Counseling and Therapy: A Practitioner's Guide to Intentional Intervention.* Thousand Oaks, CA: Sage Publications.

Chapter 13

Art Therapy as a Treatment Choice for Autism Spectrum Disorders

Deni Brancheau

"The world of children with autism is not one of confusion and baffling behaviors, but involves a different way of ordering their world. The metaphor of an inner mirror that cannot reflect may help describe their experience" (Emery 2004, p.147). Autism spectrum disorders (ASDs) and autism are interchangeable terms used to characterize a group of developmental disorders or disorders affecting brain development (Centers for Disease Control and Prevention [CDC] 2012). ASDs have become increasingly prevalent in the United States and around the world. The CDC estimates 1 in 88 children are now being diagnosed with autism. In the United States, the CDC reports 1 in 54 boys and 1 in 252 girls carry the diagnosis (2012). Frank-Briggs, referring to statistics generated by the World Health Organization (WHO), estimates that 1 in 91 to 110 children worldwide have autism (2012).

Autism spectrum disorders know no bounds; this group of disorders crosses over cultural, socio-economic, racial, and ethnic boundaries and the causes are not clearly understood. Autism is characterized by social and communication delays and behavioral issues that interfere with the ability to function effectively in society (Martin 2009). Rigidity in thinking and inflexibility lead to difficulty tolerating change and transition, incorporating the needs of others, and allowing for the acceptance of points of view different from their own (Cannon et al. 2011).

Art therapy can be an effective treatment approach for individuals with autism. Common treatment goals include improving communication, facilitating the development of social skills, strengthening self-esteem, facilitating improved self-regulation, and integrating sensory awareness. Martin (2009) notes additional treatment goals including developmental growth, facilitation of leisure skill development, addressing visual-spatial deficits, improving imagination deficits, and the promotion of abstract thinking. The Autistic Self Advocacy Network (ASAN) also describes people with autism as experiencing non-standard ways of learning and problem-solving, a need for consistency and a sense of order, and difficulty expressing and understanding social language (ASAN 2012). Gabriels (2012) suggests that art therapy can help people with autism to develop fundamental skills across academic areas, in the creation of art, and other basic skill sets in play and socialization, while assisting in the generalization of these very same skills. Betts and Martin (2010) note that inherent in the art materials is a "sensory appeal... making them a desirable tool for self-regulation and self-soothing" (p.49).

In the United States, art therapy services, along with other mental health services, are often provided in the school setting for students with special needs. School is a natural environment in which to access services as the majority of children in this country attend school throughout their formative years. In other countries where this is not the norm, community service agencies, mental health centers, and private practice providers would greatly benefit from facilitating the delivery of art therapy services to community members in such need.

In the larger sense, an autistic culture exists among individuals based on interwoven interests and patterns of thought, the assumption being that while people with autism are neurologically atypical, they are not disabled; rather, they are just different from their neurotypical counterparts (Autism-Help.org). It is also important to note that different cultures vary in their understanding and treatment of individuals with ASDs (Kim 2012).

In another way and on a different level, it might be said that individuals with ASD create their own culture, though personal awareness and understanding of this most likely varies from individual to individual. The observer looking into their world sees in a sense another world separate from their familial culture. Although distinctly a member of the primary family group, the individual appears locked inside him- or herself, often desirous of communication with the outside world but unable to fashion its expression. Art therapy may offer a pathway toward communication and connectedness. Emery notes: "The use of nonverbal expression through the experience of making art encourages children with autism to begin to represent their experiences. Forms represent objects and the very act of drawing with intention may encourage attachment to the object" (Emery 2004, p.147).

Case Study

Marshall (pseudonym) was a high school student in a nonpublic school in the eastern United States that works with students on the autism spectrum and with other special needs. He was seen over the period of two years by a Master's-level art therapy intern who met with him weekly (referred to in the case study as the "art therapist"). The art intern was supervised by the director of the high school, an art therapist, and a faculty member from the graduate art therapy program that the intern attended.

Like many students diagnosed with autism, Marshall was a "loner"; he preferred to eat lunch alone and to read instead of socializing with his peers, and generally kept to himself. He was a kind and polite young man with many interests and a strong desire to learn. He could provide you with the answer to most historical questions and had several areas where his knowledge base far exceeded that of the staff around him. He found solace in art and was recommended for individual art therapy to address needs around socialization and anxiety reduction. Ari Ne'eman, President of the Autism Self-Advocacy Network (cited in Cannon et al. 2011), when answering the question "What purpose does inflexibility serve?", said this: "For one thing, it is an effective anti-anxiety coping mechanism. It provides order in the context of a world that is confusing and illogical for us" (p.7).

Marshall, though drawn to art and the art-making process (he enjoyed going to art classes), came to the art therapy studio appearing tense and anxious. His body seemed rigid, and he worked in pencil in a tight fashion. Marshall's work lacked obvious connection, with figures and shapes floating on the page with no sense of a grounded image (Figure 13.1).

Figure 13.1 Figures and shapes
Illustrated in the color insert

Marshall preferred to use pencil or colored pencils initially and generally whenever he was given the opportunity. He dabbled in self-hardening modeling clay a few times and attempted to solve the problems of uneven drying and cracking of the structures. After a few trials, though, he elected to return to the tried and true materials of pencils and occasionally oil pastels. His willingness to use the modeling clay may have been an attempt to please the art therapist, who suggested the new material; it is difficult to know, as he often did not seem able to express what was on his mind. It was noted early in the sessions that Marshall did not connect the artwork to himself in any way, or at least in any way he was able to express in words. As a rule, Marshall did not choose to talk much about his work but would attempt to answer the art therapist's questions, posed after artwork was completed.

In a sense, you could say Marshall's responses showed a desire to "follow the rules," a common theme for students with autism, who generally function better with a good deal of structure, predictability, and consistent responses (Betts and

Martin 2010). It was important for him to follow the art therapist's directions as closely as possible. This had an effect on the nature of their work together. It limited his free expression because he did not want to ask clarifying questions or ask to be given an alternative choice, even though he may have preferred to do something else. Difficulty with social initiation is also another common characteristic of individuals with ASD (Bellini 2006; Cannon et al. 2011). Marshall worked carefully and slowly but also wanted to complete his artwork within the time frame of the session; these two variables sometimes seemed to clash, creating a sense of anxiety for him.

At times, Marshall's work was filled with space themes: planets, robots, moons. A sense of tentativeness and anxiety often characterized his work and was evident in his body posture, which was often rigid and stiff in nature. Initially he preferred a directive, but over time he self-selected the nature of his artwork more often. In response to the anxiety the art therapist felt Marshall was experiencing (he never outwardly expressed it in words), a mandala ritual was started. Mandala shapes can be found everywhere in nature and have been utilized across cultures and religions and throughout time as a centering device and a focus for meditation (Fincher 2010). Some studies have linked art making with anxiety reduction (Curry and Kasser 2005; Sandmire et al. 2012), albeit for the period of time that the activity occurs. One study (van der Vennet and Serice 2012), whose aim was to look at whether coloring mandalas reduced anxiety more effectively than engaging in other art-making activities, found that participants in the group that colored mandalas and had been deemed anxious prior to the art activity found more relief than those in the other two groups. Further research is needed to add to this finding, but in Marshall's case, the mandala creation seemed to help.

At the beginning of each session, Marshall was given a blank mandala form to work on. He seemed to take to this format and the art therapist noted some anxiety reduction. Often during the mandala creation, he would pause, take a deep breath, and stretch backwards, seeming to let go of some of his body tension. After creating the initial mandala, he usually created a second piece. It was noted that the second drawing looked less tense than previous works (Figures 13.2 and 13.3) and more grounded.

It seemed that creating mandalas allowed him to more fully engage in the art-making process and he became more able to use the art-making process for self-expression.

In the fifth month or so, the art therapist introduced the concept of a mandala journal, hoping to help Marshall use the process to aid in relaxation and anxiety reduction outside of school. In his typical way, he agreed to use the journal, though, given his compliant nature, it was never clear at the time if this was what he really wanted to do. The art therapist noted that the mandala making seemed to give Marshall a place to leave his anxiety, the mandala serving as a container for tension he often seemed to bring to the sessions. In supervision, that anxiety was explored from a different perspective in order to eliminate any potential anxiety the art therapist might be bringing to the mix herself. Marshall continued this process for many months. The significance that art therapy played in his life was evidenced one day when he chose to leave the school's Halloween dance and come to art therapy instead.

Figure 13.2 Mandala 1

Figure 13.3 Tree

As the sessions continued, Marshall became eager to share his mandala journal with his art therapist and others. The journal may have become a transitional object for him, bridging session material with his everyday life. Transitional objects, first identified in the work of Winnicott (1971), assist in the separation–individuation process and can help regulate change. Marshall carried his journal back and forth from home to school each day. In a sense, creating the mandalas seemed to contain him emotionally.

Often during a session, he could be observed engaging in what Csikszentmihalyi (1997) called a state of "flow"; he was totally absorbed in his process. As sessions continued, Marshall's artwork moved from a sense of containment to that of self-expression; the development of internal control provides the adolescent with opportunities for containment and eventually expansion (Emunah 1990). Through the mandala exercise, he seemed to be gaining some sense of connection to his feelings.

In another session, Marshall seemed to become agitated with the colored pencil medium. This was noted in the way he handled them: he was rougher than usual, spending more time manipulating the pencils as well as the box. Eventually this caused the pencils to spill out onto the table. This may have paralleled a sense of lack of control Marshall was feeling inside. He was unable to verbalize it, however; instead, the mandala served to hold the agitation, which allowed the art therapist to recognize that while he was not asking for different materials to work with, that might have been what he was trying to communicate. After that session she began to offer an array of materials including paint. She made sure other choices were available and that Marshall knew he was free to choose. He began to use the mandala to try out the new materials; the containment of the form allowed him to safely experiment. This became a place where he could now take risks. After creating a mandala in one session, he drew a river (Figures 13.4 and 13.5). The art therapist asked him about the drawing, stating, "It looks like land divided by a river." She then asked, "If you were in this picture, where would you be?" He answered, "I would be on one side." When asked how he could get to the other side, he replied, "A bridge." His drawing seemed to reflect his ability to problem solve.

While the art therapist wanted him to continue using the mandala form to reduce the sense of tension he often brought to the sessions, she wanted him to move beyond that as well. At one point, a time limit for the mandala creating was given. While this initially created some anxiety, it also allowed Marshall to create other work during the sessions.

He did, at times, resort to disjointed robotic pictorial expressions, a familiar subject matter. The use of stereotypical figures like those from cartoons or video games is often chosen when students self-select drawing topics (Henley 2000). Henley (2000, citing Williams et al. 1997) describes the use of idioms as an intervention that can "diminish stereotypical outcomes that often cloud artistic expressions in art therapy" (p.275). It was also interesting to see that when Marshall ran out of pre-drawn circle shapes in his journal, he was unable to ask the art therapist to add more. Also unable to do it for himself, he began drawing robots on the empty pages (Figure 13.6). Difficulties in social initiation and initiation of a new task are not uncommon characteristics of individuals with ASDs (Autism Speaks 2010; Emery 2004). For Marshall, initiation remained a difficult task.

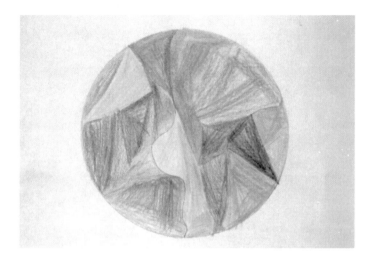

Figure 13.4 Mandala 2

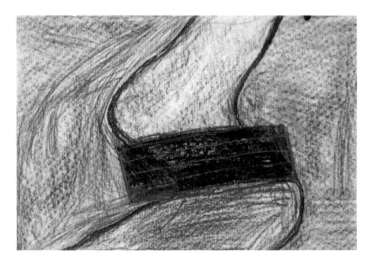

Figure 13.5 Bridge
Illustrated in the color insert

Near the end of their work together, Marshall incorporated little people on the edge of a mandala and outside the mandala for the first time. "The use of nonverbal expression through the experience of making art encourages children with autism to begin to represent their experiences. Forms represent objects and the very act of drawing with intention may encourage attachment to the object" (Emery 2004, p.145).

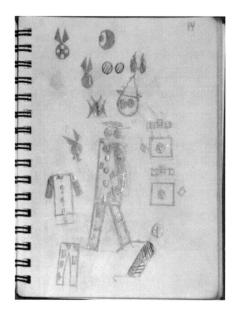

Figure 13.6 Journal

When asked to describe this, Marshall said the figure was "hanging on the arc but was strong enough to hold on." This indeed seemed to be a self-reflection. The art therapist noted the significance of his putting something outside the boundaries of the circle and wondered if he was on the precipice of some communication, perhaps a reaching out for the "other." He later did another mandala in his journal that had a clear center and a yin/yang shape inside of it, another metaphor for the whole.

Throughout their work together, Marshall seemed to become more able to freely express himself and connect his inner experience with his outer one. Art therapy became a useful tool to help him unlock his own sense of self and help him communicate with others and the outside world. What was experienced through art therapy generalized to other social situations: he became more interactive with his peers, he began to develop a sense of himself as an artist, and he was able to express himself more fully than before. One day near the end of his last year in school, he was asked by another school staff member what he was drawing. He said it was a mandala and that he had learned how to do it in art therapy. It was clear that he had internalized the meaningfulness of this experience and had learned how to use art as a vehicle for self-expression.

As illustrated through Marshall's experience, art therapy can be used to serve students with autism and can facilitate growth in many ways. It can function as a vehicle for self-expression, facilitate communication, and foster social skills. It is an important treatment modality and a useful one for this population because it can help make connections that transcend the individual's abilities or cultural background. In a sense, art was the vehicle that led Marshall to see his own reflection in the world outside him.

As the initial quote by Emery suggests, art may be able to offer the bridge between what is known on the inside and what can be expressed to the outside world.

References

Autistic Self Advocacy Network (ASAN) (2012). Available at http://autisticadvocacy.org, accessed on July 23, 2013.

Autism Speaks (2010) *What is Autism?* Available at www.autismspeaks.org/whatisit/index.php, accessed on June 17, 2013.

Autism-Help.org. *Help with Autism, Asperger's Syndrome and Related Disorders.* Available at www.autism-help.org/index.htm, accessed on June 17, 2013.

Bellini, S. (2006) *Building Social Relationships: A Systematic Approach to Teaching Social Interaction Skills to Children and Adolescents with Autism Spectrum Disorders and Other Social Difficulties.* Shawnee Misson, KS: APC Autism Asperger Publishing Co.

Betts, D. and Martin, N. (2010) "Art Therapy Approaches to Treating Autism." In K. Siri and T. Lyons (eds) *Cutting-Edge Therapies for Autism.* New York: Skyhouse Publishing.

Cannon, L., Kenworthy, L., Alexander, K., Adler-Werner, M., and Anthony, L. (2011) *Unstuck and on Target: An Executive Function Curriculum to Improve Flexibility for Children with Autism Spectrum Disorders, Research Edition.* Baltimore, MD: Paul Brookes Publishing Co.

Centers for Disease Control and Prevention (2012) *Autism Spectrum Disorders (ASDs): Data and Statistics.* Available at www.cdc.gov/ncbddd/autism/index.html, accessed on June 17, 2013.

Csikszentmihalyi, M. (1997) *Creativity: Flow and the Psychology of Discovery and Invention.* New York: HarperCollins.

Curry, N. and Kasser, T. (2005) "Can coloring mandalas reduce anxiety?" *Art Therapy: Journal of the American Art Therapy Association 22,* 2, 81–85.

Emery, M. (2004) "Art therapy as an intervention for autism." *Art Therapy: Journal of the American Art Therapy Association 21,* 3, 143–147.

Emunah, R. (1990) "Expression and expansion in adolescence: The significance of creative arts therapy." *The Arts in Psychotherapy 17,* 101–107.

Fincher, S. (2010) *Creating Mandalas: For Insight, Healing and Self-Expression.* Boston: Shambhala Publications.

Frank-Briggs, A. I. (2012) "Autism in children: A review." *The Nigerian Health Journal 12,* 2, 27–30.

Gabriels, R. (2012) "Art Therapy with Children who have Autism and their Families." In C. Malchiodi (ed.) *Handbook of Art Therapy, Second Edition.* New York: Guilford Press.

Henley, D. (2000) "Blessings in disguise: Idiomatic expression as a stimulus in group art therapy with children." *Art Therapy: Journal of the American Art Therapy Association 17*, 4, 270–275.

Kim, H. U. (2012) "Autism across cultures: Rethinking autism." *Disability and Society 27*, 4, 535–545.

Martin, N. (2009) "Art therapy and autism: Overview and recommendations." *Art Therapy: Journal of the American Art Therapy Association 26*, 4, 187–190.

Sandmire, D. A., Gorham, S. R., Rankin, N. E., and Grimm, D. R. (2012) "The influence of art making on anxiety: A pilot study." *Art Therapy: Journal of the American Art Therapy Association 29*, 2, 68–73.

van der Vennet, R. and Serice, S. (2012) "Can coloring mandalas reduce anxiety? A replication study." *Art Therapy: Journal of the American Art Therapy Association 29*, 2, 87–92.

Williams, K., Kramer, E., Henley, D., and Gerity, L. (1997) "Art, art therapy and the seductive environment." *American Journal of Art Therapy 35*, 2, 106–107.

Winnicott, D. W. (1971) *Playing and Reality.* London: Tavistock.

Resources
Online

Many applications/programs are now available for your favorite *i* device, android, or PC. See the Autism Speaks website for hundreds of autism-related apps recommended by users or search your web browser for "apps for autism" for an exhaustive list of resources.

Autism Speaks, an organization whose mission is to "improve the lives of all those on the Autism Spectrum." Available at www.autismspeaks.org.

The National Autism Resource and Information Center. Available at www.autismnow.org.

Autistic Advocacy, an organization run for and by people with autism. Available at www.autisticadvocacy.org.

Chapter 14

Giving Teens a Visual Voice
Art Therapy in a Public School Setting with Emotionally Disabled Students

Emmy Lou Glassman

Setting the Scene

The student took his time using the chalk pastels. Carefully, he drew a sophisticated and beautiful close-up view of a barn complex, complete with weathered wood boards and a fenced corral with an open gate. There were fluffy clouds that floated in the turquoise sky. The use of perspective showed accurate, strong skill. A figure in shadow, barely visible, stood in the dark doorway of the barn. The resulting piece had thick, strong layers of color which created a crisp, vivid image.

A week later, the same student chose watercolors for his project. All but a two-inch strip on the bottom of the paper was filled with streaky gray-blue clouds, creating an expansive and heavy, wet-looking sky. The bottom two inches of the paper were painted green. Set on the green strip in the middle of the scene was a one-inch square see-through house, with two "dot" windows and a small rectangular door. Above this square house sat a simple triangle as the roof. The next day the student ran away from home.

If I were to have seen this primitive painting first, I might have thought the student had limited art skills or that he wasn't as invested in his work that day. Initially, seeing the well-developed and beautifully drawn barn, with the suggestive image in the darkened doorway, merely conveyed the student's skill with developing a visual image. However, it became clear to me, when the tiny house was painted, that something was different about the boy and his life. Once I was told that he'd run away, I realized he had been "talking" to me about his home and his need to escape something or someone there.

This incident occurred during the first year of my work as an art therapist in a school for emotionally disabled students. I hadn't yet developed my skills for discerning what all of the art "messages" meant. As the years progressed, I became more astute at understanding the art and attending to what the artists were trying to say. That early incident helped me to craft a program that addressed the unique culture of my students—those with emotional disabilities. My goals were met by changing the approach of the art program from art education to one that reflected art therapy theories and techniques.

Overview

The above scenario occurred at the beginning of the 19 years (ending in 2004) that I worked for Fairfax County Public Schools in northern Virginia, now the 12th largest school system in the United States, enrolling over 170,000 students (FCPS Budget Facts). Of that number, it serves more than 24,000 students who attend special education "centers" like the ones where I worked (FCPS Special Education Handbook). The school system firmly believes in trying to serve the needs of any and all of its enrolled students, regardless of the needs or challenges they represent. It is due to this philosophy that such a broad array of programs exists within this system.

I discuss the services provided for students with emotional disabilities (ED). I also outline how I implemented an art therapy program and adapted it in a school (center) where I was called an art teacher, was expected to hold teaching credentials, and was asked to instruct art to classes (of up to 12 students) with emotional disabilities. Students in the center received credits and grades for their participation in these classes. The administration also preferred that I hold a Master's degree in art therapy in order to understand and respond to the unique demands of ED pupils in an art class.

Cultural Framework

All school districts have their distinct methods for screening students with special needs. Because this school system was conservative when diagnosing, those students found to be emotionally disabled had to go through a lengthy and rigorous screening protocol that included the following:

- initial referrals by parents, teachers, or the principal

- a review by a "Child Study Team" of the student's records, standardized test scores, teacher reports, grades, and areas of concern

- parent-signed permission for a further workup which included psychological and educational testing, a physician's examination, and development of a social history report

- further case review by an "Eligibility Committee" which made the final determination about services and placement necessary to meet the education needs of that student (FCPS Eligibility Procedures).

Once a pupil was found eligible to receive special education services, the development of an individual education plan (IEP) was designed with goals and accommodations for that individual. At an IEP meeting, a team made up of the student, a parent/guardian, and specific school officials all signed the plan to indicate their understanding of the new personalized goals and expectations.

Adolescent Development and Emotional Disability

Before discussing the scope of ED in adolescents, it may help to understand what the typical 13- to 18-year-old experiences. The teen years are widely thought of as a transition time in one's life, bridging childhood and adulthood. Many changes take place physically, emotionally, and socially. During that period teens transition through, and hopefully complete, "tasks" that will enable them to become well-adjusted adults. According to the University of Minnesota's Konopka Institute for Best Practices in Adolescent Health, some of those tasks include the following:

- adjusting to the changes in their feelings and sexually maturing bodies

- identifying meaningful personal values, moral standards, and belief systems

- establishing a sense of one's own unique individuality

- achieving emotional independence from parents and other adults

- forming mutually close and supportive friendships

- developing the ability to think abstractly and applying that skill

- developing new self-management skills such as conflict resolution, decision making, and problem solving

- identifying and clearly communicating personal emotions

- developing an understanding of the feelings of others

- preparing for one's role in society's workforce.

Over those several years, it is typical to see both progression and regression as the teen negotiates each of these areas. The challenges of this maturation process often activate feelings of isolation, indecision, emptiness, and anxiety (Hall and Lindzey 1978), making it difficult to differentiate between an average adolescent student and one with emotional disabilities. It also becomes understandable why a school system would be ethical and discerning in its process of carefully screening students for a program that would define them as ED.

According to Project IDEAL, a project of the Texas Council for Developmental Disabilities, the key characteristics of having an emotional disability often relate to issues of emotional well-being and personal identity. If a student "responds to a situation with an inappropriate behavior or emotion" such as depression or long-term unhappiness, has "a very difficult time maintaining personal relationships with others," leading to physical symptoms, or "has difficulty learning" with no intellectual or sensory cause, then an emotional disorder may be to blame. The causes of an emotional disturbance in adolescents may be due to "either biological causes, environmental causes or a combination of the two." The deficits seen in these students will be in three areas: emotional development, cognitive development, and behavioral development. As a consequence, the IEP of each student in the FCPS ED program included social, emotional, and educational goals to address those identified deficits. The primary goal was for students to develop clearer and more effective coping strategies in order to learn.

Fitting Art Therapy into the Art Classroom

Most school programs clearly outline academic objectives for their faculty. My school system was no exception, offering a Program of Studies (POS) for each subject, and, in this case, Fine Arts. It focused on art production, history, criticism, and aesthetics (FCPS Fine Arts POS). In time, new language was added to the POS that acknowledged differences in students and the need for teachers to choose from the content and skills in specific circumstances. However, long before this new language was added, my art-as-therapy program focused on the individual. My goals were reflective of the IEP goals while addressing individual needs: creating a safe environment for self-expression, fostering positive social relationships, developing problem-solving and self-advocacy skills, building ego strength, and helping to develop and maintain healthy defenses. These goals were also designed to incorporate the developmental adolescent tasks listed earlier.

The art room was always referred to as "the studio" (Figure 14.1), creating a sense that each person working there was "an artist."

Figure 14.1 Art studio

The room was carefully arranged and always in order, giving a supportive sense of structure and an unspoken message of respect for the media and space. All materials were easily found due to clear labeling. A special cabinet was designated for personal belongings to be placed upon entry to the studio. This allowed for maximum work space on the large communal art table. Each artist was assigned a shelf on the studio drying rack for wet pieces and given a personal portfolio to keep accumulated work. There was a private space to work in the room if needed, a sand tray for quiet contemplation, and a mini-library of art and reference books. The studio became a welcoming haven to the artists within its walls.

Model

The "Art Studio Guidelines" is the evolved program model of principles. During the first day in art class, these guidelines were thoroughly discussed with each student, and their signature of acknowledgment was requested below the form (see Appendix B).

Encouraging students in making daily choices and working as autonomous artists in the studio space empowered them. Acknowledging an individual's choices and helping to facilitate those choices showed respect to each of the students. Clearly outlining expectations in the Art Studio Guidelines provided a healthy structure of support.

At times, formal demonstrations, such as the techniques of successful clay handling, watercolor painting, or paper-making, were done throughout the year. Informal demonstrations were used as well. I might have dripped watercolors on paper and then looked for images to develop, or perhaps created an abstract tissue collage. Oftentimes, students became quite enticed by these informal "lessons" that were casually taught by my modeling. Regardless, as independent artists, the students were in charge of their own choices.

As an art therapist, with goals focused on individual emotional growth through artistic expression, I felt that grading a student's artwork was not acceptable. Each artist made an effort to develop and master skills with different media. Each artist progressed in order to express thoughts and feelings more fully. Therefore, all students in my art classes passed Art unless their attendance (too much tardiness or absenteeism), outlined and mandated by law, interfered with the passing grade. Many times, however, students with attendance problems had specific IEP goals and accommodations for attendance. In these cases, adjustment and modification was acceptable by law.

Case Study

Illustrating how an art-as-therapy program like this could make positive changes in the life of a student is the case of a 15-year-old sophomore I will call "R." New to our center, he had been having psychotic episodes and was demonstrating antisocial and withdrawn behaviors before going through ED screening. In the past, I had seen several students who were shy about creating artwork in front of their peers. They would often look through an art book for the first class session until they felt more comfortable in the setting. R began my program by looking through art books for two weeks, with his head lowered almost to the table, while cautiously glancing up from time to time in order to see what others were doing and what their art looked like. He said little, asked for nothing, and barely spoke when addressed. His body language and behavior indicated that he was in a state of panic.

Each day of his art book reading, I began by asking him what he'd like to work on. Each day the response was the same: "To look at books." As his acceptance of the situation changed, R began sitting up more and openly watching the work going on around him. I pointed out that everyone was doing something of his own choice and wondered what he was interested in. R responded by taking out pictures of Japanese anime characters that he liked. When he agreed to try to draw one of them, I brought paper and a pencil. Carefully he replicated one of them in a short period of time. As he worked, I slipped the set of colored pencils next to him. Before the 90-minute class period was over, he'd drawn and colored in his favorite cartoon character, one with superhero powers.

Perhaps it was those powers that fueled him to further develop other superhero characters, some in colored pencils and some, at my suggestion, with watercolor pencils. Once he had success with that new medium, he went on to try tempera paints. First drawing the details of the figure, R used the brightly colored paints to fill in the complete image, including a background (Figure 14.2).

Figure 14.2 Superhero

It seemed as though he'd exhausted his efforts with the anime characters when R approached me about learning to draw a street scene using perspective. Clearly intelligent, he easily translated the technique to create a complex image of two converging city streets. With a variety of buildings, windows, roofs, and doors, the scene was technically perfect. The scene also told me that he might be feeling at a crossroads in his life, on the verge of choosing his next direction (top of Figure 14.3).

Figure 14.3 Street scene and abstract design
Illustrated in the color insert

That new direction came without any prompting from me. Using the two-point perspective skills that he'd acquired, R went on to engineer a complicated abstract design using only pencil (bottom of Figure 14.3). Each time he entered the studio, R appeared to be single-minded about his new projects, dropping off his belongings, and starting/continuing his work. He went on to develop dozens of sophisticated geometric Op-Art pieces, first in regular pencil and then with colored pencils. Although he had a favorite color palette, R continued experimenting with various color combinations to create unique effects, blending and visually vibrating the forms.

At the end of each school year, students were asked to review and "visit" their accumulated work (see Figure 14.4). They were to select pieces that represented a variety of experiences—work that was difficult, most meaningful, and most fun, that they were most proud of/least proud of, and/or showed evidence of their own personal growth. These pieces were then arranged on our large work table for the class to look over. I directed a "critique" that focused only on noting the progress and positive value of each student's artwork. Each student was required to tell about the different media that he/she had used and talk about what the pieces represented for him/her. Although very socially awkward and reserved, R participated fully. Other classmates asked questions about his work as part of the critique, and he answered appropriately.

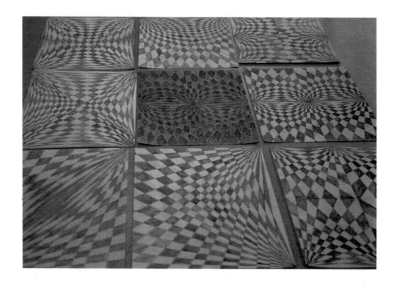

Figure 14.4 Review

As senior year evolved, R began "mapping out" new geometric designs on stretched canvases that I'd introduced to him. Each project was more complex than the next. He experimented with new colors. He used hard-to-control acrylic paints from a tube. He also seemed satisfied with his own work. After that last critique in his senior year, he asked if he could give me one of his pieces as a gift. I believe that was his thank-you note to me.

It was tradition for all of my art classes to write and draw their "farewells" to the rest of the center on a large roll of art paper, later hung on the office bulletin board for all to see. At the end of R's senior year, the art students huddled together enthusiastically, adding their messages and sentiments to the banner. R kept his distance at the bookshelves. Moments later, when his classmates were busy gathering their belongings to leave, he quietly went to the paper and wrote a message, stating in essence that at first he hadn't liked the students or the idea of attending school at the center. Now he knew that it had been a good place for him and that the teachers and staff had really helped him. R then added his thanks and signed his full name.

R never developed into a highly social or verbal person in the art studio. He did, however, grow by becoming more independent, intellectual, and interpersonal. I never witnessed the psychosis that was described by his previous school. At first he used his superheroes to give him ego strength. Then compartmentalized geometric designs helped contain and sort R's emotions, aiding his defenses. When comfortable with his feelings and mastered techniques, R moved on to use bright colors in a way that allowed personal, yet managed, freedom of expression. Even R knew that he had clearly developed his "voice."

*Figure 3.1 FSA Picture 2 completed by a normative (nonclinical)
46-year-old Korean woman in South Korea*

(page 43)

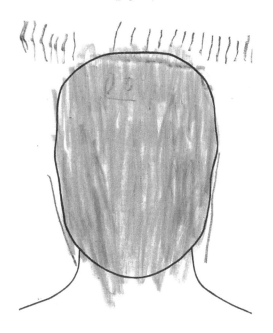

*Figure 3.2 FSA Picture 2 drawn by a "non-normative"
21-year-old Caucasian man with autism in the United States*

(page 43)

Figure 3.3 Clinical "Person Picking an Apple from a Tree" (PPAT)
by a five-year-old Asian Indian boy with possible ADHD

(page 48)

Figure 3.4 The first LECATA task, a free drawing and a story, created
by a first-grade Hispanic female aged 6 years, 11 months

(page 50)

Figure 6.2 Predrawn mandala

(page 79)

Figure 6.3 Picture of mandala with found material

(page 81)

Figure 8.1 Watercolor palette

(page 96)

Figure 8.2 "Oceania" by the author depicts the availability of the color blue to modern painters
(page 102)

Figure 9.1 "Spirit Nation," colored pencil, 4½" × 6½" paper

(page 111)

Figure 9.2 "Crossing Waterfalls," colored pencil, 4½" × 6½" paper

(page 111)

Figure 13.1 Figures and shapes

(page 145)

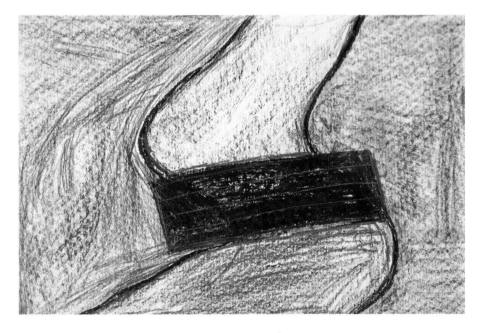

Figure 13.5 Bridge

(page 149)

Figure 14.3 Street scene and abstract design

(page 159)

Figure 16.5 Swan

(page 200)

Figure 17.1 "Surfer in a Thunderstorm"

(page 206)

Figure 17.2 Anthill

(page 207)

Figure 18.3 The future

(page 222)

Figure 19.1 Figurines used in an arts-based therapy session

(page 229)

Figure 22.1 Eight-year-old boy—Drawing of cemetery

(page 263)

Figure 22.2 Seven-year-old girl after death of her grandmother

(page 264)

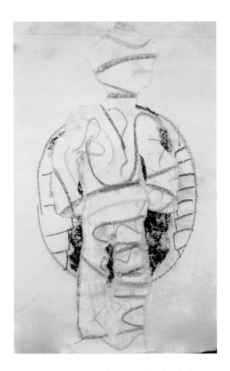

Figure 24.1 In through the back door

(page 284)

Figure 26.1 Working together

(page 301)

Figure 29.3 Draw and pass example

(page 335)

Figure 29.4 "Relationships"

(page 336)

Figure 30.1 Armenian landscape

(page 342)

Figure 30.2 Broad brush strokes

(page 343)

Figure 32.1 Figure created on newspaper 1

(page 362)

Figure 32.2 Figure created on newspaper 2

(page 363)

Variety of Roles for the School Art Therapist

Clinical Team Member

As the art therapist, I did not test my students but rather assessed their social and emotional progress through their art process and products. All of the important changes that took place in R, and in every other student in my classes, were reported at the "clinical team meetings" in our center. These meetings took place on a weekly basis and included the Principal, Department Chairperson, School Psychologist, School Social Worker, Center Counselor, and me, the art therapist. Student progress and welfare were discussed and strategies for intervention planned. I contributed a unique perspective on each student due to the fact that they worked in the art studio several times a week. I was privy to student moods, thoughts, and issues on a continuing basis. These appraisals were conveyed to the team by my sharing information necessary to student wellness and educational success.

In one case, a male student was thought to be unfocused and unorganized in most of his other classes. Amazed clinical team members changed their impressions of "K" as I kept them up to date on his progress. K had been a collector of stuff, junk really, that he had kept in his pockets and backpack. When I'd suggested that he empty all of his things onto a large tray and see if he could use any of it to make art, he started what became a two-year journey. K became a tinker, creating unique and complex three-dimensional, and sometimes moveable, sculptures. His problem-solving skills grew enormously. When I noted this ability, other classmates heard and eventually came to ask K for advice with their problem solving, about art and then also about issues with parents and/or boyfriends. He began to be held in high esteem within the group. K's skill at organizing spread to other classes. He began to regard himself differently, as more competent, as did his other teachers.

Mental Health Liaison

Keeping in close contact with the center's social worker and school psychologist was an important aspect of my position. These clinicians were acutely aware of the rich information that I could share with them about the students and their art. As a result, biweekly meetings were held so that they could look at the artwork and ask questions about students that they needed to better understand. I gave my impressions and spread out portfolio work to illustrate those impressions. Often, together with the psychological testing that they had done, a more complete picture of a student's issues and needs was created.

Art Therapist with Individuals

When indicated, clinical staff, administrative staff, and teachers from the center referred students to me for individual sessions. These were students who might not have connected with anyone at the center, who might have regularly doodled in the margins of their notebooks rather than attending to their class work, or who might have been in a temporary crisis. I saw these students on a short-term basis, perhaps for one session or a few. In doing so, I was able to offer an alternative method of self-expression and closer positive attention for students in need while further enriching the school's program.

Art Expressions Group Facilitator

A variety of support group opportunities were offered at the center to address—among other things, men's issues, freshman/senior transitions, social skills, women's issues, substance abuse, and a need to express oneself through the use of art. Students filled out interest surveys and groups were organized by the clinical staff to ensure that everyone was placed in a beneficial category. The Art Expressions Group was very different from the art-as-therapy classes. Students chose to be in this setting where they would use art to openly express their feelings and thoughts. Through the use of relevant themes, students discussed their completed art as it related to them and their lives. Always of importance was my awareness of the school setting and the need for transition from our art space and activities back to a classroom where students were to access their intellect. Themes, therefore, needed to be appropriate for the setting. Transition activities, like the use of a centering mandala drawing, were at times necessary to help students restore and/or maintain appropriate defenses for being back in the classroom. The Art Expressions Group also supported students' social-emotional needs by creating an accepting family of peers within the center.

Art Exhibit Curator

Attending a public school, rather than being a patient on a mental health hospital ward, sent a strong message to the enrolled students in our ED center. At the school, despite the fact that it was a special education center, students counted on the structure of the system in place. They counted on the rules for behavior, attendance, and grades. They counted on feeling like a student and not a patient. In addition, a key component of the Program of Studies was the expectation that student artwork would be exhibited as part of the learning process.

When students first began my art-as-therapy class, release forms were sent home to their parents/guardians. Parents were requested to discuss the form with their child and then sign it, acknowledging that the student's artwork would be exhibited later in the school year as part of the program curriculum.

As an art therapist I knew that most, if not all, of what students expressed in art class constituted their personal feelings, secrets, and fears on paper or in another medium. I also knew that much of it might not be appropriate for public viewing.

Halfway through the school year I began sifting through student portfolios, looking for work that would highlight each student's skills in a positive way, while not compromising his or her defenses and vulnerabilities. For many, it was a big step to put their work on display. Pieces selected for consideration for the art show, some completed and some not yet done, were put aside for review. Together we looked at the work and talked about what they felt comfortable sharing in the show and how they might finish those pieces that were uncompleted. I used donated professional mats from a local frame shop for student work which students helped select for their own pieces.

During the month of March, officially Youth Art Month in the United States, our center held an annual art show highlighting nearly 300 pieces of art. Named Personal Expressions," the show hosted hundreds of guests—parents, school officials, and visitors from both our center as well as other similar centers. Students volunteered to be guides, knowing that they would be required to dress up, be familiar with the different media displayed, and share that information with the parents and strangers who came. We offered our guests cookies and punch and informative tours of great art. Guests signed our comments book and talked about the impressive display. This annual event greatly bolstered egos and normalized the students' lives.

On several occasions, public art installations were created in a joint effort by students and staff alike. In order to allow everyone in the entire center to participate in creating the new piece of public art, a master art project schedule was created, taking into account the schedules of all staff and students. All involved were given the opportunity to create a unique and individual piece that was a part of the larger whole. Each of the large art assemblages was made of different materials or using different techniques than the others. Themes were student generated and work overseen by a student committee. The creation and completion of these projects brought a sense of pride to all in our work environment.

Intern Supervisor

Benefitting this special education program was the regular use of art therapy graduate school interns. Assigned for the entire school year, each intern worked first within the art-as-therapy classroom structure and later during class time in an alternate mini-studio location, with targeted individuals having further special needs. Interns also co-facilitated the Art Expressions Group and took over the art-as-therapy classroom duties in the absence of the art therapist/teacher. With this added assistance, students received closer attention and further support with their emotional and art-making needs. It was my responsibility, as a field supervisor for their university, to teach interns about the complexities of being an art therapist in a school setting and to supervise and evaluate their full experience.

Summary

When art therapy is part of a school program, it is clear that there is a true understanding of the need, benefit, and value beyond art instruction. Because of school art therapists, students learn to use art materials for reasons other than completing a piece with honed skill, and to express their thoughts and feelings. Students are encouraged to connect personally with the colors that they choose, to enjoy the journey of working with a "mistake," and to freely experiment with a variety of art materials that simply seem inviting. Art therapists may teach students how to make art, but their goals are very different from those of art teachers (Rubin 1982). Art therapists teach their students art techniques in order for them to have better ways of expressing and knowing themselves. In doing so, school art therapists provide students with new-found skills and individual powers that may fuel growth beyond the school years, and perhaps for the rest of a student's life. What may begin as tinkering with a pile of junk, creating a new superhero, or designing a complicated Op-Art design may end up as the personal key for unlocking a student's full potential.

References

Hall, C. and Lindzey, G. (1978) *Theories of Personality*. New York: John Wiley and Sons.

Rubin, J. (1982) "Art therapy: What it is and what it is not." *The American Journal of Art Therapy 21*, 57–58.

Resources

Further Reading

Blos, P. (1962) *On Adolescence: A Psychoanalytic Interpretation*. New York: The Free Press of Glencoe.

Bush, J. (1997) *The Handbook of School Art Therapy: Introducing Art Therapy into a School System*. Springfield, IL: Charles C. Thomas.

Cane, F. (1983) *The Artist in Each of Us*. Craftsbury Common, VT: Art Therapy Publications.

Isis, P., Bush, J., Siegel, C. A., and Ventura, Y. (2010) "Empowering students through creativity: Art therapy in Miami-Dade County Public Schools." *Art Therapy: Journal of the American Art Therapy Association 27*, 2, 56–61.

Linesch, D. G. (1988) *Adolescent Art Therapy*. New York: Brunner/Mazel.

Meeks, J. (1980) *The Fragile Alliance*. Malabar, IL: Robert E. Krieger Publishing Company.

Moon, B. (1998) *The Dynamics of Art as Therapy with Adolescents*. Springfield, IL: Charles C. Thomas.

Naumburg, M. (1973) *An Introduction to Art Therapy: Studies of "Free" Art Expression of Behavior Problem Children and Adolescents as a Means of Diagnosis and Therapy*. New York: Teachers College Press.

Ulman, E. and Dachinger, P. (1975) *Art Therapy in Theory and in Practice*. New York: Schocken Books.

Online

Emotional Disturbance (2008) *Project Ideal.* Available at www.projectidealonline.org/emotionalDisturbance.php, accessed on June 17, 2013.

Fairfax County Public Schools (FCPS) *Community Dialogue Meetings: Closing the Budget Gap for FY 2011.* Available at www.fairfaxcounty.gov/government/budget/fcps-budget-facts.pdf, accessed on June 17, 2013.

Procedures Required for Implementation of Special Education Regulations in Virginia's Public Schools. Available at www.fcps.edu/dss/seps/dueprocess-eligibility/procedures.pdf, accessed on June 17, 2013.

Program of Studies: High School Fine Arts (2006–2013). Available at www.fcps.edu/is/pos/hs.shtml, accessed on June 17, 2013.

Special Education Handbook. Available at www.fcps.edu/dss/sei/Handbook/handbook.pdf, accessed on June 17, 2013.

The Ten Tasks of Adolescence (2008) *Konopka Institute for Best Practices in Adolescent Health.* Available at http://adph.org/ALPHTN/assets/061109tasks.pdf, accessed on June 17, 2013.

Chapter 15

Practice of Art Therapy in Residential Schools and Group Homes

Charlotte Boston

The culture of art therapy in residential schools and group homes has provided one of the most ideal options to stabilize behavior and emotions, minimize risks, and treat youth who have been classified in special education due to the severity of their educational, emotional, or behavioral problems. A youth can struggle in his/her family, school, peer group, and community and this can impact his/her development and influence his/her success. Developmentally, the stage of adolescence (ages 11–21) has always been characterized by cognitive, social, and emotional changes. Critical components of this stage are physical, cognitive, moral, personality, identity, racial identity, and creative (Stepney 2010, p.4).

Case Study: Jay

Jay was a 15-year-old male youth with asthma. Predominant problems at home and school related to his aggressive and defiant behavior. His multiple psychiatric diagnoses related to mood, anxiety, attention deficits, hyperactivity, and a pervasive developmental disorder. In addition to his behavior problems, his trauma history—severe medical neglect and unhealthy home conditions—resulted in his removal from home and admission to a group home.

Jay resided in an eight-bedroom group home located in a quiet community. This was a suburban, single-family home where he lived with seven other male youths and two to three house staff who were consistently present. House staff were counselors, social workers, or psychiatric technicians. House rules and the daily routine were established for all the youth to follow; each was assigned regular daily chores. Jay's social worker was the liaison to the school for medical and court appointments.

Jay needed extra help with his morning routine and personal care. He often resisted the staff's efforts to help and was defiant toward rules. He would often yell and scream and refuse to shower, complete house chores, or take his medicine. Individual attention and incentive programs were effective in improving his compliance over time. He responded well to staff who talked to him privately about his behaviors.

Research indicates that the possibility for youth like Jay to have more serious problems in the future increases without a range of therapeutic interventions and additional educational support (Scott and Lorec 2007). Art therapy provides a safe and creative treatment intervention to reduce risky behavior that is sometimes associated with the stage of adolescence where there are emotional, cognitive, and physical changes that youth adjust to and struggle through. "Mental health status was also an inciting factor for risky behavior. Youths who suffered from depression, anxiety, hyperactivity, or more serious psychiatric or personality disorders were more likely to engage in antisocial or problematic behavior in the future" (Chambliss 2011, p.31).

Youth who are referred for art therapy services in residential schools and group homes have a range of conditions that can impede or arrest their emotional development and educational progress. They may have experienced multiple hospitalizations or suspensions from regular school, or failures at home, at school, and in the community. Their ability to function productively in the home, at school, and in their social community may have been greatly impaired. What complicates their condition even further are their learning disabilities, multiple diagnoses, and possible trauma history. Art therapy provides a safe, nonjudgmental, and nonintrusive, yet expressive, path toward healing and growth.

Riley says art therapy "offers a support system to adolescents experiencing abuse, depression, lack of self regard, or sudden social or academic failure" (Riley 2001, p.54). Art therapy in residential schools and group homes addresses academic issues with learning disabilities, poor concentration, self-esteem, identity, and impulse control, as it serves as a safe, nonjudgmental tool toward healing.

An alternative school is defined here as an educational setting designed to accommodate adolescents experiencing behavioral and academic problems in the mainstream educational setting, who would generally be considered at risk for dropping out or expulsion (Chambliss 2011, p.16).

In an educational setting, youth may be scheduled for art therapy to address academic issues of learning disabilities, autistic spectrum disorders, attention or concentration issues, mastery, and self-esteem (Liebmann 1999, p.25). Art therapy services for behavioral issues may also relate to poor impulse control.

Youth with severe emotional and behavioral problems, multiple diagnoses, and possible trauma history are subject to the services of residential schools and group homes because the residential setting offers a broad variety of therapeutic services, including but not limited to psychological individual and group counseling, speech/language therapy, trauma-based practices, and, in some cases, an ungraded curriculum. This type of setting also provides a higher level of supervision from a treatment team which collaborates on a comprehensive treatment plan for each youth. The additional staff attention youth receive in a residential setting may satisfy previously unmet dependency needs (Weathers and Bulock 1978, p.333) which frequently result from previous traumatic experiences.

Residential settings for treatment range from regular homes in the community to locked detention facilities for youth. Some youth are court ordered to a residential setting because they are unable to function safely or appropriately at home, in school, or in the community. Some youth are subject to the custody of a local or state agency that functioned as their guardian and monitored their services while the youth was in residential treatment. Depending upon the issues in each case, youth often have limited contact with their family. A residential setting is also more cost effective than an inpatient stay at a hospital and youth are often able to remain near their community. Group homes provide a stable, safe, structured, alternative home setting subject to rules and a daily routine which includes household chores.

A picture is often a more precise description of feelings than words and can be used to depict experiences that are hard to articulate verbally (Liebmann 1999, p.25). Art therapy bypasses normal defenses and is a safe container to express a broad range of feelings (Liebmann 1999, p.23). The benefits offered through art therapy with youth seem to stem from its nonverbal form of communication that is nonthreatening and over which the adolescent has control (Riley 2001, p.55). Youth are often unable to give voice to their experiences, especially in instances of trauma (Liebmann 2008, p.27). Art therapy can provide a means of expression.

The freedom of self-expression and self-exploration in art therapy empowers youth to develop healthier internal coping mechanisms as, prior to art therapy, their coping strategies may have been unsafe or ineffective. In addition, the creative process in art therapy may be soothing. As youth have opportunities to explore and master the art media, complete art tasks, and create within the individual session or group, there are often improvements in their social relationships, school performance, self-esteem, and mastery over tasks.

Art therapy seems to be the right fit for youth. As stated by Riley, during the developmental cycle of adolescence, depression slows the move toward independence and a secure identity. Therefore it is helpful to provide a safe outlet for the distress that has engendered the depression. Adolescents with depression motivated by situations in the family environment, or in the external world of peers and society, appear to get better when they express their anxieties through art therapy (Riley 2001, p.56).

A wonderful example of the experience of art therapy is described from a research project with boys in a detention facility. The boys' perceptions of what was most helpful about art therapy, in descending order, were stress relief and relaxation, reduction of boredom, pride and self-confidence, positive recognition, working through frustration, enjoyment and fun, improvement of ability to concentrate, and the way they were treated (Persons 2009, p.453).

The art therapy sessions in the group home described in the case study of Jay, seen earlier, were facilitated from an "art as therapy" model. This was a more flexible and practical approach given the varied cognitive levels of the youth in the home and the range of related behavioral issues to be addressed.

An example of my work with Jay, in group with the male youth in the home, relates to a combination of using therapeutic skills and being prepared with a variety of options for art tasks. There is particular attention given to the mood of the youth—individually and collectively. I would also be aware of their verbal banter and motivation. Since the art therapy sessions were monthly and a common area of the home was used for the session, I would telephone the group home staff the weekend before the session. The call helped me to consider what issues needed addressing, what their challenges had been this week, or what combination of art materials to bring. In addition, a verbal check-in with house staff, just before the group, provided general information about the youth, household issues, or any significant events.

A number of groups would begin with a warm-up activity during the first 15 or 20 minutes, as described in Liebmann's *Art Therapy for Groups*. Warm-up activities, used on various occasions with this group, included Rounds (quick sharing of personal information), Simon Says, doodles, scribbles, ink blots and butterflies, and left hand–right hand. Art materials for the art-based warm-ups were easily accessible and portable. When the youth were talkative, we would have a brief verbal check in. This supported the group's ability to focus and relaxed them enough to begin to constructively discharge any anxiety or impulses left from their day as they worked. This also assisted my ability to clearly confirm their mood and to formulate relevant themes from which to work.

Involving the youth in the decision making for the session was valuable as it eliminated power struggles. The art tasks I prepared during one art therapy session were to create a tee shirt with a self symbol or design using fabric paint or to build a model car from wood pieces and paint it. The treatment objectives were to build self-esteem, dexterity, impulse control, and concentration. Both art tasks were concretely based, would provide immediate gratification, and required a minimal amount of planning skills. This task was an opportunity for the youth to use a new medium (fabric paint); to plan and create their design; to create something they could keep; and work together to share materials. Four of the six youth in the group decided to create their own tee shirt using the fabric markers and fabric paint.

Directives for Youth

Liebmann's *Art Therapy for Groups* recommends a broad spectrum of themes for many populations. Art directives recommended for youth, learning disabled, youth on the autism spectrum, and residential populations are similar. The objectives for art therapy in educational settings most often originate from the Individual

Education Plan (IEP). Art therapy objectives identify goals such as improving communication, concentration, self-esteem, independence, and problem solving. Recommended themes for the learning disabled include those that address subjects associated with life and/or environmental occurrences, personal experiences, media exploration, and concentration/dexterity/memory (Liebmann 1999, pp.177, 178). Youth directives also include those that explore action and conflict as well as ideal places (Liebmann 1999, p.178). Recommended themes for the residential setting consist of themes or activities using murals, past/present/future, or "how you see yourself" (Liebmann 1999, pp.135, 137). In residential settings with clinical support resources, therapeutic objectives often originate from the youth's treatment plan. Art therapy objectives are based on problem-oriented goals to improve emotional and behavioral issues. Goals relating to improving mood, impulse control, concentration, task mastery, self-esteem, and social skills are also taken into account.

Within this group home's model, art therapy services could be either structured or flexible and include groups or individual sessions that best accommodated each youth's need. Each art therapist should determine which type of approach is best suited to his/her group, individual, or situation and consider the training and preparation necessary to facilitate art therapy sessions. Open studio-based groups provide freedom of choice. This is a flexible approach that is often used in long-term art therapy. Theme-based groups address specific problems, issues, or aspects of the human experience. Theme-based groups are useful for individual art therapy sessions as well. Art-based groups explore social and life issues (Liebmann 1999, pp.31–33). "One of the most valuable qualities of art therapy and personal art is the provision of a parallel frame of reference to real life, in which different ways of being can be tried out without any real-life consequences" (Liebmann 2001, p.18).

The considerations for type and range of art materials can be based on group space, storage, and portability in some cases. Basic art materials can include, but are not limited to, paper, markers, oil pastels, colored pencils, and Crayola Model Magic. Useful materials, not all related, include papermaking, sand art, and collage. Kits such as wooden car models, tie-dye, fuse beads, and plaster craft can also be used.

More About Jay

Jay participated in art therapy group sessions for three years. Art therapy sessions were held monthly and included concrete tasks. When he began in art therapy, he had problems with temper tantrums, defiant behavior, medication non-compliance, and poor basic hygiene. He also had poor school performance, and recreational and vocational issues.

Media exploration and an open-studio approach were a practical focus for this population of youth who had varied levels of cognitive functioning. The art directives for Jay were based on following directions (sequencing), improving fine motor skills, concentration and focusing attention, and improving self-esteem and mastery.

Jay was initially critical and hesitant to engage in art therapy sessions. He often questioned why he had to attend the session. He was encouraged to remain in the group and observe peers with the hope that this would improve his comfort level. Jay was in and out of group for his initial session and interrupted the group with random comments.

In subsequent months, he was asked to help with a papermaking task and this time he stood next to the art therapist curiously watching and asking questions as paper was mulched. He shared that he enjoyed tearing the paper. Jay was able to remain for the entire group session and was able to follow a simple directive. He made positive comments about making his sheet of paper. He was praised for his ability to participate and remain for the entire art therapy session.

He attended subsequent art therapy group sessions without a prompt. He met the art therapist at the door to ask what the group activity would be. He spoke loudly when he discovered the group would make wooden car models. He chattered all through the session, but was able to complete tasks and asked for help when he had problems fitting pieces that connected the wheels.

In the third year, Jay was able to work through frustration during group. He worked on a fuse bead project, a concentration task in which small beads are put on a template one by one to make a figure. He expressed being angry because the beads didn't stay on the template. This challenged his impulse control. He was encouraged through this task to completion. It was explained that the beads would move until they were melted with the iron. Peers teased him because he took longer, but he did not lose his temper and was able to complete his figure.

In Jay's group home, there were also related activities for the youth that were seasonal—for example, planning a cookout, sports, going to the pool, and/or baking. In these tasks, the youth chose roles for and applied aspects of concentration, asking for help, and working together. During a social activity, grilling hamburgers, the art therapist learned that Jay was cheerful in helping as long as no one criticized him. He was quick to respond with an angry comment when peers criticized the way he shaped hamburgers. However, with a little encouragement, he was able to quickly regroup in order to refocus his attention on completing the task. He was later able to identify one positive aspect of his work which improved his self-esteem. This experience seemed to reflect some of the work Jay addressed in art therapy sessions where he was corrected in a supportive environment.

Toward the last year of art therapy sessions, Jay had noticeable improvements in his self-esteem and mastery of tasks, as reflected in his making positive statements about his work and keeping his artwork and projects that before he would destroy and throw away. His concentration improved, as reflected in his ability to tolerate delayed gratification with multistep art tasks, being able to remain for the duration of art therapy sessions, improved conflict resolution with peers, and absence of temper tantrums.

Jay's treatment team also worked toward his success. Art therapy was one component of his progress. His experiences seemed to reflect art therapy's ability to positively influence his mood and to improve his motivation to try new things, to tolerate changes, and to improve interpersonal skills.

Jay's case describes his struggles with self-esteem, regulating his anger, and poor school performance. Over the course of the three years of regularly scheduled art therapy sessions, Jay's improved self-esteem was reflected in his ability to make positive statements about his work, and to remain on task for the entirety of the session and completion of task. Jay's frustration tolerance was very low initially, as reflected in the high incidence of conflict, tantrums, and aggression with peers in art therapy group and at school. When the art therapy sessions ended, Jay was able to control his aggression. He was able to express his anger in a healthy way without losing control. He was even able to identify three healthy ways to cope with his anger. This seemed reflected in the art therapy sessions where he was able to work through his frustration with the class by tearing up paper or using a modeling medium to discharge his impulses. He could make choices on tasks or projects in art therapy sessions, which empowered him. Jay's angry outbursts were reduced to about once every two months and even these were not as intense as when he began the sessions. House staff who worked with Jay reported that he had been accepted into a vocational program, which suggested that his ability to work with others had improved. Jay's high-risk status, given the behavior that had brought him into the group home, had significantly decreased as the art therapy sessions concluded.

The nonthreatening nature of art therapy has been a key component for behavioral, educational, and emotional progress for youth in residential settings. As noted in the review of neurobiological research by Streeck-Fischer and van der Kolk (2000), several articles describe the positive impact of art therapy as one of the creative art therapies that through the use of art materials provides a safe and concrete outlet to express and regulate feelings, regardless of cognitive ability (Carey 2006, p.23). Just as art is an integral part of any community, so is the role of art within the residential setting. Art therapy is one more tool for youth to use in their struggle to overcome life challenges and find a better future.

References

Carey, L. (2006) *Expressive and Creative Arts Methods for Trauma Survivors.* London: Jessica Kingsley Publishers.

Chambliss, W. J. (2011) *Juvenile Crime and Justice.* Thousand Oaks, CA: Sage Publications.

Liebmann, M. (1999) *Art Therapy for Groups: A Handbook of Themes, Games, and Exercises.* Florence, KY: Brunner-Routledge.

Liebmann, M. (2001) *Art Therapy for Groups: A Handbook of Themes, Games, and Exercises.* Cambridge, MA: Brookline.

Liebmann, M. (2008) *Art Therapy and Anger.* London: Jessica Kingsley Publishers.

Persons, R. W. (2009) "Art therapy with serious juvenile offenders: A phenomenological analysis." *International Journal of Offender Therapy and Comparative Criminology 53,* 4, 433–453.

Riley, S. (2001) "Art therapy with adolescents." *The Western Journal of Medicine 175,* 1, 54–57.

Scott, D. A. and Lorec, L. (2007) "A multi-tiered evaluation of adolescent therapeutic group homes." *Child and Youth Care Forum 36,* 4, 153–162.

Stepney, S. A. (2010) *Art Therapy with Students at Risk: Fostering Resilience and Growth through Self-Expression.* Chicago, IL: Charles C. Thomas Publisher.

Streeck-Fischer, A. and Van der Kolk, B. A. (2000) "Down will come baby, cradle and all: Diagnostic and therapeutic implications of chronic trauma on child development." *Australian and New Zealand Journal of Psychiatry 34,* 6, 903–918.

Weathers, O. D. and Bulock, S. C. (1978) "Therapeutic group home for adolescent girls: An interagency development." *Journal of the National Medical Association 70,* 5, 331–334.

Part IV

Understanding the Cultural Implications of Using Art Therapy in Hospital and Rehabilitation Settings

Chapter 16

Warrior Culture
Art Therapy in a Military Hospital
Paula Howie

Introduction to Inpatient Psychiatry Work

Art therapists have been working in inpatient psychiatry settings in the United States for over 50 years. In the 1960s, two of the earliest programs were at the Menninger Clinic in Topeka, Kansas, and at Bethesda Hospital in Boston (Howie and Guiterrez 1984). Until the 2000s, when there was a shift of art therapists away from traditional psychiatric hospitals to varied settings, inpatient psychiatric hospitals were the most common places for art therapists to work (Malchiodi 2007). It may follow that as art therapy is found to be a healing psychotherapeutic intervention in developing countries, the inpatient psychiatric hospital setting may be a likely area in which full-time positions in art therapy will emerge.

The Military as a Unique Culture

The work described in this chapter was performed at a large military facility in the eastern United States. The services described were developed over the course of 25 years in this program, which at one time employed eight full-time art therapists. The success of the interventions described below was the result of the dedication of many art therapy staff members and graduate students who worked in the Department of Psychiatry during that time.

As with all psychiatric hospitals in the United States, the inpatient unit underwent tremendous change during this span of time. These changes included a decrease in patient census from 140 beds to 45 beds, which was partially due to stricter criteria for admission and to the implementation of managed care standards. This also occurred, at times drastically, in civilian hospitals where hospital stays currently average two to three days. In the military, administrative paperwork can warrant keeping many individuals in the hospital for months.

Many of the active duty service or family members seen at the hospital included those from diverse cultural and ethnic backgrounds. In the 1970s, the US military became an all-voluntary force, which is a common term used to denote that individuals currently serving sign up rather than being tasked to do so by way of a draft. To date, the military mirrors the diversity seen in the general population. In 2005, the roster of active duty soldiers consisted of 22 percent blacks, 60.8 percent whites, 10.5 percent Hispanics, and 4 percent Asians. "We used to call it a melting pot," said Orlando Bridges, an instructor at Fort Lee. "I look at it as a tossed salad, rich in different colors and qualities" (Bacque 2007, p.A1). In addition, the majority of patients seen were male.

According to Mary Wertsch, the military has been called a unique culture having characteristics she describes as a "warrior culture" (Wertsch 1991, p.1). These include a rigid authoritarian organization that often extends into the structure of the home; extreme mobility resulting in isolation and alienation from both civilian communities and the extended family; and overwhelming isolation in out-of-country posts that are usually walled off from the outside culture, leading to "an oddly isolated life, one in which it is possible to delude oneself that one is still on American soil" (Wertsch 1991, p.330). Also unique to this culture are the two subcultures of the officer and enlisted ranks, each with very different lifestyles. Wertsch (1991) sees parental absence, making adults unavailable for the big moments in their children's lives, as a unique problem for this community; thus first steps such as entering school, the prom, the big football game, the drama production, or graduation, which are ordinarily seen as positive events, put an undue strain on these families. Indeed, the importance of the military mission has "historically been perceived as requiring a total commitment to the military... This is the very essence of the concept of military unit cohesion" (Martin and McClure 2000, p.15). This includes a felt sense of mission to make the world a safer place and constant preparation for disaster—that is, war, terrorist attacks, unforeseen threats. Martin and McClure (2000) state that the conditions of military family life, "including long and often unpredictable duty hours, relatively low pay and limited benefits, frequent separations, and periodic relocations...remain the major stressors of military family life" (p.3).

Art Therapy in the Military

The art therapist must enter this military culture with an open mind and an understanding presence. Unlike the treatment of our soldiers after the Vietnam War, at which time those in uniform were blamed for the war out of anger and resentment, we are now able to differentiate those serving our military from the policies that put them there. Lynn Hall (2008) cautions that the counselor must understand his or her subjective reaction to working with this population. If one does harbor resentment toward the military and its lifestyle, then working to understand this resentment and the stressors faced by these individuals helps the therapist maintain a sense of balance and empathic response.

As art therapists, we are well aware that we practice in the realities of a world that may require reporting for insurance reimbursement, using quantitative markers for treatment, defining measurable objectives, adhering to the Health Insurance Portability and Accountability Act (HIPAA 1996), and providing clinical record keeping. At the same time, we bring our knowledge of interpersonal attunement, symbols, spiritual knowing, and a deeper understanding of our patients' internal and external realities to light. Philip Bromberg (1998) asserts that therapy occurs when the artist/therapist holds the projections of the patient in a central space to affect the therapist, usually in a positive way. Those with whom we work often profoundly influence us; the impact of working in an inpatient, military environment often taps into deep feelings on the part of the therapist. These reactions may be as disparate as the therapist's protective attitude and sense of unfairness about how the military member has been treated to a sense that war is wrong and the military member may have gotten what he or she deserved for taking part in something so abhorrent. Working with a team, as well as self-exploration, peer supervision, and personal therapy, helps the art therapist deal with the deep feelings that arise while working with this client population.

In this setting, the art therapy program has a special creative mandate. The foundation of the discipline of art therapy is in the use of art as symbolic expression of feelings and thoughts while working with expressive art materials. The materials used usually include drawing materials (chalk and oil pastels, pencils, magic markers), paints, and clay, although a wide variety of materials may be available in a fully functioning art studio space. The art therapist provides a safe and welcoming environment which can allow change and independence to occur through the process of creation. In the same way that a person does not need to be an accomplished orator in order to speak understandably to someone else, a person does not need artistic skill or talents to make a picture or to use clay in order to express and communicate his/her emotions and thinking. Indeed, humankind's use of art predates written language and many of the world's alphabets are based on symbols and pictures. Elinor Ulman (Ulman and Dachinger 1996) stated that the creative experience serves to bridge the gap between the person's feelings and thoughts, and between his/her inside and outside worlds, thus aiding holistic integration. Clients can bring order to chaos and make struggles more manageable by expressing them in the presence of an art therapist who can understand visual clues and witness this journey. The process of therapy significantly improves a person's understanding of himself/herself and the world in which he/she lives.

Responsibilities and Functions of an Art Therapist

As part of a multidisciplinary treatment team including social workers, psychiatrists, psychologists, recreation therapists, occupational therapists, and horticultural therapists, the art therapist is constantly working to assess strengths and to build on these. This requires periodic modification to the treatment plan so that the individual may derive the maximum benefit from art therapy services and ensure these services are coordinated with the team. Contributing to an individualized treatment plan, the art therapist assists the individual in selecting appropriate therapeutic objectives to meet assessed needs. As a means of communication, artwork can convey a person's functional and developmental levels and his/her unique conflicts and strengths. It can also assist the treatment team in setting up treatment goals and objectives.

The therapist evaluates the patient's responses to tasks and other interventions, while continuing to assess shifting goals and maximizing progress in art therapy. Since many patients are prescribed psychotropic medications, the art therapist becomes familiar with their properties and side effects. Access to this information can be obtained through Internet resources, books, and training provided by the facility (see the Resources section at the end of this chapter). The therapist contributes to formulation of the patient's treatment for interdisciplinary conferences, where the patient's assessment pictures are often presented, using information from the assessment. The individual is then usually assigned to an art therapy treatment group, with the type of group selected on the basis of the patient's diagnosis and treatment plan as well as his/her ability to function in a more or less structured environment. There are several different types of art therapy treatment groups, but the overall goal of each is to help the patient achieve and maintain the highest possible level of self-directed functioning. Individual sessions may be scheduled for selected patients as time permits.

Art Therapy Services

The levels of art therapy treatment mirror ward advancement and begin with the most controlled level and move to the least restrictive, most open one. *Individual sessions* are provided on a case-by-case basis, when the treatment team requests a formal diagnosis or the referring clinician would like more information (e.g., suicide potential) relevant to treatment planning that has not been accessible through routine verbal or other diagnostic processes. The individual is then assigned to an Art Therapy Assessment session in which he/she is asked to draw several pictures (such as the Ulman Personality Assessment Procedure [UPAP] [Ulman 1996]; the Person Picking an Apple from a Tree [PPAT] [Gantt and Tabone 1998]; the Diagnostic Drawing Series [DDS] [Cohen, Hammer, and Singer 1998]; a scribble; a family portrait; or a theme chosen by the art therapist). The assessment, which most closely addresses the individual's presenting problem, is chosen by the art therapist. After the assessment is completed, the therapist looks at the formal elements of the picture. These include elements such as line, color content, placement, relationship of figure to ground, relative size of forms, energy level, organization, and general and personal ability to follow instructions and to respond verbally (FEATS scale; Gantt and Tabone 1998). Consequently, the art therapist has access to a tremendous amount of information about the emotional and cognitive status of the individual.

The next level is the *Themes* group, which includes five or six individuals and is held in a small, contained space on the ward. It offers those patients who have issues that preclude their leaving the ward (such as suicidal ideation, psychosis, and depression) an opportunity to use art materials in a structured small-group setting; to express their ideas about common concerns; and to communicate these ideas through artwork and group discussion to each other and the therapist (see Appendix C). All usually respond well to the clear and reality-oriented focus of this group and gain a sense of control through using the art materials. In addition, the severely withdrawn person who has difficulty communicating verbally often finds making a picture of his/her concerns less threatening than face-to-face verbal contact. Materials of choice for the themes group are more controlled materials such as pencils, chalks, and markers.

The third level, the *Creative Arts Therapy* group with six to eight participants, offers structured art experiences designed to increase knowledge through exploration of feelings and ways of interacting with others. Music and movement often supplement the artwork, enriching involvement in the creative process. Those who are recommended for this group have a less restrictive status on the ward and are able to utilize the art studio space. This group often focuses on issues such as self-esteem, as art combined with movement helps the therapist to access the individual's strengths. For the person who lacks interpersonal skills, the group offers a positive means of interacting with others. By encouraging individuals to share artwork verbally in the discussion period and to participate in group projects, such as mural making, this group allows a more insight-oriented, psychotherapeutic focus.

The final level is titled the *Expressive Art Therapy* group, which emphasizes the use of the art materials to complete individual projects. The expressive group encourages self-expression and self-understanding through the creative process itself, allowing patients choice in both subject matter and media. Long-term projects, such as water-based oil paint, acrylic paintings, or large sculptures to which patients may return over the course of a few weeks, are especially encouraged in this group and often sustain the interest and industry of its members. Patients who can most use this group are those capable of self-direction, or those who are withdrawn and more comfortable with emphasis on the symbolic communication of the art rather than with the verbal discussion periods of the *Creative Arts* group. Often, these are people who have attended the *Themes* group and *Creative Arts* group and who wish to continue working out conflicts in a less-structured environment, or to make unique artwork they can later keep.

A final option of services on an acute care ward is the *Studio Art* group (not prescribed in the treatment plan) that is open to all patients, particularly those wishing to learn new skills with the art materials and to enjoy the creative experience. Family and visitors as well as staff sometimes participate in this group.

Art Therapy Inpatient Case Study

Like many of the young active duty soldiers who enlisted after completing high school, for Seth (pseudonym) the military turned out to be a shocking experience; many hospitalized soldiers had trouble with their superior officers, became depressed, or were unable to make friends and became ostracized in their units. While on duty, they may have manifested psychotic symptoms such as loose associations, hearing voices, nightmares, blunted affect, and low energy. Unless they were deemed unfit for military service and were to be separated from the service, most had inpatient stays for a week or two. As a result of the short stay on the ward, it was not unusual for some clients to be seen only once in art therapy.

Seth was a young-looking 19-year-old when he was admitted to the inpatient service with a diagnosis of major depressive disorder. He was seen several times in art therapy during the weeks he was in the hospital. He was also placed on medications and seen in other activity treatment groups such as recreation therapy and occupational therapy.

Seth first attended an individual art assessment session. Most inpatients were seen in art therapy as attendance was considered part of their daily activity schedule. For this particular evaluation, Seth was given a modified Ulman. He was asked to draw, in this order, a free picture, a scribble, a free picture or a picture from a scribble, and a family portrait.

His first picture shows an underwater scene (Figure 16.1). He titled this "Diving to the Deep." Underwater or outer space themes were common subject matter on the ward and were thought to be a reflection of how uncomfortable and "alien" the individual felt in the military, on the ward, and in their lives. In his picture, Seth shows large rocks between which are a manta ray with a barbed tail, a large bottom-dwelling fish, and a sea anemone. Seth talked about how ferocious these creatures appear and yet how docile they are. While talking about his artwork, Seth also described himself as an "alien." Possibly a self-portrait, the manta ray picture depicts several creatures that are frightening on the outside, docile on the inside, and diving into the depths of the ocean. The ocean is often experienced as symbolic of the unconscious, a journey into which the ray, and by association Seth, may be contemplating.

His next scribble was titled "Snake Man" (Figure 16.2) and shows a rather realistic cobra with ample teeth, its body coiled but with tongue out, trying to explore its surroundings. There is little human in this picture despite its title. This scribble could be seen as a warning to others to stay away from this man-creature. Being in unfamiliar surroundings, Seth understandably felt the need to reestablish his distance and protect himself from others by presenting a frightening side.

Figure 16.1 Underwater

Figure 16.2 "Snake Man"

In his family portrait (Figure 16.3), Seth shows all family members. He is depicted as a dark shadow beside his father. Since he is a shadow, his identity seems less formed than the identity of other members of the family. Seth said that his stepmother and biological father always favored her biological children; his father married her when Seth was ten. Seth had not seen his biological mother since the time he went to live with his dad and stepmother. On the left side of the picture there is a grave with RIP (rest in peace) with his biological sister's name on it.

She was killed in an automobile accident the year before when she was 16, and Seth, who was 18 at the time, had to identify her body. Seth said that his family, especially his stepmother who is depicted as a formidable figure in front of the others, had reacted to her death by getting rid of her belongings the day after she died. "It was like they didn't want to think about it." What Seth was describing was new information for the treatment team and pointed to his feelings about the loss of his sister and loss of his family who were seen as unsupportive during this troubling time. Seth talked throughout the assessment about how he liked to make monsters and frightening creatures. Feeling like an outsider in all aspects of his life, one also has the sense from this set of pictures that Seth is desperately alone in this frightening, alien world and may be looking for, yet fearing, connection.

Figure 16.3 Family

It was clear that Seth was able to use art therapy for expression of his anger and fear, and as a way to work through some of the grief associated with the death of his sister. There is a high correlation between those who are diagnosed with major psychiatric disorders and those who have also experienced earlier trauma. For Seth, this may have begun even before the loss of his sister, perhaps prior to the loss of his mother at age ten through his parents' divorce. According to the Adverse Childhood Experiences study (Feletti 2002), there is also a connection between childhood trauma and physical illness. Without treatment for his psychiatric illness and trauma, Seth is at risk for illnesses such as diabetes, heart disease, and chronic obstructive pulmonary disease in addition to the emotional sequelae of trauma.

While on the unit, Seth continued to demonstrate his ambivalence by making frightening and not so frightening pictures. These were seen as statements of his wish to stay separate and his need to be close to others. The grim reaper and the swan (Figures 16.4 and 16.5) were two such pictures. This grim reaper shows fiery eyes and mouth, and a hooded, faceless figure. This grimacing figure is frightening, and calls to mind the untimely death of Seth's sister and his unresolved feelings about the lack of support of his family.

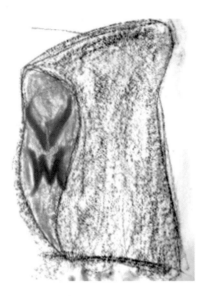

Figure 16.4 Grim reaper

Figure 16.5 Swan

Illustrated in the color insert

The swan, probably Seth's most benign figure, majestically swims in a small pond. Seth shows him making waves in an environment that seems capable of sustaining him. The swan appears to be flapping his wings and trying to fly in a confined area much as Seth is trying out new ways of "flying" by relating to and trusting others in the confines of the hospital. As this final picture demonstrates, Seth was able to use his time on the unit productively and achieve a kind of transformation and peace. It is typical that the individual is able to reveal much about himself and his issues while attending art therapy in the hospital.

Conclusion

Hospitalization may be the most fruitful time for psychotherapeutic interventions due to the individual's vulnerability and lowering of defenses. Seth certainly demonstrated this through his art. He was sent back to his military unit and referred for long-term outpatient treatment in order to work on his family and grief issues. His hospitalization, as for so many on the inpatient ward, was an extraordinarily creative time during which he opened up to other people with similar issues who were able to witness and tolerate his pain, confusion, and fear, while continuing to support his individuality and humanity.

The unique culture of the military cannot be underestimated when treating active duty service members and their families. Every facet of intervention from assessment to treatment to discharge planning provided by inpatient service personnel must take this culture into account. This, in turn, allows the client to use self-disclosure, to gain self-understanding, and to return to the military or home, becoming a more fully functioning member of his/her unit or civilian environment.

References

Bacque, P. (2007) "America's Army is looking more like America." *Richmond Times-Dispatch*, June 23, p.A1.

Bromberg, P. M. (1998) *Standing in the Spaces: Essays on Clinical Process, Trauma, and Dissociation*. New Jersey: Analytic Press.

Cohen, B. M., Hammer, J. S., and Singer, S. (1988) "The Diagnostic Drawing Series: A systematic approach to art therapy evaluation and research." *The Arts in Psychotherapy 15*, 1, 11–21.

Feletti, V. (2002) "The relation between adverse childhood experiences and adult health: Turning gold into lead." *The Permanente Journal 6*, 1, 44–47.

Gantt, L. and Tabone, C. (1998) *The Formal Elements Art Therapy Scale: The Rating Manual*. Morgantown: Gargoyle Press.

Hall, L. K. (2008) *Counseling Military Families: What Mental Health Professionals Need to Know*. New York: Routledge.

Health Insurance Portability and Accountability Act (HIPAA) (1996) Public Law 104–91, 104th Congress.

Howie, P. and Guiterrez, C. (1984) *Continuous Quality Improvement Manual*. Mundelein: American Art Therapy Association.

Malchiodi, C. (2007) "Demographic and strategic planning surveys: Highlights and preliminary results." *American Art Therapy Association Newsletter 11*, 3, pp.1 and 4.

Martin, J. A. and McClure, P. (2000) "Today's Active Duty Military Family: The Evolving Challenges of Military Family Life." In J. A. Martin, L. N. Rosen, and L. R. Sparacino (eds) *The Military Family: A Practice Guide for Human Service Providers*. Westport: Praeger Publishers.

Ulman, E. and Dachinger, P. (1996) *Art Therapy in Theory and Practice*. Chicago, IL: Magnolia Street Publishers.

Wertsch, M. E. (1991) *Military Brats: Legacies of Childhood Inside the Fortress*. New York: Harmony Books.

Resources

Agell, G. *The Ulman Personality Assessment Procedure*. Email: gladysagell@aol.com.

Barry, M., Cohen, B., Barnes, M., and Rankin, A. (1995) *Traumatic Stress Through Art: Drawing from the Center*. Brooklandville, MD: Sidran Press.

Gantt, L. and Tabone, C. (1998) *PPAT Rating Manual: The Formal Elements Art Therapy Scale (FEATS)*. Morgantown, WV: Gargoyle Press.

Liebmann, M. (2004) *Art Therapy for Groups: A Handbook of Themes and Exercises*. East Sussex: Routledge.

O'Neal, J., Preston, J., and Talaga, M. (2010) *Handbook of Clinical Psychopharmacology for Therapists*. Oakland: New Harbinger Publishers.

World Health Organization (1994) *The ICD-10 Classification of Mental and Behavioural Disorders: Diagnostic criteria for research*. Geneva: World Health Organization.

Chapter 17

Cultural Crossroads
Considerations in Medical Art Therapy
Tracy Councill and Katharine Phlegar

Cancer touches people of all ages from every walk of life and every culture. What it means to be ill, to undergo treatment, and to face death are expressed and processed through innumerable cultural practices and philosophies. Art therapists must be aware of and sensitive to the cultures of the individuals with whom they work, as well as the culture in which medical treatment takes place. In this respect, art therapists can serve as ambassadors between the two—illuminating cultural concerns of patients that may differ from institutional expectations and helping patients better understand and cope with the unfamiliar world of medicine.

What a Medical Diagnosis Means

The disease model so commonly found in Western medicine focuses on symptoms and illness. Broader views in health care also attend to the concepts of healing and wellness.

> To be psychologically well while physically sick involves the belief that your personal worth transcends physical limitations… This belief in your self-worth rarely emerges until what you have lost and grieved for stands second in importance to precious moments of inner peace and joy. (Le Maistre 1999, p.7)

Cultural traditions have varying beliefs about the meaning of illness and death, yet grief is a universal human experience. When working with seriously ill individuals and their families, it is important to remember that grief begins with the initial news of the diagnosis; mourning is not reserved solely for the end of life. Many losses occur during treatment—loss of a sense of safety, loss of physical vigor, changes in appearance, and isolation from friends and familiar routines (Councill 2012; Czamanski-Cohen 2012; Furman 2011). Processing and grieving these changes is a significant part of coping with a serious illness.

Multicultural Perspectives

Large hospitals sometimes attract patients who travel literally around the world to receive cancer treatment. Families from the same geographical locations, including those from the United States, still come from cultural and religious backgrounds with different perspectives on illness and treatment. Culturally sensitive art therapy can open avenues for expression across cultural differences. Art therapists convey respect and openness by avoiding assumptions about an individual's color choices or symbolism and instead ask about the artist's associations with the image. Art making can provide a fertile ground for conversation and education about someone's cultural beliefs and background.

When the cultural values of the patient and the family are in conflict with medical culture, treatment providers must negotiate a complex interpersonal landscape. In Western medicine, the person in the white coat has remarkable power—to treat, to heal, to make decisions. This power often goes unchallenged by individuals outside the medical culture. It can be challenging for both medical and psychosocial staff to fully align their treatment plan with an individual's or a family's cultural understanding of both the disease and treatment process.

Women are sometimes excluded from medical conversations and decision making because of the family's individual culture or the broader culture. The patient's male caregivers sit down with the medical team to discuss the prognosis and the treatment plan, and the mother stays with the child—the patient—unable to ask her questions directly to the doctors. These families may allow and even encourage the mother to be with the child during an art therapy session, while still respecting their traditionally defined role within the family. While working with the clay or paint, the mother may find another way to express herself and find a sense of support from other caregivers in a culturally appropriate way. Art therapy's facility for nonverbal expression can give voice to the voiceless, while still acknowledging cultural boundaries or expectations.

For some, the word "cancer" itself is taboo. The family of a newly diagnosed teenager did not want the medical and support staff to use cancer-related terminology in their discussions with the patient. His family escorted him around the unit to protect him from any unintentional disclosures from staff or other patients. The family then explained that cancer was essentially a death sentence in their native country because there was no treatment and certainly no expectation of cure. Additional education for staff and the family led to more open discussions, allowing staff members to more directly address the cultural perceptions of the word "cancer" and explain how treatment in the United States would be different.

Aspects of medical protocol itself may be incongruent with an individual's or a family's culture. Many people who undergo treatment for cancer require transfusions of blood products (including red blood cells and platelets), an act forbidden in some religions. Additionally, some of the medications regularly used in treatment are made from animal products. Those made from pigs can be especially offensive to some patients, including those who practice Islam or Judaism and even those with strong beliefs about the treatment of animals. Families may also want to include aspects of ritual or spiritual healing in the treatment of the patient. These practices can be met with skepticism by the medical treatment team, even if they do not interfere with medical protocols. Art therapists need to be aware of these potential cultural conflicts in order to raise awareness with the medical treatment team and encourage pastoral care or ethics consultations when needed.

Medical Art Therapy

Art therapists in medical settings can support symptom management and improve communication and understanding among patients, families, and medical care providers (Nainis 2008; Nesbitt and Tabatt-Haussmann 2008; Robb and Councill 2011). Art therapy offers opportunities for expression, processing, and a general enhancement in the quality of life for those undergoing treatment. It is an avenue that does not identify an individual solely as a patient but rather as a human being (Nainis 2008; Zammit 2001).

Choice and an Opportunity for Control

Art therapy is offered to patients undergoing medical treatment as an adjunctive or complementary service (Councill 2012; Nainis 2008; Zammit 2001). There are times when art therapy sessions must be interrupted or postponed to allow for examinations, procedures, or rest. Patients lose a great deal of personal autonomy, and art therapy offers many alternative opportunities for choice and control—from the choice of materials and subject matter to the choice of whether to participate in art therapy at all (Furman 2011; Nainis 2008). A decision to not participate should be respected as a demonstration of independence in a situation where many other choices are denied. Although refusal of services is a possibility, patients and their family members eventually engage in art therapy more often than not (Nainis 2008). Initially after diagnosis, there may be a period when patients keep primarily to themselves, allowing time to process the seemingly insurmountable information presented during the initial hospital visits. When patients and families are ready, art therapy can provide a safe space to explore their experience in a creative way.

Art pieces that express the patient's perspective on illness and treatment attest to their resilience and help them communicate with the treatment team. One 12-year-old's painting, titled "Surfer in a Thunderstorm," illustrated his experience of having leukemia. The image shows the patient as the surfer on the right side of the page facing a tremendous amount of thunder, lightning, and rain. He appears to be engulfed by the storm, but a rescue boat moves toward him. The painting (Figure 17.1) conveys both loss of control and the awareness that help is near.

When illness limits life experiences, patients can create art to express their wishes and dreams. A young adult coping with life-threatening side effects following a bone marrow transplant created a three-dimensional photo collage of a "Virtual Tour of Paris," both expressing a life-long dream and creating a piece of art that became a touchstone for guided meditation during painful medical procedures. Creating art, and showing it in the hospital or a public space when it is appropriate, can give patients a feeling of accomplishment and pride. Art therapy also offers individuals the opportunity to experience a sense of mastery over the art materials (Nesbitt and Tabatt-Haussmann 2008). This feeling of empowerment can be especially significant for people when their illness and the rest of their life seem to be beyond their control (Nainis 2008).

Figure 17.1 "Surfer in a Thunderstorm"
Illustrated in the color insert

Visual Communication

Medical care immerses patients and their loved ones in a system filled with highly specialized terminology. Even the most considerate medical staff members can sometimes forget that their everyday vernacular is foreign to many, especially to those who are recently diagnosed. Art therapy and the art therapists themselves can create visual explanations to help patients and families understand diagnoses and treatment. While adults also enjoy the benefits of concrete representations, children often respond especially well to this more active form of processing. Art therapists may ask children to draw or sculpt their conceptions of what is happening in their bodies or of what may happen during an upcoming procedure, or children may do such art pieces spontaneously. Art therapists may respond in art or play, sometimes with the assistance of other appropriate medical or psychosocial staff, to help dispel misunderstandings or to clarify steps in treatment. An 11-year-old boy was hospitalized awaiting a bone marrow transplant—a procedure that requires intensive chemotherapy and radiation to erase the patient's immune system and replace it with healthy donor bone marrow. New bone marrow is then infused through an IV, without any surgery. In art therapy the boy created puppets and performed a play in which all of the main character's bones were removed from his body. The art therapist realized that his play likely represented the patient's understanding of what happened during a bone marrow transplant. Although the patient's medical team had explained the transplant procedure to him previously, patients often require repeated explanations and sufficient time to process the mountains of information they receive. This boy's work with the art therapist allowed his emerging misconceptions and concerns to be addressed, helping him achieve a more accurate understanding of the procedure ahead.

These often metaphorical representations can also help alleviate anxieties by allowing patients to exert control over the situation in the artwork. In one case, a four-year-old girl with a brain tumor was very fearful after her initial hospitalization. She visited the art therapist after each appointment, using clay and clay tools along with medical supplies to create a "girl" and perform "surgery." As she cut and poked the clay, she explained that the surgery was taking away the cancer and that the "girl" could not feel it because she was asleep. She reenacted the process many times, rehearsing what she had been told about her treatment, and gradually gained mastery over her traumatic experiences.

Figure 17.2 Anthill

Illustrated in the color insert

A ten-year-old boy undergoing scans and tests created a complex painting of an anthill (Figure 17.2). He had intuitively created a metaphor referencing the search for cancer cells inside his body, explaining to the art therapist that

> [e]verything happens underground. You can hardly see it on the top… [The ants] are very strong and can eat much more than anyone, even though they are so small. That's why they save so much food, even more than they can eat in one meal. There is garbage and dog bones and worms underground, too. There are so many things under there that people don't know about!

Normalization and Community

In the vast majority of hospital and medical treatment centers, individuals receiving medical care are typically called "patients." Staff members sometimes also refer to these people using their particular medical diagnosis or status ("the new leukemia" or "the breast cancer recurrence"). This terminology clearly communicates medical information, but it can unconsciously distance health care providers from patients. When patients overhear this vernacular, it can challenge their sense of self: no one wants to be reduced to nothing more than a diagnosis. Art therapy in the treatment setting can be a welcome retreat to normalcy; making a unique piece of art invites patients to reclaim their individuality and personality through a "normal" activity that exists beyond the hospital walls. Treatment providers may also regard the patient's artwork as a conversation piece, allowing for connection and conversation while treatment is administered.

While receiving chemotherapy or lengthy infusions, patients are often willing and eager to participate. Rather than sitting and watching television for hours, patients and their loved ones can enjoy making art. It also provides an opportunity for patients and families to come together as a source of support for one another, demonstrating that they are not alone in their journey (Nesbitt and Tabatt-Haussmann 2008). The tedious ritual of coming to the hospital, getting medications, and having one's vital signs taken regularly can now include art making. For some patients and families, just knowing that art and the art therapists will be there for them can be an incredible relief. One mother would drive over an hour out of her way to bring her young daughter to a hospital with art therapy (rather than making an appointment at a closer facility) because art made each of her daughter's hospital visits easier and ultimately enjoyable. The often unrecognized rituals in seeing the art therapists and beginning a piece of artwork can provide a unique kind of comfort for patients and their family members. Several families from Central America were receiving care in an oncology clinic during the same period of time. An older, Spanish-speaking woman was volunteering in the art therapy program and happened to be very skilled in clay sculpture. The art therapist worked with the patients and siblings at one table in English, while the mothers worked in Spanish with the volunteer. They talked about life in their native villages while making small clay representations of home. Such depictions of home prompted conversations of cultural customs. Adults from many cultures may find their hands fashioning clay into little tortillas, pies, noodles, and stews to entertain nearby children, keep themselves distracted, and evoke comforting memories of home.

Finding a sense of community within the medical culture serves as a great source of support for patients and families (Nesbitt and Tabatt-Haussmann 2008). Because those undergoing cancer treatment may have suppressed immune systems, they are often physically isolated to prevent infections that can be harmful or even fatal. Art therapy provides a safe space where patients and families can gather to create a new community. Art therapists can facilitate these meetings and also help protect the patients by carefully attending to sanitation protocols and providing new art materials when necessary (Nainis 2008).

Therapeutic Boundaries

Boundaries essential to conducting meaningful therapy can differ somewhat in medical treatment settings, especially with children. Over time, the world of oncology becomes a second home for patients and their loved ones. Throughout treatment, patients and their families spend days and weeks in the hospital, during outpatient clinic visits and overnight as inpatients. Because there is little privacy and care is provided around the clock, the hospital itself can promote an atmosphere of over-familiarity between patients and staff. When working with terminally ill patients and families, Furman (2011) believes that art therapists "must be willing to carefully consider unconventional treatment approaches and to explore the ethical gray areas of therapist transparency and boundaries" (p.180). Art therapists need to attend to the potential blurring of these boundaries and constantly consider the appropriate therapeutic interventions and goals.

Art therapists themselves are also susceptible to the overall intensity of the cancer experience. Unfortunately, in the face of ongoing loss, many oncology staff members fail to give proper attention to processing personal grief and intentionally practiced self-care (Nainis 2005). Regular support and supervision are also necessary to ensure art therapists can continue to provide the most appropriate and effective services to patients and families.

Culture and Dying

Everyone wants to make the best medical decisions for the patient, and this can be difficult when the deeply seated beliefs of the family and the medical team do not align. One may make a case for aggressive curative treatment while the other supports palliative care in favor of a higher quality of life. These decisions can be based upon religious convictions or on the unique culture of the individual. Because such choices lack obvious solutions, everyone involved may experience regret or remorse as they struggle to identify the lesser of the two evils (Czamanski-Cohen 2012).

The family of a six-year-old in a hospice did not want him to know he was dying. A professional family from a mainstream religion, they surprised the medical team with their insistence that the boy not be told that his cancer could not be cured. This was in conflict with the medical team's commitment to telling patients the truth in an age-appropriate and compassionate way. An art therapist visited this boy in his home and was nervous about what to say, feeling strongly about respecting his parents' wishes but also not wanting to lie. The boy drew, and the art therapist sat quietly with him, as she had so often done at the hospital. When he finished his picture, he handed it to her and said, "Here, this is for you—it's a moving van" (Figure 17.3). The art therapist felt that the boy's picture illustrated the idea that the patient himself was going away. His metaphor for saying goodbye seemed to demonstrate that he understood what was happening, giving him a way to say goodbye through his art without having to speak directly about it (Robb and Councill 2011).

Figure 17.3 Moving van

Care at the end of life occurs in a very different framework than medical care with a curative intent. Much of modern medicine might characterize death as a failure of treatment. Medical caregivers burdened by a sense of failure sometimes withdraw from the family, expecting anger and blame for their loved one's death. Research on parental decision making for children with incurable cancer concluded that parents do not blame clinical staff when curative treatment options have been exhausted (Maurer et al. 2010). Rather, families look to clinicians for support and continued care. Many parents wish to express gratitude for the care they received and long to know that their child's life was meaningful to his or her caregivers. Hinds et al. (2009) and Maurer et al. (2010) encourage health care providers to stay in close communication with parents after curative treatment is no longer plausible.

Many religious and spiritual traditions provide perspectives on death, such as viewing loss as illusory rather than real or as a necessary step toward a more glorious future (ibid.). Depending on their cultural and religious backgrounds, families may wish to observe certain end-of-life rituals, spend time with the body after death, or request the presence of clergy or laypeople from their faith. The art therapist may have the opportunity to identify families' wishes and encourage them to talk with the appropriate people in advance.

Legacy Making

Both adults and children may use their time in art therapy to create gifts for family members. Adults sometimes only give themselves permission to paint when the artwork will be a gift for a child or grandchild. For children, creating gifts for the adults in their lives is a universal embodiment of affection. After a loss, the artwork serves as a precious physical memento and a legacy of the one who has died (Furman 2011).

Families facing imminent loss may work alongside their loved one to create these legacy pieces, consciously or unconsciously. Art therapists can assist in suggesting appropriate interventions, considering the physical energy and involvement of the patient. Some family members enjoy making art focused on their loved one and the fond memories they enjoyed together. Especially in the case of a dying child, caregivers seem to appreciate handprints or footprints as tactile memorials of their son or daughter. Families may also ask the art therapist to save their loved one's art or for art pieces to be brought to the memorial service.

Patients and family members frequently give artwork to staff members or the treatment center itself (Nainis 2008). Making their literal mark on the place where they have spent so much time, somewhere that has made a significant impact on their life, can be very important, even essential, to some (Furman 2011). One young adult's dying wish was to have an auction to sell the prolific artwork she had made during her treatment for leukemia; she wanted the artwork to be an inspiration to patients and staff and asked that the proceeds be used to provide a better experience for patients on the unit.

After a death, family members sometimes return to visit the treatment center, where seeing the patient's artwork still displayed can be very meaningful. This kind of memorial recognizes the impact that the patient made on staff members and demonstrates that he or she will continue to be remembered through the legacy of their artwork.

Conclusion

Though medical art therapists are part of the medical team, our work is about being with people in their experience rather than treating their medical issues. Medical art therapy augments the quality of care by attending to the whole person, as he or she exists within and outside their personal culture and the medical culture. Other chronic, life-threatening medical conditions involve similar emotional struggles. Many of the themes addressed here can be generalized to working with these people and their families.

As art therapists, we are already often familiar with cultural diversity through our knowledge of art. We draw on the influences of many cultures in our work, including worry dolls, Adinkra symbols, masks, batik, origami, and mandalas. However, we must recognize that this knowledge alone does not absolve us from continuing to seek additional opportunities and experiences to expand our cultural understanding of those with whom we work. While we cannot know every culture we encounter, practicing art therapy in a culturally sensitive way opens doors of expression to patients and families isolated from home, or simply from their normal life, in their quest for medical care and the journey toward healing.

References

Councill, T. (2012) "Medical Art Therapy with Children." In C. A. Malchiodi (ed.) *Handbook of Art Therapy, Second Edition.* New York: The Guilford Press.

Czamanski-Cohen, J. (2012) "The use of art in the medical decision-making process of oncology patients." *Art Therapy: Journal of the American Art Therapy Association 29,* 2, 60–67.

Furman, L. R. (2011) "Last breath: Art therapy with a lung cancer patient facing imminent death." *Art Therapy: Journal of the American Art Therapy Association 28,* 4, 177–180.

Hinds, P. S., Oakes, L. L., Hicks, J., Powell, B. et al. (2009) "'Trying to be a good parent'" as defined by interviews with parents who made phase I, terminal care, and resuscitation decisions for their children." *Journal of Clinical Oncology 27,* 35, 5979–5985.

LeMaistre, J. (1999) "Coping with chronic illness." *After the Diagnosis.* Dillon, CO: Alpine Guild.

Maurer, S. H., Hinds, P. S., Spunt, S. L., Furman, W. L., Kane, J. R., and Baker, J. N. (2010) "Decision making by parents of children with incurable cancer who opt for enrollment on a Phase I Trial compared with choosing a do not resuscitate/terminal care option." *Journal of Clinical Oncology 28,* 20, 3292–3298.

Nainis, N. A. (2005) "Art therapy with an oncology care team." *Art Therapy: Journal of the American Art Therapy Association 22,* 3, 150–154.

Nainis, N. A. (2008) "Approaches to art therapy for cancer inpatients: Research and practice considerations." *Art Therapy: Journal of the American Art Therapy Association 25,* 3, 115–121.

Nesbitt, L. L. and Tabatt-Haussmann, K. (2008) "The role of the creative arts therapies in the treatment of pediatric hematology and oncology patients." *Primary Psychiatry 15*, 7, 56–58, 61–62.

Robb, M. and Councill, T. (2011) "Cultural expectations in art therapy at the end of life." Proceedings of the annual conference of the American Art Therapy Association, Washington, DC.

Zammit, C. (2001) "The art of healing. A journey through cancer: Implications for art therapy." *Art Therapy: Journal of the American Art Therapy Association 18*, 1, 27–36.

Resources

Further Reading

Favara-Scacco, C., Smirne, G., Schiliró, G., and Di Cataldo, A. (2001) "Art therapy as support for children with leukemia during painful procedures." *Medical and Pediatric Oncology 36*, 474–480.

Gabriel, B., Bromberg, E., Vandenbovenkamp, J., Walka, P., Kornblith, A. B., and Luzzatto, P. (2001) "Art therapy with adult bone marrow transplant patients in isolation." *Psycho-Oncology 10*, 114–123.

Geue, K., Goetze, H., Buttstaedt, M., Kleinert, E., Richter, D., and Singer, S. (2010) "An overview of art therapy interventions for cancer patients and the results of research." *Complementary Therapies in Medicine 18*, 160–170.

Malchiodi, C. A. (2003) "Using Art Therapy with Medical Support Groups." In C. A. Malchiodi (ed.) *Handbook of Art Therapy, Second Edition.* New York: The Guilford Press.

Wood, M. J. M., Molassiotis, A., and Payne, S. (2011) "What research evidence is there for the use of art therapy in the management of symptoms in adults with cancer? A systematic review." *Psycho-Oncology 20*, 135–145.

Chapter 18

Art Therapy in Saudi Arabia

Yasmine J. Awais

This chapter describes the role of art therapy within medical rehabilitation in Saudi Arabia. The therapist's identity, particularly if the therapist is not Saudi, is of critical importance when considering the unique intersections between the cultures of medical rehabilitation and Saudi Arabia itself. Informed by first-person research and reflective practice, this chapter describes the author's personal account of working in an inpatient medical rehabilitation hospital within Saudi Arabia through investigating the intersection of various identities. This is conducted through the author's lens, one of a first-generation multicultural Asian American. Finally, a case study with drawings created by a patient being treated for spinal cord injury illustrates these themes.

Medical Rehabilitation and Art Therapy

Medical art therapy is employed for multiple reasons: "to enhance rehabilitation and recovery, to help patients cope with diagnosis, surgery, disability, medical treatments, and symptoms" (Malchiodi 1999, p.14). In 1986, Joraski made a compelling argument for the role of creative arts in cognitive rehabilitation, specifically for working with patients suffering from traumatic brain injury (TBI). She highlighted that the goal of therapy is to improve functioning in all areas of daily living, and that engaging in the arts allows for patients to connect various cognitive skills such as motor, concentration, focusing, problem solving, decision making, social interactions, and visual/spatial abilities. Art therapy has also been known to be used in stroke (cerebrovascular accident [CVA]) rehabilitation. In addition to maximizing mobility and independence, therapeutic goals specifically for CVA survivors are to assess strengths and weaknesses; increase the patient's awareness of his or her condition; teach compensatory techniques; improve cognitive and physical functioning; allow a safe space for the patient to adjust emotionally to his or her new level of functioning; provide a break from the daily routines of rehabilitation treatment; increase socialization; and introduce a nonverbal means of communication and self-expression (Wald 1999). Kim et al. (2008) name the additional goals of improving spatial perception capacity and color and shape recognition.

Art Therapy in Saudi Arabia

Alyami (2000) introduced art therapy to Saudi Arabia: first in 1995 through educational courses and then to a major medical rehabilitation center in 2005. In addition to the inherent difficulties of bringing a discipline that historically works with patients having psychiatric disorders to a medical setting, an additional challenge was that this was the first documented art therapy program brought to Saudi Arabia and the first established program in any of the Arab countries (Alyami 2000). While there are currently individual art therapists practicing throughout the Arab region (cf. Awais 2011; Ozcan 2011), it does not appear that there are art therapists practicing in Saudi Arabia outside of the program described in Alyami's paper. At the time of writing, art therapy currently has no certified training programs and is not accredited by the national body in Saudi Arabia (Saudi Commission for Health Specialties 2012). This makes increasing and promoting the practice of art therapy particularly challenging at the local level.

There are many roles that art therapy holds within the rehabilitation hospital: assessment, therapeutic intervention, adjunctive therapy, and nonverbal expression (Malchiodi 1999). Art therapy interventions are informed by the interdisciplinary treatment plan developed by doctors, physiotherapists (PTs), occupational therapists (OTs), nurses, and other professionals. The treatment plan considers the primary medical diagnosis in conjunction with the patient's goals that fit in with their role in life and society. For example, if a middle-school student is diagnosed with spinal cord injury (SCI) and his goal is to return to school, all disciplines would work toward that common goal. The PT may work toward strength and endurance training through various exercises in the gym, the OT may focus on handwriting or wheelchair skills, and art therapy would address emotional adjustment issues of reintegrating back to school through creating art in a group setting in order to promote socialization. Goals for adult males would often include ambulation to their local mosque and exercises that promote the ability to pray (Awais 2011). Malchiodi (1999) notes that "art expression is used to help people 'open up' by making visible their thoughts, feelings, and perceptions" (p.14). As a result, art therapists often hold the responsibility of assessing and encountering psychological disturbances as they are uncovered in the art-making process. Other rehabilitative therapies do not inherently lend themselves to patients discussing such feeling states, as patients often see them only as physical exercises. Dwairy (2006) emphasizes the effectiveness of working indirectly, through metaphor, with Arabs/Muslims. Working with metaphors is a natural fit to the practice of art therapy.

Themes in Imagery

Religious themes are common, as Islam is woven into daily life (e.g., the shutting down of all businesses for prayer and the separation of the sexes). Examples seen in the art therapy studio include patients writing Koranic verses when relearning how to hold a marker or sculpting depictions of the *Ka'ba* (the sacred pilgrimage site in Mecca) out of clay. As fish are often drawn by children who live on islands in Japan and skyscrapers are drawn by city dwellers, images of the desert, camels, sunrises/sunsets, and date palms are regularly depicted in art therapy sessions in Saudi Arabia. Similar to others facing some loss in functioning, themes of "loss, helplessness, hope, God, the future, uncertainty, and strength" also abound in these patients (Awais 2011, p.600).

The Role of Identity
Cultural and Ethnic Identity

Arabic and Muslim cultures, like other non-European cultures, are collectivistic in nature, in contrast to individualist cultures like those of the United States and the United Kingdom. Sue and Sue (2008) identify key values for collectivistic cultures: family being valued over the individual; the adult being valued over the child; and the importance of being perceived as polite, calm, supportive, and respectful. Islam cannot be teased out from the cultural and ethnic identity of the individual because Islam is the national religion in a collectivistic culture. Therefore, religion is a part of the society at large, which impacts the family and subsequently the individual's thoughts, feelings, and behaviors. Utilizing therapy, particularly psychodynamic-based therapy, as a tool for benefiting the individual is not common practice; instead, elders or spiritual leaders rather than therapists often give guidance.

Ability and Other Identity Markers

Some identity markers are static (e.g., race), while others can change. Health status and ability are acquired at birth yet can change due to aging or an accident. For many, ability is a part of identity that is not acknowledged until it is lost or compromised. In medical rehabilitation, age and education are tied to health status. Children and adults are able to heal quicker than the elderly, and those who are more educated and literate can understand and communicate with doctors and other providers more easily than those who are less educated. Patients come to rehabilitation with their own opinions of what it means to be disabled. Oftentimes, those with less ability are seen as weaker than others. These thoughts come into the therapeutic space and can manifest themselves through a patient's self-deprecating remarks about her or his ability to create artwork or willingness to participate in art therapy.

Identity of the Therapist

Working in a culture different from one's own has its rewards and challenges on a personal and professional level. Miller and Garran (2008) stress the importance of understanding how people in the helping professions need to understand their own place of power, which is related to the therapist's identity. The simple difference in the roles of the therapist and patient denotes power. Therapists have the power to treat or heal, while the patient is in the position of needing help; the inpatient is relegated to the hospital until discharged but the therapist can go home at the end of the day. Talwar (2010) highlights how various identity markers within the art therapist him- or herself relate to one another through the idea of "intersectionality." While it is outside of the scope of this chapter to fully investigate all identities (e.g., socioeconomic status and sexual identity), identities intersect, inform one another, and are to be considered when working in multicultural environments. Specifically, some parts of our identities may be considered "agents," which are aspects of ourselves that are powerful and privileged, and others considered "targets," defined as identity markers that are marginalized and oppressed (Miller and Garran 2008). In the author's case, ethnicity (American) and sex (female) were at times in conflict with being among people to whom I have cultural ties (collectivistic and Muslim). Every interaction within and outside of the hospital was informed by these identities.

Additional agent–target statuses may differ in Saudi Arabia from those in one's home country: religion (Muslim/not Muslim); culture (Arab/non-Arab); citizenship (Saudi/non-Saudi/refugee); race (White/people of color); and gender (male/female). What may be of agent status in one's home country may not necessarily be of agent status in another country and privileged status identities may be assumed. For example, as Christians are of agent status in the United States, it is commonly perceived that all Westerners are Christian. In the author's case, having an Arabic name and appearance may have challenged stereotypes, potentially causing internal conflict for the patient if not acknowledged in the therapeutic space.

Art therapists who are attuned to their own cultural identity and biases are more effective in working cross-culturally, and a multicultural counseling/therapy (MCT) framework is useful particularly when working with clients who are of a different culture (Sue and Sue 2008). Sue and Torino (2005) describe MCT as more than cultural competence:

> MCT broadens the perspective of the helping relationship. Rather than a singular focus on the individual, it takes a self-in-relation orientation. The individualistic approach is balanced with the collectivistic reality that we are

embedded in our families, significant others, communities, and culture. The client is perceived not solely as an individual, but as an individual who is a product of his or her social cultural context. As a result, systemic influences are seen as equally important as individual ones. (p.6)

The Kingdom of Saudi Arabia
The Expatriate Workforce

The Saudi labor market consists of 65.5 percent foreign workers (Bhuain, Al-Shammari, and Jefri 2001), while of the entire 22.7 million Saudi population only 27.1 percent are documented expatriates (Kingdom of Saudi Arabia Ministry of Foreign Affairs 2005). However, it is argued that the percentage of foreign workers is much higher. The presence of a large expatriate workforce influences the relationship between nationals and foreigners in that it is common for Saudis to have daily interactions with non-Saudis when it comes to business transactions. This is not to say that the foreign workforce lacks complexity; in Saudi Arabia, pay is based on title/position, level of education, and nationality, with the workforce from Western countries (e.g., United States, Canada, United Kingdom, and Australia) being paid more than that from non-Western countries (e.g., Philippines, Pakistan, India, and Malaysia), and there is a growing movement for Saudization (decreasing the reliance on expatriates and increasing job opportunities for Saudis). While it may not be surprising that the art therapist is of a different background than the patient, various factors impact the relationship in the hospital at large and in the art therapy studio in particular. For example, an American art therapist may be preferred over an Egyptian art therapist, even if both have the same educational training and the Egyptian art therapist shares the common language of Arabic with the patient, because of assumptions made about the superior abilities of Western expatriate workers.

Islam and Daily Life

Art therapists in Western countries with credentiated art therapy programs may not have been trained in utilizing religion in the therapeutic space and may not be aware of how important religion is in daily life in countries with a state religion, like Saudi Arabia (cf. American Art Therapy Association 2012; Australian and New Zealand Arts Therapy Association 2012; British Association of Art Therapists 2012; Canadian Art Therapy Association 2012). As with Judaism and Christianity, Islam is a monotheistic religion that believes in one God, the same God of Abraham and Moses (Esposito 1988). While the art therapist may not be Muslim, if he or she is practicing in Saudi Arabia, where Islam is the recognized religion and influences all aspects of life, he or she should become familiar with the five pillars of Islamic practice. Additionally, the ban on idol worship and some of the particulars of family law (Esposito 1988) can also impact art therapy sessions. The ban on idol worship informs the belief that there should be no depiction of any images in God's likeness, meaning that some patients may not feel comfortable drawing human figures, animals, or even vegetation. Family law outlines the guidelines and roles for women, including mandates for women to be dressed modestly.

For the art therapist, the tenets of Islam impact when clients can be seen, gender interactions, and the artwork. Prayer is required to occur five times a day, regardless of whether the person is hospitalized. While it is not expected that the patient go to a mosque, there are specific locations available within the hospital to pray. However, patients may not be able to pray in the designated areas and may instead worship in their rooms. Accommodations can be made, including ablutions without water for those patients who have difficulties with bathing independently and prayer from the seated position when one is wheelchair bound. Depending on when sessions are scheduled, the art therapist should be prepared for patients who are late to session or who ask to leave early due to prayer. A Western approach may view these behaviors as defensive rather than showing commitment to God. Patient goals may also include ambulation to their local mosque and being able to physically perform the movements required for daily prayers. These goals inform treatment when addressing the physical constraints (e.g., strength to mobilize to the mosque) and emotional concerns (e.g., how the patient will feel attending mosque when they present as physically different from others).

Gender Norms

In a gender-segregated society, the awareness of one's own gender becomes heightened. What is considered normative behavior between people of the opposite sex in a professional setting in one's home country (i.e., having a face-to-face discussion with a provider of the opposite sex) may not be considered such in Saudi Arabia. As in other orthodox communities, women are not to be seen by men unless they are related or in exceptional cases such as undergoing medical treatment (al-Baydawi as cited in Esposito 1988). For example, banks have separate branches for women; restaurants have "family sections" to separate women, women with children, and women with male family members from "single men" (this status refers not to whether the man is single or married, but to whether he is in the company of a female family member). While medical treatment is an exception where a woman can be seen by a male, the patient (particularly if female) may prefer to be seen only by a practitioner of the same sex. Exceptions occurred at the hospital where I was employed, and when a female art therapist treated a male patient, the door was kept open and groups would be co-facilitated. If a male art therapist treated a female patient, she was not expected to remove her *niqab* (veil), leaving the art therapist to interact only verbally and through the artwork and not allowing for facial expressions to be read. Western therapeutic practices value the unspoken (e.g., body language) in addition to verbalizations, making treatment of the veiled patient difficult. While hospital units are designed with separate male and female spaces, windows for female treatment areas are often covered in the event that a male staff walk by and inadvertently see a female. While maintaining professional boundaries is part of the ethical guidelines for all art therapists (Moon 2006), these boundaries may be more pronounced when working in a rehabilitation hospital in Saudi Arabia. Casual interactions between the sexes do not normally occur in hospitals, as in Arab and many orthodox cultures there is a separation between the sexes. Therefore, the intention of the art therapist to create a relaxing atmosphere by being friendly and talkative may actually result in creating an uncomfortable space because of gender differences.

Case Study

Khalid was a typical patient with SCI; he was not wearing a seatbelt while involved in a car accident. He presented as well groomed, of average height and weight, and carried prayer beads. Khalid was referred to art therapy by the treatment team as he apparently lacked motivation: sleeping during the day and missing all PT and OT sessions. Yet in the evening he was quite active, visiting others and praying/preaching to the point of disturbing other patients. His prognosis was that he would not be able to walk again and would rely on a wheelchair for the rest of his life.

During the first few sessions of rapport building, Khalid openly discussed religion and his views on women. His English skills were adequate enough that, after the initial intake session, translators were not necessary. He freely expressed his disdain for the hospital staff, especially the fact that men and women freely interacted with each other and appeared to be enjoying themselves, noting that he could see people smiling and hear people laughing. I never shared my thoughts on this, but did verbally reflect his experience back. The fact that I was a female therapist sitting in the room with Khalid did not cause him distress (or was perhaps causing him so much distress that he could not directly address it and could only discuss the behaviors between staff members). This may have been due to my nationality, which all patients were able to quickly identify by my hospital ID and by my accent.

As with other patients admitted to the rehabilitation hospital, Khalid saw artwork created by patients hung prominently in the hallways of the hospital. He was inspired by a current exhibition and was eager to draw his own story despite having no previous art background. One of Khalid's first drawings depicts a man in a wheelchair reaching for dates (Figure 18.1). Above him are the words *no life with despair*. It is clear that the man would not be able to reach the dates without assistance. In session, Khalid expressed concerns about depicting the human figure, feeling that it was against Islam; yet he drew the person. To resolve this conflict, he drew a line between the head and the body of the seated person to denote that he was not trying to create an idol or imply that his skill was better than God's (Awais 2011). The presence of a wheelchair can be seen as an acknowledgment of acceptance of his new physical condition (Wald 1999). The date palm is a reflection of the environment, a symbol of strength as the tree is bearing fruit, and possibly as another symbol of acceptance as the date palm is part of the hospital's logo. My interventions were not directive in nature, but focused on providing a space for Khalid to reflect on his own process. In this safe space, Khalid was able to discuss his own interpretations of the drawing, utilizing the metaphor of the image drawn to parallel his own experiences.

Figure 18.1 No life with despair

Khalid was able to visually express his discomfort with his new level of functioning as well as his frustration with how inaccessible places are in Saudi Arabia, including mosques. Figure 18.2 depicts a man in a wheelchair in front of a mosque. He cannot enter, as there are steps and no ramp. The *imam* tells him to leave, while the man points out that it would not cost very much for a ramp to be installed. Here, the intersection of health status, religion, and advocacy is clearly illustrated.

The final drawing created in session incorporates colors (e.g., a blue sky and various shades of brown for the mountains and road), which were not included previously (see Figure 18.3). No person is present, and a four-by-four vehicle with yellow windows (possibly reflecting the sun) is the main focus. The vehicle is driving away from the viewer into an unknown territory surrounded by mountains. These vehicles are popular in Saudi Arabia, where the terrain can be unforgiving and disparate, alternating from soft sand to hard rock. Many Saudis go four-wheeling in the desert for recreation as well. Khalid did not verbally discuss this picture, but a hopeful future can be imagined if we view the four-by-four as a strong vehicle that requires fuel to run. The vehicle replaces the figure that was prominent in previous drawings, and Khalid's fuel may be his newfound ability to see himself differently than before.

Figure 18.2 Accessibility

Figure 18.3 The future

Illustrated in the color insert

Summary

Art therapy can be a powerful intervention in medical rehabilitation, especially in Saudi Arabia where metaphor can be employed for purposes of supporting collectivistic values rather than European-centered individualistic ones. Themes surrounding religion, the environment, ability, accessibility, strength, and the future have been illustrated. Culturally sensitive art therapy techniques are possible when the therapist is aware of how identity intersects within the therapist and with the culture as a whole.

References

Alyami, A. (2000) "The integration of art therapy into physical rehabilitation in a Saudi hospital." *The Arts in Psychotherapy 36*, 5, 282–288.

American Art Therapy Association (2012) *Educational Institutions.* Available at www.americanarttherapyassociation.org/aata-educational-programs.html, accessed on June 17, 2013.

Australian and New Zealand Arts Therapy Association (2012) *Professional Training.* Available at www.anzata.org/professional-training, accessed on June 17, 2013.

Awais, Y. (2011) "Revolution calling: Rehabilitative art therapy in Saudi Arabia." *International Journal of Therapy and Rehabilitation, 18*, 11, 600–601.

Bhuain, S. N., Al-Shammari, E. S., and Jefri, O. A. (2001) "Work-related attitudes and job characteristics of expatriates in Saudi Arabia." *Thunderbird International Business Review 43*, 1, 21–31.

British Association of Art Therapists (2012) *Qualifying Training Courses for Art Therapists in the UK.* Available at www.baat.org/courses.html, accessed on June 17, 2013.

Canadian Art Therapy Association (2012) *Art Therapy Training Programs (Accredited by CATA).* Available at http://catainfo.ca/cata/study-at, accessed on June 17, 2013.

Dwairy, M. (2006) *Counseling and Psychotherapy with Arabs and Muslims: A Culturally Sensitive Approach.* New York: Teachers College Press.

Esposito, J. L. (1988) *Islam: The Straight Path.* New York: Oxford University Press.

Joraski, M. (1986) "The role of creative arts in cognitive rehabilitation." *Cognitive Rehabilitation 4*, 2, 18–23.

Kim, S., Kim, M., Lee, J., and Chun, S. (2008) "Art therapy outcomes in the rehabilitation treatment of a stroke patient: A case report." *Art Therapy: Journal of the American Art Therapy Association 25*, 3, 129–133.

Kingdom of Saudi Arabia Ministry of Foreign Affairs (2005) *Growth and Development.* Available at www.mofa.gov.sa/sites/mofaen/aboutKingDom/Pages/DevelopmentSide36146.aspx, accessed on June 17, 2013.

Malchiodi, C. (1999) "Art Therapy and Medicine: Powerful Partners in Healing." In C. Malchiodi (ed.) *Medical Art Therapy with Adults.* London: Jessica Kingsley Publishers.

Miller, J. and Garran, A. M. (2008) *Racism in the United States: Implications for the Helping Professions.* Belmont, CA: Thomson Brooks/Cole.

Moon, B. L. (2006) *Ethical Issues in Art Therapy, Second Edition.* Springfield, IL: Charles C. Thomas.

Ozcan, A. (2011) *The Mouse and the Butter: Process of Redefining Self as an Art Therapist.* Paper presented at the American Art Therapy Association's 42nd Annual Conference, Washington, DC, July.

Saudi Commission for Health Specialties (2012) *Content of Classification Examination.* Available at http://english.scfhs.org.sa/index.php?option=com_content&view=section&layout=blog&id =57&Itemid=5935, accessed on June 17, 2013.

Sue, D. W. and Sue, D. (2008) *Counseling the Culturally Diverse: Theory and Practice, Fifth Edition.* Hoboken, NJ: John Wiley and Sons.

Sue, D. W. and Torino, G. A. (2005) "Racial-Cultural Competence: Awareness, Knowledge, and Skills." In R. T. Carter (ed.) *Handbook of Racial-Cultural Psychology and Counseling: Training and Practice, Volume 2.* Hoboken, NJ: John Wiley and Sons.

Talwar, S. (2010) "An intersectional framework for race, class, gender, and sexuality in art therapy." *Art Therapy: Journal of the American Art Therapy Association 27,* 1, 11–17.

Wald, J. (1999) "The Role of Art Therapy in Post-Stroke Rehabilitation." In C. Malchiodi (ed.) *Medical Art Therapy with Adults.* London: Jessica Kingsley Publishers.

Resources
Further Reading

Hourani, A. H. (2005) *A History of the Arab Peoples.* London: Faber and Faber.

Rogan, E. (2009) *The Arabs: A History.* New York: Basic Books.

Said, E. W. (2003) *Freud and the Non-European.* London: Verso.

Chapter 19

Art-Based Therapies for Substance Users and their Families

Recognition, Deliberation, and Recovery

Shanthi Ranganathan and Reshma Malick

Impact of Addiction on Family

Addiction is called a family disease because it has an impact on each and every member of the family. Healthy relationships between husband and wife, parent and child, and siblings are jeopardized because trust, love, respect, and cooperation are eroded. There is emotional, financial, and social damage as a consequence of the addiction. The family members face a series of escalating crises which intensify over a period of time. Reality is denied by blaming and rationalizing. Despite good intentions, the family may respond to the problem inappropriately and develop dysfunctional behavior, experiencing a great deal of hurt, shame, pain, hopelessness, and lack of meaning in existence. Alcohol dependency of one individual in the family can affect other family members and change the way they interact and carry out their tasks. Over a period of time, even day-to-day functioning can be affected (Colombo Plan 2003). Understanding this mindset and creating an environment of trust and hope while setting clear boundaries and expectations makes the treatment of persons with addiction a challenge within any culture.

The T. T. Ranganathan Clinical Research Foundation (TTK) in Chennai, India, is a nongovernmental and nonprofit organization serving the field of addiction. The TTK Hospital provides one-month inpatient treatment for alcoholics and drug users with the goal of helping clients achieve total abstinence and improve their quality of life. A 14-day program is offered to the family to address their emotional needs and to empower them. The aftercare center provides a two-month extended treatment to drug-dependent persons. There is a five-day relapse management program for patients and a parallel program for family members. The center provides services for persons of all socioeconomic backgrounds. It is the policy of the organization to help all those who need treatment. No client is denied care based on financial ability. Rural camps are also conducted to provide services for people who cannot seek treatment at the center. The rehabilitation program incorporates the 12-step Alcoholics Anonymous program, which has been adapted to meet the various cultural needs of urban and rural India.

The two-month residential program aims at resolving blocks in recovery and helps in vocational rehabilitation. Treatment provided includes medical help, psychological therapy, and long-term follow-up. Computer education and special programs for families are offered. Issues related to repeated relapses are also dealt with. Cognitive behavior therapy (CBT) that emphasizes change in thoughts, feelings, and actions is used in facilitating the process of change in the client's perception of self and others. Arts-based therapy (ABT), incorporating principles of CBT, is used to address treatment goals. By using anchoring stories, colors, songs, images, and play/games, the individual is helped to sustain sobriety, which is the key therapeutic objective.

The inpatient section has an average of 950 admissions a year. Out of these, the center has only three to four female admissions. Due to cultural norms and social stigma, women are not expected to drink, and if they develop an addiction, they are more often looked down upon even by their own family. Hence, the low numbers of those seeking help are not a true reflection of how many women are dealing with alcoholism. The male admissions are usually brought in by a family member, the spouse, or the parent, when they find that all other options have failed. Often the patient is in poor physical and mental health. Most of the male population is around the age of 35 to 40 years and began drinking at the age of 16 or 18 years after graduating from high school. Despite the different socioeconomic levels of patients who are admitted for treatment, the issues presented, as well as the recovery process, are similar across various groups.

ABT is used as an adjunct group therapy with inpatients and family members, as well as in the relapse prevention program (WCCLF 2010). These sessions provide a safe and accepting environment for the individual and the family to discuss and express concerns regarding substance abuse. Use of group games in the sessions helps build rapport, which in turn helps lower the defenses and promotes more honest sharing. The process of art making provides an avenue for self-expression. Creating and working in clay gives the alcoholic family member time to contemplate and come out with his/her own recovery tools. Drawings and paintings depict their dreams in colors and images, helping them envision recovery. They provide a visual image of the patient's goals, rather than these goals remaining as words. Patients are able to take these pictures with them when they leave the program, which helps them focus on their recovery process.

ABT facilitates the expression of feelings experienced by the relapsed patients. Use of the drumming circle helps to establish rapport with others in the group and in turn creates energy that helps in the psychological detoxification. Drumming circles are an excellent complement to traditional therapy, particularly for repeated relapses and when other counseling methods have failed. The repetition of drumming with other group members brings down inhibitions and helps patients verbalize their feelings. By listening to and discussing songs that are both pleasant and discordant, joyful and melancholic, patients learn to differentiate between those feelings in themselves and to interpret the relevance of those emotions in their own lives. During this process individuals feel safer and less judged when they can project their feelings onto the song rather than discuss their own intensely personal experiences. The use of stories helps in the narration of their own relapse narrative, and in the process they are able to identify their relapse triggers.

A 21-day outcome study was conducted in 2010 to examine the effectiveness of ABT with substance abusers in the Indian context. Prior to therapy, it was found that all the participants were experiencing anger, shame, fear, and anxiety. The symptoms of these negative emotions were tiredness, lack of appetite, and insomnia. There was a lack of motivation to live. On completion of the ABT sessions, there was a remarkable decrease in the stress level and dramatic enhancement in their sense of meaning in their life.

A Family ABT Group Session

As part of family therapy, it is required that at least one family member of each hospitalized client attend five group ABT sessions. Each session lasts for one hour and meets once a week. Usually six to ten family members are present. Each session is designed to address a coping skill.

Below is an example of a session whose objective is to understand one's powerlessness over others and the alcoholic's inability to change, emphasizing the "Let Go" principle. This is metaphorically compared with the sea wave. Just like the sea wave cannot be stopped by any one person, any response from the family members cannot stop the client's addiction. Use of stories or narratives has long been a part of Indian culture. Stories are created, enacted in the form of drama, or mimed in sequence. A story related to the metaphor is shared by the therapist and all the participants reflect on the story.

The session begins with all participants engaging in a movement, for example moving their body like a sea wave. This helps them to internalize the metaphor that is going to be presented to them in this session. After this warm-up the following story is narrated to the group members by the therapist:

Story: Hanging on to the Nuts

Monkey hunters use a box with an opening at the top, big enough for the monkey to slide its hands in. Inside the box are nuts. The monkey grabs the nuts, and now its hands become a fist. The monkey tries to get its hand out. But the opening which was big enough for the hand to slide in is too small for the fist to come out. Now the monkey has a choice: to either let go of the nuts and be free or to hang on to the nuts and get caught.

What does the monkey do every time? It hangs on to the nuts and gets caught. (Jayaraman and Kanakam 2010, p.72)

The alcoholic's family (spouse, parents, or siblings) are preoccupied with the alcoholic and his behavior and in turn fail to perform their duties. They rationalize by saying, "We are unfortunate…unlucky. We are like this because… We cannot do this because…" It is pointed out that the nuts are whatever comes after "because," that the family is hanging on to, and pushes them back to their dysfunctional coping pattern of behavior.

The participants are then given a directive to create in clay anything to which they have been clinging in their lives, over which they have no control (like the sea wave). For example, a participant made a clay image of a mouth representing the verbal abuse she experienced while her husband was under the influence of alcohol. Hearing his abuse, the wife would bang her head on the wall in an attempt to stop him. Thinking about this metaphorical story and her own life, the wife realized that this self-harming behavior was something that she needed to let go of. She decided she would no longer hurt herself when her husband was abusive to her; she would instead talk to someone. This artistic creation helped her become aware of and share her dysfunctional pattern of behavior. She was able to create her own solution to the problem. To provide closure, the family members are invited to throw away the clay elements symbolizing they have made a decision to let go of the past; this "free themselves session" ends with the serenity prayer, which once more reinforces the idea that the family member has a choice to change.

> God! Grant me the serenity
> To accept the things I cannot change
> Courage to change the things I can and
> The wisdom to know the difference.
>
> *(Reinhold Niebuhr 1943)*

Case Study

PL is the 48-year-old mother of a multiple drug user. She has an advanced degree in Science (M.Sc.) and Education (M.Ed.), and works as a teacher in a boarding school. Her son has been abusing drugs for the past three years and has not attended college. During her son's withdrawals she faced verbal abuse and threats from him. This created frequent conflicts at home. PL was always anxious and constantly worried about the future. When she began ABT she avoided people, seemed preoccupied and confused, and had frequent crying spells. During a drawing of a body map, she indicated pain in the neck, back, joints, and knee.

During the course of the ABT program certain patterns emerged in her drawings and sharing. Two things were predominantly seen: a Christmas tree depicting God and a broader path narrowing down. Her interpretation was that, with the grace of God, all the problems would be sorted out. She related her childhood story with the story of Moses crossing the Red Sea. She identified herself with the story and stated that her beliefs were similar to the Jews in the story. The story she shared made her aware that belief in God and daydreaming (imagining that miracles are going to happen) were her coping mechanisms. She realized that she needed to take action rather than waste her time imagining solutions that were not practical. In the course of the session there was a noticeable change in her attitude: she was more relaxed and happy, and said that her physical pain had been reduced. She recognized her talent in drawing and painting and began to use these to relax.

Changes noticed at the end of the program as mentioned by her counselor were increased self-esteem and decreased fear, anxiety, anger, and self-blame. She was optimistic, had clarity in thinking and a better appetite, and was able to sleep well. During the last session she said, "I have never had so much fun before. Art therapy is a tool given to me by God to give me strength."

Figure 19.1 Figurines used in an arts-based therapy session
Illustrated in the color insert

Application of Art-Based Therapy in Relapse Management

See Appendix D.

Art-Based Directives for Extended Care at the After-Care Center

See Appendix E.

Cultural Adaptation

We have had to incorporate several cultural adaptations to create a culturally sensitive environment and adopt several Western techniques to address the specific needs of the population we are working with. These are a few of the adaptations made:

- The materials that are used, like clay, magazines, newspapers, and instruments, as well as the themes for songs, should be culture specific.

- Natural clay or clay dough made out of flour are more familiar to patients than colored plastic clay.

- Local newspapers and magazines in regional languages are easier to relate to than a foreign magazine, as the local ones have images or pictures of the people of that region. This helps in identifying with the images that have familiar dress, skin color, and other aspects which help with self-expression. Local magazines are also easily available.

- Instruments belonging to that country or region—like the use of various drums and bells in South India—are more common than the use of piano, which is often seen as being Western.

- Stories, folklore, and narrations from epics are easier to relate to. For example, Raja, Kumar, and Lakshmi are familiar names, unlike names such as Michelle or Florence.

- To make them comfortable with drawing, participants are invited to draw a kolam or rangoli initially, symbols with which they are familiar, and are introduced to oil pastels later on.

- Dolls or images in molds (props) that depict a particular religion or ritual of the region should be used with due respect or not used at all. For the festival of Navratri, dolls made of clay, wood, and papier-mâché are displayed. These dolls are culture and region specific. The clients use these dolls to come up with a story (Figure 19.1).

Population-Specific Issues

- Clients are not familiar with ABT, hence an orientation needs to be given on issues like the use of art material, space, seating arrangements, use of floor to sit, etc.

- Focusing on the thoughts behind the creation rather than on the images made is vital.

- Clients and family members are initially inhibited to use various mediums. They associate colors with artists, clay with sculptors, miming and drama with stage performers, and music or songs with professional singers and instrumentalists. Warming up with clay pounding, random strokes in water colors, miming as a group with the practitioner demonstrating first, and using music in groups helps to break inhibitions.

- Exposure to solvents, thinners, and adhesives, and to sharp objects like knives, scissors, and cutters in art supply kits, should be avoided as they can act as triggers for abuse. Since the clients are on disulfiram (Antabuse), the solvents in certain types of paints can cause nausea.

Conclusion

In our experience at TTK we have found that ABT plays a vital role in the recovery and relapse prevention process in addiction management. Exposure to ABT reminds the client of his or her healthy lifestyle (pre-addiction period) and also fills the immediate vacuum generated by letting go of the unhealthy lifestyle developed during addiction. The process of creating images using colors, clay, collage, stories, and music along with the sharing of thoughts associated with them helps in dealing with the past and the present, and with future life issues. Art forms are generally a source of entertainment and recreation, but when used specifically with a therapeutic objective, they facilitate recreation of healthy self, thus paving the way for recovery through recognition and deliberation.

References

Colombo Plan (2003) *Development of Family and Peer Support Groups: A Handbook on Addiction Recovery Issues.* Colombo Plan Drug Advisory Programme, Colombo.

Jayaraman and Kanakam, U. (2010) *Getting Out of Alcoholism—My Personal Recovery Tools.* T. T. Ranganathan Clinical Research Foundation.

Niebuhr, R. (1943) *Origin of the Serenity Prayer: A Brief Summary.* Alcoholics Anonymous. Available at www.aa.org/lang/en/en_pdfs/smf-141_en.pdf, accessed June 17, 2013.

World Centre for Creative Learning Foundation (WCCLF) (2010) *ABT Manual.* Available at www.wcclf.org, accessed on July 23, 2013.

Part V

Cultural Perspectives

Using Art Therapy in Outpatient Treatment Settings

Chapter 20

Stories without Words
A Cultural Understanding of Trauma and Abuse

Linda Gantt

Cultural diversity and related issues are vitally important aspects of therapy and therefore are of great interest to therapists who wish to better understand and serve the people with whom they work. In this chapter, I discuss the intersection of trauma and abuse, culture, and art therapy. Trauma is a subjective personal experience that is both intertwined with culture and independent of it due to our human physiology. As current research demonstrates, trauma is a brain-based phenomenon that we interpret through the lens of culture.

Extending the Reach of Therapy in General and of Art Therapy in Particular

The prevailing ideas about therapy in general in the United States had their genesis in Western European culture. As the demographics of our country change to include more ethnic minorities and immigrant groups, mental health programs are adapting their practices to be more sensitive to the needs of those populations. Art therapists are writing not only about such programs in the United States (Robb 2002; Rousseau et al. 2003) but also about experiences in other countries (Anderson 2011; Arrington and Yorgin 2001; Kalmanowitz, Potash, and Chan 2012; Silver 2003).

In addition, during the past three or four decades, the reach of art therapy has extended into cultures other than Western ones. This is a result of both spontaneous and independent developments and of spin-offs from the classical Western-based art therapy literature. Hocoy raises important concerns about the potential for art therapists committing "cultural malpractice" (Iijima-Hall 1997, as cited in Hocoy 2002, p.141) and he makes suggestions on how to address it. Carlier and Salom (2012) make a case for the adaptation and reworking of general art therapy principles to better fit other cultures.

Increasingly, art therapy is being recognized as a valuable component of trauma treatment. In the practice guidelines from the International Society for Traumatic Stress Studies (Foa et al. 2009) the collectively named "creative therapies" appear in their own separate sections, one for children and one for adults. As therapists in other countries become familiar with these guidelines, the potential for greater use of art therapy will no doubt increase.

Values of Different Cultures with Respect to Therapy

Whether art therapy is adopted outright or adapted for various ethnic and immigrant groups in this country or taken to other countries, it is fundamental that art therapists understand that not all participants in a therapeutic enterprise have the same framework of values and goals. A number of writers have developed important resources in the past 20 years to document different cultural perspectives on therapy. In a book on culturally sensitive play therapy edited by Gil and Drewes (2005), one can learn (among other things) that many Hispanic families often consider therapy the province of women (Hopkins, Huici, and Bermudez 2005); that self-expression through art is not necessarily a universal value (Malchiodi 2005); and that Asian parents may expect an educational component to the therapy sessions (Kao 2005). Furthermore, certain institutions (most often the church) may be more influential in clients' lives than the mental health system. Also, the community may espouse certain values (e.g., intolerance of homosexuality) that are at odds with those of many therapists (Hinds 2005). Some practices taken for granted by therapists such as the necessity of keeping regularly scheduled appointment times are not necessarily recognized as important to clients from areas such as Latin America or Russia. Traditional Native Americans see time as circular and live in the moment. They are accustomed to visiting native healers on a drop-in basis when a problem arises rather than on a weekly basis (Glover 2005). This creates a particular problem because trauma symptoms erupt unpredictably, creating a crisis mentality. Instead, clients need to understand the importance of processing traumas in a carefully planned series of sessions over a specified time.

Differences About the Concept of "Art"

In addition to different ideas and values about therapy, there are differences in the concept of *art* as it is understood and used by Western art therapists compared with artists in other cultures. For virtually all its comparatively brief history, the field of art therapy has been based on two central ideas of what constitutes art. The first is that the art produced is symbolic (an idea that comes primarily from religious art in the Middle Ages). Even if a contemporary work is an abstract or non-representational piece, it is nonetheless thought to be reflective of the person who did it. The second idea is that art can be used expressively in the service of an individual. Those of us who work with traumatized people have assumed that these two ideas explain, at least in part, the power of art therapy. However, other cultures may not see art as connected in any way to those processes that are therapeutic for trauma survivors. There are many examples of non-Western art that are done by formula or according to strict rules in which the individual artist has little personal latitude. Such cultural attitudes might influence the way a person expresses his/her own thoughts and ideas, as he/she may wish to stick to the rules of art with which he/she is familiar.

Separating the Universal from the Cultural

If trauma ranges from interpersonal violence and natural disasters to war and genocide then the possibility of some type of trauma occurs in every part of the world. According to the *Diagnostic and Statistical Manual* (DSM-IV), trauma involves "actual or threatened death or serious injury, or a threat to the physical integrity of self or others" (American Psychiatric Association 1994, p.427). Furthermore, one's response to such events is "intense fear, helplessness, or horror" (p.428). Investigations of presumed brain mechanisms involved in such a response are being conducted at an astounding pace (Lanius et al. 2006; Pain, Bluhm, and Lanius 2009).

Increasingly, researchers in the United States are documenting the overlap of many psychiatric diagnoses with trauma histories. Some theorists make the case that trauma overlaps with what appears to be symptoms of many conditions heretofore seen as schizophrenia, major depression, or bipolar disorder (Ross 2000). Others see the spectrum of trauma-related disorders as stretching from post-traumatic stress disorder (PTSD) to dissociative identity disorder (DID) (Bremner 2002).

The Instinctual Trauma Response—Is It Universal?

Clearly, trauma in general is universal, but do people in different cultures react in the same way? Several writers have considered the freeze, a phenomenon common to animals and humans, as a fundamental aspect of trauma (Scaer 2001, 2005; Schore 2002; Valent 2007). Gantt and Tinnin (2007, 2009; Tinnin, Bills, and Gantt 2002) postulate that there is a brain-based response to traumatic events that is an evolutionarily acquired process fundamental to animal survival. This is termed the *Instinctual Trauma Response* (ITR). The essential aspects of the ITR are:

- startle
- the thwarted fight/flight
- the freeze
- altered state of consciousness
- automatic obedience
- self-repair.

For further details on the ITR see Appendix F.

Body sensations accompany each aspect of the ITR (such as an elevated heart rate during attempts to fight or flee or a slower rate during the freeze). Once a person enters the freeze, the rest of the ITR is recorded in the nonverbal part of the brain. However, this material is often inaccessible to consciousness; therefore, the experience feels unfinished. Because of the dissociation that occurs during the ITR, much of the nonverbal aspects of the experience have the potential to resurface as troubling symptoms such as intrusive flashbacks, nightmares, or body memories.

The core of trauma processing using this framework is creating a series of pictures (*the graphic narrative*) based on the sequence of the ITR. In the Intensive Trauma Therapy Clinic in West Virginia, the graphic narrative is used as the principal technique for processing traumas. Regardless of the type of trauma, we find that drawing out the story by using the ITR as an outline captures dissociated material that causes the most troubling symptoms. After the drawings are completed, we put them on a large cork board and the therapist tells the story back to the client. This gives the client the experience of seeing that the story has a beginning, middle, and end, and that it is now truly over.

The first three aspects of the ITR are found in animals as well as humans. The freeze occurs when fighting or fleeing is impossible (Levine and Frederick 1997). Automatic obedience in humans corresponds to animal submission. The altered state of consciousness is uniquely human and is the most baffling of the cascade of events. Time slows down, speeds up, or is experienced as fragmented. Perceptions are distorted. One may have an out-of-body experience or the feeling of being detached from the physical pain of the trauma.

Since the nonverbal correlates of the ITR are found in a variety of animals and seem to occur across all types of trauma in humans in Western cultures, it seems likely that the same can be found in non-Western ones. Simons has demonstrated how one aspect of the ITR—the startle—begins as a "simple reflex" that then becomes "culturally elaborated" (1996, p.16). There are seemingly different manifestations, the most well known being *latah*, a culture-bound syndrome found in Malaysia and Indonesia. Certain individuals (also termed *latah*) are identified as being easily startled and exhibit exaggerated reactions that are sometimes violent or out of control. Other members of the social group target them and repeatedly provoke them with sudden surprises and physical poking or jabbing.

It seems logical to expect that the art of trauma survivors might bear some similarities across cultures given the nonverbal correlates of the ITR. Rominger (2010) investigated near-death experiences (NDEs) as depicted in the art of two research participants. One of the individuals had a positive NDE while the other had a negative one. In art the first person focused on light as an important component while the second emphasized darkness. The first man was in the middle of surgery when he had his NDE and he had the sensation of being in a light-filled space. The second had a bicycle accident. Both had an out-of-body experience (OBE) during the NDE. (The overlap between NDEs and OBEs is considerable and has yet to be understood in clinical and anthropological literature.)

In my clinical experience, OBEs are more common in trauma survivors than professional literature would indicate. Is it possible that OBEs can be recognized as a literal shift in the perspective manifest in drawings? One woman in our clinic drew a picture of her experience as a teenager of a beating she suffered at the hands of her mother. When she looked at the drawing from arm's length, she was surprised to realize that the vantage point she used was from the other side of the room and behind the couch. It was at that time that she was able to talk about the OBE she had during the beating.

Many trauma survivors have difficulty talking about their experiences. Their stories are often fragmented, disjointed, or lacking crucial details. The well-known trauma specialist Bessel van der Kolk (van der Kolk, McFarlane, and Weisaeth 1996) often comments how people are "struck dumb with terror." In his literature review of NDEs, Rominger (2010) remarks about the "ineffability" of the experience. Since the nonverbal parts of the brain record the trauma experience in images and body sensations, it stands to reason that the creative arts therapies are the most likely approaches to provide nonverbal material that eventually leads to verbal description and assimilation. Art therapists assume that once the experience is put into a drawing or sculpture then it can be imbued with words.

While Rominger's sample of art that deals with an NDE is quite small, his work is a good example of a type of comparative study we should be doing in art therapy. It is quite likely that we will get more information if we first investigate the formal variables in the "free" drawings and paintings of trauma survivors rather than the content. This may help us find out more about the universal aspects without the cultural overlay. Such elements might be the type of perspective, specific colors (particularly a preference for predominantly light or dark colors), the depiction of humans and other creatures (whether in detail or simply indicated as an outline), the treatment of outlines or shapes where the edges may be sharp or indistinct, and/or backgrounds that are hazy or foggy. This is just the beginning of a possible list to study.

Cultural Elaboration

After we study the formal elements in the art of trauma survivors, we move on to look at content and the attendant cultural meanings. As Simons (1996) shows, a complex behavior can be the intersection of neurophysiological responses (a reflex) and cultural components. There is a kind of circular process that "[b]y virtue of belonging to a given culture, a person has access to a range of interpretations, readily available to make sense of the biological event when it occurs" (Simons 1996, p.239). Cultural elaboration can almost obscure the original reflex, and thus the universal aspects (such as the startle, freeze, or an OBE) may be denied or confused with other explanations. For example, one young child who was from a southern Protestant family said she "went to heaven" during the altered state of consciousness, while another child from a secular family said she "went to Candyland."

Searching for Meaning

Being able to recognize the presence of covert meanings in art is quite a seductive aspect of art therapy. It can also be the most dangerous. Nowhere is it as dangerous as when working outside of one's own culture. Arriving at a conclusion or premature interpretation without knowing the context or hearing the artist's associations might be the cultural malpractice about which Hocoy (2002) warns us.

We can appreciate the utility of the distinction that anthropologists use when they compare explanations by those from inside a culture and explanations by those from outside a culture. This is akin to the artist's associations and the art therapist's commentary in a case report. But this seemingly clear separation starts to disintegrate when we think of subcultures having competing explanations (such as art therapists from different theoretical perspectives). Obviously, any explanation can be challenged, resulting in a constant tension about the "correct" interpretation. Keeping these distinctions in mind can lead to a more productive therapeutic experience that we understand as being co-created by the participants.

A Case Study: Putting Words to Images

The following case study gives a sense of the complex intersection of cultural, familial, personal, and universal issues.

When 40-year-old "A" came into treatment in our outpatient clinic she had already been hospitalized at least six times for severe depression and suicidal thinking. During her most recent hospital stay she was diagnosed with DID. She had been divorced for several years and her three children lived with her. Her trauma history included a number of both Type I and Type II traumas (Terr 1991). (Type I traumas are single events [such as a car accident or a natural disaster] while Type II traumas are repeated events by the same perpetrator [such as domestic violence or childhood sexual abuse].) Her first known trauma was a tonsillectomy at two and a half years of age during which she became "light" during surgery. Before she turned four, her father sexually abused her and her mother made a suicide attempt.

The family lived in considerable secrecy. Her father, a doctor, never sought psychiatric treatment for his wife, presumably because of the stigma attached to it. According to A (who had struggled to understand her mother's condition by taking some college psychology courses), her mother would have qualified for a diagnosis of paranoid schizophrenia. She and her siblings (a sister and three brothers) were brutally punished for minor transgressions. (For example, the mother broke several of one son's fingers by putting his hand in an old-fashioned washer wringer, ironically know as a "mangle.") Their mother could not maintain the house or do basic activities of daily living. Her attempts at cooking consisted of keeping a pot of beans on the back of the stove and instructing the children to serve themselves if they were hungry. In order to do so, one had to scrape the mold from the top of the beans to reach into the still edible center. Each sibling left the family as soon as he or she could. A married when she was 17 years old but her husband was as abusive as her parents. Two of the brothers later committed suicide. When A was in elementary school the general cultural climate did not include an awareness of child abuse being found in all socioeconomic strata including doctors' families. Reporting laws were just being adopted. Child protective services were rudimentary at best.

When A was seven, an uncle sexually abused her. Like many perpetrators the uncle threatened A that he would punish her if she told anyone what he had done. In treatment she could not bring herself to tell what had actually happened, but this was because of a complex intersection of familial rules and the ITR. A talented artist, A was able to do a number of sculptures during her treatment. Two of those sculptures were self-portraits. Her first self-portrait was about 18 inches high and depicted her at age two and a half, the approximate age at which she had had her first traumatic experience. After I fired the sculpture A took it home. She reported that she would carry it around most of the day as a child would carry a baby doll. She draped a small blanket over the sculpture's shoulders as if it was alive and responding to the room temperature.

After about a week, she began to carry it with her as she went from room to room doing her daily activities. After another week or two, she could leave the sculpture in one place. My thought was that this way of handling the sculpture represented a split-off part that she was able to assimilate or reintegrate into her mental representation of herself. Making the image external and concrete was a necessary step to eventually being able to develop an internal image.

After completing another clay figure to illustrate a troubling image she had in her mind's eye, she stated, "I don't know what this is." I responded, "I don't know either but we'll find out." After I fired the sculpture I put it before the two of us on a turntable on the art room table and slowly rotated it. She was mystified by the pose. I offered to stand in that same position to see if that helped her make some associations. No sooner had I clenched my hands and taken the identical pose than she exclaimed, "I know, I know!" Her words began tumbling out. She began describing the experience of her uncle taking off her underpants. She reached for the waistband and tried to pull up the garment. Her uncle then grabbed both of her wrists with one of his large hands and proceeded to finish undressing her. A noticed how the figure's head was turned away from her uncle who was trying to kiss her. Then, having been given the vocabulary of the ITR in earlier therapy sessions, she could finally put words to her experience, and she exclaimed, "I was in the freeze!" (See Figure 20.1.)

Figure 20.1 Freeze

Case Discussion

This example illustrates how images come before words and that, once an image is placed at a physical distance from the maker, it is possible to achieve a "corpus callosal bypass" (Tinnin, Gantt, and Howie 2012). This bypass or presentation to the left hemisphere of right hemisphere material makes up for the weakened connection between the two that occurs during trauma. This primacy of the image is hardly news to art therapists but we seem to have to reiterate it repeatedly to our clients and other professionals.

Therapy for A consisted of processing her traumas in chronological order and helping her obtain co-consciousness with her split-off parts. The most fundamental problem was that of externalizing the images and the body experiences for which there were no words. There were several reasons A did not have the words to process her traumas:

- some of the traumas were preverbal

- being in the ITR meant her verbal brain was "offline" (at the time she had experienced the freeze) and thus incapable of storing her experience in words

- her family valued its privacy and kept many secrets about the true condition of the home and the mental health of the mother.

The last reason refers to a value common in Appalachian and African-American cultures (as found in the expressions of "not airing one's dirty laundry in public" or "you don't put your business on the street") (Gil and Drewes 2005). This aspect of her culture did not allow her to confide in others or to use her friends, teachers, or extended family as a resource. Indeed, the need for secrecy, the fragility shown by her mother, the abuse by her father, and the abuse and threats from her uncle all conspired to make her both personally and culturally vulnerable to her perpetrators.

Conclusion

Given the ubiquity of traumatic events and the need for cultural sensitivity, those of us in the helping professions face an enormous challenge. We must develop effective models of intervention informed by an understanding of the universal, the cultural, and the individual aspects of human experience. The difficulty in telling trauma stories is transcended by the power of art therapy. The art therapist helps to take images of the unspeakable and imbues them with words. Thus, the therapist is working within the frame of universal aspects of trauma, which hearken back to our mammalian brain and are therefore ubiquitous to all human culture. As demonstrated in the case example, the therapist must also attune to the familial and individual aspects of the trauma story to allow the individual to discover her own voice and words for this story. The elaboration of this story is the most essential component of trauma therapy.

Carlier and Salom (2012, p.10) state that "a fundamental task for the profession of art therapy is to construct an identity that can navigate and adapt to the globalized world." A large part of this identity will be based on the ability of the field to make a significant contribution to trauma treatment and to be culturally sensitive when doing so.

References

American Psychiatric Association (1994) *Diagnostic and Statistical Manual of Mental Disorders: DSM-IV.* Washington: American Psychiatric Association.

Anderson, F. E. (2011) "International spotlight: A visit to Mortenson's three cups of tea country." *American Art Therapy Association Newsletter 44,* 1, 10–11. Alexandria: American Art Therapy Association.

Arrington, D. and Yorgin, P. (2001) "Art therapy as a cross-cultural means to assess psychosocial health in homeless and orphaned children in Kiev." *Art Therapy: Journal of the American Art Therapy Association 18,* 2, 80–81.

Bremner, J. (2002) *Does Stress Damage the Brain? Understanding Trauma-Related Disorders from a Mind-Body Perspective.* New York: W. W. Norton.

Carlier, N. G. and Salom, A. (2012) "When art therapy migrates: The acculturation challenge of sojourner art therapists." *Art Therapy: Journal of the American Art Therapy Association 29,* 1, 4–10.

Foa, E., Keane, T., Friedman, M., and Cohen, J. (eds) (2009) *Effective Treatment for PTSD: Practice Guidelines from the International Society for Traumatic Stress Studies, Second Edition.* New York: Guilford.

Gantt, L. and Tinnin, L. (2007) "Intensive trauma therapy of PTSD and dissociation: An outcome study." *The Arts in Psychotherapy 34,* 69–80.

Gantt, L. and Tinnin, L. (2009) "Support for a neurobiological view of trauma with implications for art therapy." *The Arts in Psychotherapy 36,* 148–153.

Gil, E. and Drewes, A. (eds) (2005) *Cultural Issues in Play Therapy.* New York: Guilford.

Glover, G. (2005) "Musings on Working with Native American Children in Play Therapy." In E. Gil and A. Drewes (eds) *Cultural Issues in Play Therapy.* New York: Guilford.

Hinds, S. (2005) "Play Therapy in the African American 'Village.'" In E. Gil and A. Drewes (eds) *Cultural Issues in Play Therapy.* New York: Guilford.

Hocoy, D. (2002) "Cross-cultural issues in art therapy." *Art Therapy: Journal of the American Art Therapy Association 19*, 4, 141–145.

Hopkins, S., Huici, V., and Bermudez, D. (2005) "Therapeutic Play with Hispanic Clients." In E. Gil and A. Drewes (eds) *Cultural Issues in Play Therapy.* New York: Guilford.

Iijima-Hall, C. C. (1997) "Cultural malpractice: The growing obsolescence of psychology with the changing U.S. population." *American Psychologist 51*, 642–651.

Kalmanowitz, D., Potash, J., and Chan, S.M. (eds) (2012) *Art Therapy in Asia: To the Bone or Wrapped in Silk.* London: Jessica Kingsley Publishers.

Kao, S. (2005) "Play Therapy with Asian Children." In E. Gil and A. Drewes (eds) *Cultural Issues in Play Therapy.* New York: Guilford.

Lanius, R., Bluhm, R., Lanius, U., and Pain, C. (2006) "A review of neuroimaging studies in PTSD: Heterogeneity of response to symptom provocation." *Journal of Psychiatric Research 40*, 709–729.

Levine, P. and Frederick, A. (1997) *Waking the Tiger: Healing Trauma.* Berkeley: North Atlantic Books.

Malchiodi, C. (2005) "The Impact of Culture on Art Therapy with Children." In E. Gil and A. Drewes (eds) *Cultural Issues in Play Therapy.* New York: Guilford.

Pain, C., Bluhm, R., and Lanius, R. (2009) "Dissociation in Patients with Chronic PTSD: Hyperactivation and Hypoactivation Patterns, Clinical and Neuroimaging Perspectives." In P. Dell and J. O'Neil (eds) *Dissociation and the Dissociative Disorders: DSM-V and Beyond.* New York: Routledge.

Robb, M. (2002) "Beyond the orphanages: Art therapy with Russian children." *Art Therapy: Journal of the American Art Therapy Association 19*, 4, 146–150.

Rominger, R. (2010) "Postcards from heaven and hell: Understanding the near-death experience through art." *Art Therapy: Journal of the American Art Therapy Association 27*, 1, 18–25.

Ross, C. (2000) *The Trauma Model: A Solution to the Problem of Comorbidity in Psychiatry.* Richardson, TX: Manitou Communications.

Rousseau, C., Lacroix, L., Bagilishya, D., and Heusch, N. (2003) "Working with myths: Creative expression workshops for immigrant and refugee children in a school setting." *Art Therapy: Journal of the American Art Therapy Association 20*, 1, 3–10.

Scaer, R. (2001) *The Body Bears the Burden: Trauma, Dissociation, and Disease.* Binghamton: Haworth Medical Press.

Scaer, R. (2005) *The Trauma Spectrum: Hidden Wounds and Human Resilience.* New York: Norton.

Schore, A. (2002) "Dysregulation of the right brain: A fundamental mechanism of traumatic attachment and the psychopathogenesis of posttraumatic stress disorder." *Australian and New Zealand Journal of Psychiatry 36*, 9–30.

Silver, R. (2003) "Cultural differences and similarities in responses to the Silver Drawing Test in the USA, Brazil, Russia, Estonia, Thailand, and Australia." *Art Therapy: Journal of the American Art Therapy Association 20*, 1, 16–20.

Simons, R. (1996) *Boo! Culture, Experience, and the Startle Reflex.* New York: Oxford University Press.

Terr, L. (1991) "Childhood traumas: An outline and overview." *American Journal of Psychiatry 148*, 10–20.

Tinnin, L., Bills, L., and Gantt, L. (2002) "Short-Term Treatment of Simple and Complex PTSD." In M. B. Williams and J. Sommer (eds) *Simple and Complex Post-Traumatic Stress Disorder*. New York: Haworth.

Tinnin, L., Gantt, L., and Howie, P. (2012) "An Art Therapy Spectrum: The Dual Brain Perspective." American Art Therapy Association Conference, Savannah, GA.

Valent, P. (2007) "Eight survival strategies in traumatic stress." *Traumatology 13*, 4–14.

van der Kolk, B., McFarlane, A., and Weisaeth, L. (eds) (1996) *Traumatic Stress: The Effects of Overwhelming Experience on Mind, Body and Society*. New York: Guilford.

Resources
Further Reading

Beals, R., Hoijer, H., and Beals, A. (1977) *An Introduction to Anthropology, Fifth Edition*. New York: Macmillan.

Bermudez, D. and ter Maat, M. (2006) "Art therapy with Hispanic clients: Results of a survey study." *Art Therapy: Journal of the American Art Therapy Association 23*, 4, 165–171.

Boyd-Franklin, N. (2003) *Black Families in Therapy: Understanding the African American Experience*. New York: Guilford.

Chu, V. (2010) "Within the box: Cross-cultural art therapy with survivors of the Rwanda genocide." *Art Therapy: Journal of the American Art Therapy Association 27*, 1, 4–10.

Ciornai, S. (1983) "Art therapy with working class Hispanic women." *The Arts in Psychotherapy 10*, 2, 63–76.

Constantine, M., and Sue, D. (eds) (2005) *Strategies for Building Multicultural Competence in Mental Health and Educational Settings*. Hoboken, NJ: Wiley.

Fitzpatrick, F. (2002) "A search for home: The role of art therapy in understanding the experiences of Bosnian refugees in Western Australia." *Art Therapy: Journal of the American Art Therapy Association 19*, 4, 151–158.

Harley, D. and Dillard, J. (eds) (2005) *Contemporary Mental Health Issues Among African-Americans*. Alexandria, VA: American Counseling Association.

Hays, D. and Erford, B. (eds) (2010) *Developing Multicultural Counseling Competence: A Systems Approach*. Upper Saddle River, NJ: Pearson Education.

Hiscox, A. and Calisch, A. (eds) (1998) *Tapestry of Cultural Issues in Art Therapy*. Philadelphia, PA: Jessica Kingsley Publishers.

Ibrahim, F. and Dykeman, C. (2011) "Counseling Muslim Americans: Cultural and spiritual assessments." *Journal of Counseling and Development 89*, 4, 387–396.

Kalmanowitz, D. and Lloyd, B. (1999) "Fragments of art at work: Art therapy in the former Yugoslavia." *The Arts in Psychotherapy 26*, 1, 15–25.

Moodley, R. and West, W. (eds) (2005) *Integrating Traditional Healing Practices into Counseling and Psychotherapy*. Thousand Oaks, CA: Sage.

Ojelade, I., McCray, K., Ashby, J., and Meyers, J. (2011) "Use of Ifá as a means of addressing mental health concerns among African American clients." *Journal of Counseling and Development 89*, 4, 406–412.

Sue, D. W. and Sue, D. (1999) *Counseling the Culturally Different: Theory and Practice, Third Edition*. New York: Wiley.

Chapter 21

Cultural Considerations in Family Art Therapy

Barbara Sobol and Paula Howie

Family therapy is unique in that its focus is upon human behavior as shaped by social context. Early psychotherapy was influenced by the assumption that therapy should be carried on with someone in private. Further experience with psychotherapy has shown that interpersonal psychology and social context are vital for the full understanding of individuals and the complexity of their lives. All human beings exist within a system, be it a family, a community, a culture, or a society. From its beginnings, the goal of family therapy was to understand the context, identify the patterns within the context that sustain the problem, change the context, and eliminate the problem (Nichols 2009).

In this chapter, the authors provide a brief history of family therapy that focuses upon the emerging field of family art therapy and upon the schools that most influence our paradigm of the eight ways of observing a family. (For a more complete listing of all family therapy schools please see Nichols 2009.)

History of Family Therapy

Many early therapists observed that when a family member became better as a result of treatment, another family member would become symptomatic. This led early therapists to identify the importance of working with the entire family.

Early family therapy drew heavily upon group theory. An important distinction, which evolved from group therapy, was the differentiation between the processes, or how people express themselves, and the content, or what they say (Nichols 2009). Warren Bennis described group development as consisting of two major phases with several subphases. Family therapists consolidated this into a theoretical model, which evolved into the concept of the family life cycle, described by Carter and McGoldrick (1999).

One of the most important influences upon family therapy has been the work of John Bowlby on attachment (Holmes 1993). Bowlby, a Scottish psychiatrist and psychoanalyst, was compelled by children's reactions to painful real-life experiences. His theory highlighted the importance of the interaction between the child and the primary caretaker in that the child will seek closeness in times of stress. Indeed, according to attachment theory, psychopathology is no longer located within an individual—it is an interpersonal dynamic. Attachment theory focuses upon an internal template or working model, from which frame the individual can judge the world as a safe and responsive place or not (Holmes 1993).

Dr. Lyman Wynne, working at the National Institute of Mental Health (NIMH) on the schizophrenia unit, linked communication deviance in families to thought disorders in schizophrenic patients (Nichols 2009).

Dr. Murray Bowen began his career by studying mothers and their schizophrenic children at the Menninger Clinic. In subsequent work at NIMH and at Georgetown University, Bowen placed emphasis on the differentiation and individuation of the self as an important aspect of maturation. If one is able to remain oneself in the face of external influences when family anxiety is high, this is a hallmark of a mature individual. All families operate on a continuum from emotional fusion to differentiation (Nichols 2009).

Dr. Salvador Minuchin worked at the Wiltwyck School for Boys where Edith Kramer also completed her pioneering work on art therapy with children (Kramer 1993). In Minuchin's structural family therapy, the therapist "joins" the family in order to restructure it so that enmeshed and disengaged families, which both lack clear lines of authority, can be helped to change (Nichols 2009).

The Family Art Evaluation and Family Art Therapy

Hanna Yaxa Kwiatkowska was the first art therapist to write about working with families. At NIMH with Lyman Wynne and Juliana Day Franz, Kwiatkowska developed the Family Art Evaluation (FAE) (Kwiatkowska 1978). In this intervention, the family is directed to make several drawings together and to briefly discuss the drawings in the presence of the therapist. By integrating their "reading" of both the artworks and the observed relationships, therapists can begin to understand family dynamics and to chart a direction for treatment. The directions include having the family complete a free picture, family portrait, abstract family portrait, scribble, family scribble, and free picture. This series of drawings transitions from a free picture to a family and an abstract family picture, which Kwiatkowska considered the most personally challenging of the series. The scribble then helps the family to decompress, after which they work together on a joint scribble. The final free picture brings closure to the series and can be compared to the first for a sense of how the family saw the FAE experience (Kwiatkowska 1978).

Dr. Harriett Wadeson also worked at NIMH. In addition to her work with families, Dr. Wadeson focused on treating couples. Her interventions were developed to shake up the homeostasis of the couple and to allow the participants to interact in new ways. These included a joint picture without talking, an abstract picture of the marital relationship, and a self-portrait given to one's spouse (Kerr et al. 2008).

As early as 1963, Dr. Judith Rubin was conducting family art therapy sessions (Kerr et al. 2008). Dr. Rubin worked for many years at the Western Psychiatric Institute and Clinic in Pittsburgh, PA. She designed a family intervention, which included a scribble, 2- or 3D family portraits, a family mural, and an extra free picture for a family member who has completed her drawings before the rest of the family.

Helen Landgarten worked at the Thalians Outpatient Clinic at Cedars-Sinai Medical Center in Los Angeles (Kerr et al. 2008). Landgarten developed an assessment that included the following tasks: a nonverbal team art task, a nonverbal family art task, and a verbal family art task. In her book, Landgarten also utilized a family-of-origin picture, where she had a parent draw himself or herself at the same age as the child client (Landgarten 1981). Maxine Junge worked closely with Helen Landgarten. Her tasks for the family included a warm-up by making their initials on 8.5" × 11" paper, embellishing these, and taking turns to make a family drawing together without talking, using one color per family member. Both therapists were interested in helping the family discover and work on coalitions and alliances (Kerr et al. 2008).

Shirley Riley drew heavily from her training in structural family therapy and, working with Cathy Malchiodi, explained her approach as an integrative one (Riley and Malchiodi 1994). She discusses the strengths of using a combination of art therapy and family therapy in this integrated approach.

Dr. Doris Arrington worked at Notre Dame de Namur University in California and describes her technique of family landscapes. She has participants think of the psychological space in their family when they were between the ages of 3 and 12. She then has them draw this as a symbolic landscape (Arrington 2001). After drawing, the artist identifies each family member and the family discusses their landscapes.

Eight Ways to Observe Family Dynamics Using Family Art Evaluation

The authors use a modified form of the FAE,[1] combining the representational and the abstract "family portrait" procedures into a single procedure and shortening the time given to complete the "individual scribble" procedure before going on to the "joint" family scribble. This is done primarily to reduce the length of time needed to complete the session. This is the way in which Kwiatkowska discussed shortening the procedure (personal communication, 1977).

The authors also use an "8 Ways" paradigm to organize the information drawn from an FAE session (see Appendix H). Through the 8 Ways paradigm, we can look at a family's artwork and interactions across several parameters to give a fuller understanding of the family. Each of the "8 Ways" reflects essential theoretical viewpoints of the major approaches of family therapy: a developmental, *life cycle* approach; a *strengths*-based resiliency approach; *communications* and behavior theory; *structural* theory; a range of theoretical approaches dealing with the *unconscious underpinnings* of family life (psychodynamic; object relations; attachment); an art-as-therapy, *themes and metaphors* approach; a recognition of "the self in the system" (Nichols 1987) or *individual issues*; and the *impact of culture* (McGoldrick, Giordano, and Garcia-Preto 2005).

Family and Cultural Context

Every family reflects assumptions, beliefs, traditions, and customs in both implicit and explicit ways—that is, as both objectively acknowledged and/or subtly embedded in the subjective life of the family. The family's experience of itself and its identity within the larger society has intergenerational implications. "Over time…a mutually reinforcing set of patterns becomes fixed, beliefs become interpreted as realities, and future generations come to believe, and enact, the same perspectives, over and over again" (Siegel 2012, p.391). This transmitted pattern of religious beliefs, customs, practices, traditions, etc., passed on through the generations, is in essence family "culture." It is a distinct part of a broader concept of family culture, which includes the unique environment or surround of each particular family.

Cultural patterns, transmitted over generations, are one stream of influence on the environment and operation of a family system. We must also keep in mind the intergenerational transmission of genetic traits, psychological traits (attachment styles, defenses against anxiety, tolerance for affect), and family vulnerability to the effects of trauma. Taken all together, one's cultural heritage can become a source of richness, a rigidified or a flexible aspect of family life, or a hidden or overt source of conflict. Whether cultural patterns are an explicit or an implicit part of family life, they are part of each adult's conscious and unconscious choices about carrying on what was given to them from previous generations. And for the children in families, culture is inextricably part of the "hand they are dealt" (Walsh 2003, p.380).

Case Study: The Family of Ms. Cindy R and Lilly R

In the case study that follows, the FAE allowed the authors to observe the relationship between a mother and daughter in real time as they made art together on two separate occasions. Using the 8 Ways paradigm, the authors were able to organize their observations of behavior and their understanding of the art into a succinct yet comprehensive profile of the family. We were also able to discern the ways that cultural impact and psychological issues were interwoven in this family. We have decided to discuss the family portrait and joint family scribble from both FAEs in order to highlight the similarities and themes, which are apparent in both sets of drawings and which remained core issues over time.

Background

Ms. R and her daughter Lilly were acquaintances of one of the authors. Ms. R first agreed in 1996 to be videotaped for the purpose of demonstrating the use of the FAE for graduate students. A second demonstration videotape with both authors present was made in 2007. Ms. R is Caucasian, the daughter of urban middle-class parents of German and Irish descent. She was raised and remains a devout Catholic. As a young adult, she joined a religious order and, before leaving the order, she traveled several times to South America where she met Mr. D. He is from a South American, middle-class, urban, Catholic family. Mr. D's family and Mr. D himself had a history of alcohol abuse, as did both Ms. R's father and one sibling. Mr. D and Ms. R never married, but they lived together for several years before the unanticipated pregnancy, and both looked forward to raising a child. However, their life together ended abruptly after a physical assault on Ms. R by Mr. D while drinking. Mr. D attended a rehabilitation program at Ms. R's insistence, but after completing it, he did not return to the relationship. Without a partner and struggling financially, Ms. R welcomed the birth of her daughter alone. Mr. D remained intermittently involved with the family until Lilly was about eight, when he moved to another part of the country.

The 1996 Family Art Evaluation

In 1996, Ms. R was 48 and Lilly was almost seven. Ms. R was concerned that Lilly had not yet begun to read. She also worried that her long work hours, financial hardship, fatigue, and the inconsistent involvement of Mr. D were a strain on her relationship with her daughter. Lilly's first drawing, which depicted the interior of a house, was hastily constructed and filled with images of danger and escape. Her second picture, the family portrait, is notably different in content and process (Figure 21.1).

The portrait is meticulously drawn and has themes of support, security, and identity. Lilly depicts her family as happily reunited, holding hands, and on their way to a dance. Her father is shown as both dapper ("I sewed his outfit!") and gentlemanly (he is carrying flowers for Ms. R). Significantly, Mr. D is wearing his artist's bag slung over his shoulder. The bag, made in his native country, identified him as a South American, an artist, and a person of note.

Both Ms. R's first drawing and her family portrait are indirect and metaphorical. The portrait is a pale, softly drawn rendering of a Japanese folding screen on which are inscribed images of wisteria vines and flowers, changing colors as if to portray the changing seasons. Lines of poetry follow the outline of the screen: Ms. R was unable to show Lilly how or where her family (herself, Lilly, and Mr. D) was depicted. She explained that the screen showed the concept of the family over time, an explanation that seemed to leave Lilly confused.

Figure 21.1 Lilly's family portrait

In their joint family scribble Ms. R and Lilly worked together harmoniously, using Lilly's scribble to develop an image of a boat at sea (Figure 21.2). High, choppy waves fill the bottom half of the page and come up over the sides of the boat. For Ms. R, the image evoked excitement, adventure, and a pleasurable memory of sailing. Lilly told a different story, once again juxtaposing themes of danger and security: "There was a man…and he was lost at sea… But he had food stored below… He had tacos. He had hamburgers. He had cheeseburgers."

Figure 21.2 Joint scribble

Using the 8 Ways Paradigm

Ms. R and Lilly were in Carter and McGoldrick's (1989) *life cycle stage* of "families with young children," a difficult time because of the felt absence of the father. Both Ms. R and Lilly had observable *strengths*. They were intelligent and articulate and able to use art making to express thoughts and feelings. Their playful cooperation on the boat scribble showed their ability to be close and caring. Ms. R maintained a *structure* in which she was clearly in the role of executive. Although at times she lowered the boundaries to share companionship and play with her daughter, she returned to her role easily. For example, she helped Lilly to clean up pastels that had spilled during the session, then guided Lilly's attention back to the drawing task. Their styles of *communication* and expression were markedly different. Ms. R was soft-spoken, intellectualizing, and at times vague. Lilly was direct, assertive, and energetic. At times during the session, she seemed confused by her mother's explanations. In terms of *unconscious internalizations*, there was an undercurrent of anxiety in Lilly's stories such as *the man lost at sea*. Lilly's family portrait was a child's fantasy of reunion and identification with the idealized father. Ms. R sometimes seemed lost within her own reverie, suggesting internal longing or sadness. Her conceptual family portrait artwork created distance from the emotional effects of Mr. D's abandonment. Lilly's artwork expressed *themes and metaphors* of danger and safety as well as reunion. Ms. R expressed both reverie and excitement. Lilly's reading problem and Ms. R's fatigue and financial stress were notable *individual issues*. Ms. R kept Latino *culture* as well as Mr. D's artistic legacy alive in their home. She was also delighted to see her daughter's integration of her North American and South American heritage. As Ms. R said, "She had tacos *and* hamburgers in the boat!"

The 2007 Family Art Evaluation

In November 2007, Lilly was approaching her 18th birthday. In the intervening 11 years, Ms. R had moved out of poverty and into a secure professional position. Lilly had begun reading in 1997. In school, she excelled in both music and art. She was fluent in two languages, Spanish and English. Between 2005 and 2007, Ms. R's mother and brother had died, and Mr. D had all but disappeared from their lives. Lilly had begun dating an older boy who had dropped out of school. Her grades plummeted, and by spring of her junior year, Lilly too had dropped out of high school against her mother's wishes. Ms. R's dream that she and Lilly would travel together to Europe and Asia was being eroded by daily clashes with a defiant adolescent who was eager to move out on her own. Lilly seemed to embody both the positive (Latina, artist) and negative (substance use, irresponsibility) aspects of her father. Although Mr. D by now was physically and emotionally distant, his presence in the family was maintained by several of his large abstract paintings still hanging on the walls of their apartment. The influence of his Latin ethnicity and artistic persona was reflected in what Ms. R called Lilly's "Latina style of dressing" and her cultivation of her own artistic persona.

For her family portrait, Lilly drew a landscape in which a single red flag or marker is planted next to a hole on a gently hilly golf course. The drawing is a tribute to her maternal uncle and a poignant expression of her sense of loss at his recent death. She took it down abruptly when her mother tried to engage her in discussing the sadness the drawing evoked in her. Lilly insisted that her uncle had had a happy life.

Ms. R's family portrait is filled with 20 sketchy purple outlines of heads without features, suggesting that many people, over time, might be considered family— again a conceptual work rather than an attempt at a portrait (Figure 21.3). Among these shadowy figures, three "heads" touch each other and have features sketched in. Ms. R identified the three connected heads as herself, Mr. D, and Lilly. As in the earlier session, Ms. R's ambiguous explanation of the relationship of the three figures evoked confusion in her daughter.

Figure 21.3 Ms. R's family portrait

As they developed the joint family scribble, Lilly took the lead in drawing, while Ms. R fell into a kind of dance, shadowing her daughter's drawing movements, echoing her forms and color, and punctuating her work at times with compliments about Lilly's talent and at other times with disapproval of her "violent" imagery (Figure 21.4). For example, when Lilly characterized one of her mother's details as "a bloody talon," Ms. R visibly recoiled and protested. Lilly, who had been mostly silent and focused on her own drawing, defensively reacted to her mother's comments. The final boldly colored image, which they titled "Bird of Paradise," twists it way down the page, visually pulling the eye of the viewer in different directions. The "face" of the bird has a masked quality, its expression ambiguous.

Figure 21.4 The joint family scribble

Using the 8 Ways Paradigm

The family had moved into a new *life cycle stage* with clear challenges brought on by Lilly's adolescence and Ms. R's aging. While their core *strengths* remained and in some ways deepened, there were now new risk factors, among them a freshly felt grief. Their inability to *communicate* clearly and compassionately was exacerbated now by the urgency of adolescence as well as their differences in style and temperament. The family *structure* was changing too. Ms. R's efforts to find the appropriate way to assert her role as the mother of an adolescent were sometimes undercut by her own active longing for the days of Lilly's childhood. Lilly's childhood longing for her absent father may have been reinforced through her mother's own fantasies of reunification and her subsequent devotion to keeping the father's *cultural* identification and associations very much alive in their small family. While at age seven Lilly longed for her father through her art themes, by 17 she embodied both the positive and negative attributes of the father. To some extent, Ms. R may have *unconsciously* projected these attributes onto Lilly. The identification of Lilly, at 17, as volatile and irresponsible threatened a reenactment of the premature break and another irreparable rupture in the family, as had happened with her father years before. The *themes and metaphors* point to struggles with loss and individuation. For Ms. R, the failed relationship, lack of social and financial stability, and the death of family members were impeding her ability to assist her daughter with individuation. *Individual issues* for Ms. R included aging and her fear of being alone. Lilly appeared to be struggling in her attempts to individuate, making choices that were ineffective or even unhealthy.

Conclusion

The ten drawings of each FAE provided a window into the inner life of both mother and daughter, as symbolized in their images. Using the 8 Ways paradigm, we looked at the family across several dimensions and, by so doing, we were able to discern a unique relationship between cultural issues and issues of object relations and attachment. The role of cultural background cannot be underestimated in this family. Embedded in Lilly's positive identification with her Latina and artistic heritage was the difficulty of internalizing the idealized father (artist and hero) while grappling throughout childhood with the reality of her father's abandonment and her own anger and sorrow. Ms. R's family portrait suggests that she herself may not have resolved the loss of Mr. D and therefore would have difficulty assisting Lilly in doing so. The preservation of Mr. D's powerful Latino and artistic influence enriched the life of Ms. R and Lilly, while in a sense it prolonged their lack of resolution. Despite the challenges faced by this pair, we viewed them as a securely attached and functional dyad. Following the 2007 FAE, Ms. R and Lilly chose to explore their relationship briefly in several sessions of art therapy. In the following years, they were able to create a successful "launching" of Lilly into young adulthood, as a student attending graduate school in the arts. Ms. R regained time to devote to her own interests and return to her love of writing. Before Lilly moved away to begin her adult life, the two traveled together to several countries in Europe and Asia. Both were able to embrace an exploration of other cultures as a healthy shared interest in the world. Despite difficulty managing some of the transitions of adolescence and early adulthood, this family demonstrated an ability to find common ground and to learn from their mistakes. This will enable them to move forward and to rise to challenges they will confront in the future.

Note

1. For a full description of the FAE process, see the original Kwiatkowska description in Kwiatkowska (1978). For a description of the modified form of the FAE, see Sobol and Williams (2001).

Acknowledgments

The authors are indebted to Patricia Ravenscroft, ATR, Mari Fleming, ATR-BC, Gail F. Edwards, ATR-BC, Carol Cox, ATR-BC, Cheryl Doby-Copeland, ATR-BC, and Elaine Parks, ATR, for their work with families and the ideas that their work inspired.

References

Arrington, D. (2001) *Home Is Where the Art Is: An Art Therapy Approach to Family Therapy.* Springfield: Charles C. Thomas.

Carter, B. and McGoldrick, M. (1989) *Changing Family Life Cycle: A Framework for Family Therapy.* Upper Saddle River, NJ: Prentice Hall.

Carter, B. and McGoldrick, M. (eds) (1999) *The Expanded Family Life Cycle: Individual, Family, and Social Perspectives, Third Edition.* Boston: Allyn and Bacon.

Holmes, J. (1993) *John Bowlby and Attachment Theory.* London: Routledge.

Kerr, C., Hoshino, J., Sutherland, J., Parashak, S., and McCarley, L. (2008) *Family Art Therapy: Foundations of Theory and Practice.* New York: Routledge.

Kramer, E. (1993) *Art as Therapy with Children, Second Edition.* Chicago: Magnolia Street Publishers.

Kwiatkowska, H. Y. (1978) *Family Therapy and Evaluation Through Art.* Springfield: Charles C. Thomas.

Landgarten, H. (1981) *Clinical Art Therapy: A Comprehensive Guide.* New York: Brunner-Routledge.

McGoldrick, M., Giordano, J., and Garcia-Preto, N. (eds) (2005) *Ethnicity and Family Therapy, Third Edition.* New York: Guilford Press.

Nichols, M. P. (1987) *The Self in the System: Expanding the Limits of Family Therapy.* New York: Brunner/Routledge.

Nichols, M. P. (2009) *The Essentials of Family Therapy, Fourth Edition.* Boston: Pearson.

Riley, S. and Malchiodi, C. (1994) *Integrative Approaches to Family Art Therapy.* Chicago: Magnolia Street Publishers.

Siegel, D. J. (2012) *Pocket Guide to Interpersonal Neurobiology: An Integrative Handbook of the Mind.* New York: W. W. Norton and Company.

Sobol, B. and Williams, K. (2001) "Art Therapy in Group and Family Systems." In J. A. Rubin (ed.) *Approaches to Art Therapy, Second Edition.* New York: Routledge.

Walsh, F. (ed.) (2003) *Normal Family Processes: Growing Diversity and Complexity, Third Edition.* New York: Guilford Press.

Chapter 22

The Universality of Grief and Loss

Heidi Bardot

Grief and loss are universal. Everyone at some point experiences loss, and every therapist at some point works with a client dealing with grief and loss issues. This may be due to death, divorce, moving, children leaving the home, job change, graduation, body changes—there are a multitude of losses that people grieve in life. A therapist must be prepared to deal with these issues. Therefore, in this chapter, I address some of the basics of grief and loss, delve deeper into some of the specific areas, describe first sessions, and provide two case examples.

What Is Grief?

Doka (2007) extended the definition of grief as a reaction to loss. Primary losses are deaths, and secondary losses come as a result of death (loss of income, friends); there are anticipatory losses (past, present, and future in the course of an illness, job layoff, retirement); tangible losses (something stolen or destroyed); intangible or symbolic losses (divorce, menopause); disenfranchised grief (no opportunity to publicly mourn—deaths of former spouse, lover, or pet; divorce, miscarriage, incarceration, infertility); ambiguous loss (missing person or missing body, dementia); and complicated grief (violent death, death coupled with trauma or abuse).

"Loss is defined by the meaning we give it" (Fiorini and Mullen 2006, p.19). Therefore, a divorce for one person may be the ending of an unhappy marriage, while for another it may be the loss of a loved life and lifestyle. The loss of a job may mean the end of a cherished career for one person, while for another it may be an opportunity to start something new. But for each person, a loss is a disruption—a change in the story of his/her life that must now be revised in order to create a new one (Bolton 2008).

When a person experiences a loss and resultant grief there are "normal" responses that occur. These may include feelings such as sadness, shock, numbness, anger, anxiety, loneliness, relief, and guilt. Physical sensations may occur such as hollowness in the stomach, tightness in the chest and throat, breathlessness, and lethargy. Certain cognitions may occur such as disbelief, confusion, and preoccupation. And many behaviors may surface such as crying, sleep and appetite disturbances, absentmindedness, avoidance of reminders, and social withdrawal (Worden 2009).

Most of what I describe here is specifically related to a loss through death; however, many of the theories and examples can be applied to the other losses previously mentioned.

Theories of Grief and Loss

There are many theories that involve the stages or phases of grief and loss. The most well known of these theories is Elizabeth Kubler-Ross's (1969) five stages of grief. Often these models are taken as absolute stages through which one must pass in sequence before moving to the next one; if they are not completed in the correct order, one has not grieved in a healthy manner (Stroebe et al. 2008; Walter and McCoyd 2009; Worden 2009). However, we must move toward the notion that there is no single way to mourn, but that each individual has a unique experience and an individual response to grief and loss (Doka 2007; Worden 2009). Worden (2009, p.50) believed that a more task-oriented approach gave control back to the client. His four tasks are: (i) to accept the reality of the loss; (ii) to process the pain of the grief; (iii) to adjust to a world without the deceased; and (iv) to find an enduring connection with the deceased in the midst of embarking on a new life. While I have never approached my grief work in this specific framework, most of my sessions have achieved these very tasks. Neimeyer (2001, 2012) introduced a different approach to grief work that focused on meaning making—stating that grief work is a mutual relationship between client and therapist of being present in grief, listening to personal stories, validating emotions, and eventually making meaning out of the loss and moving into the future without the person. This theory works particularly well in art therapy because much of the creation of art and exploration of the art piece is making meaning out of that which is expressed.

Essentials of Grief Art Therapy

One of the core aspects of grief therapy is to allow the client to tell his/her story—and to repeat it often (Neimeyer 2012). It seems that in the repetition there is learning and healing being addressed. The key attribute for the therapist in this process, then, is the willingness to listen and to be present in the grief. Often people are "not allowed" to speak of the death, their feelings, or the overpowering grief that has changed their life because of the discomfort or unwillingness of friends and family. Many times this is not due to their lack of caring or love, but because of society's discomfort with death and the client's sometimes insatiable need to revisit the details. Therefore, as a therapist, the key to success with grief and loss clients is your willingness to be present in their pain and to explore what they need to when they need to.

Another essential understanding is that there is no correct or normal time frame for dealing with grief. Clients are often told by their well-meaning family and friends that they "should be over it by now" or, conversely, asked, "Why aren't you still grieving?" For some people, if there is an illness, the loss is something for which they have been preparing for months or years. For others it may take years to begin to accept that the loss has occurred or that the person is no longer with them. Additionally, in the case of death, the grief may return with each new life event that the survivor must experience without the deceased (i.e., graduation, wedding, birth of a child). Each person and relationship is individual; therefore, the response to the loss is individual.

An advantage that comes with grief art therapy is the use of images. Often I discuss with clients that when they experience a terrible loss it can be difficult to describe the feelings with words, because there are no words to describe the loss and pain they might be feeling. But sometimes we can create art about it—we can put colors and shapes and emotion into creating an image. This acknowledgment of those inexpressible feelings and the offer to support them in finding a method to express a small piece of what they are feeling usually begins the therapeutic alliance.

Developmental Understanding of Grief and Loss

Each person responds differently when dealing with a loss; however, there are some developmental guidelines for children and adolescents that are important to keep in mind. Additionally, please note that children may be advanced, delayed, or moving between stages. Very young children (two to four years old) will not understand the concept of loss, but they will know that something has changed in the household and may act out as an expression of their confusion or fear. As they begin to understand the cycle of life and death (ages four to seven), they will begin to ask a lot of questions. They may be protective of family members and may withhold their emotions so as to not upset anyone. They also may feel responsible in some way for the death and for the well-being of the family. By age seven to ten, they realize death is final and will happen to everyone; therefore, they may begin exploring what happens after death. Behavior at school or home can change, as often they feel different from their peers. With older children and teens, grief may be complicated as the teen needs to separate from caregivers in order to become independent; however, he/she is separating at a time when he/she most needs their support. Peers often become the primary support at this time (McCaw 2012; Walter and McCoyd 2009).

Because of this developmental process, a child may continue or return to grieving as he/she ages and understands more about death. This is especially true on special days or during life events when the person who died would naturally have been present. It is normal and healthy for these thoughts and feelings to resurface throughout a lifetime.

Basics of Initial Sessions

As I mentioned earlier, grief work is unique to each client; however, there are some specifics that need to be determined in the early sessions in order to guide future sessions.

My sessions begin with a phone call to the client or client's family, if a minor. During this phone call I am gathering factual information and assessing the issues. Factual information would include type of loss, date of occurrence, relationship with the deceased, how the client responded to the loss, whether this is their first experience with death, how other family members are responding, and what support systems are available. Assessment of the issues would include exploring current behaviors (e.g., difficulties in school, sleep disturbances, anxiety, angry outbursts); previous behaviors, characteristics, issues prior to the loss (i.e., whether this is a change or a worsening); any medical, developmental, and mental health diagnoses; what the client or family members believe is the issue; and questions to which the client might be seeking answers. Though this is an assessment and fact-gathering phone call, it is also a therapeutic interaction. Therefore, empathic responses and words of support are important and essential in beginning a therapeutic alliance. In addition to working out the details of meeting, it is important to explain what to expect in the first session (i.e., we will meet as a family, this will be an individual session, and I will meet with the parents afterward), and an explanation of these decisions.

I will focus this description of the session on children because of the hands-on and interactive approach that must be used; however, much of what I share can be used with adolescents and adults in an age-appropriate manner. At the beginning of the session I explain who I am and, if needed, what art therapy is. I also ask the client why they think they are meeting with me. Particularly with children, it is important to determine what the parents have told the child. This helps me to assess how open the parents are with the children and also addresses the issue up front: we are meeting because someone in your life has died. If the child does not know why he/she is there, I explain that his/her parents told me someone in their life has died, I ask who it is so he/she can tell me in his/her own words, and I share that the parents thought it would be important to meet with me to talk and create art about what this experience was like for him/her. I also explain that I meet with many people just like them who have had someone in their life who died. This statement usually gets the child's attention because most likely they have not met anyone else who is in the same situation. This allows them to feel less different and less isolated.

Once settled, I explore more about the death and, depending upon the child's openness and willingness to share, I ask questions such as: how did he die, were you there when he died, did you know he was sick, was he sick for a long time, did you know he was going to die, did your family talk to you about it, what happened after the death, was there a service? Throughout this I am assessing whether the child needs to transition from the verbal to art (decreased verbal response, ignoring questions, looking away, seeming uncomfortable). At this specific point we transition to the art and I suggest that I would like to know the person that died better. I say that since I did not get to meet him/her, it would be helpful if the child could create an image of a memory of something he/she used to do with that person—maybe something they loved to do together either before or after the person got sick, or something the whole family did together.

The idea behind this directive is to determine the strength and connection of their relationship. Oftentimes if there is a strong connection then the grief process is more difficult (Worden 2009). What I am looking for in the artwork and the follow-up description or story by the child is the depth of relationship—was it a daily or occasional occurrence, is it a positive or negative memory, is it focused on the family relationship or an individual relationship with the deceased, is it an interaction the loss of which will affect their current functioning (i.e., grandpa picked me up from school every day), do they seem like they are sharing an important story with me or merely completing the task that I have requested of them? Additionally, I am exploring feelings and behaviors attached to the death, such as anxiety, fear, anger, and acting out in response to these feelings.

After this initial session, I usually meet with the parents in order to provide feedback and educational materials about children and grief. I give them my assessment of the situation and methods to support their child, and ask whether it seems appropriate to continue sessions. This educational period is one of the most important aspects of the session, as the parents inevitably will be supporting their child through the grief process. I offer methods of exploring their child's feelings (i.e., discussions on walks or in the car, sharing some of their own emotions, reading books focused on grief such as *When Dinosaurs Die: A Guide to Understanding Death* [Brown and Brown 1996]). I provide information on the developmental understanding of death dependent upon their age, as well as behavior to be concerned about and when to seek additional help (McCaw 2012). Also, I discuss what may be happening if a child does not seem to need art therapy at this time. Some of these instances may be when the parent is having a strong natural grief response, while their child is not because the relationship to the deceased is different (i.e., mother is grieving her father's death, but child is not connected to his grandfather in the same way). I usually then suggest that perhaps the mother seek counseling knowing now that her child is fine. Another instance of this can occur when the parent is having a strong grief response and the child feels that it is "unsafe" for him/her to grieve at the same time. He/she will then unconsciously wait until his/her parent has finished grieving and there is an emotional support system available for him/her. Surprisingly I have seen this many times particularly when a parent loses a spouse. The grief may be so all-encompassing that the child needs to remain strong for the surviving parent. Usually, this is a brief process of perhaps a few weeks to a month when the parent regains functioning and focuses on the child and then the child is given "permission" to grieve their loss. During this time it is possible to therapeutically support the family; however, it is impossible and inadvisable to force the child to address his/ her own grief. If you create the therapeutic alliance, they will approach the topic when they are ready. A therapist must use his/her skills to determine the difference between therapeutic waiting and avoidance on the part of the child.

As long as the child is not in crisis, I schedule art therapy grief counseling every other week. This allows the child to process the grief in a natural manner with their family and with focused art therapy sessions with me to check in and explore deeper areas. By their very nature, children cannot maintain focus on death for very long, but must go in and out of the topic. Therefore, even during a single session, we might discuss the death, then sports, then school, then the death, then weekend activities, and then the death in a cyclical pattern. Initially this feels unfocused or counterproductive; however, I have seen children be incredibly insightful in these moments because it is an unforced method of interaction. Additionally, it is sometimes while discussing a seemingly unrelated topic that the most insightful thoughts are expressed.

During the second session, I generally explore feelings in response to the death. With a set of laminated expressions and feelings cards (created from *Feelings Poster*, Creative Therapy Associates 1994) we explore all the possible feelings—expected ones such as sadness, loneliness, anger, shock, and fear, and unexpected ones like happiness, guilt, and shame. I explore what each one means to the child. We talk about the unspoken feelings of anger at the doctors, at the surviving parent, at family members, at friends who haven't experienced loss, at God, and at the deceased. Sometimes we discuss the guilt that children often carry when they have "magical thinking" and believe that the person died because they were angry with them or did something "wrong." I validate each feeling, which provides the child with relief that these are normal emotions when someone dies: for example, because you are angry with someone does not mean that you do not love them, or because you are sad, it does not mean that you cannot also have fun and laugh when you are with your friends. We explore healthy ways to express feelings and how important it is to talk about them. During this discussion I also explore what their beliefs are about death—do they have unexplored fears that everyone will die, are they afraid of getting sick or falling asleep, do they have separation anxiety, or do they view death as something that happens when you are old or very sick? What do they believe happens after death and would making artwork of that be helpful? Do they have unspoken opinions they need to voice to the deceased? All of these responses determine how and whether I proceed with future sessions.

These future sessions become more individualized dependent upon what areas the client is struggling with and determine how best to interact with the client. Sessions might include other family members and focus generally on the actual death and the resultant grief, and eventually move into adjusting to life in the present and future without the deceased person.

This final phase in the therapeutic process is one of the most important in healing as the client must be able to figure out how to maintain a connection with the deceased, but in a new type of relationship (Worden 2009). Often with children this person is viewed as a "guardian angel" who watches over them. This is viewed as a comforting aspect and should not be confused with viewing the deceased as a ghost, which is connected to their fears. The guardian angel is also seen in adults, but more often adults reintegrate the person in their life as inherited or learned strengths that are now within them since the death. This is a very healthy method of recognizing the importance the person held in their life and transferring that attribute to the self. Therefore, the survivor now is stronger because of having had a relationship with the deceased. This new strength can then support them in the future.

Cultural and Spiritual Aspects

Another extremely important area that must be taken into consideration when working with grief and loss is determining your client's cultural heritage and spiritual beliefs. Sometimes these two are intrinsically linked. We have already discussed that there should be no "norms" in a client's grief response; however, it is important to determine what responses are expected within the client's culture or spiritual belief in order to recognize what expectations are being placed on your client by himself/ herself and by his/her support system. Additionally, people can be bicultural and multicultural and have blended traditions and practices; therefore, it becomes imperative to determine what your client specifically believes (Fiorini and Mullen 2006). Recognizing the effect of spirituality on a client's responses to loss is essential (Doka 2007; Wolfelt 1996; Worden 2009). Often in Western therapy, spirituality is a taboo subject; however, in grief work it is essential as beliefs and death are often inseparable and can be the issues most discussed in the processing of loss. Therefore, the therapist must have great self-awareness of his/her own beliefs, disbeliefs, and biases about spirituality and religion. Spirituality comes into play in rituals after the death, during the mourning period, and in beliefs about what happens after death. Generally, I explore the client's beliefs with a simple question: "What do you think happens after death?" This can be a natural question after exploring how the death occurred and what rituals they had after the death, and as the client begins to explore his/her life without the deceased. With adults this can often lead to an existential and spiritual discussion about life and death, allowing them to integrate the loss into their life and also to begin to attach meaning to the loss. With children, this usually results in artwork detailing the place where their loved one now lives. This allows the child to imagine a safe place for this person, free of disease and danger, surrounded by beautiful things and loving people and animals; creating this place in their mind and in their art provides comfort to the child, so they no longer have to worry about the person who died. In all of my years working with grieving children, every single child, from every culture, background, and belief system, believed that there was a place where the deceased went after death.

Case Studies

I wanted to include two examples of grief work: an image from an eight-year-old boy who was grieving in a healthy manner and one from a seven-year-old girl who was having a difficult time with her grief. In both cases, these were first session drawings after their grandmother, who lived with them, had died.

In the first example (Figure 22.1), the boy created a scene from the funeral and, in this case, burial of his grandmother. He described the cemetery and how she was buried next to his grandfather, who had died before he was born. He separated out the two graves from the others, making them special, and he spent a great deal of time in the session creating the fence that separated the graves from where his family parked on the road. At the end he quickly added in the "closed" sign and commented that no other family members could die now. His image and comments portray a positive connection to his grandmother, but also the fear he was feeling regarding his first exposure to death and the wish to protect his family. This was a natural response and led to helpful and supportive discussions in our future sessions as well as within his family. This boy moved through the grief process as his family had been open with him while his grandmother was ill and after she died and regularly explored his feelings and shared theirs with him; therefore, the family worked together to heal as a family.

Figure 22.1 Eight-year-old boy—Drawing of cemetery

Illustrated in the color insert

In the young girl's artwork (Figure 22.2), she was also dealing with death for the first time; however, in this case the parents felt they had kept her protected from the illness and death and their emotional response to it and did not feel that she was negatively affected or in need of therapy. The image very clearly portrays a different viewpoint. She described the picture as a little girl all by herself on the top of a hill when a lightning storm swept in with dark clouds, rain, and chaotic lightning overtaking the very small figure, portrayed with wide eyes and an open, screaming mouth. She did not directly connect the picture to her grandmother's death, but many children find it safer to "stay within the metaphor" and describe a story when they are really speaking of themselves. Therefore, as a therapist, it is best to stay within the metaphor and explore the story with them. By the end of the session, she was able to admit that her grandmother's death had been "scary." There are many times when a child responds very emotionally to a death. In this case it may have been because her parents had not prepared her for the death and had not shared their own grief, and she felt alone in her feelings; it may have been because they did not feel she had been affected and had therefore not explored the possible emotions she might feel; or there may have been other underlying issues within the family that produced this negative reaction. However, the art therapy allowed her a safe place to express what she was feeling and I was able then to share with her parents her current struggles and give them information on how to better support her. This is a perfect example of how one should never assume what a child is feeling or not feeling, and how much better it is to explore and find out the reality.

Figure 22.2 Seven-year-old girl after death of her grandmother

Illustrated in the color insert

The Essential Quality of Self-Awareness

Grief is a normal reaction to loss, something everyone must deal with repeatedly throughout their life; therefore, it is natural for therapists working with grief and loss to revisit their own past losses, worry about future losses, and even ponder their own inevitable death (Doka and Davidson 1998; Worden 2009). Additionally, therapists may connect on an emotional level with their clients, even mourning the death themselves, which may then, after multiple losses, lead to bereavement overload (Bardot 2008; Herman 1997; Rando 1984). Imperative in this work is constant attention to self-awareness, specifically in healing one's own issues of grief and loss. You cannot do this work on a regular basis unless you are aware of how it is affecting you. This can only be achieved by seeking support through supervision or personal therapy in order to heal past losses, address additional grief, remain empathically connected to clients, and make meaning out of seeming meaninglessness (Bardot 2008; Hardy 2005).

Conclusion

Grief is something that one never "recovers" from; the bond continues with the deceased, but in a different form (Doka 2007; Worden 2009). Clients often tell me about losses they have experienced many years in the past and how they can still feel the pain of the absence in their lives. However, there is healing—over time and with a refocus on life without the person. This healing process is what makes this work so rewarding. We are given entrance into a person's or family's life when they may be at their most vulnerable; we are asked to walk that journey with them, and we are there when they begin to appreciate life again. So, though there is no end point to our grief, there is a revised meaning to life.

This chapter is but a very small insight into grief work, specifically with art therapy. If you are interested in this topic I encourage you to explore the myriad resources, many of which are included in the References.

References

Bardot, H. (2008) "Expressing the inexpressible: The resilient healing of client and art therapist." *Art Therapy: Journal of the American Art Therapy Association 25*, 4, 183–186.

Bolton, G. (ed.) (2008) *Dying, Bereavement and the Healing Arts.* Philadelphia: Jessica Kingsley Publishers.

Brown, L. and Brown, M. (1996) *When Dinosaurs Die: A Guide to Understanding Death.* Boston: Little, Brown and Company.

Creative Therapy Associates (1994) *Feelings Poster.* Available at www.ctherapy.com, accessed on June 17, 2013.

Doka, K. (2007) *Living with Grief: Before and After Death.* Washington: Hospice Foundation of America.

Doka, K. and Davidson, J. D. (eds) (1998) *Living with Grief: Who We Are, How We Grieve.* Philadelphia: Brunner/Mazel.

Fiorini, J. and Mullen, J. (2006) *Counseling Children and Adolescents Through Grief and Loss.* Champaign: Research Press.

Hardy, D. (2005) "Creating Through Loss: How Art Therapists Sustain their Practice in Palliative Care." In D. Waller and C. Sibbett (eds) *Facing Death: Art Therapy and Cancer Care.* Maidenhead: Open University Press.

Herman, J. (1997) *Trauma and Recovery: The Aftermath of Violence—From Domestic Abuse to Political Terror.* New York: Basic Books.

Kubler-Ross, E. (1969) *On Death and Dying.* New York: Scribner.

McCaw, J. (2012) *Touching Grief: Frequently Asked Questions about Child and Adolescent Grief.* Fairfax: Walker's Cove Publishing.

Neimeyer, R. (2001) *Meaning Reconstruction and the Experience of Loss.* Washington: American Psychological Association.

Neimeyer, R. (2012) *Techniques of Grief Therapy: Creative Practices for Counseling the Bereaved.* New York: Routledge.

Rando, T. (1984) *Grief, Dying, and Death: Clinical Interventions for Caregivers.* Champaign, IL: Research Press Co.

Stroebe, M., Hansson, R., Schut, H., and Stroebe, W. (eds) (2008) *Handbook of Bereavement Research and Practice.* Washington: American Psychological Association.

Walter, C. and McCoyd, J. (2009) *Grief and Loss across the Lifespan: A Biopsychosocial Perspective.* New York: Springer Publishing.

Wolfelt, A. (1996) *Healing the Bereaved Child.* London: Routledge.

Worden, J. W. (2009) *Grief Counseling and Grief Therapy: A Handbook for the Mental Health Practitioner, Fourth Edition.* New York: Springer Publishing.

Chapter 23

HIV/AIDS

Reflecting on 15 Years in New York City

Daniel Blausey and Yasmine J. Awais

Disclaimer/Notes for the Text

The authors alternate between *client* and *patient* in this text when discussing the population that is being served as both terms speak to the roles that are taken. In the nonprofit setting, the term client is usually preferred while patient is used in hospital/medical settings. In this chapter, people living with HIV/AIDS (PLWHA) take on the roles of both client and patient. The term *affected* refers to a person who has a close family member or partner that has HIV or AIDS.

The sight of the small table abruptly silenced the echoes of voices in the great hall. On it, a candle flickered in the daylight, highlighting a paper with the names of those who had died the night and days before. A moment of grieving was always allowed for those who had died.

It was 1995 and the long-term acquired immune deficiency syndrome (AIDS) facility had opened a few months earlier in the shadow of New York City. This was shortly before highly active antiretroviral therapy (HAART) altered the course of treatment and well over a decade after the haunting discovery of human immunodeficiency virus (HIV)/AIDS. The role of the art therapist was to ease the emotional and physical suffering while preparing clients for a potential early death. Depending on the individual's physical health, art therapy was conducted at bedside or in a multiple-use room.

The population was as diverse as the surrounding urban sprawl. Paths that would normally only cross on the tangle of local expressways were brought together by AIDS. Former prominent professionals, the chronically mentally ill, disenfranchised populations, and blue-collar workers filled the rooms. Family involvement varied greatly, with some left to die in the arms of strangers and others with generations of loved ones at their side. The means of transmission, from the first author's memory, rarely had any hierarchy in this setting among the staff or fellow clients.

Engagement was not determined on whether the whiteness of the first author's skin contrasted nicely or blended easily with the varied hues of the clients. Nor was it determined by his Midwestern movements or accent, which were decidedly different when compared to the East Coast accents and urban vernacular. His race and gender were firmly established and accepted as those of a white male but his perceived sexual orientation and HIV status changed with the gender, race, and sexual orientation of the clients. For example, a white gay male patient may perceive the first author as a white gay male, while a black straight male patient may perceive the first author as a white straight male. This unconscious transference onto the therapist has remained a constant experience for the first author in working with this population across states and in various settings. Engagement appeared to hinge on the patient's individual responses to the dying process, physical pain, and the ability to empathize and establish a safe environment.

HIV and AIDS are not simply viruses or a collection of symptoms or opportunistic infections. It is a challenge to identify another topic that holds more stigma than HIV/AIDS. Topics considered taboo in many cultures (sex and drugs, for example) were brought out into the open in the early years of the epidemic as gay men and injection drug users were hardest hit. Over the HIV/AIDS timeline, socioeconomic status, race, sexual identity, gender, homelessness, and family ties become salient in everyday life. Planning for the future, including death, becomes more urgent. In this chapter, we chronicle the disease from the mid-1990s, when the first author began his work and AIDS was a diagnosis of almost certain death, through 2012, when the second author began her work at a camp for families impacted by HIV/AIDS. The authors reflect on the role of the art therapist in community-based settings in the New York City area in this 15-year period.

HIV/AIDS: An Overview

From a Terminal Disease to a Chronic Illness

Symptomatic gay male patients were first identified in 1981. "By the summer of 1982, scientists had convincing evidence that AIDS must be caused by a blood-borne and sexually transmitted virus" (Cohen et al. 2010, p.94). This further burdened populations stigmatized by race, gender, sexual orientation, drug use, and lifestyle, as illness-related stigmas are often directly connected to the mode of infection, especially in cases of sexually transmitted diseases (STDs) (Cohen et al. 2010). Discriminatory fears were heightened in 1984 by discoveries that a retrovirus was the cause of AIDS and that HIV contained properties that would make it next to impossible to vaccinate against AIDS (The Office of History, National Institutes of Health 2010).

HIV stigma and discrimination has been a tremendous and costly hindrance. Bayer and Oppenheimer recall in *The New England Journal of Medicine* that there was "pervasive institutional and professional resistance to caring for patients with AIDS during the early 1980s" (2006, p.2273). As a result, extreme societal hostility impacted access to primary medical care and community support in fighting a terrifying and unknown disease.

As HAART medical advances dramatically increased the life expectancy of individuals with access to health care, mental health needs correspondingly changed. Many people living with HIV/AIDS (PLWHA) found themselves emotionally and financially adrift. Living with a draining terminal illness leading to disability, immobilizing medication side effects, and fairly certain early death overshadowed long-term financial responsibility, career aspirations, and life planning. Some clients, literally on their deathbeds, were revived by HAART to lead unexpected and unplanned extended lives.

Living with HIV: The Stages

"Despite the medical advances an estimated 17,774 people with AIDS died in 2009, and nearly 619,400 people with AIDS in the U.S. have died since the epidemic began. Meanwhile an estimated 1.2 million people in the United States are living with HIV infection" (Centers for Disease Control and Prevention 2012a, p.1). While feelings of helplessness, fear, depression, vulnerability, anger, and other issues are often seen across the course of the disease, mental health treatment needs are best tailored to the fairly clear-cut stages of living with HIV: seroconversion (the point where HIV antibodies are detectable in the blood serum after infection), the newly diagnosed person, mid-term survivors, and long-term survivors.

Stage lengths are determined by disease progression and are dependent on time between seroconversion, HIV testing, medical treatment planning and adherence, and multimorbidity factors that impact health (e.g., other illnesses that are associated with HIV/AIDS, such as anemia and kidney disease). A person can be diagnosed with HIV and simultaneously with AIDS if there is a considerable length of time between seroconversion and HIV testing. Thus a lack of medical intervention results in disease progression. This example highlights the need for routine testing and importance of HIV status awareness. To be newly diagnosed, a person must be exposed to HIV antibodies through bodily fluids such as blood, semen, vaginal fluid, or breast milk. After exposure, the body undergoes seroconversion; at this point, after obtaining a HIV-specific test, one can receive an HIV diagnosis. The newly diagnosed stage is a pivotal time frame and lasts for several years. At this juncture in the illness, acceptance, understanding, transmission education, and connection to medical care are critical for the individual.

The largest and most diverse group, the mid-term survivors, often live healthy, active, and productive lives impacted by living with a chronic and transmittable illness. They navigate careers, relationships, and families in a normative fashion. We are categorizing this stage by those who have accepted their HIV-positive status, attempt to make long-term behavioral changes to maintain routine HIV medical care, and adhere to lifelong medication regimens. Mental health issues include depression, anxiety, and lack of social connectedness. For persons with drug abuse histories, this stage often coincides with a commitment to active harm-reduction practices or sobriety.

Some people move from the mid-term phase to the role of long-term survivor with little disease progression. Long-term survivors have been living with HIV for decades and most probably have experienced the epidemic from the early years. This is a time that is often experienced with increased HIV medical and mental health symptoms that may lead to disability and less severe decreased physical ability. Depression may also become an issue as long-term survivors have witnessed the death of friends made in social support groups and at medical care facilities. This raises concerns about their own mortality and issues surrounding death and dying. Concrete concerns such as future planning (e.g., who cares for the children after death, estate planning, etc.) as well as emotion-related ones (e.g., was a full life lived?) are common themes.

The Role of Art Therapy

Art therapy took many forms in the long-term care facility. Some patients too ill to draw would describe homelands or weave stories in great detail. The art therapist would often draw the clients' images or their faces as they talked. The storytelling provided an opportunity to be heard and to share personal stories that allay fears of being forgotten or having lived a life with minimum purpose. Other clients expanded our understanding of art materials, culture, and death. For example, the first author's resistance to glitter as an art form was overcome as a young man from the Caribbean created abstract paintings with glitter, glue, and paper with flair. The art swirled with life and eased his pain. In his words, it was the most productive he had ever been. As his death came nearer, some days the pain would be so strong that he would spend the session contemplating his completed work in silence.

Piccirillo (1999a) identified five skills useful in working with PLWHA: knowledge of HIV/AIDS; knowledge of death and bereavement; cultural competence; self-knowledge; and tolerance for frustration. These skills are most certainly relevant today. Additionally, people in the helping professions may also benefit from skills in advocacy and social justice. It could be argued that anyone working with PLWHA is a social activist, as the work requires confronting the systematic imbalance of power on a daily basis that manifests itself in issues such as homelessness, child custody battles, drug use, and immigration. There are various models that the art therapist can adopt to become an active advocate through dismantling racism and utilizing art therapy as a tool for social change (cf. Hocoy 2007; Miller and Garran 2008).

Before work can be done, it is beneficial for art therapists to be aware of how their presence impacts others. Because of the stigma surrounding how HIV/AIDS transmission occurs, clients may wonder why professionals work with a population that is subject to prejudice and being judged. Projections such as HIV status, sexual orientation, and socioeconomic status will be put onto the art therapist. For the first author, being a white male could allow for projections of power and authority, while being "one of us" (the author's skin color, perceived HIV status, etc.) can simultaneously occur. For the second author, a petite female of mixed Asian heritage, projections of needing to be protected and educated about HIV/AIDS are common. How the art therapist addresses these projections impacts the therapeutic work and goals. Through various art interventions and materials, these projections can become opportunities to address concerns with lack of autonomy, feelings of isolation, the need for protection, and education in the group setting.

Art therapy's benefits have been noted in working with PLWHA of all ages and settings (Bien 2005; Hrenko 2005; Piccirillo 1999a, 1999b; Rao et al. 2009). The bridge between developing prevention programs to decrease new infection rates while simultaneously providing effective services for PLWHA is often a parallel process. We outline below some art therapy interventions used to address prevention; to disclose to intimate partners, friends, and family; to cope with social issues (e.g., homelessness, stigma); to deal with denial; to address drug use and recovery; and to handle medical concerns, including medication compliance.

Art Therapy in the Early Stages

The newly diagnosed individual faces the emotional impact of the diagnosis, disclosure issues with family and friends, potential HIV stigma and discrimination, negotiation with sexual partners to prevent HIV transmission, navigation of medical care, and managing mental health issues related to living with a chronic and transmittable illness. Additionally, a partial list of fears includes abandonment and isolation, symptom onset and uncertainty of disease progression, medication side effects, transmitting the virus to others, threat of an early death, and exhibiting physical symptoms associated with HIV/AIDS. For example, facial wasting is a common identifying feature for PLWHA and for patients taking certain HIV medications, which results in a significant loss of fat in the patient's face. Psychosocial support groups are a common method to address the fear engendered by this and other disfigurements.

Newly diagnosed clients often respond well to the structure of a psychoeducational group to gain access to educational resources and peer support in a safe environment. Clients are still understanding the disclosure process, specifically who to disclose to outside of where they are receiving medical and psychosocial care. PLWHA often will disclose personal matters in a group that inherently has self-disclosed such as a group at an AIDS Service Organization where it is known that all of the members are HIV positive. Art therapy interventions can be successful when they support the educational aspects of the session and address feelings of contamination, identity and HIV, self-perception, and internalized feelings of stigma and shame. Often these feelings are still forming and are difficult to articulate.

Individual and group art therapy goals for early-stage clients include validating the individual art expressions; encouraging appropriate risk-taking behaviors through art making (i.e., sharing emotions creatively instead of holding them in, as sharing emotions can sometimes be seen as unsafe for clients); reflecting on the art-making process and products in order to make the unconscious or unseen seen; and promoting a space that values community. In general, both authors recommend nondirective approaches in the art therapy sessions during the early stages in order to promote the aforementioned goals. In addition, the authors employ exploratory directives to enhance knowledge attainment within the psychoeducational group structure. The directives provide a shared focus and the art often visually strengthens clients' understanding of the group goals.

Art Therapy in the Mid-Term

Despite being asymptomatic and healthy, the mid-term survivor must maintain the required ongoing critical commitment to an often burdensome HIV medical care regimen, strict medication adherence, navigation of potentially severe medication side effects, and the constant monitoring of medical interventions. Connection to a responsive and accessible primary care provider is essential to success. The fervor of the newly diagnosed phase fades and the monotonous aspect of living with HIV threatens treatment adherence, safer sexual practices, and self-care. Poor or inconsistent adherence leads to disease progression. Those who are not reliable with their medication and follow-up care often want the least amount of medical intervention, yet medical care involvement increases as the disease progresses.

Art therapy can be beneficial at this stage to assist in treatment, medication adherence, and risk reduction, as well as addressing unrelated mental health issues. Since many people living with HIV have histories of trauma, physical and sexual abuse, and addiction, addressing these issues is crucial to long-term adherence success. Engagement with art therapy in a group setting can create a productive opportunity for growth and has been used to address issues raised mid-term (e.g., Bien 2005; Hrenko 2005; Piccirillo 1999a). "Artistic activity is a bridge between inner and outer realities and it is often cathartic, organizing, and integrative. Making art in the presence of others can evoke and intensify feelings while at the same time provide safe, concrete structures for their expressions" (Moon 2010, p.73). Individual, nondirective art therapy has also been found to be beneficial in decreasing physical and psychological symptoms in PLWHA (Rao et al. 2009).

While working with PLWHA who were also housing insecure, such as those experiencing periods of homelessness or those who were at risk of becoming homeless, the second author found three-dimensional media to be a material of choice. Besides the usual drawing, painting, and sculpture materials that are generally found in art therapy studios, it was important to offer pieces of wood, wood burning tools, chisels, files, and sandpaper. Clients enjoyed the physicality of altering a piece of wood, carving, and burning designs. Often, glitter or other embellishments would be incorporated with photographs of loved ones (see Figure 23.1). The pieces were completed by ritualistically pouring a thick coating of clear epoxy over the entire work. On a practical and metaphoric level, this final step of pouring resin provides protection (waterproofing) and extends the life of the artist (artwork) in the face of an uncertain future. Because of the nature of the materials, an open studio model was utilized. The studio was open for only three hours at a time, but clients were given the freedom to work for extended periods. The open studio parallels the mid-term stage experience: with clients being at different levels of acceptance and treatment in their medical care, they are able to tolerate and process nonverbally for different lengths of time.

Figure 23.1 Response art

Art Therapy, Prevention, and Disclosure

For someone who is HIV negative, prevention entails eliminating or reducing behaviors that put someone at risk (e.g., eliminate IV drug use or only partake when clean needles are available; abstain from sex or only engage when safer sex practices are utilized). Disclosure (Obermeyer, Baijal, and Pegurri 2011) to sexual partners and family is considered to be a key role in prevention. For pregnant mothers, prevention also includes reducing perinatal HIV transmission, which can occur during pregnancy, labor, childbirth, and breastfeeding, so that the child will be born without seroconverting (Centers for Disease Control and Prevention 2007; Murphy 2008).

The second author focused on prevention through disclosure between parents and their children at a family camp for those impacted by HIV/AIDS. It has been noted that HIV/AIDS is multigenerational (Havens, Mellins, and Pilowski 1996; Piccirillo 1999a), and in the United States, people in urban areas and people of color, specifically women of black and Latino descent, are disproportionately affected (Centers for Disease Control and Prevention 2011, 2012b). Therefore education plays an important role in prevention. Looking at the family as a microcosm of society, disclosure among family members can positively impact the community at large. The second author's role at camp was to educate adults that disclosure is a process and not a one-time event, especially when it comes to children (Obermeyer et al. 2011). In Obermeyer et al.'s review of adult HIV disclosure literature, they found that "the majority of people disclosed their status to *someone*" (p.1012; emphasis added). Identified factors that increase disclosure include the individual's status being HIV negative; disclosure to relatives as opposed to friends; and disclosure to steady partners versus casual partners (Obermeyer et al. 2011). Benefits of disclosing include emotional support, medical care, and resources (Obermeyer et al. 2011). Risks of disclosing include fears of abandonment and discrimination.

Art Therapy with Those Affected by HIV/AIDS

Little has been written about working with the HIV/AIDS-affected population (Hrenko 2005). This may be a result of the fact that for art therapy to be practiced with those affected by HIV/AIDS, disclosure is required. A secondary factor is how the disclosure occurred: was the affected person told directly by the infected person? Or was the affected person informed of their loved one's HIV status during a period of crisis such as sickness, hospitalization, or death? In a nondirective manner, art therapists can address the affected person's emotional needs; these may include anger, shame, guilt, and uncertainty. The authors again promote nondirective and supportive art therapy techniques. Affected individuals are at different stages of acceptance that depend on their age, relationship to the PLWHA, understanding of HIV/AIDS, and the loved one's current health status (e.g., asymptomatic, symptomatic, or deceased).

Art Therapy and Long-Term Survivors

Although PLWHA are living longer and healthier lives since the introduction of HAART, "the frequency of endocrine, metabolic, cardiovascular, renal, dermatological, neoplastic, hepatic, pulmonary, and gastrointestinal multimorbid medical conditions remains very significant and [is] in some cases increasing" (Cohen et al. 2010, p.235). Thus the normal aging process, onset of ancillary health problems, and the emotional toll of living with a transmittable disease complicate the mental health needs of long-term survivors. Common issues include sex, relationships, isolation, depression, and loss of peer group. Emotional well-being hinges on establishing support systems, a stable sense of self, and a life with purpose and meaning.

Art therapy that invites exploration of life's purpose and deeper meaning in combination with issues of death and dying may provide emotional stability. Moon writes: "Art provides an avenue for self-expression that is desperately lacking and frantically longed for by those who suffer with existential emptiness. The studio space becomes a sacred stage upon which the artist enacts the drama of soul restoration" (Moon 1997, p.21). Sharing is important during the long-term survivor stage. Art therapy groups allow for the sharing of artworks, feelings, and emotions, while allowing for the sharing of resources such as lawyers for end-of-life issues (e.g., living wills). The second author has utilized the creation of prayer flags in working with long-term survivors at an HIV family camp. Individuals paint personal symbols onto fabric that reflect strengths they have obtained through their family, community, or religion. These individual pieces are then strung together as a collective whole for the group to embrace.

Conclusion

The HIV/AIDS epidemic continues to be a problem in the United States and throughout the world despite extraordinary medical advances in treatment. Over the decades of treatment in the United States, overt professional and community stigma and discrimination have largely been dissipated. For instance, many churches have AIDS ministries and many communities offer AIDS treatment services. In addition, Gay Men's Health Crisis has an annual AIDS Walk fundraiser engaging 40,000 walkers; prominent athletes and entertainers spotlight the need for an AIDS-free world.

Art therapy can ease the anxiety of a newly diagnosed person, provide insight into the mid-term client's medical adherence issues, and assist with decreased physical health and end-of-life issues for long-term survivors. Feelings of isolation and fear for PLWHA can be addressed and healing begun in the art therapy studio, particularly when members of the group have already disclosed their serostatus. Community support can be gained through the art therapist creating a safe environment where emotions can be expressed utilizing a wide range of materials and where reflection from the art therapist, other group members, and the client is valued.

References

Bayer, R. and Oppenheimer, G. M. (2006) "Pioneers in AIDS care: Reflections on the epidemic's early years." *The New England Journal of Medicine 355*, 2273–2275.

Bien, M. B. (2005) "Art therapy as emotional and spiritual medicine for Native Americans living with HIV/AIDS." *Journal of Psychoactive Drugs 37*, 3, 281–292.

Centers for Disease Control and Prevention (2007) *Mother-to-Child (Perinatal) HIV Transmission and Prevention* (CDC HIV/AIDS Fact Sheet). Available at www.cdc.gov/hiv/topics/perinatal/resources/factsheets/pdf/perinatal.pdf, accessed on June 17, 2013.

Centers for Disease Control and Prevention (2011) *HIV Among Women.* Available at www.cdc.gov/hiv/topics/women/index.htm, accessed on June 17, 2013.

Centers for Disease Control and Prevention (2012a) *HIV in the United States: At a Glance* (CDC HIV/AIDS Fact Sheet). Available at www.cdc.gov/hiv/resources/factsheets/us.htm, accessed on June 17, 2013.

Centers for Disease Control and Prevention (2012b) *HIV Surveillance in Urban and Nonurban Areas.* Available at www.cdc.gov/hiv/topics/surveillance/resources/slides/urban-nonurban/index.htm, accessed on June 17, 2013.

Cohen, M. A., Goforth, H., Lux, J. Z., Batista, S. M., et al. (2010) *Handbook of AIDS Psychiatry.* New York: Oxford University Press.

Havens, J. F., Mellins, C. A. and Pilowski, D. (1996) "Mental health issues in HIV-affected women and children." *International Review of Psychiatry 8*, 23, 217–225.

Hocoy, D. (2007) "Art Therapy as a Tool for Social Change: A Conceptual Model." In F. F. Kaplan (ed.) *Art Therapy and Social Action.* London: Jessica Kingsley Publishers.

Hrenko, K. D. (2005) "Remembering Camp Dreamcatcher: Art therapy with children whose lives have been touched by HIV/AIDS." *Art Therapy: The Journal of the American Art Therapy Association 22*, 39–43.

Miller, J. and Garran, A. M. (2008) *Racism in the United States: Implications for the Helping Professions.* Belmont: Thomson Brooks/Cole.

Moon, B. L. (1997) *Art and Soul: Reflections on An Artistic Psychology.* Springfield, IL: Charles C. Thomas.

Moon, B. L. (2010) *Art-Based Group Therapy: Theory and Practice.* Springfield, IL: Charles C. Thomas.

Murphy, D. A. (2008) "HIV-positive mothers' disclosure of their serostatus to their young children: A review." *Clinical Child Psychology and Psychiatry 13*, 1, 105–122.

Obermeyer, C. M., Baijal, P., and Pegurri, E. (2011) "Facilitating HIV disclosure across diverse settings: A review." *American Journal of Public Health 101*, 1011–1023.

Piccirillo, E. (1999a) "Beyond Words: The Art of Living with AIDS." In C. Malchiodi (ed.) *Medical Art Therapy with Adults.* London: Jessica Kingsley Publishers.

Piccirillo, E. (1999b) "Hide and Seek: The Art of Living with HIV/AIDS." In C. Malchiodi (ed.) *Medical Art Therapy with Children.* London: Jessica Kingsley Publishers.

Rao, D., Nainis, N., Williams, L., Langner, D., Eisin, A., and Paice, J. (2009) "Art therapy for relief of symptoms associated with HIV/AIDS." *AIDS Care 21*, 64–69.

The Office of History, National Institutes of Health (2010) *In Their Own Words: NIH Researchers Recall the Early Years of AIDS.* Bethesda: NIH.

Chapter 24

Cultural Considerations of Eating Disorders through Art Therapy

Michelle L. Dean

While biological, genetic, and psychological factors contribute to the etiology of eating disorders, the influence of cultural beliefs and attitudes has long been appreciated as a significant factor to the continuum of disordered eating behaviors (Hesse-Biber et al. 2006; Keel and Klump 2003; Miller and Pumariega 2001; Nasser 1997). "[C]ulture is a term used to define a group of people who share a system of meaning" (Markey 2004, p.142), which is not as easy to identify as race or ethnicity due to a multitude of complex factors both seen and unseen (e.g., customs and habits, beliefs and values). Culture is a pervasive part of human experience; cultural attitudes lay out a relational context, or fabric, into which influences, attitudes, beliefs, and actions are woven.

Cultural beliefs and attitudes are meant to assist in societal structure and relationships within an identifiable group of people, and are passed down to future generations through messages about ideals and values; they may be seen in food rituals, as well as traditions, gender roles, body size, and beauty, as well as personal, spiritual, and ascetic values. They often are carried via images such as views of family life, holidays, illustrations of religious scenes, imagery of myths and fables, and popular culture as seen in art, on television, in movie theaters, and, more insidiously, through advertising campaigns. With the expeditious development of a global society and rapid social change, exposure to different cultures and beliefs brings a wake of potential clashes. These cultural fissures may create a disavowal of social customs and beliefs that, in many regards, are considered to be the glue that holds communities and societies together. The resulting loss of stability in a cultural foundation, a loss of purpose, a loss of meaning, and a loss of personal value that leads in turn to a heightened need for control may contribute to the emergence of eating disorder behaviors (Forbes et al. 2012; Katsounari 2009; Soh et al. 2007). Cultural instabilities and clashes are often not perceptible, just as words may be understood differently, even by people of the same cultural background.

In practice, the nuances and complexities of language as well as cultural issues are often overlooked in treatment. Amplifying meaning and understanding through a visual and symbolic process such as art therapy may be beneficial for illuminating individual and cultural meaning with all of its subtlety. For example, creating a graphic image such as a representation of one's family as food and placing this depiction of a meal in a setting (Earley 1999a, 1999b) can provide opportunities to explore family dynamics and food preferences, and initiate dialogue regarding cultural beliefs as they pertain to food, family, and society. For example, as an art therapist, I have assisted clients in utilizing their artwork to explore attitudes about food, including the messages about food imparted by family, food rituals related to personal and societal practice, and messages portrayed in the media that may polarize "good/bad" foods; thus the artwork provides a metaphorical canvas for understanding cultural beliefs and individual meaning.

Food rituals may be seen in all cultures and may include when and how to eat, what foods are to be eaten or avoided, and how foods are prepared. This includes what foods are to be eaten at celebratory events and holidays (e.g., wedding cakes, Christmas cookies, Seder dinner) and customs around foods to assist with grief and loss (e.g., bread made with eggs). The foods in these circumstances hold symbolic purpose in the lives of a community. They offer comfort, symbolic significance, and value. Rituals that lose their cultural significance and take on idiosyncratic meaning are ripe for modification into eating disorder symptoms and behaviors. Art, and its symbolic nature, offers an outlet for understanding these meanings in treatment.

"[S]ymptoms of eating disorders may be recognized among diverse populations; the meaning of these symptoms, and their etiology, is culturally influenced" (Markey 2004, p.144). Although once thought of as affecting only Western, upper- and middle-class white women, gender, ethnic, and racial differences do not make one immune to eating disorder symptoms (Katsounari 2009). According to Hesse-Biber et al. (2006), this previous, erroneous belief may have led to "misdiagnosis as well as under-representation among people of different gender, racial, ethnic, sexuality and class backgrounds with eating disorders" (p.211). While diversity in research on eating disorders has increased in the last decade, it is still skewed toward white, middle-class women (Hesse-Biber et al. 2006). Research has shown that eating disorders and subclinical disordered eating (problematic eating issues that do not meet all of the criteria for a diagnosis as listed in the *Diagnostic Statistical Manual-IV-TR* [*DSM-IV-TR*] [American Psychiatric Association 2000] may be found in populations once considered impervious due to strong cultural values and limited Western media exposure. This includes African-Americans; Hispanics; people from the cultures of China, Cyprus, Fiji, and Singapore; South Americans, especially from Argentina and Brazil; and Eastern European women (Forbes et al. 2004; Forbes et al. 2012; Humphry and Ricciardelli 2003; Katsounari 2009; Shuttlesworth and Zotter 2011; Soh et al. 2007).

The emergence of eating disorder symptoms and their meanings are constantly in flux as they are influenced by a plethora of factors, many of which still are not fully understood due to their complexity, symbolic meaning, and evolution. Eating disorder behaviors may be conceptualized as a "system of signs and symbols with multiple meanings" (Brumberg 2000, p.7). "Rates of these disorders appear to vary among different racial/ethnic and national groups, and they also change across time as culture evolves" (Miller and Pumariega 2001, p.93). Like the disorder itself, it is a shape-shifting expression of symbolic conflict and issues that take shape as a physical voice through the overindulgence, purging, and/or restriction of food.

In the United States, 20 million women and 10 million men suffer from a clinically significant eating disorder, including anorexia nervosa, bulimia nervosa, binge-eating disorder (which has been included in the *DSM-V* (American Psychiatric Association 2013) as binge eating/purging type, 307.IF50.02), or an eating disorder not otherwise specified (EDNOS) (Wade, Keski-Rahkonen, and Hudson 2011). According to the National Eating Disorders Association (NEDA) (2012):

- there has been a rise in the incidence of anorexia in young women aged 15–19 in each decade since 1930 (Hoek and van Hoeken 2003)

- the incidence of bulimia in 10- to 39-year-old women tripled between 1988 and 1993 (Hoek and van Hoeken 2003)

- the prevalence of eating disorders is similar among non-Hispanic whites, Hispanics, African-Americans, and Asians in the United States, with the exception that anorexia nervosa is more common among non-Hispanic whites (Hudson et al. 2007; Wade et al. 2011).

For various reasons, including cultural differences, many cases are not reported, and thus statistics about this global epidemic are likely to be underreported. In addition, many individuals struggle with body dissatisfaction, which is a known contributor to the development of an eating disorder (Stice 2002). This dissatisfaction may be linked to cultural issues explained later in this chapter.

Symptoms such as those described in the *DSM-IV-TR* (American Psychiatric Association 2000) define static classifications of behavioral symptoms and fail to account for the polyvalent nature of such symptoms or the significance of such symptoms in a larger cultural context. This may be a limitation of the *DSM-IV-TR*, as it does not consider cultural context or the fluid, symbolic nature of the illness. It is not uncommon to find multiple manifestations of symptoms over a lifespan such as anorexia in adolescents, followed by binging and purging behaviors in adulthood, or any combination of these, reflecting a shifting of symptomatic response to changing life conditions. Eating disorder behaviors are best thought of as a symbolic continuum and are not necessarily confined to issues of eating; they also may manifest in other physical expressions such as somatic complaints and illnesses, while the origins may remain the same (Costello 2006; Finell 1997; McDougall 1989; Minuchin, Rosman, and Baker 1978; Ramos 2004; Sidoli 2000). Classifications such as those found in the *DSM-IV-TR* reduce the eating disorder symptoms to fixed unchangeable criteria which are stripped of any acknowledgment of its dynamic and symbolic process. This leaves cultural influences invisible and unacknowledged in many forms of treatment. Cultural considerations are extremely important in the prevention and treatment of eating disorders due to the idiosyncratic nuances and meanings of the symbolic symptoms as well as the staggering lethality and frequency of eating disorders. These disorders have the highest mortality rate of any psychiatric disorder (Arcelus et al. 2011), with a 5 to 20 percent death rate for anorexics. It is reported that only 30 to 40 percent fully recover (Costin 1997).

A Brief Historical Perspective

Throughout history, symptoms of eating disorders were apparent with varied regularity in a variety of manifestations but were not diagnosed before the 1870s, as there were no "cultural contexts [to] provide necessary information for the interpretation of the behavioral patterns as either conventional or problematic" (Markey 2004, p.149). For example, it was recorded that ancient Greeks and Egyptians participated in ritualized fasting for brief periods (Miller and Pumariega 2001), quite akin to many religious practices today that promote restriction as a means of spiritual piety and asceticism, a practice of extreme self-discipline. More extreme practices of prolonged self-starvation exist in various religions as a means of rejecting the hedonism and materialism of that time (Miller and Pumariega 2001).

Although eating disorder behaviors have been reported for thousands of years, anorexia nervosa did not appear as a diagnosis until the 1870s, as noted above, and originally did not include the fear of fatness (which was included in the 1930s), now an essential part of current diagnosis criteria. It was almost 100 years later, in the 1970s, that bulimia nervosa was introduced as a formal diagnosis. At the time, culture-dependent psychological hypotheses for causes of anorexia included pituitary atrophy and other biological factors (Miller and Pumariega 2001). Bruch (1973) was among the first to recognize that girls with anorexia struggled with a lack of autonomy and differentiation from their mothers. The control issues stemming from the individuation and separation processes of adolescence in eating-disordered girls are now widely accepted as a contributing factor to eating disorder symptoms. Current hypotheses about etiology tend to focus on the individual's limitations or circumstances, such as family dynamics (Minuchin et al. 1978), economic class, biological factors, endocrine systems (e.g., depression), or genetic make-up. The current focus on these factors reflects the current trends in emerging realms of technology, such as genetics and psychopharmacology, with limited regard to the complex cultural issues of our time.

Specific Social/Cultural Issues

Hesse-Biber et al. (2006) suggested shifting focus from a medical/psychological view to a sociocultural/economic perspective that examines messages that perpetuate derogatory values in gender roles as well as the mind/body dichotomy. While cultural attitudes may be seen in images portrayed in media that idealize thinness and other attributes, they are not the only sources of cultural information, nor are they a singular cause of disordered eating. Lee (1995) stated that "self-starvation has metaphorical significance that varies across cultures" (as cited in Markey 2004, p.150) and that the "fat phobia" is often absent in many Asian eating-disordered patients. It has been hypothesized that Western standards for beauty may be rejected by women living in non-Western cultures who have a strong ethnic identity. However, many studies have shown that non-Western immigrants moving to Western societies increase their dieting behaviors and are more prone to depression, body-image dissatisfaction, and eating disorders. This finding has included immigrant groups such as female Arab students attending universities in London (Nasser 1986), Kenyan Britons (Furnhan and Alibhai 1983), and Hispanic-American adolescent girls (Gowen et al. 1999). Literature indicates that being exposed to unattainable ideals through media and other commercial outlets cultivates a sense of dissatisfaction, a drive for thinness, increased consumerism, and consumptive/addictive behaviors (Bishop et al. 2012; Brumberg 1997; Kilbourne 2000; Slim Hopes 1995). A promise of aesthetic perfection is falsely given by purchasing products to "fix" perceived shortcomings, longings, losses, or disappointments. Brumberg (1997) wrote: "Although elevated body angst is a great boost to corporate profits, it saps the creativity of girls and threatens their mental and physical health" (p.xxiii).

It is thought that "[t]he experience and exposure to the *difference* between two cultures, rather than a particular culture itself, is also hypothesized to contribute to the aetiology [sic] of eating and body image disturbances" (Soh et al. 2006, p.58), and that it is a "culture-change syndrome of communities modernizing" (Miller and Pumariega 2001, p.103). Although the above authors were referring to immigrants or cultures whose community ideals have been influenced by another society's cultural values, it would be the cause of an assimilation clash as is so often the case when Western capitalism or consumer–corporate culture meets the individual's original culture. It may not be the industrialization itself that is so problematic, but rather the "parasitic" attitude that accompanies it. In other words, a cultural attitude latches onto the host culture (invaded by the new ideals) and is consumed by it or at least radically changed, altered, or ravished by the invading culture. Often working from the inside out, this most affects those with poor esteem, unstable cultural identities, and a host of other factors including trauma, childhood ruptures, and attachment issues. The external conflict of the differing cultures and internalization of the cultural conflict provide the pregnant constellation of factors necessary for the emergence of eating disorder symptoms. In other words, when there is a conflict of cultural ideals, those conflicts are experienced both internally within the individual and externally within the environment, creating conditions that are ripe for the emergence of eating disorder symptoms. "Women struggle with making sense of this incompatibility, as they are socialized into a society that often devalues women's roles and social positions, especially during adolescence" (Macsween 1993, as cited in Hesse-Biber et al. 2006, p.210). Being detached from traditional roles that are typically in direct relationship to the earth, such as the cycles of the seasons, food gathering, production or preparation, and childbearing and rearing, leaves a separation or split between oneself and the environment, a source from which many cultural values and traditions arise. From an ecopsychology viewpoint, as cultures become fragmented and communities are severed in order to seek economic development and opportunity, meaning and relational aspects of our environment, place, and culture are lost. Rudderless and vulnerable in these modern roles, women in particular are more prone to enact the conflict symbolically through the dismembered remnants of a central core of prior value: food for sustenance and well-being. As Jackson (1996) stated:

> In what has become dubbed a consumer society, however, maniacally gobbling the earth's resources and presenting us with ever-expanding sets of choices, new food-related anxieties have arisen. (p.8)

Thus, the material substance of food becomes a symbolically charged element in the psychic structure where it at once manifests psychic disturbance and masks its genuine nature. "This confusion of spirit and body is quite understandable in a culture where spirit and body [are] concretized in magnificent skyscrapers, where cathedrals have become museums for tourists…and nature is raped for any deplorable excuse" (Woodman 1980, p.100). The prevailing attitude toward one's environment, or the lack of relationship with the environment, thus creates a mirroring of the stance of possessiveness and manipulation of the body to the exploitation and manipulation of the earth and the minimization of feminine ideals.

The issues surrounding eating disorders are paradoxical. At the threshold of individuating and becoming an increasingly independent adolescent or young adult, an eating disorder robs one of the ability to truly nurture oneself in the most basic way, thus creating an external expression of an internal conflict. This increased conflict creates problematic dependence on parents and a shattering of parental hope that their daughter will be able to care for herself with greater self-sufficiency. Additionally, Brumberg (1997) and others have noted that, "at the very time when social changes have greatly increased available roles and opportunities for women, social expectations of female body types have become increasingly rigid and unrealistic" (cited in Forbes et al. 2004, p.331). Traditional roles for women have become devalued, and women no longer link their security to their ability to secure a mate and their role as a mother; instead, they are forced to compete with men for the same jobs and incomes. Further discussion of patriarchal roles and feminism is beyond the scope of this chapter but is significant as another layer of cultural consideration in the emergence of eating disorders.

The Symbolic Voice in Treatment: A Sociocultural Sensitive Method

According to Woodman (1980), "This one sided consciousness can be corrected by focusing attention on a creative approach to the body loving-understanding of its mechanism" (p.45). Likewise, "People who are in touch with the spontaneous archetypal creative/imaginative impulse are always in a state of creative ferment" (Taylor 1992, p.113). Art and image making carry the dichotomy of cultural bias and conflicts simultaneously. Art images create distance while also providing opportunities for relatedness. Thus, this mirroring in the image becomes the individual's response to a cultural attitude or pattern and can be related to and engaged in a therapeutic dialogue (Dallett 2008; Woodman 1980). In art therapy, the image may be the carrier of new meaning and offer opportunities for reintegration of splits or voids that once were filled by actions of the eating disorder. According to Taylor (1992), a "relationship with our imaginative life is an absolutely crucial part of any authentic and effective individual or collective liberation" (p.113).

Symptoms are symbolic and cannot therefore be extracted from their context without losing meaning; so too the therapeutic framework must include the finding of meaning. A therapeutic approach that is able to work with the complex symbolism of the eating disorder offers an opportunity for relatedness and meaning making which is essential for recovery. It is the "process of finding meaning, coherence and wholeness in relationship" (Goodwin 2007, p.13) that is critical in stabilizing cultural values and conflicts. Meaning "permeates the creative cosmos that we know" (Goodwin 2007, p.13). Treatment, which emphasizes the relational and symbolic aspects of expression in its receptive, compassionate, and mirroring abilities, supports the integration and well-being that manifest eating disorders in a sociocultural sensitive means. Research and clinical observation support the use of "modified psychotherapy," such as art psychotherapy, to improve verbalization and symbolic expression, which often are impaired due to damaging early childhood experiences that may include invasive cultural values such as devaluing the role of motherhood and attachment, attentiveness to emotional receptivity, and the importance of food production and preparation (Bruch 1973; Dean 2006a, 2006b, 2008; Earley 1999a, 1999b; Makin 2000; Matto 1997; Milia 2000; van der Kolk, Perry, and Herman 1991). With an eating disorder, creative development becomes stilled, starved, and arrested. By reengaging in a creative process, such as art therapy, there is an opportunity to amplify the emergent nature of the image that holds the symbolic content of the individual and the culture in a polyvalent way.

Art Therapy: A Relational Treatment

When working within an art therapy framework with patients with an eating disorder, the ability to address the emergent individual content and cultural context of the disorder becomes visible simultaneously through the art image and the process of the art therapy. The art therapist is able to amplify associations to the created imagery in order to offer opportunities of awareness and meaning to the symptoms, which often lie beyond verbal recognition.

For example, in the drawing/collage that Maya (a pseudonym) created during an art therapy session (Figure 24.1), she was able to recognize, through her associations, that the encoded images were relevant and revealed a relational pattern with her hovering mother that was destructive. The directive, which is explained in Appendix H (Dean 2006a, 2006b; Earley 1999a, 1999b), encourages the use of abstract imagery and time limitations in order to reveal latent content related to body image and the relationship between self and environment or others. After completing the six images, she was asked to create a single image out of two of the pages by ripping one into the shape of her body and sticking it onto the second one.

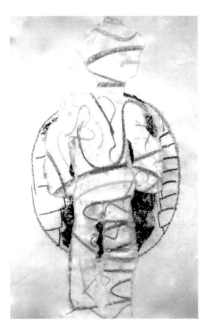

Figure 24.1 In through the back door

Illustrated in the color insert

Maya's initial response was one of doubt that the seemingly random images she created could relate to issues pertaining to the development of her eating disorder. As she spoke of the marks that looked like chaos that occupied her body, she thought it remarkable that the heart shape appeared "right where my heart would be." She also gave associations about feeling bound and "tied up" as she pointed to the areas of her abdomen and arms. She said that when she was creating the background she thought of the city streets where she lived and the cold, dark night skies. After turning the page and gazing at it again, she said it looked like "a big mouth getting ready to chomp me down." This association then was followed quickly by much discussion about how she felt overwhelmed and depressed because of her mother's hovering and her mother's perceived desire to consume her every move. Discussions about her mother's "Old World" conservative, Jewish expectations for her were in conflict with the things she wanted for herself, including the coursework she wished to pursue in college and her eventual career. Maya was eventually able to see that she had been restricting food as an unconscious way of "getting back" at her mother. Although this was only one of many sessions in a long recovery from her eating disorder, it was helpful in illuminating how the image carries much of the emergent symbolic material, about both the self and one's cultural environment—information that would otherwise be difficult to reach through verbal therapy alone.

Conclusion

Cultural factors, including values of consumerism and assimilation clashes, are cited among many significant contributing factors to eating disorder behaviors. Those who are particularly vulnerable to eating disorders are those without solidified and stable cultural identities. The cultural foundation of human experience and its valuing or devaluing forces often are unseen in both their communal and divisive nature. Utilizing art and symbolic imagery within a therapeutic framework allows the symbolic material of cultural values and potential ruptures to emerge in a visible and relatable entity. For art psychotherapists, patients, and the collective culture this means "cultivating new skills and enlarging our scientific horizons so that there is room for the creativity that is a part of our everyday experience of living" (Goodwin 2007, p.31). Bringing art and images into the therapeutic process provides an experience and creates the necessary therapeutic framework large enough to conceptualize the symbolic manifestations of a culture. This simultaneously provides an adequate therapeutic forum for reflection and relatedness to the inexhaustible complexities associated with humanity and our relationship to food.

References

American Psychiatric Association (2000) *Diagnostic and Statistical Manual of Mental Disorders, Fourth Edition, Text Revision.* Washington, DC: American Psychiatric Association.

American Psychiatric Association (2013) *Diagnostic and Statistical Manual of Mental Disorders, Fifth Edition.* Washington, DC: American Psychiatric Association.

Arcelus, J., Mitchell, A. J., Wales, J., and Nielsen, S. (2011) "Mortality rates in patients with anorexia nervosa and other eating disorders." *Archives of General Psychiatry 68*, 7, 724–731.

Bishop, E., Jr., Talucci, L., Dean, M. L., Isis, P., and Bechtel, A. (2012) "Recognition and treatment of eating disorders: Art therapy's impact on body image and healthy eating." The American Art Therapy Association Conference, Savannah, GA.

Bruch, H. (1973) *Eating Disorders: Obesity, Anorexia Nervosa and the Person Within.* New York: HarperCollins.

Brumberg, J. J. (1997) *The Body Project: An Intimate History of American Girls.* New York: Vintage Books.

Brumberg, J. J. (2000) *Fasting Girls: The History of Anorexia Nervosa.* New York: Vintage Books.

Costello, M. S. (2006) *Imagination, Illness and Injury: Jungian Psychology and the Somatic Dimensions of Perception.* London: Routledge.

Costin, C. (1997) *The Eating Disorder Sourcebook: A Comprehensive Guide to the Causes, Treatments, and Preventions of Eating Disorders.* Los Angeles: Lowell House.

Dallett, J. O. (2008) *Listening to the Rhino: Violence and Healing in a Scientific Age.* New York: Aequiteas Book from Pleasure Boat Studio: A Literary Press.

Dean, M. L. (2006a) "Creative destruction: Art based interventions with eating disordered clients who self-injure." The 16th Renfrew Center Conference, Philadelphia, PA.

Dean, M. L. (2006b) "Preserving the self: Art psychotherapy applications with eating disordered clients who self-injure." The American Art Therapy Association Conference, New Orleans, LA.

Dean, M. L. (2008) "Preserving the Self: Treating Eating Disordered Individuals Who Self-Injure with Art Therapy." In S. Brooke (ed.) *Creative Arts Therapies with Patients Who Have Eating Disorders.* New York: Charles C. Thomas.

Earley, M. L. (1999a) "Art therapy: Body image, media and art." The American Art Therapy Association Conference, Orlando, FL.

Earley, M. L. (1999b) "Art therapy with eating disordered clients." The Renfrew Center Conference, Philadelphia, PA.

Finell, J. S. (ed.) (1997) *Mind-Body Problems: Psychotherapy with Psychosomatic Disorders.* Northvale: Jason Aronson.

Forbes, G. B., Doroszewicz, K., Card, K., and Adams-Curtis, L. (2004) "Association of the thin ideal, ambivalent sexism, and self-esteem with body acceptance and the preferred body size of college women in Poland and the United States." *Sex Roles 50*, 5/6, 331–345.

Forbes, B. G., Jung, J., Vaamonde, J. D., Omar, A., Paris, L., and Formiga, N. S. (2012) "Body dissatisfaction and disordered eating in three cultures: Argentina, Brazil, and the U.S." *Sex Roles 66*, 677–694.

Furnham, A. C. and Alibhai, N. (1983) "Cross-cultural differences in the perception of female body shape." *Psychological Medicine 13*, 829–837.

Goodwin, B. (2007) *Nature's Due: Healing Our Fragmented Culture.* Edinburgh: Floris Books.

Gowen, L. K., Hayward, C., Killen, J. D., Robinson, T. N., and Taylor, C. B. (1999) "Acculturation and eating disorder symptoms in adolescent girls." *Journal of Research on Adolescence 9*, 67–83.

Hesse-Biber, S., Leavy, P., Quinn, C. E., and Zoino, J. (2006) "The mass marketing of disordered eating and eating disorders: The social psychology of women, thinness, and culture." *Women's Studies International Forum 29*, 208–224.

Hoek, H. W. and van Hoeken, D. (2003) "Review of the prevalence and incidence of eating disorders." *International Journal of Eating Disorders 3*, 4, 383–396.

Hudson, J. I., Hiripi, E., Pope, H. G. Jr., and Kessler, R. C. (2007) "The prevalence and correlates of eating disorders in the National Comorbidity Survey replication." *Biological Psychiatry 61*, 348–358.

Humphry, T. A. and Ricciardelli, L. A. (2003) "The development of eating pathology in Chinese-Australian women: Acculturation versus culture clash." *International Journal of Eating Disorders 35*, 579–588.

Jackson, E. (1996) *Food and Transformation: Imagery and Symbolism of Eating.* Toronto: Inner City Books.

Katsounari, I. (2009) "Self-esteem, depression and eating disordered attitude: A cross cultural comparison between Cypriot and British young women." *European Eating Disorders Review 17*, 455–461.

Keel, P. K. and Klump, K. L. (2003) "Are eating disorders culture-bound syndromes? Implications for conceptualizing their etiology." *American Psychological Association, Psychological Bulletin 129*, 5, 747–769.

Kilbourne, J. (2000) *Can't Buy My Love: How Advertising Changes the Way We Think and Feel.* New York: Simon and Schuster.

Makin, S. (2000) *More Than Just a Meal: The Art of Eating Disorders.* London: Jessica Kingsley Publishers.

Markey, C. N. (2004) "Culture and the development of eating disorders: A tripartite model." *Eating Disorders 12*, 139–156.

Matto, H. (1997) "An integrative approach to the treatment of women with eating disorders." *The Arts in Psychotherapy 24*, 4, 347–354.

McDougall, J. (1989) *Theaters of the Body: A Psychoanalytic Approach to Psychosomatic Illness.* New York: W. W. Norton and Company.

Milia, D. (2000) *Self-Mutilation and Art Therapy: Violent Creation.* London: Jessica Kingsley Publishers.

Miller, M. N. and Pumariega, A. J. (2001) "Culture and eating disorders: A historical and cross-cultural review." *Psychiatry 64*, 2, 93–110.

Minuchin, S., Rosman, B. L., and Baker, L. (1978) *Psychosomatic Families: Anorexia Nervosa in Context.* Cambridge, MA: Harvard University Press.

Nasser, M. (1986) "Comparative study of the prevalence of abnormal eating attitudes among Arab female students of both London and Cairo universities." *Psychological Medicine 16*, 621–625.

Nasser, M. (1997) *Culture and Weight Consciousness.* London: Routledge.

National Eating Disorders Association (NEDA) (2012) *Facts on Eating Disorders.* New York: NEDA.

Ramos, D. G. (2004) *The Psyche of the Body: A Jungian Approach to Psychosomatics.* New York: Brunner-Routledge.

Shuttlesworth, M. E. and Zotter, D. (2011) "Disordered eating in African American and Caucasian women: The role of ethnic identity." *Journal of Black Studies 42*, 6, 906–922.

Sidoli, M. (2000) *When the Body Speaks: The Archetypes in the Body.* London: Routledge.

Slim Hopes (1995) Directed by J. Kilboune; executive producer Sut Jhally. Media Education Foundation [VHS].

Soh, N., Surgenor, L. J., Touyz, S., and Walter, G. (2007) "Eating disorders across two cultures: Does the expression of psychological control vary?" *Australian and New Zealand Journal of Psychiatry 41*, 357–358.

Stice, E. (2002) "Risk and maintenance factors for eating pathology: A meta-analytic review." *Psychological Bulletin 128*, 825–848.

Taylor, J. (1992) *Where People Fly and Water Runs Uphill: Using Dreams to Tap the Wisdom of the Unconscious.* New York: Warner Books.

van der Kolk, B. A., Perry, J. C., and Herman, J. L. (1991) "Childhood origins of self-destructive behavior." *American Journal of Psychiatry 148*, 1665–1671.

Wade, T. D., Keski-Rahkonen, A., and Hudson, J. (2011) "Epidemiology of Eating Disorders." In M. Tsuang and M. Tohen (eds) *Textbook in Psychiatric Epidemiology, Third Edition.* New York: Wiley.

Woodman, M. (1980) *The Owl was a Baker's Daughter: Obesity, Anorexia Nervosa and the Repressed Feminine.* Toronto: Inner City Books.

Resources

Further Reading

Bayles, D. and Orland, T. (1993) *Art and Fear: Observations on the Perils (and Rewards) of Art Making.* St. Paul, MN: The Image Continuum Press.

Edinger, E. (1994) *The Anatomy of the Psyche: Alchemical Symbolism in Psychotherapy.* Chicago, IL: Open Court.

Littlewood, R. (2004) "Commentary: Globalization, culture, body image, and eating disorders." *Culture, Medicine and Psychiatry 28*, 597–602.

Qualls-Corbett, N. (1988) *The Sacred Prostitute: Eternal Aspect of the Feminine.* Toronto: Inner City Books.

Smolak, L. (2011) "Body Image Development in Childhood." In T. Cash and L. Smolak (eds) *Body Image: A Handbook of Science, Practice, and Prevention, Second Edition.* New York: Guilford.

Streigel-Moore, R. H. and Franko, D. L. (2003) "Epidemiology of binge eating disorder." *International Journal of Eating Disorders 34*, S19–S29.

Wilfley, D. E. and Rodin, J. (1995) "Cultural Influences on Eating Disorders." In K. D. Brownell and C. G. Fairburn (eds) *Eating Disorders and Obesity: A Comprehensive Handbook.* New York: Guilford Press.

Part VI

Cultural Influences in Community-Based Art Therapy

Chapter 25

Art Therapy in Private Practice
What Does It Take?

Jennie Kristel and Paula Howie

Many art therapists have considered providing services to private clients at some time during their career. In part, this is due to the appeal of working for oneself and to the freedom that this type of work promises. Also, if one is unable to find a suitable art therapy position, private practice may be seen as a viable alternative.

The Art Therapy Credentials Board (ATCB 2007) requires that independent practitioners of art therapy maintain their registration (ATR) with the ATCB, which takes several years of full-time, supervised work experience to obtain. In addition to registration, prior to setting up a private practice one must have at least two full years of full-time practice or 3000 hours of paid clinical art therapy experience. The amount of experience required before setting up an independent practice makes this an untenable option for a recent graduate. Despite these substantial requirements, the American Art Therapy Association (AATA) membership survey in 2009 found that approximately 18 percent, around one-fifth of members, are in private practice either as full- or part-time employees and that "private practice, 'other' settings, outpatient mental health clinics, and psychiatric hospitals are among the top four primary work settings" (Elkins and Deaver 2010, p.141).

Private practitioners are responsible for the delivery of services to clients where the client pays the therapist directly or through insurance for art therapy services rendered. Due to the importance of providing this type of intervention for clients and the number of art therapists who work in it, the authors explore private practice by examining two unique work settings and discussing what is entailed in setting up a practice, in complying with ethics or regulatory standards, and in providing culturally competent services.

Jennie has a private practice in collaboration with one other person in a relatively small community of 43,000 people where she provides expressive therapy, psychotherapy, shamanic healing (her partner is a Cherokee Elder), and energy work. She and her partner work with a variety of populations such as returning veterans, couples, and families and with a wide range of diagnoses, including posttraumatic stress disorder (PTSD). Expressive therapy services are usually sought as a creative counterbalance to the restrictions that impede an individual from being able to move through his/her life with ease, with a sense of creativity, and with an inner freedom. The expressive arts have become more accepted as a therapeutic technique as therapists have proven the validity of using such alternative forms of therapy. Some therapists undertake home visits as a way to support a client who may be unable to come to the office for one reason or another.

Jennie's office is located in the back of the building complex sufficiently away from other offices and provides a strong sound barrier (Figure 25.1). It is approximately 950 square feet, allowing for movement and drama therapies to be provided. There is an art room and an area with a couch and chairs, which can also be a quiet meditation area. Having a space that is large enough for movement and drama work was a big consideration when securing space, as was having a space to create art and to be a little messy. On an average day in the life of an expressive therapies group, there might be one person who is using movement, another person who is playing music, a third sitting on the couch writing a story, and two others in the art space painting. Having a space that allows for this level of flexibility is supportive in allowing individuals to explore and create individually as well as together. In this manner, they receive support not just from the therapist, but from one another as well. A space such as this is conducive to collaborative networking partnerships within the community. Therapists working or contracting with outside agencies have more flexibility to do so either by running groups or seeing individual clients. It can take some experimentation to find what physical setting works best for each practitioner.

Figure 25.1 Jennie's office space

Paula has a more traditional art therapy practice in a large, urban area with a population of around 4.5 million people. She has a relatively small room (around 180 square feet) in a high-rise office suite in which three psychologists and two psychiatrists also have offices (Figures 25.2). This suite has a shared waiting room. Paula is a licensed counselor (LPC) in the states of DC and VA. In the aforementioned AATA survey (2009), 32.9 percent (about a third) of respondents were licensed as Professional Counselors (LPC), making this the license most frequently held by art therapists. Paula focuses as an art therapist and does not routinely offer music or movement aspects to therapy, since in her urban area there are specialists available for referral. In her work with children, adults, couples, and families, she utilizes the healing properties of the visual arts. She specializes in working with trauma and PTSD. Materials include visual arts supplies such as papers, markers, pencils, paints, collage supplies, model magic, self-hardening clay, sand trays and figures, and some craft materials.

Figure 25.2 Paula's office space

As mentioned above, a compelling reason to consider private practice is the flexibility and autonomy, which allows one to set one's own hours. The therapist is able to decide where and how long sessions may be, making evening and weekend work possible. Indeed, these may be the most advantageous times for clients if they are employed during weekdays. Also, evenings are good times to see children who are in school during the day.

As art therapists, we create and offer art therapy in unique ways based on who we are and what our focus is. Both authors can increase sessions to 1.5 hours in length to allow for the creative aspects of art therapy to take place or to work on a trauma story. Jennie works internationally and often uses Skype in order to be able to have face-to-face sessions with clients continents away. Skyping and other technological advances have made this kind of work more feasible, but this does need to be done with great care and consideration. The ethics concerning the use of this kind of communication are being developed as technology becomes more widely used in therapy.

Private practice allows the practitioner to set his/her own ways of working and to develop an individual style that is not framed by agency regulations. Developing a private practice allows you to create the space you need in which to work (Bollas and Sundelson 1995).

How an office is set up also supports the identity that is projected to the community. An office space that accommodates children would be different from one that primarily serves adults. The materials and interventions provided must be appropriate for the ages and developmental levels of those we treat. The autonomy of private practice has the capacity to allow for expansion as we grow as therapists. Having so much autonomy means that one takes on many more responsibilities concerning marketing, networking, and supervision. The practitioner will have to pay independently for clinical supervision and to be able to maintain any regulatory licensing and association fees (Beigel and Earle 1990).

One of the drawbacks of private practice may be the lack of a team to consult with and the loneliness this can sometimes engender. It may be advantageous to have a supervisor or peer group with whom to discuss clients that are of concern. The private practitioner must handle appointments, billing, and insurance issues. Many art therapy practitioners do not take insurance due to the time required to fill out the paperwork in order to obtain reimbursement.

Maintaining a clear code of ethics is important for any therapist. Those who live in a relatively small community have to be both flexible and clear about their boundaries. This is in part due to the possibility of seeing clients in another setting such as at church or at a local gym. Making it clear in a client contract what will happen if one is seen outside the office helps define the boundaries necessary between the client and therapist. For instance, in the case of meeting in a public space, mirroring the response of the client, which gives the client the ability to greet or not greet as they feel comfortable, is one approach. Another aspect of setting clear boundaries is whether or not to touch a client. If the therapist intends to use touch as a therapeutic intervention, this needs to be specified in the intake forms that a client signs.

Many expressive therapists and therapists who follow a more person-centered approach, based on the work of Carl Rogers, may use touch therapeutically in the form of a hand on a shoulder, or a hug (Rogers 1993). Touch has been used over many centuries in healing practices, shamanic and religious ceremonies, and rituals. Over the last few years, the role of touch has increased in psychotherapy, as research has pointed in the direction that appropriate touch is vital to our physical and emotional well-being (Bonitz 2008). When doing energy work, touch will need to be discussed and its therapeutic underpinnings reinforced throughout the therapy work. Clients often need to be reminded that they are in control and have the right to say no at any given time, so each client can make a choice. Clarity and transparency are paramount in this process. In a traditional psychotherapy practice, one may also be confronted with whether or not to touch a client. Paula often has children who hug her as they are leaving sessions or adults who request a hug after processing a particularly difficult trauma. This is always handled on a case-by-case basis, keeping in mind the therapeutic rationale for using touch. There are many instances in which touch is not appropriate. When a client is experiencing deep emotion, the act of putting one's hands on the client's shoulders can be grounding and centering, but it can also potentially retraumatize a client who has had negative experiences of being touched in the past. Before touching a client in this situation, the therapist should ask and say what they are going to do ("Would it be all right to put my hands on your shoulders to help ground you?"). Oftentimes, grounding can be accomplished without touch by use of a "grounding stone," by referring the client to his/her safe place picture, or by having the person notice what is above their line of vision, at their line of vision, and below their line of vision.

Other ethical issues that must be considered by the private practitioner are documenting, confidentiality, where the art is stored, who stores the art, and what happens with the art after the therapy is complete. The AATA (2011) recommends keeping the art in storage for seven years. This may entail finding a suitable space for long-term storage of artwork. There are also ethical issues related to documenting interactions which are unique to art therapy such as taking photographs and having client art exhibits. Many of these are covered in the AATA Ethical Principles for Art Therapists (AATA 2011) or in the ATCB Code of Professional Practice (ATCB 2007). As a rule, in private practice, artwork should be given the same due consideration, concern for confidentiality, and protection as other forms of communication (Malchiodi 2012).

Cultural Considerations in Private Practice

The arts have been used for centuries in healing ceremonies where whole communities come together to support healing for one another. Cultural considerations with private practice include one's self-awareness and self-knowledge, level of skill, and therapeutic framework in order for the practitioner to make culturally appropriate decisions about treatment (Wells 2005). It is important that art therapists make a special effort to take advantage of opportunities that support their growth around the cultural needs of their community and their practice. Being culturally aware means offering multicultural materials and framing conversations in such a way as to allow for cultural diversity to exist within the relationship. Part of this can be collecting art materials and musical instruments from around the world that add a variety of texture and sound and heighten the level of creativity within the art process. It is necessary to have available art and collage materials that represent a variety of cultures, ethnicity, abilities, and races. This gives clients choices about how to frame a particular exercise and can deepen the understanding and connections made by clients during therapy.

Art therapists come with their own set of biases and cultural norms and may unintentionally miss important cues that stem from cultural differences. If therapists "do not integrate awareness of diversity factors into their work they may be violating their clients' cultural integrity and infringing on basic human rights" (Moon 2006, p.203). This can be avoided when the art therapist understands that the client's story is in some respects framed by his or her culture. It is the understanding of this "bigger story" that becomes the basis of culturally sensitive therapy. In many cultures, psychotherapy can bring up issues of shame. There are often misperceptions around psychotherapy that can lead to a stigma— of the individual or even the whole family (Howie et al. 2002). Any negative implications of therapy have to be illuminated, understood, and worked through. Talwar, Iyer, and Doby-Copeland (2004) discuss the importance of the therapist understanding privilege and racial attitudes on a visceral level so as not to be a color-blind therapist. This must occur in the clinical situation to allow the therapist and the client to encounter each other in such a way that authentic interaction and deep awareness are possible. For instance, one of the authors who is White was working with a Black woman, helping her to process past trauma. While speaking of her abuse, the woman also spoke of how her father was treated unfairly in the southern town in which she grew up. No one had ever used "mister" in front of her father when speaking to him; he was simply called by his last name. The therapist was taken aback by this and other issues the client brought up about how she and her family couldn't use the public park even though her father had paid taxes. This material helped the therapist, whose father was called "mister" and who was able to use the parks, to understand the pervasive manner in which prejudice had permeated the client's earliest memories and how out of touch the therapist was with her own privileged upbringing. Brown (2009), when speaking of working with members of other cultures, asserts: "I must also know that I have benefited from the unearned privileges associated with my phenotype of European-appearing skin and they, in turn, have experienced undeserved social disadvantage associated with their phenotype with darker skin than mine" (p.42).

Conclusion

The art therapy private practitioner has the capacity to allow clients to explore core issues in a way that can honor their traditions and can acknowledge the influence of the therapist's and client's cultures. Culture has many aspects to it. It can encompass one's gender, color, country of origin, ethnicity, socioeconomic status, disability, and sexual preference. It is the willingness of the therapist to ask questions and her ability to assess appropriately based on her understanding of the client's cultural norms that allows the highest standards of art therapy services. Asking questions is a core way for each one of us to understand the symbols, metaphors, and references that come up in the artwork. Listening with sensitivity and understanding the importance of one's culture can guide interventions, improve effectiveness, and assist empathic interventions with our clients.

References

American Art Therapy Association (2009) *Membership Survey.* Washington, DC: American Art Therapy Association.

American Art Therapy Association (2011) *Ethical Principles for Art Therapists.* Washington, DC: American Art Therapy Association.

Art Therapy Credentials Board (2007) *Code of Professional Practice.* Greensboro: Art Therapy Credentials Board.

Beigel, J. and Earle, R. (1990) *Successful Private Practice in the 1990s: A New Guide for the Mental Health Professional.* New York: Brunner/Mazel.

Bollas, C. and Sundelson, D. (1995) *The New Informants: The Betrayal of Confidentiality in Psychoanalysis and Psychotherapy.* New York: Jason Aronson.

Bonitz, V. (2008) "Use of physical touch in the 'talking cure': A journey to the outskirts of psychotherapy." *Psychotherapy: Theory, Research, Practice, Training 45,* 3, 391–404.

Brown, L. (2009) *Cultural Competence in Trauma Therapy: Beyond the Flashback, Second Edition.* Washington, DC: American Psychological Association.

Elkins, D. and Deaver, S. (2010) "2009 Membership Survey Report." *Art Therapy: Journal of the American Art Therapy Association 27,* 3, 141–147.

Howie, P., Gantt, L., Rubin, J., Williams, K., and Wilson, L. (2002) "Therapeutic Boundaries: Common ground, Changing Perspectives." Panel at the 33rd American Art Therapy Association Conference, Washington, DC.

Malchiodi, C. (2012) *Handbook of Art Therapy.* New York: Guilford Press.

Moon, B. (2006) *Ethical Issues in Art Therapy.* New York: Charles Thomas.

Rogers, N. (1993) *The Creative Connection.* Palo Alto: Science and Behavior Books.

Talwar, S., Iyer, J., and Doby-Copeland, C. (2004) "The invisible veil: Changing paradigms in the art therapy profession." *Art Therapy: Journal of the American Art Therapy Association 21,* 1, 44–48.

Wells, S. A. (2005) "An Ethic of Diversity." In R. Purtilo, G. Jensen, and C. Royeen (eds) *Educating for Moral Action: A Sourcebook in Health and Rehabilitation Ethics.* Philadelphia: Davis Books.

Chapter 26

The Community Art Studio
Creating a Space of Solidarity and Inclusion

Catherine Hyland Moon and Valery Shuman

Introduction

The first iteration of ArtWorks was an open art studio established in 2007 in the Uptown neighborhood of Chicago, a gradually gentrifying area of the city characterized by racial, ethnic, and class diversity. Beginning in the 1960s, the Uptown neighborhood, because of its inexpensive lodging, became a magnet for newly deinstitutionalized mental hospital patients. As a result, a network of social service organizations developed to meet the needs of those who required services. This heavy concentration of social service agencies has persisted, despite a sustained increase over time in the number of affluent people moving into the neighborhood (Henderson 2007; "Uptown" 2005). A culture of NIMBYism (not in my backyard-ism) has grown, with some well-to-do neighbors expressing discomfort about living in the same area as a large contingent of people who are homeless or have mental illness and/or substance use disorders (Marx and Jackson 2009).

In response to this divide, we conceived of ArtWorks, a place where people with and without social stigmas could come together to create art, culture, and community, and where neighbors with vastly different social positions could get to know one another. Everyone was welcome in the community art space; there were no referrals, intake procedures, or criteria for participation.

The first iteration of ArtWorks closed its doors after just a year and a half, due to state health care funding cuts, but the project has not ended. During the life of the ArtWorks Uptown studio, we learned from our challenges and successes. We have applied that knowledge to the development of ArtWorks Edgewater in Chicago, and are discussing plans for opening additional studios in the city. This chapter reflects our experiences at the first ArtWorks site, where we developed the project's mission, values, and corresponding cultural activities, as well as its practical operations, ethical guidelines, and collective practices.

Theoretical Underpinnings

There have been multiple theoretical and practice models—including critical psychology, disability studies, harm reduction, and socially engaged art and art therapy practices—that have influenced ArtWorks' ongoing development. Before discussing the various facets of ArtWorks, each of these interlocking foundational strands is briefly discussed.

Critical psychology, which emerged from liberation and feminist psychologies and from antiracist critiques of psychology (Austin and Prilleltensky 2001), is focused on the examination of the personal as it is embedded in larger social structures, and aimed at bringing to light inequities of power. Its practitioners challenge widely accepted psychological diagnoses and interventions that mistakenly identify problems as purely or primarily individual in nature, reinforce imbalances of power, perpetuate the stigma of mental illness, and contribute to unjust social conditions (Fox and Prilleltensky 1997; Hare-Mustin and Marecek 2001).

At ArtWorks, we engaged in healthy skepticism regarding the hegemony of neuroscience as an explanation for emotional distress, and the predominance of pharmaceutical solutions for treating psychiatric conditions. We attached greater emphasis to social factors, such as unemployment, inadequate housing, poverty, stigma, and social isolation. We also promoted recognition of values, ideas, and perspectives of people whose versions of reality have rarely been acknowledged or given legitimacy (Sampson 2000).

Disability studies, an interdisciplinary field that challenges prevailing deficit models of disability and examines the social, cultural, medical, ethical, and policy implications of how disability is constructed and functions in society, also informed our work. Disability scholars and activists contest the idea that disability is primarily a medical issue and instead view it as a social construction imposed on individuals with impairments, resulting in their exclusion from full participation in society (Corker and Shakespeare 2002; Lewis 2006; Titchkosky 2002). This is not to deny that there are biochemical and biophysical aspects of a disability such as mental illness, but these experiences of the body are complicated by prejudice, discrimination, sexism, racism, homophobia, classism, marginalization, and other manifestations of social inequalities (Nicki 2001).

Harm reduction, initially a public health response to the HIV and Hepatitis C crises, has provided a theoretical and practical platform for ArtWorks' stance of radical acceptance of all people. A particularly useful concept put forth by harm reduction experts Denning and Little (2012) is the exploration of safety versus comfort. Community discomfort is often framed as a safety issue and people are banned from spaces due to their differences in appearance or behavior, or due to fears around their use of alcohol or other drugs. This concept of safety versus comfort provides a framework for exploring one's reactions and responses to other people, particularly those reactions influenced by societal attitudes or formative personal experiences. Such a framework also can help community members change their perspectives and expectations of the community pariah; they may come to understand and even appreciate the adaptive nature of unorthodox behaviors

(Denning and Little 2012). "Reintegration is emphasized over social exclusion… The philosophy of harm reduction encourages us to reach those outside of the circle and welcome them back in" (Aboriginal Peer Project, as cited in Centre for Addiction and Mental Health n.d., para. 21).

Socially engaged art—also known as relational, participatory, dialogic, littoral, community, new genre public, social practice, or interventionist art—is characterized by participation, sociality, critical dialogue, and civic and political engagement (Thompson 2012). Bourriaud (2002) defines relational art as "a set of artistic practices which take as their theoretical and practical point of departure the whole of human relations and their social context, rather than an independent and private space" (p.113). Of particular influence on the development of ArtWorks have been the conceptions of the artist as social change agent, of participants as our collaborators in personal and social transformation (Kester 2004), and of ArtWorks itself—not just the objects we make—as a product of our collective creativity (Moon 2010).

While the body of literature on socially engaged art therapy has been slow to develop, recent books devoted to social action (Kaplan 2007) and social change (Levine and Levine 2011) in art therapy indicate growing interest in the topic. We have been most influenced by the work of art therapist Janis Timm-Bottos (1995, 2001, 2006, 2011a, 2011b), who has developed a number of free community art studios in the United States and Canada. Her commitment to social inclusion and collaborative community building has directly inspired and informed the development of ArtWorks.

Organizational Structure

ArtWorks was created under the umbrella of a nonprofit social service organization, affording us 501(c)3 status and administrative support. This arrangement held both advantages and disadvantages. We had access to staff whose sole purpose was researching and applying for grant opportunities, but were limited in some of the grants we could apply for due to the size of the organization and potential internal competition for funding. We had administrative support for budget and IT management, as well as for legal issues, but had to negotiate approval for many of our decisions. For example, the organization was focused on creating a sustainable business model, but we were devoted to maintaining accessibility to people with low incomes by offering free or minimally priced programming. Another example was the long, laborious process of deciding on a logo for the project. Multiple levels of staff at the organization had to weigh in on and approve the logo design, as ours was the most visible organizational project within the local area. We also benefited from the organization's social and business networks, but sometimes were met with suspicion or skepticism by local residents because we were identified with a social service organization.

Mission, Values, and Corresponding Cultural Activities

The purpose and aims of ArtWorks are captured in its mission statement:

> ArtWorks is dedicated to serving as a bridge between diverse groups of people. Through the arts and cultural exchange, we work toward personal empowerment and meaningful social change. Our aim is to foster the development of understanding and compassion between all members of the community, including those marginalized due to mental, physical, or social differences. (ArtWorks, n.d., para. 2)

The core values coming out of this mission statement are that (1) democratic negotiation of public space and a shared sense of belonging occur when the perspective of every member of the community is valued and represented; (2) everyone has the right to equal representation in the cultural life of the community; (3) diversity is a positive feature of society that requires care, cultivation, and protection; and (4) cultural and creative expression and exchange are catalysts for meaningful and lasting social transformation.

These values led to the development of four main areas of cultural activity. First, we offered lectures and workshops led by community members to recognize local expertise, reinforce a broad definition of art and culture, foster the development of practical skills, and engender collective empowerment. Second, through the establishment of open studios and a knit and crochet circle, and through partnering with other community arts organizations, we created forums for multidirectional cultural dialogues. Third, we stimulated the flow of cultural resources and cultural capital through performances, exhibits, community events, and sales of artwork. Our fourth aim, to foster collaboration and representation among the various constituencies that made up ArtWorks by creating an advisory board and engaging in participatory action research, was not fully realized due to the premature termination of ArtWorks Uptown.

Creating a Space of Solidarity and Inclusion

On the surface, ArtWorks functioned as a comfortable, nurturing art space. But just below that surface was a quiet, restrained form of activism (Phillips 1995) focused on (1) radical inclusivity; (2) stigma reduction; (3) collective community building; and (4) emancipatory intent.

Our vision of radical inclusion is grounded in solidarity with those who are oppressed and marginalized (Freire 1996). Therefore, we did not create a space for people with "special needs," but rather aimed to bring together the neighborhood's housed and homeless, poor and middle or upper middle class, old and young, mentally/physically ill and healthy, substance users and abstainers, and so on (Figure 26.1).

Figure 26.1 Working together
Illustrated in the color insert

Among the participants were people who had serious mental illness, people whose mental health status was unknown to us, and people who were therapists at mental health centers. Of the regular participants, there was one gentleman whose substance use resulted in intermittent periods of homelessness, and a mother and two young daughters who expressed no concerns regarding sustained, comfortable housing. When two men who were obviously intoxicated entered the space one day, we talked with the men and the other participants about what kinds of behavior we were able or unable to tolerate in the space, thereby working together to differentiate between perceived danger and genuine requirements for community safety. Though we were clear about our roles as facilitators, we also functioned in the space as artists, collaborators, and co-participants.

Our efforts directed toward stigma reduction were based on our understanding that people with differing social positions have few opportunities to interact with one another in a meaningful way, and that this separation reinforces stereotyping, marginalization, and stigmatization. In contemporary society, "normality" and the "pathological" have become co-constituted cultural divisions that structure both professional and social understandings (Oliver, as cited in Lewis 2006). Minor faults or incidental quirky behavior may easily be interpreted as evidence of stigmatized difference (Goffman 2006). The radically inclusive, open-to-the-public, art-based format of ArtWorks was based on research indicating that the most effective way to reduce stigma associated with mental illness is through contact that occurs in real—rather than contrived—situations, with individuals having equal status in the interaction and engaging in activities that are friendly and informal (Figure 26.2) (Corrigan and Lundin 2001).

Our aims toward collective community building led us to reconsider our roles as art therapists. As those holding the keys to the space, we understood that it was impossible to entirely collapse the power differential, but we minimized it as much as possible. Upon entering the space we signed in like everyone else; we made art alongside others; we offered and received assistance; we taught and learned new skills; we functioned as leaders and enthusiastically supported the leadership of others. While we shared our expertise, we also benefited from the diverse skills, knowledge, and abilities of community co-participants. We even shared in the therapeutic benefits of co-creating a community of art and culture makers! In contrast to the traditional role of therapists, our participation was most often characterized by doing with rather than for or to others.

Figure 26.2 Open to the public

Some people who had heard about ArtWorks from mental health professionals knew we were art therapists; others knew only that we were artists or simply participants. We sometimes struggled to free ourselves of the mantle of art therapists, as participants with previous experiences in art therapy persisted in viewing our activities within the framework of traditional art therapy and, consequently, viewing themselves within the limiting construct of client. At the same time, we recognized that our skills and knowledge were valuable assets for the ArtWorks community. Our contributions included relational sensitivity, observational skills, organizational abilities, a wealth of knowledge about art materials and practices, experience of facilitating group communication and managing group dynamics, knowledge of local resources, and understanding of how to create psychologically safe and nurturing environments.

Collaborative community building was cultivated through co-creating an atmosphere of mutual respect and belief in each individual's capacity for adding something of value to the collective. Participants contributed to the community through informally sharing skills, leading workshops, participating in group problem-solving, bringing food or music to share, and helping maintain the studio. This collaborative approach fostered an environment where stigmatized individuals were able to try on new identities and determine the best fit for themselves, rather than stay mired in a socially prescribed identity. For example, Steven, one of the people referred from a community mental health agency, gradually came to relish the task of greeting new people and orienting them to the space. Over time, he focused less on his psychiatric symptoms and more on his skills as an artist, abilities as a guide, and identity as an experienced and valued member of the community.

The emancipatory intent of ArtWorks was enacted through fostering the capacity of participants to materialize personal and collective resources for the purpose of individual and social transformation. Traditional psychology and counseling practices often function as instruments of social control, working to mask, modify, or eradicate behaviors that are at odds with dominant social norms and values. The emphasis is often on labeling and "fixing" individuals so they conform to the status quo, or on segregating nonconformists from mainstream social and communal life (Prilleltensky and Nelson 2002). In contrast, we attempted to resist individualizing problems that were better understood in the context of family, community, and society (Lewis 2006; Lupton 1997). We also contested aspects of the psychiatric discourse—such as clinical records and psychiatric diagnoses—that objectify "mental illness" (Wilson and Beresford 2002). For example, administrators from our parent organization expected us to write progress notes on participants who were also service users in their system. We vigorously contested this requirement because it caused invisible but real discrimination and undermined our mission to bring people from diverse social positions together. Eventually, the administrators conceded to our wishes and we eliminated note writing altogether. Our overall intent for ArtWorks was to create a transformational setting focused on social change, rather than an ameliorative setting that simply provided individualized help or support (Hocoy 2007; Prilleltensky and Nelson 2002; Timm-Bottos 1995, 2001, 2006, 2011a).

Steven's Story

To illustrate some of the concepts discussed above, we describe Steven's participation in ArtWorks and how his personal transformation was knitted together with the transformation of the community.

When Steven first came to ArtWorks he made it clear—both subtly and overtly—that he identified as a mental health client. He spoke in an intense, pressured way, and often discussed his psychiatric symptoms. He brought in an art history book and painted copies of masterworks, soliciting feedback from others on his work, but rarely seeming to consider the feedback or offering his own reflections on his work. His interactions with other participants were initially focused on getting cigarettes and buying or selling things, while his encounters with us were characterized by constantly seeking approval for his behavior and artwork. At times, he also interpreted our innocent comments as personal attacks. For example, one of the authors could not find her iPod and inquired whether anyone in the studio had seen it. Steven immediately assumed she was accusing him of taking it, and responded by becoming angry and raising his voice at her.

Another time, Steven attended a participant-led workshop that focused on mapping one's sense of home in relation to travel, places lived, and people. The workshop evoked in him traumatic memories of his home life, to which he responded with intense crying. He did not seem to know how to soothe himself, and other community members seemed unsure of how to respond to him. On yet another day, when we put up an anti-domestic violence sign in the space, Steven became visibly angry. He said he had suffered the consequences of being wrongfully accused of violence toward a woman, and wanted us to take the sign down. However, other community members believed the antiviolence message was important and decided to leave the sign up.

These experiences provided all of us with opportunities to collectively navigate the boundaries between private and public spheres, within a shared physical and conceptual space. While uncomfortable and awkward at times, witnessing intense emotions most often elicited empathy and acceptance from other participants. It also served to normalize the common experience of intense emotion, offered alternative perspectives to the paradigm of mental wellness associated with dispassionate self-control, and engaged us all in considering how best to take care of ourselves during times of distress. But we were also concerned with Steven's emotional well-being. We talked to him about whether his participation at ArtWorks was helpful to him, and asked him to think about both what he needed and what he could contribute to the community. He decided to take a break from the space for about two weeks.

When he returned he began to engage with the studio in a new way. He seemed more trusting that we had his best interests at heart, and gave us permission to ask him to take a break if he was becoming overly aggressive or disruptive. He also checked in with other community members about the impact of his behavior, and attempted to recalibrate his demeanor accordingly. He began to learn more about materials, and to develop his own sense of what he liked or didn't like in his artwork. He contributed to the studio by orienting newcomers to the space, bringing salvaged materials to share, and helping with cleanup. When we encountered challenges in the studio, he contributed to finding solutions. For example, when a young boy who had accompanied his grandmother to the studio was running amuck in our small space, making it difficult for anyone to concentrate, Steven took it upon himself to serve as a mentor/big brother to the boy. In a masterful move, he asked for the boy's feedback about his (Steven's) painting-in-progress, and began to teach the boy basic painting techniques. In no time, the boy was calmly painting and talking with Steven, as the rest of us looked on with admiration.

In general, Steven's identity shifted from client to artist and valued community member. After he had been part of the studio for over a year, we were faced with budget realities that threatened the closure of ArtWorks. Steven rallied other ArtWorks members to write testimonials about how the studio had impacted their lives, and then compiled them into a document he shared with Department of Mental Health representatives. In his moving and heartfelt statement, he spoke for the collective by saying how he and other participants no longer perceived themselves as "different" or "less than," but rather had acquired self-worth and a sense of belonging. When the closing of ArtWorks became inevitable, we had a final exhibit celebration. Steven enacted this sense of community identity by using his modest income to buy or trade art pieces so that everyone sold something or had a memento of the experience to take with him or her.

Figure 26.3 Creating community

Conclusion

ArtWorks became a space of solidarity and inclusion because of its emphasis on radical inclusivity, stigma reduction, collective community building, and emancipatory intent. This ethos was effectively captured by a photo of some of the sock monkeys made at one of our workshops. These monkeys are no standard Rockford sock monkeys! Instead, they are a rather motley crew of quirky characters and unlikely comrades, sitting side by side, arm in arm (Figure 26.3). In their charmingly accessible and subtly subversive way, they convey what ArtWorks was all about.

References

ArtWorks (n.d.) "History and mission." Available at www.artworkscommunity.org/history.php, accessed on June 17, 2013.

Austin, S. and Prilleltensky, I. (2001) "Diverse origins, common aims: Challenges of critical psychology." *Journal of Radical Psychology 2*, 2.

Bourriaud, N. (2002) *Relational Aesthetics*. Dijon: Les presses du reel.

Centre for Addiction and Mental Health (n.d.) "CAMH and harm reduction: A background paper on its meaning and application for substance use issues." Available at www.camh.ca/en/hospital/about_camh/influencing_public_policy/public_policy_submissions/harm_reduction/Pages/harmreductionbackground.aspx, accessed on June 17, 2013.

Corker, M. and Shakespeare, T. (eds) (2002) *Disability/Postmodernity: Embodying Disability Theory*. London: Continuum.

Corrigan, P. and Lundin, R. (2001) *Don't Call Me Nuts! Coping with the Stigma of Mental Illness*. Tinley Park: Recovery Press.

Denning, P. and Little, J. (2012) *Practicing Harm Reduction Psychotherapy: An Alternative Approach to Addictions*. New York: Guilford.

Fox, D. and Prilleltensky, I. (eds) (1997) *Critical Psychology: An Introduction*. London: Sage.

Freire, P. (1996) *Pedagogy of the Oppressed*. New York: Continuum International.

Goffman, E. (2006) "Selections from Stigma." In L. J. Davis (ed.) *The Disability Studies Reader, Second Edition*. New York: Routledge.

Hare-Mustin, R. T. and Marecek, J. (2001) "Abnormal and Clinical Psychology: The Politics of Madness." In D. Fox and I. Prilleltensky (eds) *Critical Psychology: An Introduction*. London: Sage Publications.

Henderson, H. (2007) "The high ground." *Chicago Reader*. Available at www1.chicagoreader.com/features/stories/uptown/ history, accessed on June 17, 2013.

Hocoy, D. (2007) "Art Therapy as a Tool for Social Change: A Conceptual Model." In F. F. Kaplan (ed.) *Art Therapy and Social Action*. London: Jessica Kingsley Publishers.

Kaplan, F. F. (ed.) (2007) *Art Therapy and Social Action*. London: Jessica Kingsley Publishers.

Kester, G. (2004) *Conversation Pieces: Community and Communication in Modern Art*. Berkeley: University of California Press.

Levine, E. G. and Levine, S. K. (2011) *Art in Action: Expressive Arts Therapy and Social Change*. London: Jessica Kingsley Publishers.

Lewis, B. (2006) "A Mad Fight: Psychiatry and Disability Activism." In L. J. Davis (ed.) *The Disability Studies Reader, Second Edition*. London: Routledge.

Lupton, D. (1997) "Foreword." In S. Hogan (ed.) *Feminist Approaches to Art Therapy*. London: Routledge.

Marx, G. and Jackson, D. (2009) "Chicago nursing homes: Slaying of nursing home resident in nearby hotel shows how violence can spill into neighborhoods." *Chicago Tribune*, December 1. Available at www.chicagotribune.com/health/chi-uptown-edgewaterdec01,0,6291662.story, accessed on June 17, 2013.

Moon, C. H. (2010) *Materials and Media in Art Therapy: Critical Understandings of Diverse Artistic Vocabularies.* New York: Routledge.

Nicki, A. (2001) "The abused mind: Feminist theory, psychiatric disability, and trauma." *Hypatia 16,* 4, 80–104.

Phillips, P. C. (1995) "Peggy Diggs: Private Acts and Public Art." In N. Felshin (ed.) *But is it Art? The Spirit of Art as Activism.* Seattle, WA: Bay Press.

Prilleltensky, I. and Nelson, G. (2002) *Doing Psychology Critically: Making a Difference in Diverse Settings.* New York: Palgrave Macmillan.

Sampson, E. (2000) "Of Rainbows and Differences." In T. Sloan (ed.) *Critical Psychology: Voices for Change.* London: Macmillan.

Thompson, N. (2012) *Living as Form: Socially Engaged Art from 1991–2011.* Cambridge, MA: MIT Press.

Timm-Bottos, J. (1995) "ArtStreet: Joining community through art." *Art Therapy: Journal of the American Art Therapy Association 12,* 3, 184–187.

Timm-Bottos, J. (2001) "The Heart of the Lion: Joining Community Through Art Making." In M. Farrelly-Hansen (ed.) *Spirituality and Art Therapy: Living the Connection.* London: Jessica Kingsley Publishers.

Timm-Bottos, J. (2006) "Constructing creative community: Restoring health and justice through community arts." *The Canadian Art Therapy Association Journal 19,* 2, 12–26.

Timm-Bottos, J. (2011a) "Endangered threads: Socially committed community art action." *Art Therapy: Journal of the American Art Therapy Association 28,* 2, 57–63.

Timm-Bottos, J. (2011b) "The Five and Dime: Developing a Community's Access to Art-Based Research." In H. Burt (ed.) *Art Therapy and Postmodernism: Creative Healing Through a Prism.* London: Jessica Kingsley Publishers.

Titchkosky, T. (2002) "Cultural Maps: Which Way to Disability?" In M. Corker and T. Shakespeare (eds) *Disability/Postmodernity: Embodying Disability Theory.* London: Continuum.

"Uptown" (2005) *The Electronic Encyclopedia of Chicago.* Chicago: Chicago Historical Society. Available at www.encyclopedia.chicagohistory.org/pages/1293.html, accessed on June 17, 2013.

Wilson, A. and Beresford, P. (2002) "Madness, Distress, and Postmodernity: Putting the Record Straight." In M. Corker and T. Shakespeare (eds) *Disability/Postmodernity: Embodying Disability Theory.* London: Continuum.

Chapter 27

A Self to Call Home

Community-Based Art Therapy and Homelessness

Kate Baasch

Introduction: Welcome to an Open Art Studio in Washington, DC

It is another weekday afternoon and we are getting ready to open for our afternoon arts studio. We have one large dining room in the basement of a church in which we offer a variety of social services and therapeutic programming. In our organization, space is at a premium and we carve it up to host an abundance of services. Using materials on hand such as extra chairs to create visual cues, we indicate that various programs will take place in different parts of the room. It is 2:30 p.m.; the artists' drop cloths have been put on eight tables, about half the tables in the room, to denote where the artists who utilize our studio can paint, bead, sculpt, or knit. The art cart has been wheeled out and has been stocked with classroom-standard two- and three-dimensional art supplies (see Figure 27.1).

Figure 27.1 The art studio

The case management desk is stocked with referral forms. There are two tables set up for a creative writing group, and today chairs are lined up to create a barrier for yoga. A doctor doing outreach is waiting in one of the offices in the back of the room so people can drop in to see her. There is a queue of 50 people, most of whom are chronically homeless, waiting at the door for the program to open. The five of us on staff are trained and energized to find ways to welcome guests into the room, to create space for one another, and to create a sense of community. We create opportunities for clinical relationships that lead to collaborative treatment plans. Some of the clients are here to make art; some are here because they like today's writing instructor; and some have come simply for "help," to talk to a caseworker, or because they have heard there is a doctor, as well as good coffee. Some are hungry and are here to seek shelter from the weather; some may also have voices telling them that the president told them to come here, or...all or none of the above.

Welcome to the therapeutic arts studio! The studio program is one of four programs. The others are meals, case management, and a coffeehouse-style café. All four programs work hand-in-hand to welcome people into a non-threatening space so we can talk about available services and how to access them, identify needs, and work together to remove barriers. We use a nontraditional clinical model where the emphasis at intake is a spirit of hospitality in which we welcome strangers by making space for people to "come as they are." Most of the clients we work with are currently homeless and live literally outside on the street or in an emergency shelter. At our agency there is no formal intake and all services are free and accessed voluntarily. We do this in order to build a community that is accessible. The philosophy here is that everyone needs a place to *be*. Relationship building is our first priority, and I believe this is the way to help any stereotyped population of clients feel valued in a treatment setting. Our clinical team refers to clients as guests. It is my clinical opinion that the first need in any therapeutic relationship with persons experiencing chronic homelessness is to be welcomed and to feel invited, as a guest would. In this way they build trust and can get to know the services offered and explore what needs to be done collaboratively. This structure is not meant to be imposing but ensures that services are relevant.

This chapter demonstrates that working collaboratively through art therapy with people experiencing homelessness creates opportunities to recover and/ or redefine identity. The community-based open art studio model can create a space for homeless clients to name who they are, exert their individual identity, internalize ego strength, and, in essence, feel at home with themselves. If, as McNiff (1995) suggests, in art therapy we fill emptiness with people and images (p.179), then this chapter serves as one response on how to use the tools of art therapy to fill an intrapsychic emptiness and how to invite others to use those tools. This chapter also examines and contributes to the iterations articulated throughout art therapy literature about the development of the open art studio approach. The open art studio approach as a clinical model has limitations. However, the model is extremely versatile because it is full of unique possibilities. Using creativity and clinical acumen, an open studio can be tailored to effectively address both programmatic and client needs.

Homelessness: An Experience, Not an Identity

Art therapy with people who are experiencing homelessness can create opportunities to redefine identity. The definition of homelessness comes from sources other than personal agency. It is a label that carries a social stigma and is not a chosen identity. This definition is, among other things, often cited as a starting point for heated political opinions, discussions, advocacy movements, and policies. In this chapter, the definition serves as a way to begin to look at the categories of homelessness that come from it. It is also referenced as a way to challenge readers to move beyond stereotyped thinking, including expanding the understanding that homelessness is an experience that could happen to anyone. Most importantly, though, it is referenced to illustrate the intrapsychic implications to the notion of the loss of home.

The United States Department of Housing and Urban Development (HUD) provides one definition of the experience of homelessness. In general, it encompasses individuals or families without a place to sleep, people staying in a place not meant for habitation, people who will soon lose their primary place to sleep, unaccompanied youth, persons defined as homeless under different federal statutes, and individuals and families fleeing life-threatening situations (Department of Housing and Urban Development 2009).

This definition is further fleshed out into categories of homelessness: transitional, episodic, and chronic. This chapter specifically looks at the *chronically homeless*, whom HUD describes as "disabled persons who have been homeless for more than a year or who have been homeless three times in the last four years" (Department of Housing and Urban Development 2009). The word *disabled* implies major physical and/or mental illness that creates a high level of vulnerability in daily function for the person that is disproportionate to that experienced by the general population.

This definition is important to consider when working therapeutically with an individual or group experiencing homelessness, because it is a systematic summary that by its purposed function cannot capture the significance of these experiences and therefore it cannot critically inform us as to the specific clinical needs of individuals or groups. Simply put, this definition identifies a social issue and not the therapeutic needs of an individual. This is important to keep in mind for a few reasons. First, HUD's goal is to find a systemic solution and deliver services to a multitude of people. Second, the people whom the definition identifies did not get to define their experience themselves. Most importantly though, no matter what cultural context you work within, a single definition of a problem tends to flatten the individual's experience and does not adequately address the complexities of individual need. An art therapist should keep in mind how external definitions and labels can restrict and/or pathologize a client and instead utilize the art made in art therapy to explore issues of identity.

Perspectives on Therapeutic Work and Homelessness

Other examples of using therapeutic interventions and/or art therapy with homeless individuals come from a variety of perspectives. For the purpose of this chapter the following examples from the literature have been highlighted: O'Connor (2003) discusses homelessness in terms of intrapsychic conflict; Davis (1997) reviews the practical application of object-relations theory in treating the homeless; and specific art therapy perspectives and approaches are exemplified and examined in Allen (1995, 2001), Braun (1997), McGraw (1995), and McNiff (1995).

O'Connor's (2003) discussion on homelessness as an intrapsychic conflict, in part, is perhaps most compelling because it illuminates the role insecure early childhood attachment plays on the pattern of behaviors of those experiencing homelessness. While this is one factor among many, it may be central to informing therapeutic treatment. Poverty and social issues are external factors in a complex array of the experience of homelessness. O'Connor (2003) suggests that framing homelessness in any social system alone can be detrimental to finding a long-term solution for the individual. It is important to consider the pervasive effects of family dynamics and/or dysfunction as well as instability and early childhood trauma that underpin chronic homelessness. He suggests that treatment should attempt to get closer to the internal experience of homelessness. He writes: "Homelessness is the realization of an internal situation—a shifting of personal struggle into a new and more visible stage" (p.111). This new and more visible stage can be contextualized within the residual effects of trauma, where our attachments inform who we think we are and result in our somatic experiences—that is, our perspectives, actions, and ultimately our behavior. O'Connor (2003) writes that the internal conflict results in a person literally feeling "on the outside" (p.114) or on the margin of their family, and as a result never feeling at home with himself/herself. Finally, Martens (cited in O'Connor 2003) highlights the ways in which this experience is traumatic and can be central to the recurring trauma inherent in the experience of homelessness.

O'Connor (2003) finds that safety and security are crucial to recovering identity. Robbins (cited in Davis 1997) suggests "that object constancy comes from finally internalizing a structure" (p.212). Assisting a client in reestablishing his identity and locating his internalized referent for his *self* comes from "creating a home through art" because the "house" or "home" is representative of the self (Davis 1997, p.211). The open studio can be a tool to harness group dynamics to recreate secure family dynamics and object constancy. An atmosphere of hospitality and welcoming addresses the intrapsychic marginalization that O'Connor (2003) observed. The idea that an open studio can be a community in which clinicians can foster secure attachment and transference of the feelings of "home" (e.g., comfort, security, and familiarity) through artwork and consistency is what gives the open studio approach its clinical potency in working with clients experiencing homelessness and/or chronic mental illness.

History of the Community-Based Studio

Art therapists have been innovative in the development of the community-based open studio approach since the beginning of the field (B. Moon 1999; C. Moon 2002; Rhyne 1984). The tradition of the open studio in the United States can nominally be traced back to early programs such as the Art Studio in Cleveland, Ohio, founded in 1967 by art therapist Mickie McGraw and psychiatrist Dr. George Streeter (McGraw 1995). Moreover, the concept of the open art studio may have an even older tradition in Europe (Vick 2008). In his comparative study, Vick (2008) cites Adamson's notion of "the healing studio" (p.4), an idea linked to an older paradigm of treating pathology. Vick (2008) and Kapitan (2008) reference the use of community-based studios as a legitimate practice found throughout the evolution of the field of art therapy. Timm-Bottos (1995) and Franklin (1996) (cited in Vick 2008) were noted as "authors who ventured beyond [the traditional] template by taking positions more conducive to community practice" (p.4). Each of the ways of utilizing an open arts studio is seen as vital to the future of the field.

The terms "open studio" or "open art studio" refer to one general idea within art therapy. Looking specifically throughout art therapy literature at various examples of open studio models reveals that each studio seems to take on a structure of its own based on the needs of the community, the artists/clients who use it, and the art therapists who facilitate it. This suggests that there is not one formula for operating a therapeutic open studio; perhaps this is part of the "openness" of the studio. For example, Allen (2001), when coining the phrase "the open studio process," practices her unique expression of the term with a protocol of intention, attention, and witnessing. Allen's open studio process includes journaling and more formal group process techniques, which may not be appropriate for every open studio. It is interesting to note that Allen (2008) later stated that, from its inception, the open studio she helped to found was not considered art therapy. Allen states that this choice came from the founders' desire for creativity to be associated with health above any association of a "disease process." The founders also wanted to "abandon the role of expert...in favor of the role of artist-in-residence" (p.11).

Yet, some elements seem to be present in every open studio. Patients/clients identify as artists, and necessarily an art therapist should respect this identity (Allen 1995; McGraw 1995; McNiff 1995; Vick 2008). Similarly, art therapists openly identify themselves as artists within the therapeutic relationship and often make art alongside client-artists (Allen 1995, 2001; McGraw 1995; McNiff 1995). A variety of materials and processes are offered (Allen 1995; Braun 1997; Davis 1997; McGraw 1995; Vick 2008), even extending into workshop-style classes within the open studio (Allen 1995; Braun 1997; McGraw 1995; Vick 2008). The artwork belongs to the client and he/she chooses what to do with it (Allen 1995; McGraw 1995). Art exhibitions both on- and off-site are integral components to the open studio experience (Allen 1995; Braun 1997; McGraw 1995; McNiff 1995; Vick 2008). The group should be organized and generate energy. Allen (1995) and McNiff (1995) reasoned that the group's energy would be reflective of how the studio space is used and advised that special attention be paid to the environment of the studio. Studio space is often carved first out of unlikely spaces before being given a space of its own, such as a storefront or thrift store (Allen 1995; Timm-Bottos 2011), offices within a homeless shelter (Davis 1997), a shelter space itself (Braun 1997), and even abandoned cottages on hospital grounds (McNiff 1995). Additionally, Vick's (2008) study surveyed community-based studios in the United States and Europe to look at the similarities and differences. His comparative approach was noteworthy because it considered the larger question of what constitutes the clinical work of art therapy.

It is clear from this brief review that an open studio can be tailored to the needs of a therapeutic community and to individual clients while still offering a unique opportunity to structure a group that encompasses the program's therapeutic goals and artistic vision. When developing a therapeutic open studio it is essential to collaborate with the clients you work with to understand their needs and desires. This collaboration may be distinctly different from that of more traditional art therapy processes and directives. It is also essential to review the history of what has been done in art therapy with both the population and an open studio. Finally, the structure of the open studio must be flexible while maintaining concrete therapeutic opportunities that meet the specific needs of the clients and the community. The tenets of the open studio I facilitate are organization, opportunities, and containment.

Organization

I try to strike a balance between flexibility and structure relative to the needs of the community. Keeping an organized studio allows for better choices in materials and projects. Being organized also allows for more cohesive therapeutic opportunities and helps maintain the integrity of the therapeutic space. Therapeutic opportunities are often new experiences for people. New experiences are often the first step in any process of growth and are fundamental to understanding the *self*. New experiences can also be extremely anxiety producing, and keeping the open studio organized can ease this anxiety by providing an aspect of predictability.

Organization also tacitly communicates the intentional structure of an open studio and is a component of a "good enough environment" (Winnicott 1971, p.95).

Containment

Braun (1997) suggests that an open studio can be a way for a person defined by a stereotype to choose a new identity. The open studio can also be an opportunity for this identity to be actualized and ultimately, as Davis (1997) suggested, internalized. Containment is essential for this type of growth to be realized. Based on O'Connor's (2003) research, and the open studio models reviewed, I suggest that identity formation is inherent to therapeutic work and that a community-based open studio can play a unique role in this. If, as O'Connor (2003) suggested, the therapeutic needs of homeless individuals begin within a person's intrapsychic knowing, then a community-based open studio can be made to create a "good enough" experience of the self as "home." The community-based model can be a space in which a person is safe enough to experience embodied secure attachment by reintegrating experiences of acceptance.

The community-based open studio model presented earlier seeks to create opportunities for reintegration each time a client names himself and is welcomed for whoever he is. The therapeutic group dynamic is presented with intention and provides the opportunity for an intrapsychic shift in adaptation, be it healthier interpersonal dynamics, a shift in daily functioning, or a transformation of self-concept or self-care. Art making in the community-based model answers the goals of McNiff (1995) and Allen (1995) to know the self, while also providing a deeply therapeutic experience naturally found in art making and made present by the finesse of a clinical team holding the community space.

The way to create opportunities for a client to recover and/or redefine identity is to find ways for him/her to feel at home in himself/herself. A community-based open studio model is one way to do this because of the ways it can interrupt the effects of traumatic attachment. Rooted in a psychodynamic understanding of human consciousness, identity is an internalized understanding of the value a person comes to understand himself/herself to have, based on his/her earliest experiences of how he/she was cared for and who cared about him/her (Klein, cited in O'Connor 2003; Robbins, cited in Davis 1997). Through the therapeutic relationship clients can be present for this process and in their art making create a space for themselves that is safe enough to allow them to move toward security, name who he or she is, and internalize ego strength from the balance that is provided by the art therapist and the open studio community. In my experience, an effective open art studio is aware of the needs of the community and retains the ability to set the stage for safe experiences to be explored and shared.

Thoughts on Expressing an Internal Space

Finally, a currently homeless individual named Kwes (his pseudonym) offered to share his thoughts as a way to highlight the uniquely participatory nature of a community-based open studio and the inherent potential it offers him to give voice to his identity. He began by reflecting on his experience of making art in art therapy. Kwes offered:

> I've been thinking about art a lot. How we use it to communicate, to carve out space. How people use space affects other people and there is a certain power behind that. I claim my space even though I don't own it. Some people have more comforts but we're all in similar situations. The world is made up of personal property and space that isn't yours. Art provides you your own space. Inside it's yours, you transfer your experience to paper and it is unique every time, it is my internal space every time.

Figure 27.2 is one of Kwes's drawings made in art therapy. He experimented with using lines and shapes to create an image with a narrative. The image holds his expression and the opportunity to be heard as he chooses. In art therapy Kwes often asks the question of who he thinks he is perceived to be. He asks me, "Am I an angry black man, Katie? What is an angry black man?" Through his art in the context of a valuing community, Kwes answers this question himself. In response to this drawing, Kwes saw a new side of himself taking shape: a visual storyteller, able to bring fragments together. When reflecting on his exercise in lines and shapes, he said he sees a woman sitting at a table. There's a heart he did not intend to make, but she's sitting there waiting; it is Valentine's Day. Throughout the art group we talked about philosophy, love, using our minds, the penultimate meaning of life… Yet we did not arrive at any definite answers, only more ground to be explored.

Figure 27.2 Inner space

Conclusion

Our work as clinicians is really about making space for people and consistently providing opportunities in art therapy to form a new experience of a caring relationship. This exploration is toward a sense of self-concept. Acceptance and containment allow for reintegration. When space is made for others to come as they are, the art made in a community-based studio can shift feelings of marginalization to those of inclusion. Art therapists and clients can collaborate in a studio space to create a home—that is, the feeling of home through art and art making. If this is possible, perhaps the community-based model is paramount in also creating instances of embodied identity formation through instances of secure attachment.

References

Allen, P. (1995) "Coyote comes in from the cold: The evolution of the open studio concept." *Journal of the American Art Therapy Association 12*, 3, 161–166.

Allen, P. (2001) "Art Making as a Spiritual Path: The Open Studio." In J. Rubin (ed.) *Approaches to Art Therapy Theory and Practice, Second Edition.* New York: Brunner-Routledge.

Allen, P. (2008) "Commentary on community-based art studios: Underlying principles." *Journal of the American Art Therapy Association 25*, 1, 11–12.

Braun, L. N. (1997) "In from the cold: Art therapy with homeless men." *Journal of the American Art Therapy Association 14*, 2, 118–122.

Davis, J. (1997) "Building from the scraps: Art therapy within a homeless community." *Journal of the American Art Therapy Association 14*, 3, 210–213.

Department of Housing and Urban Development (2009) *The McKinney-Vento Homeless Assistance Act, 42 U.S.C.11431 et seq.* Washington: Department of Housing and Urban Development.

Kapitan, L. (2008) "Not art therapy: Revisiting the therapeutic studio in the narrative of the profession." *Journal of the American Art Therapy Association 25*, 1, 2–3.

McGraw, M. (1995) "The art studio: A studio-based art therapy program." *Journal of the American Art Therapy Association 12*, 3, 167–174.

McNiff, S. (1995) "Keeping the studio." *Journal of the American Art Therapy Association 12*, 3, 179–183.

Moon, B. (1999) "The tears make me paint: The role of responsive artmaking in adolescent art therapy." *Journal of the American Art Therapy Association 16*, 2, 78–82.

Moon, C. (2002) *Studio Art Therapy: Cultivating the Artist Identity in the Art Therapist.* London: Jessica Kingsley Publishers.

O'Connor, J. (2003) "Homelessness and the problem of containment." *European Journal of Psychotherapy, Counseling, and Health 6*, 2, 111–128.

Rhyne, J. (1984) *The Gestalt Art Experience: Patterns that Connect.* Chicago: Magnolia Street.

Timm-Bottos, J. (2011) "Endangered threads: Socially committed community art action." *Journal of the American Art Therapy Association 28*, 2, 57–63.

Vick, R. (2008) "Community-based art studios in Europe and the United States: A comparative study." *Journal of the American Art Therapy Association 25*, 1, 4–10.

Winnicott, D.W. (1971) *Playing and Reality.* London: Tavistock.

Chapter 28

Utilizing a Thematic Approach to Art Therapy with Seniors
Enhancing Cognitive Abilities and Social Interactions

Linda Levine Madori

One afternoon during a group, after talking for a few minutes with the participants, I played relaxing music and then led the group into a body relaxation and guided imagery session using the change in seasons as a theme. On completing this I asked the participants what they had visualized and then asked them to capture this image on paper. They were given a choice of materials to work with. John (not his real name) drew a picture of a house and tree (see Figure 28.1). This drawing looked like random marks on paper. John described his picture as the house he had bought 60 years ago. He said that there was a very old tree behind the house and he went into details about how his own children grew up under this tree and how now, at 80, he celebrates with his grandchildren under the same tree. The group shared their images and talked about their lives and memories. Themes like this evoke memories from the past and bring out experiences that others may relate to.

Figure 28.1 John—House and tree

During another session, participants were again given a body relaxation and guided imagery session and asked to visualize a safe, secure, and peaceful place where they could relax and quiet their mind and body. One individual, who I will call Dorothy, drew an image (shown in Figure 28.2) and shared her story with the group. She envisioned herself sitting high on a cliff looking out over a beautiful body of water. Her story sounded very ordinary until she continued to share with the group a very personal story. She had been scared of heights her entire life and yet, in this guided imagery, she was unafraid and calm, sitting high up above a large body of water. One of the other participants in the group asked her, "How do you feel drawing this picture knowing you are afraid of heights?" Dorothy responded by stating, "I think this represents the fact that what I was once scared of I am now confronting, and this parallels my feelings about having just been diagnosed with Alzheimer's disease. I was once very fearful about my diagnosis, and now I am facing my fears!" The ability to go within and "see into" one's life allows participants to share meaningful, emotional memories, and sharing stories which enhance a supportive group atmosphere.

Figure 28.2 Dorothy—Cliff

I begin this chapter with depictions of typical art therapy sessions to illustrate how simple childlike marks on paper have a story to tell, which is done using rich verbal language. It is the memories expressed in these stories that make up a person's life. Erickson calls this stage of an individual's development "ego"; its gift is wisdom and its tasks are to achieve integrity versus despair (Vogel-Scibilia et al. 2009). Here the person reflects on the past while looking into the future, which might include accepting the end. Advances in medicine and technology have created an increase in life expectancy worldwide. In the twenty-first century, we will have more senior citizens, in terms of percentage of the population, than ever before. With changing lifestyles and working environments, generations within families live separately. Some members may live in the same city while others may live in different parts of the world. Due to this dramatic increase in the aging population, fragmentation of the family structure, and decreased support systems, an increasing number of community-based services will be needed to serve the needs of adults over 65 years of age.

As more people will be living longer and healthier, seniors' centers, assisted living facilities, and skilled nursing facilities will be expanding their services in countries around the globe. While some seniors may have family members and hobbies that will keep them active in their old age, many others will have to go through this stage alone. Physical limitations plus other personal factors can cause feelings of isolation, which in turn may lead to feelings of loss, rejection, withdrawal, low self-esteem, and resistance to interacting. Retirement communities will need to find various ways to engage and keep the population motivated. Many times members' physical abilities are deteriorating while their mental faculties remain intact; the reverse may also be true. Today we have to find ways to provide avenues to help seniors continue to feel part of the society in which they live. Art therapy is one way of helping seniors to cope with their present situation, to reflect on the past, present, and future, and to feel productive.

> At times emotional needs can be inadvertently overlooked because of the many physical health problems the client is experiencing. Art therapy is one way to address—respectfully, efficiently, and comprehensively—the emotional needs of the frail elderly in a culturally competent manner. Art therapy offers healing by providing social connection, the experience of control and the opportunity to both express and manage emotions. It offers hope by facilitating nonverbal communication and providing opportunity to create meaning through life review. (Johnson and Sullivan-Marx 2006, p.309)

This chapter addresses how art therapy is useful. It also outlines how a theme-based approach known as Therapeutic Thematic Arts Programming, or the TTAP method, developed by the author, has been clinically proven to stimulate social interactions, enhance cognitive functioning, and decrease depression while directly affecting self-esteem in this rapidly growing population.

Art therapists work in day care, residential, medical, psychiatric, or assisted living facilities for the elderly. They may also work with seniors in private practice or in the community at church groups or other special events. In each of these settings, goals can vary from an art-as-therapy approach to a more insight-oriented group or individual process-oriented approach. This variance in approaches occurs many times as the participants are often not in groups specifically to gain insight into their problems or to find solutions to them; rather, they may be in a group simply because art is part of their everyday schedule. An art therapist will have to develop her method of working within any given setting. The American Art Therapy Association

Tool Kit (AATA 2012) provides a list of different programs that art therapists have set up in the United States. In each of these facilities the goals are varied and the approaches are different in order to serve the needs of a particular population. In any of these settings, participants come from a wide range of cultures, countries, and backgrounds. Servicing these culturally diverse populations can be challenging because, as individuals, we all come from unique perspectives and experiences that influence how we react to this stage in life. When we speak about cultural differences we can identify six significant factors: environment, language, food, music, religion, and rituals (Spector 2002). When a diverse group of individuals are brought together for therapeutic programming, the art therapist is commonly challenged with the following issues:

1. The group lacks common interests.

2. There is a lack of understanding among the individuals in the group.

3. The direction of the group is unclear due to the complexity of the participants.

4. The participants may have deeply rooted cultural points of view including stereotypes and prejudices.

5. There is a lack of a common language.

One of my first employment opportunities was working in a seniors' housing facility that provided continuum of care. This includes residential buildings for seniors, assisted living units for those needing some help, a long-term care unit for those who need 24-hour care, and an entire three-storey building for those diagnosed with Alzheimer's disease. In my role as director of the Creative Arts program, I was responsible for developing art therapy programming for all levels of residential care and I worked in this facility for over 12 years.

 I witnessed certain patterns of behavior occurring especially in the groups of people with Alzheimer's disease. The basic theories based on free choice of materials were not working as they would with younger adults or children. Instead, I was finding a natural resistance from older adults to trying art materials or getting involved in the actual process of making art. These were individuals who grew up in times of war and depression. Most had not graduated from high school, as they had had to work to support their families and earn an income very early in life. So I decided to try something different: I started my group with meditation, music, and body relaxation. The residents seemed to really enjoy this process and shared with me that they were seeing meaningful and emotional life memories in their guided imagery experiences.

 I decided to conduct all my sessions in this manner and started to realize that the art therapy sessions became more meaningful in that each session built upon the first session and had a past, present, and future orientation. Each session wasn't just an art therapy session: the sessions now had a personal meaning that came out of the guided imagery. Each session had a past: we could reminisce on what people had shared during the last session and look to the future with what could be possible. This illustrates a person-centered approach: art activities stem directly out of personal and meaningful events.

When the session starts with a theme discussion, individuals are better able to project ideas and thoughts into their artwork. I observed that the residents started to use rich, detailed language when speaking about clear and concise memories. These shared conversations started to get longer. People started to become social with one another after the session was over, and I believe this was all due in part to the deep emotional and meaningful personal stories that were brought into the group conversation through the use of themes.

In my quest to understand what was happening, I developed the TTAP method, which is rooted in the belief that the use of themes—social, cultural, environmental, or personal—creates a framework to provide a person-centered approach to art programming which is fundamental to the care and treatment of all populations (Levine Madori 2005, 2012).

I developed a 12-step approach (see Appendix I). Each of the 12 steps is a creative arts modality which can be incorporated into a thematic approach, and is designed so that the therapist can chart through identification of exactly which learning process occurs and exactly which brain region is stimulated. This application of assessment enhances documentation and raises the efficacy of art with the aging population. The steps can be followed in sequence, or conducted out of order. The TTAP method utilizes art therapy programming first through conversation about a specific theme; the group then is asked to do a body relaxation and guided imagery. The group can decide to then move to painting (Step 3) an image of what they saw in the mind's eye, create a sculpture (Step 4), create a dance (Step 5), or write a song (Step 6) about what they witness in their meditation. The TTAP approach structures all the creative arts so the therapist can ask the individual, "Would you like to create your own piece of poetry or story, or write about a memory?" The participant also has the freedom of deciding to create a recipe from what they are reminiscing about or use photographs for the next session. This ability to choose is often what is lacking at the end stages of life. The TTAP approach allows a flow to naturally occur due to the freedom of choice, direction, and materials. I believe this process brings intrinsic value, increased socialization, and enhanced cognition, and helps develop self-motivation for older adults.

Enhancing Cohesion in Culturally Diverse Groups

Using themes as a guide to structure group programming naturally taps into the personal fibers of the participants. By doing so, the common problems that arise in culturally diverse groups are minimized. Below is a description of how each of these problems is addressed.

1. Lack of Common Interests

By using a thematic approach to art therapy, participants can further explore what they *do* have in common. For example, if the theme is wintertime, even those individuals who live in geographic locations that don't have seasons can now explore this through another group member's shared memory of going out into the snow. These commonalities create strong social bonds, which in turn establish the foundation of a social support structure within the program and after the program ends. In two different facilities the residents reported a significant growth in social bonds that was seen after the program ended. Residents reported that they started to sit with and speak to each other in a way that they had never done before.

2. Lack of Understanding of Each Other and the Therapist

The incorporation of art therapy programming into the exploration of environmental themes and personal themes naturally fosters a richer understanding of every individual's cultural complexities. A thematic approach opens the door to enhanced communication and clarification about language, food, music, religion, and rituals. The older person loves to learn, even at the later stages of life. The ability to learn from each other provides a richer dialogue, more meaningful conversation, and longer moments of engagement with each other. This dialogue fosters the relationship between therapists and clients as well as directly impacting cognition. An example of this dynamic happened after I had conducted a TTAP Method Certification Training in a large rehabilitation facility in Ithaca, New York. The first day covered language usage, objects, and how to communicate with the group members. The next morning, a male nurse who had taken the training came in early and told me he would like to speak with me privately. He told me that he had been working in the dementia unit for seven years and that one woman that he cared for had never spoken; in fact, when he was hired he was told that she didn't speak. But the previous night a very unusual event had happened. He was on the unit and this woman, who I will call Mary, was holding a pencil without a point. The male nurse bent down and asked her "Would you like me to sharpen that pencil for you?" and Mary shook her head to mean "Yes." The nurse brought back a pencil and paper and was suddenly called away to an emergency. When he returned, Mary had drawn a square with nine small circles evenly placed within the square. The nurse asked her, "What did you draw?" (not imagining she would reply). But Mary looked up and said, "I was a teacher and this is my classroom." The nurse was stunned, and continued the conversation, saying, "What did you teach, Mary?" Mary replied, "I was a science teacher!" The nurse shared this story with me, stating that he had brought in his old elementary school books for her to see and discuss with him.

3. Lack of Group Direction

The innate structure of the therapeutic thematic approach in art therapy gives the therapist a clear focus by choosing a theme to explore. Once the theme has been chosen, the 12 steps of the TTAP method provide clear directions to the therapist. Therapists who are just starting to practice can take advantage of this structured approach which enables the therapist to explore all the creative art expressions.

4. Deep-Rooted Stereotypes and Prejudices

During a group session with two women diagnosed with moderate stage Alzheimer's, the topic was favorite childhood books. However, due to the participants being encouraged to speak about their memories during their childhood, one woman who had grown up in northern New Jersey and another who had grown up in southern Tennessee started to discuss racial prejudices that they each had experienced in their childhood days. Sharing and discussing personal themes like this naturally breaks down the stereotypes and prejudices people hold by exposure through conversation. The TTAP method's structure, which starts with conversation, allows intimate and meaningful sharing at each art therapy session. The lack of understanding among the participants is no longer problematic because the group members develop an understanding of each other through the exploration of personal and environmental themes.

Appendix I illustrates how the TTAP method weaves each of these steps together, identifies each step with a specific learning style, and indicates brain regions stimulated to facilitate the creation of programming around themes. I have witnessed, over two decades, deep meaningful conversations (Levine Madori 2009) being initiated between individuals who had lived together side by side for years in long-term care facilities and who had never spoken to each other prior to this approach. This art therapy process changes individual behaviors in the group in three significant ways: the participants are intrinsically motivated to share memories, actual time in the program increases, and cognition increases, according to clinical research (Alders and Levine Madori 2010). In a recent study of this approach, after all staff were certified in the TTAP method in a geropsychiatric hospital, the aggressive behaviors and falls among patients decreased so significantly that it was documented to have saved the hospital $160,000 in direct healthcare costs (Levine Madori 2012, p.170).

12-Step Process: Learning Brain Function

Through the TTAP method's 12-step process (see Appendix I), the group has clear direction, which naturally provides the therapist with multiple options for developing programming (Levine Madori 2007b). Time and again students entering an internship of fieldwork state that this process freed them from the "worry" of what they were going to do in the next session, because the direction of the next session was an important part of each group meeting. The art therapy sessions have a past, present, and future direction. Even when a therapist is only seeing a patient once or twice, there is still the opportunity to reflect on what was done in the last session and what direction the art therapy session is going to take in the moment.

It is hoped that through this chapter you were able to broaden your understanding of themes and of how the use of all the creative arts can further the multiple challenges that can arise when serving groups of aging individuals from diverse populations. The usefulness of thematic approaches has been proven through research to not only stimulate socialization among participants but also to enhance cognitive functioning. We are living in a global community; with the use of this approach, diverse populations, cultures, and abilities can be engaged through meaningful art therapy processes (Levine Madori 2007a).

References

Alders, A. and Levine Madori, L. (2010) "The effect of art therapy on cognitive performance of Hispanic/Latino adults." *American Art Therapy Association Journal 27*, 3, 127–135.

American Art Therapy Association (AATA) (2012) *Art Therapy Tool Kit Art Programs: Enhancing the Lives of Older Adults.* Available at www.arttherapy.org/ALFAToolkit/alfatoolkit.pdf, accessed on June 17, 2013.

Johnson, C. and Sullivan-Marx, E. (2006) "Art therapy: Using the creative process for healing and hope among African American older adults." *Geriatric Nursing 27*, 5, 309–316.

Levine Madori, L. (2005) "The effect of therapy session participation on cognitive functioning and psychosocial well-being among elderly individuals with mild to moderate Alzheimer's disease." *VMI Doctoral Dissertation Services.* New York: New York University.

Levine Madori, L. (2007a) *Therapeutic Thematic Arts Programming for Older Adults.* Baltimore: Health Professions Press.

Levine Madori, L. (2007b) *Therapeutic Thematic Arts Programming Workbook for Healthcare Professionals.* Baltimore: Health Professions Press.

Levine Madori, L. (2009) "Using the TTAP method for cognitive and psychosocial wellbeing." *American Journal of Therapeutic Recreation 7*, 14–11.

Levine Madori, L. (2012) *Transcending Dementia through the TTAP Method: A New Psychology of Art, Brain and Cognition.* Baltimore: Health Professions Press.

Spector, R. (2002) "Cultural diversity in health and illness." *Journal of Transcultural Nursing 3*, 197–199.

Vogel-Scibilia, S. E., Cohan McNulty, K., Baxter, B., Miller, S., Dine, M., and Frese, F. J. (2009) "The recovery process utilizing Erikson's stages of human development." *Community Mental Health Journal 45*, 6, 405–414.

Resources

Further Reading

Bloom, S. and Krathwohl, D. (1956) *Taxonomy of Educational Objectives: The Classification of Educational Goals.* New York: Longmans.

Burgener, S., Gilbert, R., and Mathy, R. (2007) "The effects of a multi-modal intervention on cognitive, physical, and affective outcomes of persons with early stage dementia." *Journal of Alzheimer's Disease and Related Disorders 12*, 143–156.

Gardner, H. (1982) *Art, Mind, and Brain.* New York: Basic Books.

Hass-Cohen, N. and Carr, R. (eds) (2008) *Art Therapy and Clinical Neuroscience.* London: Jessica Kingsley Publishers.

Rentz, C. (2002) "Memories in the making: Outcome-based evaluation of an art based program for individuals with dementing illnesses." *American Journal of Alzheimer's Disease and Other Dementias 17*, 3, 175–181.

Snowdon, D. (2001) *Aging with Grace: What the Nun Study Teaches Us About Leading Longer, Healthier, and More Meaningful Lives.* New York: Bantam Books.

Part VII

Cultural Implications for Practicing Art Therapy with Unique Populations

Chapter 29

Therapy in the Prison Subculture
Maintaining Boundaries while Breaking Barriers

David Gussak

All settings and environments where art therapists work vary greatly in their focus, execution, and mission. This chapter contends that prisons and other correctional milieu have a separate and distinct subculture with their own rules and rites. Concurrently, they are among the few blatantly antitherapeutic places resistive to psychological well-being. In fact, the punitive intention of some members of the correctional community may lead them to view such services as antithetical to their overall mission—to punish the guilty and protect the public.

On the other end of the correctional spectrum, "prison inmates build rigid defenses and put on 'masks,' which ensure survival" (Gussak 1997a, p.1). In essence, inmates remain silent about their vulnerabilities to avoid appearing weak, making verbal therapy an especially daunting task. The therapist may find himself or herself battling both ends of these difficult continua to provide services. While the health and mental health care that inmates receive fluctuates depending on the current legislative or social climates—both at the national and state level—the dynamics within the system remain somewhat consistent.

This chapter examines how art therapy can work within such a system. It demonstrates how an art therapist can use creativity to provide services while still meeting the charge of safety and security despite the challenges inherent within this milieu. It provides an overview of the history of the arts in prisons and explores how and why the arts are prevalent and the benefits of art therapy within this subculture. This chapter concludes with a discussion on the challenges an art therapist may find to the necessary boundaries significant for this setting.

The Arts in Prison
A Brief History
Creativity and artistic expression are inherent within the correctional subculture. In an environment where little is respected, the ability to create tangible, tradable artistic items is a status builder. Inmates can earn coveted respect and friendship from peers and correctional officers (Gussak 1997a; Kornfeld 1997). Their art

is prolifically displayed "through prison craft shops, inmate painted wall murals, decorative envelopes that inmates can 'buy' from each other to send letters to loved ones, and intricate tattoos" (Gussak and Ploumis-Devick 2004, p.35). Although the correctional milieu is often seen as a desolate environment and, as such, an unlikely breeding ground for objects of beauty, history demonstrates that inmates have a drive to create.

Ursprung recognized that "prison art is probably as old as the institution of prison itself" (1997, p.18) The writings of Plato and Socrates were inspired by their respective incarcerations (Rojcewicz 1997). In the first century AD, gladiators enslaved in the Pompeii arena scratched graffiti onto the walls of their imprisoning barracks (Kornfeld 1997). Historically, prisoners traded their handcrafted products to their jailers for food and clothing. The excavation of a Pennsylvania prison built in 1829 yielded inmate handicrafts, specifically wooden toys, figurines, and gaming pieces (Ursprung 1997). Many famous artists and writers completed great works of art while imprisoned in asylums and early forms of penitentiaries (Rojcewicz 1997). Oscar Wilde and Villon wrote and composed poems about their respective prison experiences. Art making in prison has inspired and interested many scholars (Prinzhorn 1926, 1972), and the art of such notorious prison inmates as Charles Manson and convicted serial killer John Wayne Gacy Jr. continues to intrigue and baffle us: we wonder how someone so seemingly inhumane can create.

Why Art Is So Prevalent

Creative expression in the prison subculture is not surprising, as the act of creating art has been directly linked to aggression, sexuality, and escape—primitive instinctual impulses prevalent but institutionally controlled in correctional settings (Fox 1997). Generally, such impulses require release, but to do so within this subculture may have dire consequences for those venting these impulses and for those around them. However, creating art may provide a safe outlet and expression of these libidinal urges.

Art and sex are "each primal behaviors that have become elaborated in the essential service of affiliation and bonding" (Dissanayake 1992, p.193), and "the impulses that drive some people to create are perhaps alike primarily in the fact that both can be considered expressions and agents of feelings" (Dissanayake 1988, p.140). Creative expression can be a socially acceptable by-product of sublimating aggressive and libidinal impulses (Kramer 1993; Rank 1932; Rubin 1984). The act of creating also allows the inmate to "escape," if only for a few moments or hours, into his or her created world; it provides a diversion from this primitive subculture (Gussak 1997b; Gussak and Cohen-Liebman 2001; Hall 1997).

Resistance to the Arts in Prison

Understandably, the establishment resists these impulses if expressed in their pure form (Fox 1997); thus, the redirection of these instincts into creative, artistic expression is more acceptable to the establishment, even if the institution is not aware of the strength of such redirection. Using the art permits the inmate to express himself or herself in a manner acceptable to both the inside and outside culture. Art therapists take advantage of this ability of the art to allow those libidinal expressions while simultaneously providing an avenue for expressing personal issues without having to voice them.

One challenge, however, is that, in the name of safety and security, the environment limits the tools that may be available, even commonplace, in other settings. At times, it may even seem that such regulations are arbitrary given that they may vary from setting to setting, or even from week to week in a single institution. Determining what tools can be used, and how to work within the regulations established, becomes an ongoing challenge.

For example, in one facility, it made sense that scissors had been completely banned. However, several months prior, safety scissors were considered appropriate. The decision the facility made was that safety scissors obtained long ago could still be used, but new ones could not come through the gate. Moreover, this rule was specific to this one agency.

Some programs deem long pencils as dangerous, replacing them with short "golf" pencils, whereas others allow them. In many settings, clay is considered contraband, the rationale being less that it could be used as a weapon but more that it could be used to jam locks or make impressions of keys. Oil pastels may not be used in some settings, as there is a concern that some inmates may be able to extract oil from them to make a flammable weapon. Consequently, art therapists find themselves becoming adept at developing alternative directives to work around these limitations. Paper may be ripped instead of cut, the inmates may be directed to make three-dimensional paper sculptures to replace clay, masks may be made from paper plates rather than plaster or preformed plastic, and all materials used may need to be nontoxic and nonflammable.

Art Therapy in the Prison Subculture

The prison milieu as a therapeutic agency may also be counterintuitive in that any expression of weakness and vulnerability by an inmate may be taken advantage of by others within the subculture, where survival of the fittest is the credo. This primitive subculture maintains its own mores; to violate such unspoken rites may leave one suspect. Admitting to a mental illness, sadness about one's circumstances, or an inability to adjust to the setting may be seen as a weakness. Thus, the inmate with such issues may find that he or she is unable to express them without fear of retaliation or revile. "There is an inherent mistrust for such verbal disclosure, and a well-grounded fear of prisoners taking advantage of others' voiced vulnerabilities; rigid defenses are built to achieve basic survival" (Fenner and Gussak 2006, p.414).

To survive, many of those inhabiting the prison may adopt sociopathic tendencies, even if they did not have such tendencies prior to arriving. Unfortunately, inmates must adapt to their new subculture and learn that they may not be able to trust anyone, including therapists.

> If a therapist tries to break through necessary barriers, the inmate/patient may become dangerous even if initially charming and cooperative. The inmate's defenses take over, making him anxious and angry, perhaps even violent, to a much greater extent…than clinicians are accustomed to with the general population. (Gussak 1997a, p.1)

To compensate, a therapist must be prepared to work with inmates in a way that does not raise suspicion or increase their vulnerability. While this might be a challenge in talk therapy, art therapy has mechanisms to work around these limitations (Gussak 1997b).

The Benefits of Art Therapy in Prison

Previous publications have delineated several benefits of art therapy in prison (Gussak 1997a, 2004; Gussak and Cohen-Liebman 2001). In most cases, the art created during therapy becomes a hidden resource in the therapist's arsenal, since art has the ability to disguise the therapeutic process. The act of making art allows the expression of the instinctual libidinal impulses, while the "environment" remains unaware. In this sense, the hidden process becomes the core of the art therapy. It allows disclosure without vulnerability. It allows the inmate/patient to express himself/herself in most situations with little fear of retaliation from the environment, as his/her means of creative expression is valued by both the inside and outside culture. It provides a simpler form of expression when, due to illiteracy or diminished capacity, the inmate may not be able to utilize verbal communication. It has the advantage of bypassing certain conscious and unconscious defenses, which may emerge through lying or reconstructing reality. It provides a much-needed diversion and allows for emotional escape. What is more, it does not require that the inmate/client discuss or even know what he or she has disclosed through the art. The environment is dangerous, and any unintended disclosure can be threatening. The art process can diminish pathological symptoms without verbal interpretation.

The art process also allows for the reemergence of the self, of personal identity, even in an environment where control is reinforced through objectifying the inmate. In a subculture where the inmates are identified by numbers and are forced to wear the same uniform, the reinforcement of self and identity are compromised. The art allows the opportunity to reverse this. For example, one directive used with this population, known as *making the most out of nothing*, focuses on self-efficacy, identity, and esteem. All of the participants in the group are provided with two simple materials: white paper and glue. They are then asked to create a paper sculpture. Despite the uniformity of the materials, the end results are often varied and well designed (see Figures 29.1 and 29.2). Many are intricate, and they reinforce the notion that although participants may all start with the same materials, and are limited in terms of what they are given, with ingenuity, problem-solving, and risk-taking they may succeed in maintaining a unique identity.

Figure 29.1 White paper sculpture 1

Figure 29.2 White paper sculpture 2

Along with these benefits previously supported through case vignettes, recent studies have demonstrated that art therapy helps decrease depression while increasing locus of control, problem-solving, and socialization (Gussak 2004, 2007, 2009). Such benefits create a safer environment for all those who comprise an institution and can facilitate the transition into society following release. Of course, as in any setting, boundaries are necessary in order to maintain healthy therapeutic relationships. However, in this subculture, boundary crossings are magnified and provide yet more challenges and obstacles. Simply put, it is the job of the institution to create and guard boundaries; it is the objective of the inmate to challenge them.

Boundary Crossings

Boundary considerations and manipulations are a natural part of the therapeutic alliance and environment in order to decrease or magnify transferential relationships and examine personal issues. However, they pose a significant challenge within the correctional subculture. Bridges (1999) defines a boundary, when effective, as a psychological holding environment, established by the therapist to help a client feel comfortable in expressing himself or herself. Relying simultaneously on predictability, an effective boundary makes for a safer environment for both the therapist and the client. However, as Gutheil and Gabbard (1993) indicated, boundaries can also be somewhat amorphous, tailored specifically to the needs of the client and the culture, varying across types of therapy offered.

Interactions that define the boundary construction fall among the continua of rigidity and fluidity, opacity and transparency. Maintaining an awareness of how clients may challenge boundaries, therapists, in turn, need to remain vigilant regarding their own boundary transgressions. Such challenges may include any degree of self-disclosure, physical touch during time of trauma, or succumbing to transferential issues. They may also include dual relationships, bartering for goods and services, or overt sexual contact (Agell, Goodman, and Williams 1995; Bridges 1999; Gutheil and Gabbard 1998).

Along with the natural sociopathic tendencies prison inmates maintain to survive in the prison environment, boundaries may be unwittingly—or wittingly—challenged in order to garner attention or to maintain a sense of control or power. In fact, the sociopathic tendencies may lead directly to the testing of boundaries to determine any opportunity for manipulation. In some cases, if a clinician violates the boundaries, the inmates may find themselves in a position to take advantage of such weakness for personal gain or attention. Fenner and Gussak (2006), in discussing supervisory issues that arose during an internship experience in the prison setting, reflected that certain boundary violations are prevalent for the art therapist: those of time, space, materials, and self-disclosure.

Time is carefully structured through regularity and dependability within prison to maintain security and control. Inmates naturally ask for additional time from the therapists. They enjoy the attention and focus while perhaps using this mechanism to see how much they can disrupt or take control. While art therapists may wish to provide additional time to a client so that they may complete an especially well-done piece, such boundary crossings are antithetical to the safety of the institution. Ultimately, it is up to the clinician to carefully weigh the benefits of extending the time as a therapeutic compromise against the possibility that it may be a boundary crossing.

Similarly, personal and environmental space is constantly being evaluated, and something as simple as a handshake is suspect within the correctional arena. In any setting, the art therapist has to consider issues as simple as whether to "touch client artwork, is the space adequate for the production of those tasks clients are asked to perform, is the water supply adequate, where does the art therapist position him or herself in the group as various tasks are being performed and simply, where are the exits?" (Fenner and Gussak 2006, p.415). Such protection of space and personal output is even more prevalent in prison, where there is a lack of both. In addition, whereas art therapy is dependent on an adequate distribution of materials in order to complete the requested directives, the art therapist finds himself or herself constantly being challenged by the inmates and the setting to maintain strict control of the materials.

However, to challenge the notion of environmental and personal boundaries while simultaneously reinforcing them, oftentimes a *Draw and Pass* exercise may be encouraged. The group members, who are sitting around a table, are asked to draw a particular image or images using semi-structured materials like colored pencils or markers on the sheet of paper in front of them. After a short period of time, they are directed to pass it to the person sitting next to them, who then adds to the composition; all drawings shift over one. When they receive their initial sheet of paper in front of them, they are given the opportunity to add to it for a couple more minutes and make their finishing marks. Ultimately, this directive reinforces their own sense and identity of personal boundaries, and the environmental challenges to these boundaries. This directive helps reinforce frustration tolerance, address loss of control, and strengthen socialization skills. The participating inmates can also learn to recognize their own contribution to a larger, creative endeavor, augmenting their sense of identity. Figure 29.3 is an example of a completed Draw and Pass by a group of eight male inmates who had been working together for six weeks prior to its completion.

There is also the question of self-disclosure by the inmates and by the therapists. Whereas clinicians may find themselves in certain situations where some self-disclosure may be beneficial to the trajectory of care, it is a commonly held concern in the correctional milieu that any form of self-disclosure may be detrimental. Whether this is accurate or not, the prison clinician must be especially aware of what information he or she may provide. This is just as true in the art. While the therapist may feel that it is fairly safe to show his or her own artwork, it may be just as revealing to the client and can provide more information than what the therapist intended. Nowhere is this more dangerous than in prison where it is believed that inmates can take advantage of such personal information. For example, an inmate who was seen in the facility as strong and unaffected by his surroundings was asked to complete an image that represented "Relationships" (shown in Figure 29.4). Despite how he presented himself, this "death mask's" lines, shapes, and composition seem to reveal anxiety, identity issues, and vulnerabilities, characteristics that belied what he chose to show others in the institution. Presenting such feelings verbally may have left this particular inmate appearing weak. By providing an outlet for him to express these tendencies in the art piece without giving voice to the underlying attributes, the therapist kept the inmate safe and allowed him a healthier means of self-expression.

Consequently, while in some cases the art therapist may find it easier to break through barriers and work behind the self-imposed masks to facilitate therapeutic development, he or she may find greater challenges in maintaining strong boundaries than verbal therapists. Therefore, it is in the art therapist's best interest to remember where he/she works and recognize that art may facilitate boundary crossing, inconvenient within most settings but potentially dangerous in the correctional institution.

Figure 29.3 Draw and pass example

Illustrated in the color insert

Figure 29.4 "Relationships"
Illustrated in the color insert

Conclusion

As a distinct subculture, prisons are a unique and, at times, antitherapeutic environment in which art therapists may find themselves. However, despite—or because of—the environment's primitive us-versus-them dynamics, most prison inmates have a natural need to create. Art therapists can use this need to redirect the primitive and, at times, detrimental impulses inmates may have to provide them with a means to express their weaknesses and difficulties without leaving them vulnerable. In order to do so, therapists may discover that they have to simultaneously address the natural sociopathic tendencies and boundary violations induced by the inmates, and the institutional resistance to provide services for people that "have nothing coming to them" in order to provide care. However, as this chapter elucidates, art therapists have the nonverbal tools in their arsenal to bring about change that can ultimately decrease depression and increase locus of control, problem-solving, and socialization to create a safer, more productive environment.

References

Agell, G., Goodman, R., and Williams, K. (1995) "The professional relationship: Ethics." *American Journal of Art Therapy 33*, 4, 99–109.

Bridges, N. A. (1999) "Psychodynamic perspective on therapeutic boundaries: Creative clinical possibilities." *The Journal of Psychotherapy Practice and Research 8*, 4, 292.

Dissanayake, E. (1988) *What is Art For?* Seattle, WA: University of Washington Press.

Dissanayake, E. (1992) *Homoaestheticus: Where Art Comes From and Why.* New York: The Free Press.

Fenner, L. and Gussak, D. (2006) "Therapeutic boundaries in a prison setting: A dialogue between an intern and her supervisor." *The Arts in Psychotherapy 33,* 414–421.

Fox, W. M. (1997) "The Hidden Weapon: Psychodynamics of Forensic Institutions." In D. Gussak and E. Virshup (eds) *Drawing Time: Art Therapy in Prisons and Other Correctional Settings.* Chicago, IL: Magnolia Street Publishers.

Gussak, D. (1997a) "The Ultimate Hidden Weapon: Art Therapy and the Compromise Option." In D. Gussak and E. Virshup (eds) *Drawing Time: Art Therapy in Prisons and Other Correctional Settings.* Chicago, IL: Magnolia Street Publishers.

Gussak, D. (1997b) "Breaking through Barriers: Advantages of Art Therapy in Prison." In D. Gussak and E. Virshup (eds) *Drawing Time: Art Therapy in Prisons and Other Correctional Settings.* Chicago, IL: Magnolia Street Publishers.

Gussak, D. (2004) "Art therapy with prison inmates: A pilot study." *The Arts in Psychotherapy 31,* 4, 245–259.

Gussak, D. (2007) "The effectiveness of art therapy in reducing depression in prison populations." *International Journal of Offender Therapy and Comparative Criminology 5,* 4, 444–460.

Gussak, D. (2009) "The effects of art therapy on male and female inmates: Advancing the research base." *The Arts in Psychotherapy 36,* 1, 5–12.

Gussak, D. and Cohen-Liebman, M. S. (2001) "Investigation vs. intervention: Forensic art therapy and art therapy in forensic settings." *The American Journal of Art Therapy 40,* 2, 123–135.

Gussak, D. and Ploumis-Devick, E. (2004) "Creating wellness in forensic populations through the arts: A proposed interdisciplinary model." *Visual Arts Research 29,* 1, 35–43.

Gutheil, G. B. and Gabbard, G. O. (1993) "The concept of boundaries in clinical practice: Theoretical and risk management dimensions." *The American Journal of Psychiatry 150,* 2, 188.

Gutheil, G. B. and Gabbard, G. O. (1998) "Misuses and misunderstandings of boundary theory in clinical and regulatory settings." *The American Journal of Psychiatry 155,* 3, 409.

Hall, N. (1997) "Creativity and Incarceration: The Purpose of Art in a Prison Culture." In D. Gussak and E. Virshup (eds) *Drawing Time: Art Therapy in Prisons and Other Correctional Settings.* Chicago, IL: Magnolia Street Publishers.

Kornfeld, P. (1997) *Cellblock Visions: Prison Art in America.* Princeton, NJ: Princeton University Press.

Kramer, E. (1993) *Art as Therapy with Children, Second Edition.* Chicago, IL: Magnolia Street Publishers.

Prinzhorn, H. (1926) *Bildenerei der gefangenen: Studie zur bildernerischen gestaltung unbegabter (Artistry of Convicts).* Berlin, Germany: Alex Juncker Verlag.

Prinzhorn, H. (1972) *Artistry of the Mentally Ill.* (trans. E.V. Brockdorff). Berlin, Germany: Springer Verlag.

Rank, O. (1932) *Art and artist.* New York: W. W. Norton.

Rojcewicz, S. (1997) "No Artist Rants and Raves when He Creates: Creative Arts Therapists and Psychiatry in Forensic Settings." In D. Gussak and E. Virshup (eds) *Drawing Time: Art Therapy in Prisons and Other Correctional Settings.* Chicago, IL: Magnolia Street Publishers.

Rubin, J. A. (1984) *The Art of Art Therapy.* New York: Brunner/Mazel Publishing.

Ursprung, W. (1997) "Insider Art: The Creative Ingenuity of the Incarcerated Artist." In D. Gussak and E. Virshup (eds) *Drawing Time: Art Therapy in Prisons and Other Correctional Settings.* Chicago, IL: Magnolia Street Publishers.

Chapter 30

Working with Asylum Seekers and Refugees

Marian Liebmann

Introduction

This chapter discusses some of the issues in using art therapy with asylum seekers and refugees, such as language barriers, cultural differences, time boundaries, trust, stability, and practical help. These may mean going beyond the conventional therapeutic boundaries, but if they can be negotiated well, art therapy can be a powerful means of healing for traumatized asylum seekers and refugees. The chapter is illustrated by the case study of an Armenian asylum seeker/refugee.

The Setting

I work for a community mental health team in central Bristol, the United Kingdom (UK), a city of about 400,000 inhabitants. The team covers an inner-city patch with considerable diversity—white British people, immigrants from Europe, Asia, Africa, the West Indies, and the Far East, and the children of immigrants born in Bristol. Since it is a port city, Bristol has had minority ethnic people settling there for several centuries. In recent years, some of those coming to Bristol have been asylum seekers from a variety of war-torn countries.

Being an asylum seeker has many stresses, so it is not surprising that some succumb to depression, posttraumatic stress disorder (PTSD), or psychotic illnesses. Most of them are treated by their family doctors but a few develop serious mental health problems and are referred to our team. Often English is their second language, and though art therapy treatment does not rely totally on words and hence can be effective, an interpreter is often needed.

The community mental health team is multidisciplinary and includes psychiatrists, community psychiatric nurses, social workers, mental health workers (who undertake practical tasks such as helping clients find transport or courses), psychologists, and a part-time art therapist. Several staff are from minority ethnic groups, for example Europe, Asia, Africa, and black British, with knowledge of many languages. Clients are visited at home or in counseling rooms at the team base. The art therapy room where I work doubles as a multipurpose room for other activities when I am not there. Most of my work with clients (including asylum seekers) is with individuals, usually in weekly hour-long appointments. Occasionally I run theme-based groups on specific topics.

Asylum Seekers and Refugees

A refugee is defined by the 1951 United Nations Convention on Refugees as "a person who seeks safety in another country, due to a well-founded fear of persecution in her/his country of origin on grounds of race, religion, ethnicity, political beliefs or membership of particular social groups. Someone who applies for asylum is called an asylum seeker while they are waiting for a decision" (Bristol Refugee Rights 2012).

It can take several years before a decision is reached, during which time asylum seekers' lives are "on hold." They are forbidden to work, and receive a minimal money allowance. They are allocated housing by the National Asylum Support Service (NASS) and can be moved anywhere in the UK without notice.

If people are granted humanitarian protection or refugee status, they have "leave to remain," usually for five years in the first instance. Then they face a new set of challenges—finding accommodation, finding work, settling into UK life, working toward British citizenship, acquiring British passports, making friends, and improving their English.

Issues in Working with Asylum Seekers and Refugees

Most asylum seekers have limited familiarity with the way things work in Britain, so I explain even more carefully than usual what the options are and what I can offer. Even initial appointments often require interpreters, who need good briefing as they are unlikely to have worked with an art therapist before. Sometimes whole families arrive, as they rarely have access to child care.

It would be preferable for people to access therapy through their mother tongue, but this is often not feasible. I have found it possible to do good therapy through interpreters—maybe because art therapy has a life of its own and does not rely entirely on words (though these are necessary too). It is important to lay out boundaries, such as translating everything both ways. For an ongoing piece of work, I have insisted on the same interpreter throughout, who can then be integrated into the session in a seamless way.

The usual time boundaries of therapy—the hour-long slot at an appointed time—may be difficult for asylum seekers and refugees. Before I went to Africa, a friend told me, "Europeans have watches, Africans have time." Asylum seekers also have many official appointments, and often have difficulty with transport, so arriving on time can be problematic.

One young woman was referred to me by her psychologist who felt therapy was stuck. The client would arrive 45 minutes late, so their sessions were truncated. The psychologist and I then worked with her alternate weeks. There was no language problem, as she spoke five languages, two African and three European. But despite my careful explanations that art therapy could not be done in 15 minutes, she still arrived 45 minutes late. She felt bad about it but seemed unable to change. One day it dawned on me that maybe I could change. I altered my following session to 30 minutes later, and when she arrived apologetically at her normal time, I said, "This week my next session is not till 3:30, so we have 45 minutes to do something." She then used the art therapy sessions in a very constructive way. While I understood that this might reflect a cultural issue of keeping time, I also felt that she struggled with low self-esteem and an inability to motivate herself to come to the sessions. In making the change without letting her know about the change in time, I was able to accommodate her and work with her, thereby overcoming the issue of lack of time to do the artwork.

Professional helpers may assume that asylum seekers would benefit from talking about the traumas they have suffered. This may be true for some people; however, in my experience, clients need some stability before they are able to talk about these. They do not have enough stability while they are waiting for their case to be heard, or coping with the fear of removal if their claim is rejected. One of the main tasks of therapy with refugees is that of safety and containment (Kalmanowitz and Lloyd 2009; Kovacevic 2012).

Organizations working with asylum seekers and refugees have pointed out that therapists need to be more flexible and offer help with other tasks normally seen as beyond the remit of therapy. For instance, I have found myself signing passport application forms (as I am the only professional person they have known long enough), or making referrals to other resources, or helping them to get bus passes.

Case Study: Asylum Seeker from Armenia

Arman and his wife Anna were arrested and beaten up in Armenia because of their anti-government views—they worried particularly because Anna was pregnant. She fled to the UK with their first child. Arman fled to Georgia and Russia until he could join his wife two years later. They were first based in London, where they had access to Armenian contacts and the organization Freedom from Torture. Then they were moved by NASS to Swansea, South Wales, where they became very isolated. Anna suffered postnatal depression after the birth of their second child, and Arman's mental health deteriorated. He could not sleep and had visual hallucinations of his attackers. When he did sleep he had nightmares of them. He lived in a constant state of fear that he would be pursued by them. He did not go out. He had suicidal thoughts, so that Anna was afraid to leave him alone. They were seen by Swansea Mental Health Services, who supported their request for a transfer back to London, and were rehoused by NASS in Bristol, halfway to London. This was a good move, and some of Arman's symptoms subsided, but he was still very depressed, cutting his wrists and suffering from auditory hallucinations. Their doctor referred Arman to our team. His diagnosis was mild to moderate depression with PTSD.

He was allocated a care coordinator to oversee his care. The care plan included a variety of services (gym sessions, English lessons, vocational training) and a mental health worker to help him to access these. Arman was referred to art therapy because of his expressed need for therapy and his interest in art and sculpture. I set up an assessment session, and the mental health worker organized an interpreter. There were no Armenian interpreters in Bristol, so a Russian-speaking interpreter was found (Arman's second language). Even though Arman had been in the UK for about three years, he spoke no English at all. He was simply too traumatized to learn.

Throughout our contact, we often had to shift our sessions because of important appointments the couple had with authorities about their application for refugee status. That meant shifting the interpreter too, and it was hard to keep up with this. The family had contacts in London, so went there frequently (friends sent them tickets). They were moved to different accommodations by NASS. They had very little money, existing on the Home Office voucher scheme. Working with these obstacles, they became part of the therapy and we built up a good rapport among Arman, the interpreter Ivan, and me. His art therapy fell into four phases, described below.

Starting: Holding on Tight

Arman arrived for the assessment session with his wife Anna and two children (aged four and two). I briefed Ivan, the interpreter, carefully. We found drawing materials for the children. I discussed art therapy with Arman and asked him what he wanted from it. He said he wanted to take his mind off his problems, especially the fear and uncertainty about his future, and to cope better with life in general. We listed Arman's problems and strengths, and I showed him the art materials. We agreed to meet weekly or every two weeks (depending on other appointments).

Next session the whole family arrived again and expected to come into the session, but I asked them to go to the local park for an hour. Arman chose plasticine and modeled an Armenian cross. He had no particular associations with this symbol, but said he had modeled churches from paper and little people from bread (however, bread was too expensive in the UK for this). I had to remind Ivan to translate everything. Arman took great care over the cross, and I commented that he was clearly a perfectionist. He agreed, and we had a useful conversation about the pros and cons of perfectionism—mostly it seemed to be a burden to him, a way of coping that led to migraines, self-criticism, and frustration.

The following session he used pencils to draw a picture of Mount Ararat in Armenia and its neighboring peak, then colored it in neatly with thick felt-tip pens (see Figure 30.1). He talked about being homesick and missing the landscape and his friends in Armenia.

Figure 30.1 Armenian landscape

Illustrated in the color insert

Next session Arman seemed a bit brighter. He drew a pencil landscape of a boat with its reflection between two cliffs of stone, with a tree and the moon. The finished picture gave him a feeling of calmness, and he took it home to help continue this feeling. The session after he used pencils again, this time drawing a house in which he delineated every single brick. This time he was very dissatisfied with himself and talked again about the problems caused by his perfectionism, saying how difficult it made life for all the family. I asked him if we might use art therapy to try out a different way of being, and he was agreeable.

Loosening Up

Arman arrived at his fifth session having walked on his own, a big step forward. I explained the idea of using art materials to "loosen up" and help him relax more. I had written out cards with loosening-up exercises in large letters, with space underneath for Ivan to write the Russian translation. I wanted Arman to have a choice and feel a sense of empowerment. The cards included the following:

- "Make marks with paint"
- "Fill the paper with colors"
- "Butterfly paintings (create by adding dabs of paint and then fold the paper to create an image)"
- "Relaxation—imagine a peaceful place"

- "Take a line for a walk—eyes closed/left hand"

- "Make a mess and work with it"

- "Take prints from paintings"

Arman looked at all the cards and then chose "Make marks with paint." He gathered blue, green, yellow, and red paint. I gave him a clutch of large brushes and rollers and asked him to make marks without worrying about what it looked like (Figure 30.2). He enjoyed doing big strokes of color in blue, green, and yellow, and then started to do narrow lines and worry about making all the edges perfect. He said he wanted to try working on larger paper the next time. We also tried to find something small in his life which he could contemplate changing—he suggested finding a place for his shoes that didn't lead to conflict with his children.

Figure 30.2 Broad brush strokes
Illustrated in the color insert

The following session he came alone again, and reported that he had found a better place for his shoes. He used large paper with thick brushes and foam sticks. He painted a sun (symbolizing clarity and honesty for him), blue sky, raindrops, rainbow, grass, and a tree. He talked about Armenia, how he liked looking at the rain, sun, and rainbows, which also symbolized dark times getting better. He did not retreat into perfectionism this time, and liked what he had done. He joked about selling it for lots of money and told me he had been the "joker" of his circle. It seemed a good sign that his sense of humor was returning.

The next session he chose "Fill the paper with colors" and used colored pencils to do bands of color diagonally across the paper. He liked it and declared it a "masterpiece." We discussed the fact that he could work quickly without being too much of a perfectionist, and still produce satisfying images. He asked for a recipe for play dough to get back to sculpting again.

Just before our eighth session, the family received the good news that they had "indefinite leave to remain" in the UK. However, Arman said he felt worse than before, as he couldn't quite believe it and worried that it would be reversed. During the session, he retreated to his perfectionist style and got frustrated with the result. He expressed fears that his mental health problems were chronic (his mother had committed suicide), but I encouraged him to see them as a phase of his life rather than permanent.

Beginning of New Life

Our next session was nearly a month later owing to other commitments. Arman was beginning to feel good about his new status. He chose "butterfly paintings" from the set of cards, and squeezed purple, blue, and black paints from the bottles, then folded the paper. As he opened up the paper, a look of surprise and delight came over his face—he really liked the result. He could see all sorts of animals in it—a deer, a peacock, and more. We discussed "nice surprises," compared with the unpleasant ones he had experienced. He then used felt-tip pens to draw a butterfly—"a new species of butterfly." A butterfly is often a symbol of new life and transformation.

The next few sessions were confusing for Arman; there was so much going on that he found it hard to focus. I suggested doing smooth bands of color. Arman chose soft colored pencils and liked the result, especially the more fluid parts. He continued this picture over three sessions and found that it was calming and helped him to concentrate. We were still trying to find him an art class and English lessons, but neither seemed to materialize.

Arman tried watercolor paints and liked them. He painted three trees in spring, two with flowers and one chopped off but beginning to sprout again, with leaves but no flowers yet. I asked him if that was like his life, and he looked at his picture and nodded.

Next session he painted a picture of a scene in Armenia (Figure 30.3), where his family had a dacha by the river, between two steep mountains. There was a little church on top of the mountain, some trees at the bottom, and a little bridge. He talked a lot about his life in Armenia, his schooling, his qualifications in welding and carpentry, and his continued telephone contact with his father. He finished the picture in the next session, adding the house, an old mill, a bathing pool, and stones for diving in and drying clothes. It seemed important for him to remember his former life in Armenia.

Figure 30.3 Favorite place in Armenia

Break

By this time practical issues became a priority. There was another house move, welfare benefits to rearrange, bills to pay, English classes to apply for, passports to get, and more. The mental health team wanted to discharge Arman, but he and I (and his wife) felt he needed a few more sessions. So we arranged a break of several months while the family moved to a council house (in another part of Bristol) and got settled. Initially it was a family effort to get him to art therapy, but he learnt to find his own way. We restarted nine months later. I had to make a special request for Ivan as interpreter, to maintain continuity.

Final Phase: Integration

We managed these final ten sessions fairly regularly. His first painting was of a symbol of eternity, painted in many colors, very balanced, "unlike real life," he said. He had many aspirations—ability to speak English, good job, car, etc.—but these still seemed unattainable. He made a step toward work by enrolling on a voluntary railway project, painting old engines, and drew these in one of our sessions.

He worried about his memory, and thought he had too much "old stuff" in there: I suggested he could use art therapy sessions to depict some of these memories if he wished. He thought this was a good idea, and decided to start with good memories, going back to the scene he had drawn before (Figure 30.3), but this time using colored pencils in a soft and warm style. He was now using the colored pencils consistently, drawing swiftly and freely, concentrating well, enjoying the results, and talking more about his life. We discussed the importance of being able to share good memories, and he said he had two friends in Brussels with whom he could share.

He ran out of positive memories to work on, and did not want to go back to bad memories. He looked again at the cards and chose "Relaxation—imagine a peaceful place." I took him through a relaxation and visualization and he drew a beautiful picture of a pond, lily pads, waterfall, trees, and flowers. His next picture was of the view from the back of his house, over a local park; he included the back garden that he had worked hard on. He was enjoying the peace and quiet of their situation on the edge of Bristol. The next session the whole family came, as I needed to see the children to verify their photos for their passport forms. But the children drew and played quietly, and Arman was able to draw in peace. He drew "his landscape"—rocks on one side, trees on the other, with water in between. His penultimate picture was of the view from his local bus stop—houses and trees, a peaceful scene. He said he was noticing things around him more, and generally thinking in a more positive way. His final picture was of a new swimming complex in Armenia, from a video brought back by a friend who had visited: he had been shocked at the changes. (Quite often migrants imagine their homeland staying exactly as they last saw it.) Arman used colored pencils for all the latter pictures (sadly they would not reproduce well for this chapter). We said goodbye and thanked Ivan, who had been part of the whole process.

Arman at last had a place on an English course, and (on appeal) a bus pass for the six-mile round trip. He was now less traumatized and able to learn. I made a home visit, at their request, and saw how Arman had improved the house with beautiful craftsmanship. There was a final Care Plan meeting, attended by the whole family, and Arman was discharged from art therapy and the mental health service. The whole process had taken two years.

Conclusion

The case study demonstrates how art therapy can help an asylum seeker/refugee to work through stages of trauma, find a source of healing, and achieve stability and a more normal life. Art therapy in such cases needs to include the flexibility to respond to rapidly changing circumstances, often involving activities normally seen as beyond the boundaries of therapy, to create a secure enough space to use therapeutically. The use of art as a means of communication can then help clients to work through life issues in a practical way.

References

Bristol Refugee Rights (2012) Information leaflet. Bristol: Bristol Refugee Rights.

Kalmanowitz, D. and Lloyd, B. (eds) (2009) *Art Therapy and Political Violence: With Art, Without Illusion.* London and New York: Routledge.

Kovacevic, K. (2012) "The exploration of therapeutic boundaries and containment in the context of art therapy with refugees." Unpublished research essay, University of Roehampton, London.

Chapter 31

Art as Healing with Children and Adults in Cambodia, China, Ethiopia, and the Ukraine

Doris Arrington

People of all ages and cultures have used art as a language and a healing for physical and spiritual pain. Art and image descend into the unconscious, stirring memories, empowering values, and healing loss. Art engages the mind, body, and spirit of humankind, opening each person to "the life of soul" (Jung 1972, pp.38–40). This chapter addresses how therapeutic art directives from trained staff helped individuals throughout the world recover from the "spectrum of trauma" (Nebrosky 2003, p.291). When language is an issue, an interpreter is always part of the treatment process.

Art as Healing in China

In 2005, I was invited to join the *Let Them Hear* medical team that traveled to China where we worked with hearing-impaired children and their families. Our team provided 75 hearing aids and performed five cochlear implants on five children. There, I came to understand why medical mission teams need to travel with art therapists. While members of the medical team are attending to the physical needs of clients, the art therapist is often the only one who has the occasion and the experience to ask the child or the parent to tell or draw what happened and how they felt about it. The art therapist can then provide directives that establish dialogue with the client and the family. Therapeutic art directives provide a vehicle to access the very core of trauma and loss (Arrington 2007).

In China, each year 10,000 children lose their hearing because of improper medication given by country doctors with limited training. Lu, an 11-year-old boy, was one of these children. Lu was the top of his class. When he lost his hearing due to meningitis and an improper dosage of medication, he could no longer attend school because he and his teacher could no longer communicate. His remote village had few books and no TV. Lu, with a bright and inquisitive mind, was impeded in his intellectual growth. Although he was loved by his parents, there was a real possibility that he would be unable to support them as they grew older; villagers thus saw Lu as a burden and often mistreated him. Without a cochlear implant or an effective hearing aid, Lu's future would be that of a beggar or a thief. If Lu had been a girl, the future would likely have included both those options as well as being sex-trafficked by a Chinese gang. Throughout the world, orphans and physically or emotionally challenged children are often kidnapped by gangs who traffic them into various criminal enterprises.

Today, art therapists travel throughout the world and share therapeutic art experiences with caregivers, counselors, teachers, and educators. Although we are not teaching these fellow helping professionals to become art therapists, as art therapy requires graduate training and a clinical internship, we are teaching them to understand how art is communication, why it is healing, and when to use it.

When I travel in a foreign country and teach art as a healing modality to local caregivers, it is not long before someone in the area, working as a counselor, comes to me and asks if I can come to their agency and teach them how to use art therapeutically. The Bridge (an assumed name), an agency in a large Chinese city, had seen the need for and established a safe house for sex-trafficked girls and women. When they asked me to come and share art directives, I agreed to meet with the group the following morning. Due to the need for secrecy, I was told where to go, where to wait, and who to look for. Eventually a guide met me and we found our way to a dark and crowded apartment. There, five or more young girls (10–12-year-olds), previously sold as virgins to businessmen to help secure their good business fortunes, were living with sex-trafficked girls (13 and older) and a small staff of women. Staff explained that every night they went to the street to talk to girls and invite them to come live in the shelter and change their lives. They told us that when the girls see staff regularly on the street and hear about the women who have been rescued, they become more trusting and decide to leave the brothels and go home with the caregivers. If, however, the girl is a brothel favorite, loud and angry men will come to the shelter beating on the door, yelling and threatening violence to everyone in the building if the girl is not returned to the brothel. Frightened by both the angry men and the building residences, women in the agency, advised by police who have been bribed by the pimps and criminals, return the girl to the brothel.

Therapeutic art directives help clients communicate their thoughts and feelings and often make spiritual and cultural sense of their abuse. Usually, wanting to help clients feel safe and in control, I begin an art therapy session by asking them to draw a safe place, or a safe person. However, with sex-trafficked and severely abused women who have rarely known a safe place or person, it is more meaningful to ask them to draw a calm place or a calm person. This is the directive I helped the caregivers at the brothel to utilize with these young women.

Art Materials

To help decide on the appropriate art materials to use, it is also helpful to know what, if anything, has happened in the shelter earlier in the day. Materials I usually carry with me include 3" × 5" index cards for motivation or care cards, small white paper bags for grief bags, multicolored paper cutouts of 12-inch circles, paper plates for mandalas, and magazine pictures of animals, birds, and fish for metaphorical exploration. I also bring a few boxes of thin or broad-tipped markers, oil pastels, scissors, glitter, glue, and multicolored feathers. Children and adults universally enjoy glitter and feathers.

When working with abused clients, I try to provide structure by explaining to the group what we will do together and by showing examples. After that, we make what we discussed out of the available materials and then group members are encouraged to talk about the experience. The young women at The Bridge were shown care cards and asked to make one for someone in the agency whom they cared for or who cared for them. Knowing that a girl had been returned to the brothel that evening, I was apprehensive about whether all the girls would be able to follow this directive. One of the agency staff, knowing what had occurred the night before, had gone by the flower market and purchased floral wire and several large bouquets of colorful, fragrant flowers. After the women had exchanged the care cards, staff helped them make flower crowns, wreaths, and necklaces and to discuss their experience that day in the group. The beauty, the texture, and the fragrance of the fresh flowers were therapeutic. Not everyone could talk about their fear from the prior evening, but many of the girls were able to think metaphorically and compare their lives to the fragile and beautiful flowers.

Art as Healing in the Ukraine

In 1991, the Ukraine, like other states that broke from the Soviet Union, faced economic hardships, few jobs, and significant increases in alcohol use. In addition, the government was unable to provide adequate funds for the unemployed and pensioners. As a result, 10,000 to 50,000 children moved from villages to cities, and then to the streets to find food and escape abusive caregivers. On the street, these cold and hungry children were exposed to illicit drugs and to the Ukrainian Mafia that trafficked street kids as either street soldiers or sex workers. In 2000, not realizing that it would change my life forever, I joined a health care team going to Kiev to assist doctors who were treating rescued children and to discern through the use of art therapy what these children were thinking and feeling. Members of our health care team had been invited to visit Kiev by Dr. Roman, a physician who began to be involved with these children by bringing them into his home. When he had 20 children in his small apartment, he raised funds and started an orphanage he called Father's House. Despite 30 years of training and experience in art therapy and psychology, I found myself being apprehensive.

However, this proved to be unwarranted as art therapy was readily accepted in his orphanage and other agencies in Kiev as a healing intervention for street children. Despite knowing very little about art therapy, Dr. Roman quickly recognized how helpful art was in identifying feelings for these traumatized children (Arrington 2007; Arrington and Yorgin 2001).

Initially, I worked with 50 children living in Father's House. The team agreed that we needed to gather information on the children's health, intelligence, educational history, and family situation so we would be able to evaluate what the children's strengths were and what we could expect from them (Arrington 2001; Gilroy, Tipple, and Brown 2012). Working with children in age and gender groups, I began by sharing my simple rules written in Ukrainian: "We respect group members, ourselves, our artwork, and our materials." This provided structure, which made the children feel safe and taught them to care for artwork, their own and that of others, the materials they were using, and each other. Next, we talked about their limited experiences with art materials. Encouraging them to use the materials, I suggested they draw their "favorite kind of day" (Manning 1987). When they reflected on their artwork, the children's sad or fantasized stories were revealed. Often they shared stories about the loss of their homes or the loss of their parents.

Whether or not they were able to speak about their art, the pictures, with their sharp points and lonely figures, revealed their pain (Arrington 2007). The art therapy sessions, with little children sitting on a caregiver's lap and middle-school children sitting close to staff, modeled to the children how to listen to honor each other's experiences.

After observing the art therapy group, Dr. Roman noted that he would like to be more involved in the art sessions since they provided him with insight into what the children were experiencing. Seeking help and wanting to share the art-as-healing experience, Dr. Roman made arrangements for our team to visit a state residential shelter staffed by untrained personnel where approximately 100 malnourished children lived. Known as the Isolator, it is one of approximately 35 similar agencies in the city of Kiev. At the Isolator, regardless of gender, each child's hair was shaved to eliminate lice. Their nicks and bruises were treated with purple merthiolate and their clothing was old and gray. It was not unusual for the children to be disciplined with sticks or switches carried by staff. The Isolator was a significant contrast to the orphanage run by Dr. Roman.

We began to get to know the children through various art exercises. Each child was then interviewed and meticulous notes were recorded in order to prepare a report for the staff the next day. In the afternoon, working on a small table, our team, including the interpreter, worked with four groups of 16 boys and girls; 20 staff members sat in chairs around the walls prepared to correct the children's behavior if needed. However, once the children were given art materials and a directive, they drew willingly. The children responded positively to the structure. My 30 years of experience with difficult children has been that if there are good art materials and an interesting art assignment children are willing participants. Only one teenager drew a naked person with breasts and a penis (Arrington 2001). He scratched through it and then threw it away. His art was later retrieved.

Our small team worked late into the evening matching pictures and information. The next day we were able to give the Isolator staff each child's entire name, village name, family, and educational history. Never had the staff at Father's House or the Isolator kept records on any of the children, not even their last names. Six months later, when I returned to the orphanage and the Isolator in Kiev, I was met by staff members who proudly shared their notes on the children who were in their care. Now they could tell who the children were, what village they were coming from, and how many times they had been brought to the Isolator by the authorities.

The art-based directives and assessments I used with the sexually and physically abused orphans at Father's House and at the Isolator are outlined in Appendix J.

With the assigned art-based directives and assessments, I was looking for common patterns in the children's art using my knowledge of the use of line, color, tones, form, and space as an art teacher, an art therapist, and a psychologist, and as found in specific scales in the Formal Elements Art Therapy Scale (FEATS) by Gantt and Tabone (1998).

Human trafficking is currently the number one crime worldwide (Kristof and WuDunn 2009). Through experience, however, we believe that directives used for art as healing are helpful in rehabilitating abused and trafficked victims (Arrington 2007). These directives help victims clarify their thoughts, get in touch with their feelings, and share both with staff and others. I often use magazine cutouts of animals. The children choose several they like and then the group looks for their strengths, weaknesses, opportunities, and threats (SWOT). The Instinctual Trauma Response (ITR) helps participants realize that the traumas they have suffered are just part of their life and not their whole life (Gantt and Tinnin 2007a, 2007b). Art therapy directives are also helpful with participants who want to learn how to forgive others and themselves (Luskin 2003).

Art as Healing with Ex-Prostitutes in Ethiopia

In spring 2007, my husband and I led a health care team to Ellilta, one of the few agencies in Addis Ababa, Ethiopia, that attempts to rehabilitate ex-prostitutes. There are few agencies concerned with rehabilitating ex-prostitutes. For ten days team members and staff sat on rugs on mud floors in corrugated steel housing. With the help of staff and interpreters, the art therapists taught 15 women and men how to heal trauma using art directives (Arrington 2001; Gantt and Tinnin 2007a, 2007b; Solomon and Siegel 2003; Tinnin, Bills, and Gantt 2002). Within each culture there are acceptable and unacceptable behaviors. In Ethiopia, the art experiences opened communication and healed sexual trauma for the women who, due to family poverty and culture, were often victims of rape or human trafficking.

Harla was one of these clients. According to the customs of her tribe Harla's family, when she was ten years old, married her to an older man. She was very unhappy and ran away to Addis where she worked first as a housekeeper and later as a construction worker. When work was hard to get and she felt she had no other option, Harla worked as a prostitute. Like many others in her condition, she lived in fear. Her only sense of safety emerged when she went home one evening with a counselor from Ellilta and found care, hope, and safety. Harla was illiterate. Until we offered her one, she had never held a crayon in her hand. However, once the ITR protocol was explained, she used it to tell her story (Tinnin et al. 2002). Each picture in the set of figures below (Figures 31.1 to 31.9) is representative of one stage of the ITR protocol. The pictures are in ITR order: Safe Place, Before Picture, Startle, Thwarted Intention, Freeze, Altered State of Consciousness, Body Sensations, Automatic Obedience, Self-repair. Often there is an After Picture requested.

Figure 31.1 Safe Place—"A calm place"

Figure 31.2 Before Picture—"Meeting the resource person" (Betti, counselor)

Figure 31.3 Startle—"What happened?"

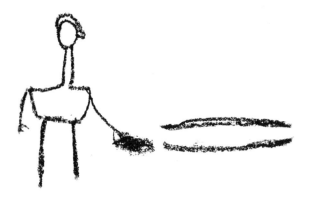

Figure 31.4 Thwarted Intentions—"Urge to escape"

Figure 31.5 Freeze—"Emotional numbing"

Figure 31.6 Altered State of Consciousness—"Where did your mind go?"

Figure 31.7 Body Sensations—"How I felt"

Figure 31.8 Automatic Obedience—"Following"

Figure 31.9 Self-repair—"Healing"

Art directives taught were focused on helping the women recover from their fearful experiences. They included a brief history of art as healing, paying particular attention to Ethiopian cultural norms, noting that their trauma was not their fault. We used art directives that emphasized how all of their feelings were okay, particularly grief or loss over family or childhood trauma. We taught the women how to take care of themselves by learning ways to support themselves and other women creatively (cooking, beading, tie-dying, etc.) (Moe 1993). In Ethiopia, team members found that when art didn't open up relationship channels, native music and dance had the power to do so.

Art as Treatment with Sex-Trafficked Children in Cambodia

In 2010, I traveled with a team to Phnom Phen, Cambodia, and the infamous village of Svay Pak, where in the recent past small children were sold to pedophiles for brief periods (Kristof and WuDunn 2009). Getting into the rehabilitative agencies requires a thorough identification check, but once inside our job was to help staff working with sex-trafficked children in agencies like Hagar and Agape integrate therapeutic art directives and material use into their skill sets. I was impressed at how young but well trained their staff was. As with Ethiopian groups, we worked sitting on the floor. For those working with younger children we suggested age-appropriate interventions like *I am special* and *All of my feelings are OK* using crayons, markers, clay, and poster paints (Moe 1993). For older children and adults, art interventions included making projects for specific goals like warming up, building coping skills, practicing self-soothing directives, identifying places and people who were calm or even safe, collecting a circle of feelings, decorating worry bags, and practicing forgiveness (Luskin 2003). Directives included a scribble chase, drawing a bridge, making care cards, making mandalas, and decorating grief bags using natural materials or those we had brought. As we do often, art materials were left with the agencies where we trained staff.

Return to Kiev

In spring 2011, with an invitation from the government, my husband and I returned to Kiev with four art therapists and three psychologists. For four days at Father's House and the Isolator we trained college-educated staff working in government and private agencies how to use therapeutic art directives with social orphans (their parents had given them up) and abused children. Our team, invited by Children's Hope Chest, traveled on to Russia where we worked with staff at Rybnoe, Ryazan, and Vladimir orphanages helping the older children build self-esteem so they could take care of themselves by making good life choices. The youth graduate from the orphanages at 16. Many are fearful because they have limited, if any, support. Without adult support these young people often find their limited choices lead them into crime, poverty, physical and sexual abuse, and death. Our hope is that, by teaching staff ways to use art directives, they can develop tools to bring about change and healing, leading to a better future for these children.

Conclusion

For me, art therapy has long been a calling. It is a ministry of compassion for children and adults who, because a human need was not met or met intermittently, or because a traumatic event occurred, live as victims in despair, fear, mistrust, rage, and threat. Therapeutic art is healing not only to the individuals but also to their families and the communities in which they live. When I first went to Kiev in 2000, the government did not acknowledge that there were homeless and abused children living on the streets. However, caring people in Kiev's agencies, communities, and government have brought change. They have sought out and hired compassionate caregivers and trained them how to care for traumatized and grieving children and youth. In 2010, recognizing that there is and has been a child crisis, the Ukrainian Parliament honored Dr. Roman for his leadership in the care of Ukraine's street children.

Today, my life goal to train others how to use art as healing continues to be supported. But I am not alone: many art therapists travel with art materials, teaching directives used for art as healing. Participating in therapeutic art can reduce fear. It can awaken creativity, bringing "life to the soul."

References

Arrington, D. (2001) *Home Is Where the Art Is: An Art Therapy Approach to Family Therapy.* Springfield, IL: Charles C. Thomas.

Arrington, D., (2007) *Art, Angst, and Trauma: Right Brain Interventions with Developmental Issues.* Springfield, IL: Charles C. Thomas.

Arrington, D. and Yorgin, P. (2001) "Art therapy as a cross-cultural means to assess psychosocial health in homeless and orphaned children in Kiev." *Art Therapy: Journal of the American Art Therapy Association 18,* 2, 80–86.

Gantt, L. and Tabone, C. (1998) *The Formal Elements Art Therapy Scale.* Morgantown, WV: Gargoyle Press.

Gantt, L. and Tinnin, L. (2007a) "Intensive trauma therapy of PTSD and dissociation: An outcome study." *Arts in Psychotherapy 34,* 69–80.

Gantt, L. and Tinnin, L. (2007b) "The Instinctual Trauma Response." In D. B. Arrington (ed.) *Art, Angst, and Trauma.* Springfield, IL: Charles C. Thomas.

Gilroy, A., Tipple, R., and Brown, C. (2012) *Assessment in Art Therapy.* London: Routledge.

Jung, C. (1972) *Mandala Symbolism* (trans. R.F.C. Hull). Princeton, NJ: Princeton University Press.

Kristof, N. and WuDunn, S. (2009) *Half the Sky: Turning Oppression into Opportunity for Women Worldwide.* New York: Alfred A. Knopf.

Luskin, F. (2003) *Forgive for Good.* New York: HarperCollins.

Manning, T. (1987) "Aggression depicted in abused children's drawings." *The Arts in Psychotherapy 14,* 5–24.

Moe, J. (1993) *Discovery: Finding the Buried Treasure.* Tucson, AZ: Stem Publications.

Neborsky, R. (2003) "A Clinical Model for the Comprehensive Treatment of Trauma Using an Affect Experiencing Attachment Theory Approach." In M. Solomon and D. Siegel (eds) *Healing Trauma: Attachment, Mind, Body, and Brain.* New York: W. W. Norton.

Solomon, M. and Siegel, D. (2003) *Healing Trauma: Attachment, Mind, Body, and Brain.* New York: W. W. Norton.

Tinnin, L., Bills, L., and Gantt, L. (2002) "Short-Term Treatment of Simple and Complex PTSD." In M. Williams and J. Sommer (eds) *Simple and Complex Post-Traumatic Stress Disorder: Strategies for Comprehensive Treatment in Clinical Practice.* New York: Haworth Press.

Chapter 32

Overseas Art Therapy Journeys

Frances E. Anderson

Global art therapy is about practicing one's passion (art therapy) "in the most adventurous place possible," knowing it will help others (Anderson 2011). This chapter offers many avenues to achieve this goal. Some of these ideas and actions are already known and some are not. A few best practices that I have utilized with a wide range of people from different countries and cultures are also included.

Starting the Journey

The journey starts with personal connections. It is from these contacts that overseas invitations emerge. I have been fortunate to have overseas contacts due to friendships developed during my graduate work. I have traveled to Australia and Yugoslavia to teach, to keynote conferences for the International Society for Education Through Art (INSEA), and to various art therapy organizations around the world. Other contacts have been made through involvement in professional associations. There are a growing number of presenters from other countries at the national American Art Therapy Association (AATA) conferences. Attending these presentations and making an effort to meet the lecturer may offer a way to establish a connection that could lead to an overseas art therapy endeavor. Another venue through which to make contacts is the European Consortium for Art Therapies Education (ECArTE). This organization holds conferences throughout Europe. Several websites list various art therapy organizations throughout the world. The International Expressive Arts Therapy Association (www.ieata.org), the International Art Therapy Association (www.internationalarttherapy.org), and the International Society for the Psychopathology of Expression (www.uia. be/s/or/en/1100052868) are a few. One may search on the Internet to locate other art therapy organizations. Examples not listed above include the Lithuanian Association of Arts Therapy (www.menoterapija.org), the Korean Art Therapy Association (www.korean-arttherapy.or.kr), and the East European Arts Therapy Association (http://eeata.net).

Travel Funds

Most countries and foreign institutions might want to have an art therapist give a workshop, teach, or do clinical work but many have no funds for travel, housing, or meals. Having an entrepreneurial spirit will help the art therapist to raise funds for the trip. One art therapist worked two jobs to get the travel money; another raised funds from her church by giving presentations about the country she hoped to visit. Many church mission trips would welcome the involvement of an art therapist. Once again, the caveat is that the travel funds have to be raised by each participant. Sometimes these mission trips provide financial assistance and, in a few rare cases, it might be possible to travel as part of a medical team. Some universities have an interest in global outreach and in providing overseas experience to their students. Many art therapy training programs have incorporated overseas experiences as part of their multicultural curriculum. The programs at Notre Dame de Namur University, the George Washington University, the Art Institute of Chicago, Lesley University, Loyola Marymount, Florida State University, Mount Mary College, Converse College, Emporia State University, and New York University come to mind, but there are many other art therapy training programs that do this. University study abroad and social justice programs may fund travel for students. For example, Florida State University's Center for Social Justice has sponsored undergraduate art therapy students who have worked with sex-trafficked girls in Thailand and with earthquake victims in Haiti. These university programs may not specify students in art therapy, but that does not mean the programs could not fund them. Because each academic institution is different, specifics cannot be provided here. Persistence and a willingness to investigate campus programs and identify similar programs and opportunities may well yield funding for an overseas art therapy endeavor.

Grants

The Foundation Directory is one of the best sources to find potential funders as there is an international grants section. There are two versions of the directory: one is a hard copy and the other is online. University grants offices and some community foundations may have access to the online version (http://fconline. foundationcenter.org). Contacting the community foundation in your geographic area can also lead to some outside funding. Often, there are businesses that have overseas offices or manufacture items in other countries. Contacting the specific community liaison for a particular business may provide information and "leads" for a program that addresses a particular need evident in that company's overseas locations. For example, Rotary Club International has programs to foster overseas connections. One art therapist received two such grants that took her to Australia and to Brazil. It is important to have personal connections with the civic group providing the funds.

    Having academic experience, credentials, and a publications record can qualify you for one of the grants offered by the Council on the International Exchange of Scholars (CIES) (www.cies.org). One must be a citizen of the United States to apply for most Fulbright awards. The most difficult award to obtain is the Fulbright Senior Scholar Award (FSSA). There are two types of FSSAs. One has a focus on teaching and the other focuses on both research and teaching. The FSSAs are limited to applicants with doctorates in specific fields. Applicants must demonstrate excellence in both scholarship and teaching. These grants can run from four months to a year. Fewer than half a dozen art therapists have received an FSSA.

The CIES also has other kinds of awards. The Fulbright Senior Specialist (FSS) has more flexibility and more opportunities than the FSSA. The FSS's goal is to help various overseas institutions with special projects or teaching. FSS grants provide travel expenses and a stipend and can run from two to six weeks. The overseas host institution must provide housing and meals. Several art therapists have been successful in obtaining these awards. If you are considering applying for a Fulbright award, talk with an art therapist who has been successful in obtaining one. Under the sponsorship of the FSS (as of this writing), art therapists have traveled to Australia, Ukraine, Taiwan, Thailand, and Pakistan. It is important to remember that these opportunities do not come to you: you have to seek them out. The only way to apply for the Fulbright programs is online. To qualify for an FSS one must have a doctorate in one of the fields listed on their website. There are about 12 eligible fields including education, public health, and social work. Art therapy is not on the list.

The reader may not be aware that the CIES also awards Fulbrights to overseas students and scholars to study in the United States. It also offers overseas teaching exchanges and these are administered through a specific country's local Fulbright Office.

Existing Resources for Overseas Travel
See Appendix K.

Research the Country's Culture
It helps to investigate the culture in which you might work. This is important even when making initial contacts (Hocoy 2002). I was invited to Thailand twice but found out that this was an invitation only, with no offer of travel funds. It was only through an FSS in 2008 that I was able to go to Thailand. It is always helpful to speak with someone who has recently traveled to the country that might be your destination. If there is a local newspaper in English, it will help in understanding the culture of the country you plan to visit if you do not speak the language.

Making Assumptions

Keeping an open mind will help prevent you from making assumptions—negative or positive—about the country or the specific workshop location in which you have an interest. For instance, do not make assumptions about available projection or computer equipment. In my case, I had requested projection equipment to give a presentation in an Asian country. I was assured the equipment would be there at my lecture, but when I arrived at the lecture hall the equipment was nowhere to be found. So I had to completely revamp my lecture immediately.

It is also important to make no assumptions about the participants attending a lecture or workshop. For instance, I was to speak about art therapy to a group of university-educated students in Pakistan. My first question was "How many of you have had any art [lessons]? Please raise your hands." Of the 200 students in the lecture hall, only one hand was raised. Again, I had to totally change my presentation. Fortunately I had my own laptop with several PowerPoint presentations that I used to provide an introduction to the topic of child development as it relates to the artistic stages of children's art. I also discussed the impact of the arts on learning in other subjects (Jansen 2001). I also worked with children who had been victims of flooding in Pakistan. Pakistan being a Muslim country, I worried about religious beliefs that dictated no artistic rendering of any human form. I happily discovered that there were no such restrictions.

Other Issues

How one dresses can have unforeseen consequences. On my first Thailand visit, the country was in mourning over the death of the monarch's sister. I could only wear black or white colored clothes. In other countries, women do not wear dresses. On several occasions, I had to buy some cloth, go to a tailor, and have some slacks made, as there were no stores with ready-made clothes. In some cultures it is considered a compliment to dress in the same manner as the local women or men. If this is the custom, in some instances specific cultural dress can be purchased via the Internet.

Art Materials

In some countries there are no art materials available and it is advisable to bring your own. Find out before you leave and ask the organizers what they may provide and whether there are specific art media available that are typically used in that culture. If so, it will be important to utilize these same materials. In planning for work with the Pakistani flood victims, I found that the only materials available were used plastic bottles and used paper. While there is the possibility that a culture cannot obtain the kinds of art materials that art therapists use in the West, I think it is important to provide an opportunity to use these art materials. After students have had direct experience using the art materials one provides, these students often make creative adaptations to fit their situations. Art media might include markers, crayons, pencils, brushes, pairs of scissors, glue, clear and masking tape, colored paper, stickers, feathers, and any other material that you utilize in your clinical practice. It is important to have enough recycled materials for each member of the group.

Before my first FSS trip to Pakistan in 2010, I was not told what I was to present or anything about the workshop participants. While I did ask about this, my question was not specifically answered. Sometimes it is wise to refrain from pressing this point due to cultural customs, as it could be considered impolite. Additionally, communication is never easy or clear in a long-distance situation. As I packed, I threw in a roll of masking tape and a few boxes of markers along with body outlines and my laptop with many PowerPoint files. I found out 30 minutes before my lecture that I would be speaking to teachers in training. Since only one student had had any art training and none knew about children's artistic development, I thought making a life-size body trace would be a great way of introducing them to art materials and the creative process. However, I had no large drawing paper of any kind. Then I remembered my masking tape and thought that sheets of old newspapers could be taped together to make a large drawing/tracing surface. So I asked the students to bring old newspapers for the next day's lecture. Due to time constraints I divided the 200 students into groups of five or six and had each group create one body trace. Thus, it took only three sheets of old newspaper taped together to create each body trace. I discussed the ways this activity could be used with children and adults with adaptations. The results were astounding (see Figures 32.1–32.3).

Figure 32.1 Figure created on newspaper 1

Illustrated in the color insert

Figure 32.2 Figure created on newspaper 2

Illustrated in the color insert

Figure 32.3 Picture of the group with author

Plastic Bottles, Newspapers, Paper Plates, and Dirt

When I was preparing to do clinical work with flood victims on my second visit to Pakistan in the fall of 2010, I found that the only available "art materials" were used paper and empty plastic bottles. After some experimentation, I discovered I could use the paper and bottles to create puppets. (A permanent marker and clear or masking tape are of great help in these creations.) I worried that there might not even be a flat surface on which to draw. I experimented with various sticks and found that wood chopsticks worked very well to draw on the ground. (One may need water to make the dirt moist enough so that marks can be made.)

I also thought that the paper could be used to make paper airplanes. There are several kinds of paper airplanes that can be made in this way. When I contacted one of the art therapists who had extensive overseas experience, including in Cambodia, she suggested feathers, small sacks, and paper plates (for making three-dimensional work) (Arrington, personal communication, 2012). After some research and experimentation, I discovered that many different art experiences could be accomplished using paper plates. The center of the plate is a great surface for drawing.

Who Pays for the Art Materials?

Be prepared to pay for art materials and do not be afraid to ask for help from friends, family, and other contacts. Before going on my second FSS trip to Pakistan, I sent out an email to my friends and others in my exercise classes. I included a list of specific art materials and asked if each person could bring something from the list. I also quickly added that people did not have to bring anything and that their prayers were the most important "material." A restaurant supplier donated 500 (plain) paper plates. Others gave me money for art materials. A public school art director donated construction paper, computer paper, markers, colored pencils, and some other items. I took two large duffle bags of 50 pounds each of art materials. Every airline has a specific baggage size and weight limits. It will be important to know the limits that pertain to the airline you are using. The issue of providing art materials can be both an inspiration and problematic— especially if the materials you bring are too expensive or impossible to obtain in that culture. However, it has been my experience that workshop participants can be very creative in utilizing locally available materials.

Some children and adults have never held a crayon or used any other art medium. Incorporate some basic instruction on the use of art materials. Flexibility is essential because you may have to make some adaptations. What art materials are considered taboo or inappropriate? If there are art materials available, are they nontoxic? What attitude does the culture have toward making art? In some cultures making art is considered frivolous. In others, making images is so powerful that both the act of making images and the images themselves are considered taboo (Hocoy 2002).

Ethical Issues

Because most overseas visits may range from three days to two weeks, the kind of art therapy practiced is often brief art as therapy (Kramer 1971) or creating art for healing (Arrington, personal communication, 2012). With brief art as healing, one may have only 20 minutes, 1 hour, or 3 hours. I never knew how long my sessions were going to last or how many participants would attend. I always explain the ethical issues in providing brief workshops for non-art therapists (Kalmanowitz and Potash 2010; Moon 2006). I believe that one or two weeks of art as healing is better than having none.

Keep in mind that art therapy interventions are culturally influenced. One must always be sensitive to the culture of the clients and workshop participants. Flexibility and a willingness to make adaptations are essential (Gomez Carlier and Salom 2012). I frequently talk about the need to develop art therapy practices that are reflective of or influenced by the cultures in which I am presenting, as well as how art therapists are trained in the United States. I always add that each country has to develop its own education programs reflecting its culture. That may mean keeping in mind that university education is unobtainable or unavailable (Anderson 2011; Arrington 2005; Gomez Carlier and Salom 2012; Hocoy 2002; Kalmanowitz and Potash 2010; Kapitan, Litell, and Torre 2011; Stoll 2005). A recent article by Potash and Bardot (2012) addressed this issue with sensitivity and in considerable detail.

There are ethical issues associated with giving participants a completion certificate that specifically uses the term "art therapy." Pakistan, Thailand, and Argentina are countries where certificates are often given to workshop participants. Because "art therapy" in the United States refers to a two-year graduate study program, I have encouraged the use of the term "art as healing" or "art for expression" instead of the term "art therapy" on these certificates. I do this to clarify that having a certificate that says one has completed a workshop in "art therapy" does not mean one is an art therapist.

Copying Lectures and Interventions

Some cultures do not have the concept of "copyright." In other cultures, copyrights are simply ignored. Give some thought to this issue before giving a lecture or making a presentation. The information *will* be copied. On a positive note, I like to think that this copying is done out of an eagerness for information. In this context I believe it is important to share as much information as possible.

Ideas for Art Expression Activities
Art Material Exploration

As I mentioned previously, many children and adults may have little or no experience with art materials. If there is no drawing paper, I use old newspapers. I might begin with markers and have participants make large sweeping strokes on the page. If the participants are adults, I sometimes ask, "What age would allow you to be able to be freer and express yourself?" and encourage them to pretend to be six, nine, or even four years old. This takes away the "I do not know how to draw" anxiety. In one Asian culture, art was understood to consist of drawing with rulers in a very tight copying technique. Thus, having the participants do large sweeping lines helped define art in a different way. I might then talk about how lines can have meanings or can stand for a word or feeling (always keeping in mind language and cultural differences). So we might draw a "happy" line, an "angry" line, and a "sad" line. Or, we might draw a line that represents a situation such as going to a party, dancing, etc. I generally prefer markers because they are easily transported, produce a bright color, and are not messy like crayons or oil pastels, which tend to melt.

Manning's Draw Your Favorite Kind of Day

Manning's research is based on climatic details shown in the drawings of aggressive children (Manning 1987). I often use this directive as an icebreaker with children. When I asked Argentine children to draw their favorite kind of day, most of the drawings had nothing to do with climate. One child drew the day he got his dog; several drew pictures of their birthday parties. Others drew going to the beach. The word "favorite" can be interpreted differently depending on the cultural context (Cirlot 1971). Children's drawings in Argentina tend to include their families. Family occasions are very reflective of their culture (Anderson 2002).

Body (Person) Outlines

I have found pre-prepared art activities (Anderson 1992, 1994; Vick 1999) to be very helpful in encouraging participation. They can provide some idea as to the developmental ages of the children and are also especially useful with adults. I carry about 20 copies of these with me when I travel. If I need more, I can draw them myself on plain paper or on used newspapers if other paper is not available. This activity was an adaptation made by one of my art therapy students. She scaled down a larger body outline used by Kristine Mendenhal among others and shown in the film *Drawing from the Fire* (1995). Using a sheet of 8.5" × 11" paper (or longer standard legal size in some cultures) makes the outlines easier to transport and reproduce. Participants are encouraged to complete the outline. I give some suggestions. For example, I might say, "If you have a headache, the head might be larger, or covered in red or black or some other cultural color meaning pain." I also encourage adding additional items to the outline. Children may complete the picture in a more concrete way by using the same colors as they are wearing.

In my work in Pakistan, I made one important cultural change in the body outlines because of the traditional clothes that Pakistani men and women wear. In that country the women wear a kind of shirt called a kameez that comes below the knees. The men also wear a kameez, but it is simpler and has a Chinese collar. Educated Pakistani men often wear Western clothes instead of the kameez. So I provided a choice of outlines. Some were based on Western clothing and some had a kameez incorporated into the outline (see Appendices M and N: Body Outline for Pakistani Male and Body Outline for Pakistani Female; Figure 32.4 shows an example of a completed Pakistani male outline).

In addition to differences in language, there are other cultural differences. In one group of 60 flood victims, the four- to seven-year-old children (both male and female) immediately began working on a body trace. The older girls were not expected to do a life-sized body trace because, in Muslim culture, women are always covered up. However, the culture does permit women to wear jewelry, so the older girls gathered around a large table where they used markers, shiny stickers, and feathers to create jewelry out of paper plates. Others created hats and crowns. I had brought 1000 shiny stickers and they were all gone in less than 30 minutes. (I had meant to cut the roll in half so I could use the stickers with other children. I should have done this before I placed the roll on the table.) So, I learned to put out only the art materials that would be used, not everything that I had. Using up all those stickers reminded me that these were very poor children and few, if any, "owned" anything of their own.

Figure 32.4 Pakistani man

In working with the flood victims, I had some local high school volunteers. After I showed examples of the kinds of art that was age appropriate for the children, the volunteers nodded, indicating that they understood. In reality, no volunteer understood (and would not have done so unless they had used the same art materials that the children were to use). There was no time for the volunteers to experiment with the art materials, so they worked right along with the children.

Conclusion

I began with a statement that paraphrased remarks by Diane Sawyer about the advice her father had given her: "Find something you are passionate about, practice it in the most remote places on earth, and be certain that it helps others" (Diane Sawyer, interviewed by Oprah Winfrey) (Anderson 2011). It is my sincere hope that you find this advice helpful in your many overseas adventures.

References

Anderson, F. E. (1992) *Art for All the Children: Approaches to Art Therapy for Children with Disabilities.* Springfield, IL: Charles C. Thomas.

Anderson, F. E. (1994) *Art-Centered Education and Therapy for Children with Disabilities.* Springfield, IL: Charles C. Thomas.

Anderson, F. E. (2002) *Final Report: Cross-Cultural Research on Argentine Children's Drawings.* Council on the International Exchange of Scholars, Buenos Aires, Argentina. Unpublished report.

Anderson, F. E. (2011) "International spotlight: A visit to Mortenson's three cups of tea country." *American Art Therapy Association Newsletter, Winter, 2011.* Washington, DC: American Art Therapy Association.

Arrington, D. B. (2005) "Global art therapy training—Now and before." *The Arts in Psychotherapy 32,* 3, 193–203.

Art Therapy India Group Members. Retrieved July 24, 2012. From group-digests@linkedin.com.

Cirlot, J. E. (1971) *A Dictionary of Symbols, Second Edition.* New York: Vail-Ballou Press.

Council on the International Exchange of Scholars. Retrieved June 20, 2012. From www.cies.org.

The Foundation Directory. Retrieved June 18, 2012. From http://fconline.foundationcenter.org.

Florida State University's Center for the Advancement of Social Justice. Retrieved June 20, 2012. From www.cahr.fsu.edu/sub_category/_field_placement.html.

Gomez Carlier, N. and Salom, A. (2012) "When art therapy migrates: The acculturation challenge of sojourner art therapists." *Art Therapy: Journal of the American Art Therapy Association 29,* 1, 4–10.

Hocoy, D. (2002) "Cross-cultural issues in art therapy." *Art Therapy: Journal of the American Art Therapy Association 19,* 4, 141–145.

Jansen, E. (2001) *Art with the Brain in Mind.* Reston, VA: Association for Supervision and Curriculum Development.

Kalmanowitz, D. and Potash, J. (2010) "Ethical considerations in the global teaching and promotion of art therapy to non-art therapists." *The Arts in Psychotherapy 37,* 1, 20–26.

Kapitan, L., Litell, M., and Torres, A. (2011) "Creative Art Therapy in a Community's Participatory Research and Social Transformation." *Art Therapy: Journal of the American Art Therapy Association 28,* 2, 64-73.

Kramer. E. (1971) *Art as Therapy with Children.* New York: Schocken Books. Revised edition Magnolia Street Publishers, Chicago, IL, 1994.

Kramer, E. (1993) *Art as Therapy with Children, Second Edition.* Chicago, IL: Magnolia Street Publishers.

Manning, T. (1987) "Aggression depicted in abused children's drawings." *The Arts in Psychotherapy 14,* 1,15–24.

Moon, B. (2006) *Ethical Issues in Art Therapy.* Springfield, IL: Charles C. Thomas.

Potash, J. S. and Bardot, H. (2012) "Conceptualizing international art therapy education standards." *The Arts in Psychotherapy 39*, 2, 143–150.

Stoll, B. (2005) "Growing pains: The international development of art therapy." *The Arts in Psychotherapy 32*, 3, 171–191.

Vick, R. (1999) "Utilizing prestructured art elements in brief group art therapy with adolescents." *Art Therapy: Journal of the American Art Therapy Association 16*, 2, 67–77.

Chapter 33

Developing Therapeutic Arts Programs in Kenya and Tanzania
A Collaborative Consultation Approach
Catherine Hyland Moon

Introduction

As increasing numbers of art therapists cross international borders to engage in research, consultation, and educational initiatives, it is essential to critically evaluate these practices with the aims of undermining tendencies toward ethnocentrism and of promoting a decolonizing approach to the work. This chapter proposes a model of international collaborative consultation that emphasizes reflexivity, power sharing, and cultural relevance. An ongoing project to develop therapeutic arts programs in Kenya and Tanzania provides an example of the challenges and benefits of this collaborative model.

Organizational Context

Since 2007 I have served as a consultant with Global Alliance for Africa (GAA), a not-for-profit organization that addresses the needs of orphans and other vulnerable children impacted by the AIDS pandemic in sub-Saharan Africa. GAA, in partnership with local grassroots organizations, designs and implements economic strengthening programs as the basis for providing sustainable care. The organization employs a multidimensional approach, implemented by a primarily African staff, to address the shelter, food security, educational, vocational, legal, health care, and psychosocial needs of the children (Global Alliance for Africa n.d.).

The analogous mission of GAA's Therapeutic Arts Program (TAP), developed in collaboration with partners in East Africa, is to "provide emotionally and physically safe spaces where orphaned and vulnerable children and youth are valued and respected as contributing members of the community, and where they can use the arts to freely express themselves, be unburdened of whatever troubles them, learn from each other, gain confidence in their skills and abilities, and experience a sense of belonging" (Therapeutic Arts Program consultants and partners, personal communication, 2011).

Development of the Therapeutic Arts Program

In 2008 I became a consultant for GAA to assist in developing the TAP. Since that time I have worked with US art therapist Angela Lyonsmith and African colleagues Sane and Eunice Wadu, who are well-known visual artists in Kenya, and Haji Maeda, a drama and music instructor at the Bagamoyo College of Art in Tanzania. Together we have been developing the TAP program, with the input of GAA staff and partners and the art therapists, artists, and other cultural workers who have traveled to Africa with us each year. In this chapter I frequently use the pronoun *we*, which reflects the collaborative nature of the project.

My involvement in the TAP began with a trip to Tanzania and Kenya sponsored by GAA. We traveled as a group from the United States and East Africa, participating in cultural exchange workshops, facilitating art camps for children, and visiting GAA's partner programs. When the rest of the group members returned to their respective homelands, I stayed in East Africa an additional week to visit social service sites and engage in conversations with artists, social workers, mental health workers, teachers, and vocational counselors about local arts and healing resources and about the potential of developing a therapeutic arts program in the region. As a result of these conversations, and in consultation with GAA staff, the TAP was born. It is based on a model of identifying East African artists and cultural workers who provide valued services to local children, and then partnering with them to build art programs that promote children's psychosocial health. Given the absence of infrastructure in East Africa to support art therapy education and professionalization, we provide *therapeutic arts* trainings aimed at a paraprofessional level. Similar to situations in other impoverished locales, this alternative approach to education and training has placed the benefits of art therapy within reach (Kapitan, Litell, and Torres 2011). To support the trainings, Angela Lyonsmith and I authored a draft training manual that incorporates accessible language and a multi-arts focus. We wrote it with the intention of eventually enlisting our African partners as co-authors, to incorporate culture-specific experience and knowledge in relation to indigenous arts and healing practices.

Beginning in the summer of 2008 I have returned annually to East Africa, each year traveling with a group of cultural workers from the United States, Africa, and sometimes other countries. Those from the United States share their knowledge and skills related to the arts and art therapies, and African artists share their knowledge and skills related to East African cultural resources, indigenous healing practices, and the use of the arts to help vulnerable children and youth. Based on a *train the trainers* model, the eventual aim is for East Africans to become the trainers, implementing the therapeutic arts trainings and programs in culture-specific ways that meet the needs of local communities. Economic sustainability is being facilitated through our African partners' involvement in GAA's microfinancing programs.

Theoretical Foundations

> Theory is never a disinterested relay of the happening of a world out there...
> Theory also writes the world in its image. (Jazeel and McFarlane 2010, p.113)

In this section I briefly discuss the developing theoretical foundations that inform the work we do in East Africa. The theory building is complicated by multiple factors: the contested value of humanitarian aid in sub-Saharan Africa, the complex nature of cross-cultural work between White, Western art therapists working with collaborators from the Global South (in hierarchical terms, "Third World" or "developing" countries), and the scarcity of literature about international art therapy consultations. Add to that the dearth of literature by Kenyan and Tanzanian theorists and practitioners on the subjects of counseling, therapy, and indigenous healing practices, and the theoretical base is, of necessity, contingent and evolving. The theoretical strands that have proven most useful thus far are postcolonial theory, liberation theory, and literature on the internationalization of psychology, counseling, and art therapy.

Postcolonial Theory

Postcolonial theory provides a framework for critically analyzing the internationalization of art therapy, particularly in relation to the exporting of art therapy from the Global North to the Global South. *Postcolonialism* refers to the historical legacy of control imposed on a culture or country by an invading force, as well as its afterlife of cultural traumas, inherited institutional structures, and unequal distributions of social power and privilege (Good et al. 2008; Norsworthy and Khuankaew 2006). Postcolonial theory exposes the propensity of dominant groups to define constructs like *developed* and *undeveloped* (Ladson-Billings and Donner 2008). It also acknowledges the voices and perspectives of those who have been marginalized (Racine and Petrucka 2011) and fosters decolonizing ways of theorizing and practicing cross-cultural work.

Colonization can be psychological as well as physical. It is reinforced when dominant values, beliefs, and practices are promoted as superior and the perspectives of the colonized are viewed as inferior and thus rendered insignificant or invisible. US psychology and, by extension, art therapy have been implicated in the imposition of dominant ideologies such as individualism and scientism, along with exoticizing, trivializing, or disregarding other countries' indigenous psychological constructs and healing practices (Leung 2003; Norsworthy and Khuankaew 2006; Misra, as cited in Marsella 1998). This has resulted in a loss of globally diverse ways of conceptualizing and responding to trauma and mental distress (Watters 2010).

Postcolonial theory has helped me recognize the evidence of colonized mentalities in the Kenyan and Tanzanian artists when they persist in deferring to the supposed superiority of my knowledge and skills. Likewise, I have had to resist slipping into a colonizer mentality by assuming the role of the expert, particularly given that I am the cultural outsider and thus often largely ignorant of local cultural complexities. Assuming the expert role without attention to the power and privilege I hold in the situation serves to reinforce the postcolonial dynamics of domination and subordination.

Liberation Theory

Liberation theory, based on Freire's (1993/1970) educational model and Martín-Baró's (1994) approach to psychology, provides an antidote to colonization by proposing that those who are oppressed have the capacity to identify, analyze, and take collective action against oppressive situations for the purpose of liberating themselves. It positions disenfranchised citizens as the authorities of their own experiences, and as the ones most capable of developing solutions. The liberatory therapist stands in solidarity with those who are marginalized by facilitating the development of critical consciousness, supporting the emergence of collective solutions, and collaborating in actions directed toward social change (Freire 1993/1970; Golub 2005; Martín-Baró 1994; Norsworthy and Khuankaew 2006). Watkins and Shulman (2008) suggest that, through liberatory arts practices, communities are able to reconnect with traditional cultural forms, strengthen social networks, interrupt social amnesia, restore capacities for meaning making, and move from silence toward transformative action.

An important aspect of my work in Tanzania and Kenya has been to become acquainted with locally generated liberatory arts practices. For example, while visiting the Kibera slum in Nairobi, a few of us involved with the TAP met and worked alongside a youth artists' collective. The youth incorporated dance, drama, and poetry in performances aimed at addressing critical social and political issues affecting the community. The youth, all orphans, spoke movingly about how the collective had become their family and provided them with a sense of security. They expressed excitement about working with Eunice and Sane Wadu, TAP collaborators and famous Kenyan artists. Later that evening, Sane became tearful as he talked about the encounter with the youth. He said they reminded him of his own experiences as a young adult, when the activist arts community he joined saved him from becoming a social outcast and gave him a sense of purpose in life.

There have been many other such encounters with liberatory arts practices in my travels in East Africa, such as a college art instructor who used drama to engage local villages in pressing social issues; a group of disabled artists who reclaimed their social dignity and economic stability by developing a business selling one-of-a-kind handicrafts made from recycled materials; and Masai Mbeli, an artist collective in the Kibera slum that organized the Art for Peace Healing Project after the post-election violence in 2007. In all these instances, the knowledge I received about sub-Saharan Africa as a place of greed, corruption, instability, and ineffectiveness has been disrupted and replaced with experiences characterized by generosity, creativity, resourcefulness, critical consciousness, political savvy, and commitment to social change.

International Consultation Work in Counseling, Psychology, and Art Therapy

In international collaborative consultation it is important to recognize that Western models of therapy are themselves indigenous, and to be aware of the consequences of their use in non-Western contexts. The aim is to encourage the development of indigenous psychologies that address locally defined problems and generate culturally relevant solutions. The likelihood of success is enhanced when the collaborative relationships are reciprocal and mutually beneficial, characterized by respect, solidarity, and power sharing (Horne and Mathews 2006; Kalmanowitz and Lloyd 2005, 2011; Leung et al. 2009; Marsella 1998; Norsworthy and Khuankaew 2006).

I have come to appreciate that, as a cultural outsider, my knowledge of Kenya and Tanzania is limited and incomplete. Therefore, I try to listen more than talk. As much as possible, I focus on "decentering myself in the learning process in the service of supporting collaborators in finding their own voices to language their experiences and…[access] their own knowledge, wisdom, and solutions" (Norsworthy and Khuankaew 2006, p.437). I judiciously share my knowledge and experiences, with attention to how it is being received, conscious of the potential for my perspectives to be either idealized or rejected.

After working together for five years, I see evidence that my African colleagues and I are progressing in our collaborative relationships. During my last visit, Salum, a new African collaborating artist, noted that our training manual addresses the incidents of mental illness that arise as a result of everyday life, but not those that arise as a result of witchcraft. I admitted my lack of knowledge and experience in relation to witchcraft and said that I would have to rely on them to educate me. A fascinating conversation about various manifestations of witchcraft ensued. The African artists expressed a multitude of perspectives in relation to witchcraft— belief in its power, awareness of it being used as a front by scam artists, anger at its assumed role in causing disability or illness, and evidence of negative bias toward "backward" ethnic groups whose practice of it is believed to be widespread. My African colleagues' freedom in speaking to me about witchcraft was evidence of their growing trust in me.

At the end of the conversation, Eunice suggested that next year we focus on rewriting the manual so that it better reflects the local context. I silently rejoiced at this sign of progress in our collaborative relationship. Yet I wonder if it will be enough to revise a training manual that is based on a Western psychology paradigm and worldview. We might need to scrap it entirely, replacing it with a manual that privileges the values, knowledge, wisdom, and practices of the East Africans, supplemented by complementary Western counseling and therapy perspectives (Norsworthy et al. 2009).

Sharing Knowledge through Collaborative Consultation

Over time, we have recognized that the most fitting and productive way to frame our work in East Africa is through the lens of cross-cultural exchange rather than the hierarchical paradigm of training and supervision. Kester (2011) proposes that the most successful socially engaged art practices are characterized by "a pragmatic openness to site and situation, a willingness to engage with specific sites and communities in a creative and improvisational manner, a concern with non-hierarchical and participatory processes, and a critical and self-reflexive relationship to practice itself" (p.125). These characteristics also are relevant for successful international art therapy work. In Kenya and Tanzania, our collaborative model of consultation emphasizes reflexivity, power sharing, cultural relevance, and openness.

Reflexivity

> The tension between doing "good works" and the recognition that this may be seen in the future as contributing to the continued oppression of Indigenous people ought not to be sought to be resolved… It provides the motivation to continue to reflect on…whether interventions have positive social consequences, have negative consequences, or help promote the status quo. (Bishop et al. 2002, pp.617–618)

Those of us from the United States who work in East Africa cultivate "a state of mind in which we are interested and open but always tentative about what we understand" (Dean 2001, p.629). We practice reflexivity, an ongoing process of reflecting and acting in which we acknowledge our privileged social positions, make explicit our values, biases, and prejudices, and challenge our cultural and professional assumptions. We see the value of being "inside messy spaces of immersion and involvement" (Jazeel and McFarlane 2010, p.114) through which we may come to understand our East African collaborators' lived experiences within historical, social, gendered, and cultural contexts (Racine and Petrucka 2011; Sparks and Park 2000).

For example, one year we traveled to a rural area of Kenya to work with children at a facility run by Catholic nuns. The accommodations for the women in our group were in the same residence where the nuns lived. However, Maeda, a male, and Eunice and Sane, a married couple, stayed in a separate building. One morning while we were there, Eunice told me that she and Sane had become alarmed during the night by the gagging noises coming from Maeda's room. I asked Maeda what had happened. He told me that his ancestors had choked him. Maeda, a Muslim, said his ancestors were displeased with him for three reasons: for mistakenly having eaten pork the day before, for having skipped his nighttime prayers, and for staying at a Catholic compound. He looked directly at me and said, "This was not a dream. My ancestors visited me." Later, when I was back in Chicago and told a colleague this story, the colleague raised an eyebrow, cocked his head, and said, "That's pretty primitive thinking, isn't it?" I was disturbed by his response, but also had to admit that my own initial internal reaction had been similar. This recognition caused me to call into question my cultural assumptions. Who am I to say that Maeda's ancestors did not visit him that night? The dominant US culture that privileges logic and rationalism would locate Maeda's experience in the realm of dreams or imagination. But maybe Maeda is acutely attuned to ancestral relationships that I cannot even fathom. Who is to say that my more limited, rationally based perspective is not the more primitive one? Why is it that the theoretical construct of dreaming is legitimized while communicating with one's ancestors is denigrated? By asking these questions, I decenter my privileged position and enter "into the messy space of immersion and involvement" wherein Maeda's experiences are foregrounded and I recognize that my own are historically and culturally situated. It is a space where understanding is tentative, inclusive, and open-ended.

Power Sharing

True collaboration cannot take place without ongoing attention to power sharing based on mutual respect and recognition of each other's strengths and expertise. Despite the reality that our African collaborators live in areas of extreme hardship, they have resources that include histories, knowledge, skills, hopes, and dreams (Denborough and Wakhungu 2006). Each year we begin our collaborative consultations by asking the African artists how their work with the children has gone, and by enlisting their help in setting the agenda for our time together. Over the years, we have moved toward more equal exchanges of ideas, information, and skills, along with a more recent development of collaboratively led trainings.

Despite all our efforts, power sharing has not come easily. Our lack of a common mother tongue requires frequent checks to make sure we understand each other, punctuated by translations in Kiswahili among the Africans. To bypass some of these language barriers, we have focused on experiential learning whenever possible. However, misunderstandings persist. In a number of instances, the arts activities for children facilitated by our collaborators have borne little resemblance to the plan upon which we had all "agreed." More recently, our differences in perspective and opinion have been overtly expressed, yet another positive sign that our collaboration is maturing.

Even the writing of this chapter is problematic in relation to power sharing. As the author, my voice becomes authoritative, while our local collaborators are relegated to the role of informants whose perspectives and experiences I interpret. I determine "which topics are addressed and which are not, what is questioned and what is taken for granted, even whether a discussion takes place at all" (Jagger 1998, p.11). To rectify this situation, I am discussing strategies with my African colleagues for co-authoring publications.

Cultural Relevance and Openness

While the cultural value placed on the arts in Kenya and Tanzania might suggest that the arts therapies would be a good fit for addressing trauma, loss, and mental distress in these countries, the reality is that 80 percent of the population in sub-Saharan Africa seek health care services from traditional healers (Levers, as cited in Gerstein et al. 2009). Therapy and counseling are not widely understood social constructs; institutionalized structures of care are scarce, while informal community-based care is common. Further, critical engagement in the work requires "resistance to an 'all arts heal' discourse" (MacLeod 2011, p.151).

We attempt, therefore, to suspend imposing our Western perspectives and practices until we understand the impact and relevance they will have in the local context (Horne and Mathews 2006). We engage in "social perspective taking" (Ibrahim 1996, p.83) whereby we refrain from immediately passing judgment when faced with unfamiliar practices or beliefs, and instead bear witness to what is happening and attempt to understand the underlying rationale or perspectives. We value the ongoing process of gathering information and experience from and with our collaborators, judiciously sharing our Western ideas and practices, reflecting on their relevance in the local context, revising our approaches and perspectives, and mutually co-constructing new ways of working and thinking.

It is not always easy, however, to remain open and nonjudgmental in this process, particularly when culturally relevant practices are dissonant with Western counseling values. For example, one day Eunice and Sane told one of my US colleagues, Angela, and me about an experience they had had with a young boy working in their home-based studio. The boy was behaving aggressively toward other children. After being told he had to leave the space, the boy went outside and began throwing stones at the studio windows. Knowing they had to establish limits with him, Sane and Eunice asked two of the older boys to go get the younger boy and return him to the studio. When they had done so, Eunice reprimanded the young boy for his behavior and then caned him. Though Sane reassured us that it was a very light caning and only on the boy's feet, we were stunned. The use of corporal punishment is so antithetical to our approach to art therapy! However, we held our tongues for the moment, and simply listened to their story. They went on to say that the young boy, from that time forward, became a regular and contributing member of their studio program. They said he needed this sort of discipline to become part of the community. I thought about all the resources I have at my disposal as an art therapist in the United States. I have professional colleagues with whom I can consult and programs to which I can refer. Sane and Eunice have little more than each other. I began to wonder what I would do were I in their situation. While I disagreed with their method of setting limits, I understood both their need to set limits and the fact that their method was culturally relevant. As Simoneaux (2011) notes, it is common for adults in Kenya to recall the physical punishments they received as children in a positive light, as experiences that made them become better people.

In the end, what I said to Sane and Eunice was that I too understand the importance of setting limits with children, but that as therapists in the United States, we are not permitted to do that through physical punishment; we have to find other means. With effort, I was able to remain open to their way of handling the situation, while also respectfully introducing the idea that there are alternative methods. Providing an interpersonal space of openness where culturally incongruent values and practices can be held and considered is an essential aspect of collaborative consultation aimed at cultural relevance.

Conclusion

For our African collaborators, incorporating a therapeutic arts approach has led to increased awareness of the specific burdens individual children carry in relation to poverty, illness, homelessness, hunger, loss, and trauma. It also has led to a more pronounced sense of helplessness in the face of these overwhelming burdens. Yet, there is cause for *tumaini* (hope). While the resources for addressing the children's problems are sorely lacking, through the TAP we provide spaces where children are relieved of the additional burden of having to bear their troubles all alone. Within the context of humble art spaces facilitated by therapeutic artists, children have the chance to develop skills, resilience, and a sense of belonging.

The TAP, developed through long-term collaborative consultation, provides a sustainable and culturally relevant model for the internationalization of art therapy. It has been heartening to return each year to hear the stories of the artists' work with children, and to witness the development of their unique approaches to therapeutic arts in East Africa.

References

Bishop, B. J., Higgins, D., Casella, F., and Contos, N. (2002) "Reflections on practice: Ethics, race, and worldviews." *Journal of Community Psychology 30*, 6, 611–621.

Dean, R. G. (2001) "The myth of cross-cultural competence." *Families in Society: The Journal of Contemporary Human Services 82*, 6, 623–630.

Denborough, D. (ed.) and Wakhungu, C. (2006) *Raising Our Heads Above the Clouds: The Use of Narrative Practices to Motivate Social Action and Economic Development.* Adelaide, Australia: Dulwich Centre Foundation International.

Freire, P. (1993) *Pedagogy of the Oppressed.* New York: Continuum International. (Original work published 1970.)

Gerstein, L. H., Heppner, P. P., Ægisdóttir, S., and Leung, S. A. (eds) (2009) *International Handbook of Cross-Cultural Counseling: Cultural Assumptions and Practices Worldwide.* Los Angeles, CA: Sage Publications.

Global Alliance for Africa (n.d.) *Our Mission.* Available at www.globalallianceafrica.org/our-mission-and-goals, accessed on June 17, 2013.

Golub, D. (2005) "Social action art therapy." *Art Therapy: Journal of the American Art Therapy Association 22,* 1, 17–23.

Good, M. D., Hyde, S. T., Pinto, S., and Good, B. J. (2008) *Postcolonial Disorders.* Berkeley, CA: University of California Press.

Horne, S. G. and Mathews, S. S. (2006) "A Social Justice Approach to International Collaborative Consultation." In R. L. Toporek, L. H. Gerstein, N. A. Fouad, G. Roysircar, and T. Israel (eds) *Handbook for Social Justice in Counseling Psychology: Leadership, Vision, and Action.* Thousand Oaks, CA: Sage Publications.

Ibrahim, F. A. (1996) "A multicultural perspective on principle and virtue ethics." *The Counseling Psychologist 24*, 1, 78–85.

Jagger, A. M. (1998) "Globalizing feminist ethics." *Hypatia 13*, 2, 8–31.

Jazeel, T. and McFarlane, C. (2010) "The limits of responsibility: A postcolonial politics of academic knowledge production." *Transactions of the Institute of British Geographers 35*, 1, 109–124.

Kalmanowitz, D. and Lloyd, B. (2005) *Art Therapy and Political Violence: With Art, Without Illusion.* London: Routledge.

Kalmanowiz, D. and Lloyd, B. (2011) "Inside-Out Outside-In: Found Object and Portable Studio." In E. G. Levine and S. K. Levine (eds) *Arts in Action: Expressive Arts Therapy and Social Change.* London: Jessica Kingsley Publishers.

Kapitan, L., Litell, M., and Torres, A. (2011) "Creative art therapy in a community's participatory research and social transformation." *Art Therapy: Journal of the American Art Therapy Association 28*, 2, 64–73.

Kester, G. H. (2011) *The One and the Many: Contemporary Collaborative Art in a Global Context.* Durham, NC: Duke University Press.

Ladson-Billings, G. and Donner, J. (2008) "The Moral Activist Role of Critical Race Theory." In N. K. Denzin and Y. S. Lincoln (eds) *The Landscape of Qualitative Research.* Thousand Oaks, CA: Sage Publications.

Leung, S. A. (2003) "A journey worth travelling: Globalization of counseling psychology." *The Counseling Psychologist 31*, 4, 412–419.

Leung, S. A., Clawson, T., Norsworthy, K. L., Tena, A., Szilagiya, A., and Rogers, J. (2009) "Internationalization of the Counseling Profession: An Indigenous Perspective." In L. H. Gerstein, P. P. Heppner, S. Ægisdóttir, and S. A. Leung (eds) *International Handbook of Cross-Cultural Counseling: Cultural Assumptions and Practices Worldwide.* Los Angeles, CA: Sage Publications.

MacLeod, C. (2011) "The Choreography of Absence." In E. G. Levine and S. K. Levine (eds) *Arts in Action: Expressive Arts Therapy and Social Change.* London: Jessica Kingsley Publishers.

Marsella, A. J. (1998) "Toward a 'global-community psychology': Meeting the needs of a changing world." *American Psychologist 53*, 12, 1282–1291.

Martín-Baró, I. (1994) *Writings for a Liberation Psychology.* Cambridge, MA: Harvard University Press.

Norsworthy, K. L. and Khuankaew, O. (2006) "Bringing Social Justice to International Practices of Counseling Psychology." In R. L. Toporek, L. H. Gerstein, N. A. Fouad, G. Roysircar, and T. Israel (eds) *Handbook for Social Justice in Counseling Psychology: Leadership, Vision, and Action.* Thousand Oaks, CA: Sage Publications.

Norsworthy, K. L., Leung, S. A., Heppner, P. P., and Wang, L. (2009) "Crossing Borders in Collaboration." In L. H. Gerstein, P. P. Heppner, S. Ægisdóttir, S. A. Leung, and K. L. Norsworthy (eds) *International Handbook of Cross-Cultural Counseling: Cultural Assumptions and Practices Worldwide.* Los Angeles, CA: Sage Publications.

Racine, L. and Petrucka, P. (2011) "Enhancing decolonization and knowledge transfer in nursing research with non-Western populations: Examining the congruence between primary healthcare and postcolonial feminist approaches." *Nursing Inquiry 18*, 1, 12–20.

Simoneaux, G. (2011) "Creating Space for Change: The Use of Expressive Arts with Vulnerable Children and Women Prisoners in Sub-Saharan Africa." In E. G. Levine and S. K. Levine (eds) *Arts in Action: Expressive Arts Therapy and Social Change.* London: Jessica Kingsley Publishers.

Sparks, E. E. and Park, A. H. (2000) "The Integration of Feminism and Multiculturalism: Ethical Dilemmas at the Border." In M. M. Brabeck (ed.) *Practicing Feminist Ethics in Psychology.* Washington, DC: American Psychological Association.

Watkins, M. and Shulman, H. (2008) *Toward Psychologies of Liberation.* Basingstoke: Palgrave Macmillan Publishers.

Watters, E. (2010) *Crazy Like Us: The Globalization of the American Psyche.* New York: Free Press.

Appendices

R/CID Models

(Chapter 10)

These racial/cultural identity development models will facilitate an examination of the possible therapist and client stage combinations of racial/cultural identity development and should sensitize art therapists to provide more effective cross-cultural therapy.

Asian American Identity Development Models (Kitano 1982; Sodowsky, Kwan, and Pannu 1995; Sue and Sue 1971)

Biracial Identity Development (Poston 1990)

Black Identity Development Models (Cross 1971, 1995; Jackson 1975; Thomas 1971)

Feminist Identity Development (Downing and Roush 1985)

Latino/Hispanic American Identity Development Models (Bernal and Knight 1993; Casas and Pytluk 1995)

Multi-Homosexual Identity Development (Cass 1979; Coleman 1981/1982)

Native American and Alaska Native Identity Development (Dixon and Portman 2010)

Native Hawaiian Identity Development (McCubbin and Dang 2010)

Racial and Personal Affiliation (Choi-Misailidis 2010)

White Racial Identity Development (Hardiman 1982; Helms 1984, 1990, 1994, 1995)

References

Bernal, M. E. and Knight, G. P. (1993) *Ethnic Identity: Formation and Transmission Among Hispanics and Other Minorities.* Albany: State University of New York Press.

Casas, J. M. and Pytluk, S. D. (1995) "Hispanic Identity Development." In J. G. Ponterotto, J. M. Casas, L. A. Suzuki, and C. M. Alexander (eds) *Handbook of Multicultural Counseling.* Thousand Oaks, CA: Sage.

Cass, V. C. (1979) "Homosexual identity formation: A theoretical model." *Journal of Homosexuality* 4, 219–235.

Choi-Misailidis, S. (2010) "Multiracial-Heritage Awareness and Personal Affiliation (M-HAPA): Understanding Identity in People of Mixed-Race Descent." In J. G. Ponterotto, J. M Casas, L. A. Suzuki, and C. M. Alexander (eds) *Handbook of Multicultural Counseling, Third Edition.* Thousand Oaks, CA: Sage.

Coleman, E. (1981/1982) "Developmental stages of the coming out process." *Journal of Homosexuality* 7, 31–43.

Cross, W. E. (1971) "The Negro-to-Black conversion experience: Towards a psychology of Black liberation." *Black World 30*, 13–27.

Cross, W. E. (1995) "The Psychology of Nigrescence: Revising the Cross Model." In J. G. Ponterotto, J. M. Casas, L. A. Suzuki, and C. M. Alexander (eds) *Handbook of Multicultural Counseling*. Thousand Oaks, CA: Sage.

Dixon, A. L. and Portman, T. A. (2010) "The Beauty of Being Native: The Nature of Native American and Alaska Native Identity Development." In J. G. Ponterotto, J. M Casas, L. A. Suzuki, and C. M. Alexander (eds) *Handbook of Multicultural Counseling, Third Edition*. Thousand, Oaks, CA: Sage.

Downing, N. E. and Roush, K. L. (1985) "From passive acceptance to active commitment: A model of feminist identity development for women." *Counseling Psychologist 13*, 695–709.

Hardiman, R. (1982) "White identity development: A process oriented model for describing the racial consciousness of White Americans." *Dissertation Abstracts International 43*, 104A (University Microfilms No. 82-10330).

Helms, J. E. (1984) "Toward a theoretical explanation of the effects of race on counseling: A black and white model." *Counseling Psychologist 12*, 153–165.

Helms, J. E. (1990) *Black and White Racial Identity: Theory, Research, and Practice*. New York: Greenwood Press.

Helms, J. E. (1995) "An Update of Helm's White and People of Color Racial Identity Models." In J. G. Ponterotto, J. M. Casas, L. A. Suzuki, and C. M. Alexander (eds) *Handbook of Multicultural Counseling*. Thousand Oaks, CA: Sage.

Jackson, B. (1975) "Black identity development." *Journal of Educational Diversity 2*, 19–25.

Kitano, H. H. L. (1982) "Mental Health in the Japanese American Community." In E. E. Jones and S. J. Korchin (eds) *Minority Mental Health*. New York: Praeger.

McCubbin, L. D. and Dang, T. A. (2010) "Native Hawaiian Identity and Measurement: An Ecological Perspective of Indigenous Identity Development." In J. G. Ponterotto, J. M. Casas, L. A. Suzuki, and C. M. Alexander (eds) *Handbook of Multicultural Counseling, Third Edition*. Thousand, Oaks, CA: Sage.

Poston, W. S. C. (1990) "The biracial identity development model: A needed edition." *Journal of Counseling and Development 69*, 152–155.

Sodowsky, G. R., Kwan, K. K., and Pannu, R. (1995) "Ethnic Identity of Asians in the United States." In J. G. Ponterotto, J. M. Casas, L. A. Suzuki, and C. M. Alexander (eds) *Handbook of Multicultural Counseling*. Thousand Oaks, CA: Sage.

Sue, S. and Sue, D. W. (1971) "Chinese-American personality and mental health." *American Journal 1*, 39–49.

Thomas, C. W. (1971) *Boys No More*. Beverly Hills, CA: Glencoe Press.

Art Studio Guidelines
(Chapter 14)

You May

- Enjoy the freedom of choice of projects and materials within the art studio. (There are no formal assignments; however, individual assignments and due dates may be assigned at the request of the student and/or at teacher discretion.) Each student must aim to experience drawing, painting, and clay/ceramic media during the school year.

- Explore and use the "Art Library" in the studio whenever you have "artist's block." There you will find information about artists, art history, and art techniques.

- Choose to begin your studio experience any day by working on a "mandala" design. Paper with the mandala outline is available with other papers.

- Work at your own pace. (Take the time you need, but do not waste time.)

- Listen to music while working. (Use good judgment in choosing your communal music. Tapes and CDs should be appropriate.) Music is a bonus and should not interfere with the art process. Music is turned on after all students are working and may be turned off if the art process is disrupted.

- Use this period as your time to relax, unwind, create, and express yourself artistically. Mistakes and experimenting are expected and encouraged.

- Fill the period with a variety of art activities that *you* prefer.

You Are Asked To

- Be respectful of your fellow students and their artwork. Group members should aim to support one another. An environment of acceptance should prevail in the studio.

- Never, ever touch someone else's artwork without their permission.

- Be respectful of the art studio and art materials. You are responsible for setting up and cleaning each day.

- Get your materials out and begin work upon entry to the art studio. Fill the entire period with art activities.

- Save all work done in class. Everything will be collected in your personal portfolio and become part of an end-of-year critique, your final examination.

Art Studio Grading System

- Each student receives a daily grade and may earn as many as 4 points per class period.

- Points will be deducted for acting-out behavior, disrespect of others in the studio, inappropriate language, inconsistent involvement, disturbing the art process, or touching another student's work without his/her permission.

- Individual projects are not graded.

- Daily grades reflect how supportive a student is of others in the group, level of appropriate behaviors, respect of the room and materials, and *particularly how much each student involves and develops himself/herself with the art process.*

- Daily grades will then be averaged at the end of each marking period.

- No one is graded on talent!

I understand all of the above guidelines and expectations for my time in the art studio.

Student name (printed):

Signature:

Date:

Appendix C

Themes List
(Chapter 16)

The general purpose of using themes in art therapy treatment is to provide structure and a holding experience for the client. Some themes invite more disclosure than others, while some support adaptive defenses and containment.

Assessment Themes (Disclosure)

- Draw your family (in an activity) (Burns and Kaufman 1970)
- A problem I want help with
- Person Picking an Apple from a Tree (Gantt and Tabone 1998)
- Draw a first memory, childhood memory, or best memory
- Past, present, and future
- How I see myself
- One thing I want to change
- Safe place
- Three things to introduce yourself to the group
- "I" statements such as I feel, I need, I have, I wish, I want, I love, I am, I hope, I have
- Draw a house, a tree, a person (Buck 1948)
- Draw a person
- Your favorite place
- Map of highlights and low points of day
- Tree to represent your life
- Animal, plant, or object as self
- Seed representing your life

- Feelings list: a feeling experienced now or in the last 24 hours, uncomfortable/ones you avoid, those you want more of, etc.

- Identify a personal strength

- Represent yourself as an animal

- Create your most ideal place to live

- Create an island and place everything you will need to live on it

- Draw yourself as a tree in the most ideal environment

- Draw your mood using a type of weather

- Create a character (4 to 6 frames) and tell a story that has a beginning, middle, and an end

- Draw the problem that brought you to the hospital

- Draw a treasure chest and what is inside it

Stabilization and Containment (Support of Adaptive Defenses)

- Draw a safe or favorite landscape

- Create a mandala (Kellogg 1978)

- Create a container and place in it what you need to discard

- Create a picture of a goal and three steps toward it

- Draw a still life using only warm colors (relate feelings to warm colors, situations that bring out frustration or anger) as a way to handle feelings

- Draw a still life using only cool colors (associate feelings and how to generate relaxation) as a way to handle feelings

- Introduce an art technique such as watercolor, drawing with pastel, printmaking

Group Themes

- Self symbol: Let color, line, shape, and texture express your many and unique meanings. Show how you are whole, integrated, fractured, scattered

- Barriers/obstacles

- Volcano

- Most ideal environment

- Bridge: Going from and to somewhere (Hayes 1981)

- Door: Fold paper in half, door on outside, door opens to? (on inside)

- Mask: Inside and outside (Inner/outer self; Fears; Public self/private self)

- Self-portrait: Draw a picture of yourself starting from the bottom up

- Create the cover for your autobiography

- The weather as a reflection of your mood

- Draw yourself in an activity

- How I handle frustration

- Something you like about yourself, something you would like to change

- Haiku (three-line poem) to describe your picture: First line, 5 syllables; second line, 7 syllables; third line, 5 syllables

- Using clay, work on a "this is me, I am" clay piece (Rhyne 1974)

- Clay scribbles

- Keep a drawing journal

- Draw an animal that expresses a characteristic you have or would like to have; can be an imaginary creature

- Find articles in the world and create a collage from them/recognize your environment

References

Buck, J. N. (1948) "House tree person (HTP): The projective device." *American Journal of Mental Deficiency 51*, 606–610.

Burns, R. and Kaufman, S. H. (1970) *Kinetic family drawings (K-F-D): An introduction to understanding children through kinetic drawings.* Ann Arbor, MI: University of Michigan Press.

Gantt, L. and Tarbone. C. (1998) *The Formal Elements Art Therapy Scale.* Morgantown, WV: Gargoyle Press.

Hayes R. (1981) "The bridge drawing: A projective technique for assessment in art therapy. *The Arts in Psychotherapy 8*, 207–217.

Kellogg, J. (1978) *Mandala: Path of Beauty.* Towson, MD: Mandala Assessment and Research Institute.

Rhyne, J. (1974) *The Gestalt Art Experience.* Salt Lake City, UT: Brooks/Cole.

Application of Art-Based Therapy in Relapse Management
(Chapter 19)

Objective	Art form/medium	Benefits
Sharing: relapse story	Making use of props (miniatures, models, toys) that help them to actually see what precipitated the relapse.	Identifying the triggers that lead to craving. The position in which they place the props, the details they add, the various meanings they give to each prop—all reveal their thoughts in image form.
Expression of feelings	Use of rhythm, songs, lyrics to express emotions, anchor themselves to positive feelings. Drum circle use of instruments like djembe, drums, etc.	A client who is less verbal, silent, and apprehensive to talk openly can choose songs that convey the mood he experiences. The lyrics he sings portray the meaning of his thoughts in words and the instruments can be used as a form of catharsis. The roles they choose to enact, discussions that follow, the dialogues they add, the facial expressions, and physical movements, apart from being a form of catharsis, give them a chance to envision a more positive image of themselves.

Objective	Art form/medium	Benefits
Identifying goals in life	Drawings and paintings	Self-image drawings: How the client perceives himself is clearly depicted through his drawings and paintings. It is a confession he makes through use of colors in an art form. The differences seen in pre- and post-self-image indicate the shift in his thought process. Envisioning the future through using colors to draw and paint is like talking aloud through colors. The choice of colors, the strokes, the size of the drawings, along with their reflection of what it means to them are truly unconscious leaks of the mind that help make conscious efforts and decisions. Due to post-acute withdrawal symptoms (PAWS) like tremors, holding a pastel or a paint brush may be difficult for some, which helps them to accept their physical damage.
Planning their recovery tools	Clay or collage work identifying their recovery tools, things that will make them hold on to recovery.	Various forms: some perfect, out of molds like models, and some abstract; some three-dimensional, others two-dimensional; varies with each client. Images taken from magazines, newspapers, captions, and statements help in expression of thoughts; the whole process of making, creating, and contemplating in the process helps to throw light on their future decisions.

Appendix E

Art-Based Directives for Extended Care at the After-Care Centre

(Chapter 19)

Objective	Art form/medium	Benefits
To have an insight into what addiction has done to them What are the resulting thoughts, feelings, and actions?	Clay sculpting	Through the help of sculpting with clay, an image to reflect their thoughts is created that helps in verbalizing. Phrases or one-liners are written or shared. **Anchoring positive thoughts in clay images:** When asked to create an image in clay that reminds them of recovery tasks or sobriety, it turns out to be a souvenir of positive thoughts.
Anchoring positive feelings and actions	Miming/music/colors	Engaging in drums circle and finding **a song to get anchored to**, diverts their attention while experiencing craving and provides a different way of engaging with people. Miming initiates physical movements: this reduces inhibitions and forces them to interact with others, build rapport, and communicate with others through actions.

Objective	Art form/medium	Benefits
To rebuild relationships by seeing the positives in others	Story and drama	**Drama:** Creating a demon and destroying it followed by listening to the story narration (story of Kalinga war) gives the client an opportunity to bring out the resentments they hold within themselves toward their drug abuse and is cathartic. Once this is done, when they look back at the relationships they have lost or distanced themselves from due to addiction, sharing stories can help them heal. **Anchoring to stories:** Sharing personal real-life stories or stories that help them to reconcile with their lost relations helps them to shift their perceptions and focus on positive qualities in others.
Enhancing whole-person recovery by working on the recovery capital	Music with relaxation and use of color cards	Colors are used to represent various aspects that support recovery, good qualities, support system, etc. They can be anchored to act as reminders for distractions. For example, if a client chooses the color blue to anchor a relaxed feeling, then he can look up at the sky to distract himself during stressful moments. Listening to music during a relaxation exercise and getting **anchored to a particular color** provides a relaxing effect to the client and acts as a take-home healing metaphor.
Mapping the recovery journey by marking hurdles, obstacles in recovery, and planned goals	Play or games	Play and games create an environment where the client is encouraged to engage in an activity, loosen his inhibitions, and participate in a healthy means of fun. The play acts as a warm-up and introduces the client to the theme of the session. (For example, the "Hurdles and Helpmates" game.)

Appendix F

The Instinctual Trauma Response
(Chapter 20)

The following chart, created by Tinnin, Bills, and Gantt (2002) assists the clinical with the sequence of the Trauma Response Model when working with traumatized subjects.

The Instinctual Trauma Response

Begin with a safe place drawing and a butterfly hug	
Adults	Children
What's happening first? *Startle—A state of high alert*: ready Ready action	Lions and tigers, oh, my
Thwarted intention (fight or flight): I am out of fundamental survival mechanisms here	Oh, no! #$%*
Freeze: Momentary state of immobility or paralysis	I think I am dead
Altered state of consciousness: An "out of the ordinary" experience, a dream-like state in which time and perception are changed May involve an out-of-body experience	This can't be happening This must be a dream
Body sensations: The body remembers sensations of the trauma but cannot code the experience in words	What's happening to my body!
Automatic obedience: Unthinking compliance with any perpetrator or helper (e.g., medical personnel)	Yes sir! Anything you say, sir!

Self-repair: Sleeping, eating, washing, rocking Withdrawing to a quiet place	Boy, I'm glad that's over...what a relief! Where's my blankie?
End with a butterfly hug	

Source: Revised with personal permission from Tinnin, Bills, and Gantt (2002), The Trauma Recovery Institute, WV.

Reference

Tinnin, L., Bills, L., and Gantt, L. (2002) "Short-Term Treatment of Simple and Complex PTSD." In M. B. Williams and J. Sommer (eds) *Simple and Complex Post-Traumatic Stress Disorder*. New York: Haworth.

The 8 Ways Paradigm
(Chapter 21)

1. Families have a natural course of development or life cycle with identifiable events and dynamics of preceding generations, which influence how a family handles any particular phase (Carter and McGoldrick 1999).

2. Every family has its strengths or qualities of resiliency that can sustain the family and its individual members through difficult times (Walsh 2003).

3. Every family has observable, unique patterns of behavior and communication. These patterns operate in a circular rather than a linear way (Nichols 2009). "All behavior's communication" (Watzlawick et al. 2011).

4. Every family has a discernible structure or the underlying and implicit rules or principles that govern relationships within the family (Nichols 2009).

5. Every family has a largely unconscious emotional life that has its roots in the past and that influences current relationships (Nichols 2009).

6. Every family expresses its emotional life through behavior, structure, and words and at another level through themes, content, and metaphors in their art.

7. Every individual may be seen as part of the whole system and as an individual self (Nichols 1987). It is often a symptom of an individual family member that overwhelms the family's coping resources and brings the family into therapy (Nichols 2009).

8. Every family operates in a culture and society and both influences and is influenced by the society that surrounds them (McGoldrick et al. 2005).

References

Carter, B. and McGoldrick, M. (eds) (1999) *The Expanded Family Life Cycle: Individual, Family, and Social Perspectives, Third Edition*. Boston: Allyn and Bacon.

McGoldrick, M., Giordano, J., and Garcia-Preto, N. (eds) (2005) *Ethnicity and Family Therapy, Third Edition*. New York: Guilford Press.

Nichols, M. P. (1987) *The Self in the System: Expanding the Limits of Family Therapy.* New York: Brunner/Routledge.

Nichols, M. P. (2009) *The Essentials of Family Therapy, Fourth Edition.* Boston: Pearson.

Walsh, F. (ed.) (2003) *Normal Family Processes: Growing Diversity and Complexity, Third Edition.* New York: Guilford Press.

Watzlawick, P., Beavin, J., and Jackson, D. (1967) *Pragmatics of Human Communication: A Study of Interactional Patterns, Pathologies, and Paradoxes.* New York: Norton.

Appendix H

"In Through the Backdoor"—A Directive for Working with Patients with an Eating Disorder

(Chapter 24)

The directive often cited by the author as "In through the backdoor" has been shown to be effective in reducing defensiveness often associated with persons with an eating disorder by employing abstract art methods (Dean 2006a, 2006b; Earley 1999a, 1999b). The task requires six pieces of white 12" × 18" paper, a glue stick, and drawing materials (colored markers, oil pastels, and chalk pastels) for each person. The participants are asked to fill the page as best they can with "lines, marks, and textures" within the time allotment. Encouragement is given before commencing to discourage participants from working in a small corner of the page and so that each expression may be different and unique, using as many or as few colors as the participant likes.

The facilitator of the session will be responsible for keeping the time for each drawing and encouraging the participants to mark the back of each image with the corresponding number for each image in the series. The time limits for filling each page are as follows:

1. 1 minute

2. 1 minute

3. 30 seconds

4. 15 seconds

5. 2 minutes

6. 1 minute.

Once complete, spread out all six images so they may be seen simultaneously, if space allows, and instruct the participants to choose the drawing that is the most affectively charged, either positively or negatively. Then have them choose the second most affectively charged image. The first image chosen is then to be ripped out into the shape of the participant's body and adhered to the second chosen drawing, creating a ground or environment for the body-shaped image.

The rationale behind this directive is multifaceted, with many possibilities for discussion, associations, and amplifications to the emergent imagery that carries the underlying symbolic material. Briefly, some significant questions include: Is the self-image created from a page that took longer to make than the environment, or a shorter time, or the same amount of time? Does this resonate with the person's energy to look inward in a self-absorbed way, being preoccupied with external feedback, or feel like equal amounts of time are devoted internally and externally? Is there congruency between the foreground and background (i.e., do lines merge or overlap)? Visually, is there a pattern to the marks or forms? Do they cross or demarcate a significant part of the body, and what are the participant's feelings about this part of his or her body? Does the merged image create other interesting imagery or does the body feature blend in or disappear into the background? How does this reflect the person's experience in his or her daily life, if at all? These are just a few questions used to engage associations, but many more implications and discussions of this directive and its yielded responses lie beyond the scope of this appendix.

References

Dean, M. L. (2006a) "Creative destruction: Art based interventions with eating disordered clients who self-injure." The 16th Renfrew Center Conference, Philadelphia, PA.

Dean, M. L. (2006b) "Preserving the self: Art psychotherapy applications with eating disordered clients who self-injure." The American Art Therapy Association Conference, New Orleans, LA.

Earley, M. L. (1999a) "Art therapy: Body image, media and art." The American Art Therapy Association Conference, Orlando, FL.

Earley, M. L. (1999b) "Art therapy with eating disordered clients." The Renfrew Center Conference, Philadelphia, PA.

The 12-Step Approach for the TTAP Method

(Chapter 28)

Steps in TTAP	Process	Brain stimulation/ learning style	Brain region(s)
Step 1 CONVERSATION	Individual thought to group conversation	Linguistic/interpersonal	Broca's area
Step 2 MUSIC and MEDITATION	Listening to music and reflection on images	Musical/intrapersonal	Temporal lobe
Step 3 DRAWING and PAINTING	Drawing and painting any images "seen" in the mind's eye	Visual/interpersonal	Parietal lobe
Step 4 SCULPTURE	Creating a three-dimensional form	Spatial/kinesthetic	Motor cortex/ cerebellum/ temporal lobe
Step 5 MOVEMENT and DANCE	Movement/ dance	Gross motor/kinesthetic	Motor cortex/ cerebellum/ temporal lobe
Step 6 POETRY and WRITING	Creating personal or group writing experience	Fine motor/linguistic	Frontal lobe/ Wernicke's area

Steps in TTAP	Process	Brain stimulation/ learning style	Brain region(s)
Step 7 FOOD PROGRAMMING	Words into food	Spatial/kinesthetic	Sensory cortex/ reticular formation
Step 8 THEME EVENT	Food into event	Visual/kinesthetic	Reticular formation
Step 9 PHOTOTHERAPY	Event to picture	Visual/spatial/kinesthetic	Broca's area
Step 10 SENSORY STIMULATION	Touch, taste, sight, hearing, feeling	Spatial/kinesthetic/ music/linguistic/ inter–intrapersonal	All regions of the brain
Step 11 DRAMA, THEATER	Drama, theater, and acting out scenes	Spatial/kinesthetic/ music/linguistic/ inter–intrapersonal	All regions of the brain
Step 12 PERSONAL EVALUATION OF PROGRAM	Personal value of participants' feedback and satisfaction, guaranteeing person-centered programming	Any level the individual is capable of, written or verbal response	Frontal lobe/ Wernicke's area

Art-Based Directives and Assessments Used by the Art Therapist with Sexually and Physically Abused Orphans at Father's House Orphanage and at the Isolator (State Shelter)

(Chapter 31)

Father's House Orphanage	The Isolator (State Shelter)
Favorite Kind of Day (Manning 1987)	Bridge Drawings; Hayes and Lyons (Hayes 1981)
Mandala drawings (Kellogg 1978)	Draw a Person Picking an Apple from a Tree (Gantt and Tabone 1998)
House/tree/person (Buck 1948)	Free drawing
Make your own island	Draw how you got here
Group work	Feeling mural

References

Buck, J. (1948) "H.T.P.: The projective device." *American Journal of Mental Deficiency 51*, 606–610.

Gantt, L. and Tabone, C. (1998) *The Formal Elements Art Therapy Scale.* Morgantown, WV: Gargoyle Press.

Hayes, R. (1981) "The bridge drawing: A projective technique for assessment in art therapy." *The Arts in Psychotherapy 8*, 207–217.

Kellogg, J. (1978) *Mandala: Path of Beauty.* Towson, MD: Mandala Assessment and Research Institute.

Manning, T. (1987) "Aggression depicted in abused children's drawings." *The Arts in Psychotherapy 14*, 5–24.

Appendix K

Existing Resources for Overseas Travel
(Chapter 32)

There are existing organizations that foster overseas involvement. For example, Communities Healing Through Art (CHART) emerged from a group of artists who worked with the tsunami victims in Thailand in 2005 (www.atwb.org/AdvisoryCouncil.html and www.facebook.com/pages/CHART-Communities-Healing-Through-Art/7644242543). CHART's projects include facilitating art therapists to work with earthquake victims in Chile, New Zealand, and Japan. Since 2012 CHART has been involved in at least seven trips to Haiti. Other venues include projects in India, Thailand, Lebanon, and Pakistan (to assist victims of the 2010 floods). Baxter Garcia is the liaison helping to connect art therapists and art therapy projects around the world. Gaelynn Wolf Bordinaro, Art Therapy Professor at Emporia State University, is the Clinical Director of CHART. She has traveled to Haiti, India, and the Bahamas, bringing art therapy students along to assist her.

Art Therapists Without Borders (www.atwb.org/AdvisoryCouncil.html) is an organization with an overseas focus. This project and others may be interested in having art therapy volunteers.

Art Therapy India Group Members (group-digests@linkedin.com) often wants volunteers in New Delhi.

Another resource is the book *Half the Sky: Turning Oppression into Opportunity for Women Worldwide* (2010) by N. D. Kristof and S. WuDunn (New York: Knopf Doubleday Publishing). The book has vignettes of women around the world who have survived sex trafficking, poverty, rape, mutilation, and other abuses. It includes a chapter on how readers can get involved to help these women. At the end of the book is a list of organizations that welcome support.

Appendix L

Body Outline for Pakistani Male
(Chapter 32)

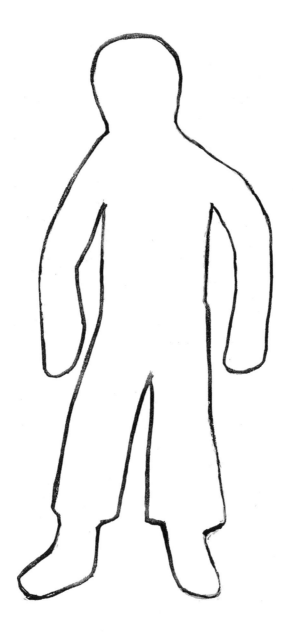

Body Outline for Pakistani Female
(Chapter 32)

The Contributors

Frances E. Anderson, Ed.D, ATR-BC, HLM, is a founding member of the American Art Therapy Association (AATA). She spent several semesters as Visiting Professor at six universities and founded the art therapy programs at Illinois State University (ISU) and the Florida State University (FSY). She has published over 90 articles and four books. Her work with individuals with physical and mental challenges, and children and women who have been sexually abused, was funded by 40 grants. After 35 years as Distinguished Professor at the School of Art at ISU, Frances received five Fulbright awards to research and teach overseas in Argentina (2002), Taiwan (2005), Thailand (2008), and Pakistan (2010). In 2012, Very Special Arts and the National Art Education Association gave her the Lifetime Achievement Award for Work with Special Needs Children. She served the AATA as Journal Editor, and continues as the Video and Non-Print Media Editor for *The Arts in Psychotherapy*.

Doris Arrington, Ed.D, ATR-BC, HLM, is an artist, art educator, art therapist, author, and international speaker. She served for 28 years as founding director and professor in the Art Therapy Psychology Department at Notre Dame de Namur University in Belmont, CA. A Fulbright Senior Specialist to the Ukraine, Doris has trained caregivers of the abused and traumatized in Cambodia, China, Ethiopia, Ireland, Mexico, Poland, South Korea, Spain, Taiwan, Great Britain, Ukraine, and the United States. Her book publications include *Home Is Where the Art Is: An Art Therapy Approach to Family Therapy* and *Art, Angst and Trauma: Right Hemisphere Interventions of Developmental Issues*. Doris exhibits art through Arts of the Covenant in Menlo Park, CA, and Peninsula Art Institute in Burlingame, CA.

Yasmine J. Awais, MAAT, ATR-BC, ATCS, LCAT, is an American art therapist with extensive cross-cultural clinical and supervisory experience, working in Chicago, Boston, New York, Japan, and Saudi Arabia. Her art therapy practice is informed by multicultural counseling/therapy, social and restorative justice. Her personal artwork is an examination of identity through photographing artificial and natural environments. Her clinical experience includes working as Senior Art Therapist at King Fahad Medical City in Riyadh, Saudi Arabia, and with families directly impacted by HIV and AIDS as the Psychosocial Director of One Heartland, and housing insecure PLWHA at Housing Works and young people infected and affected by HIV/AIDS at The Door. Yasmine is currently a Clinical Assistant Professor at Drexel University in Philadelphia, Pennsylvania.

Kate Baasch, ATR-BC, began her career as an art therapist at Miriam's Kitchen in 2008 as an art therapy intern and became a full-time art therapist and case manager in September

2009 after she received her Master of Arts in Art Therapy from the George Washington University. Kate is a registered, board certified art therapist and holds a Professional Counseling License in the state of Pennsylvania. She has a diverse professional background and has experience working in recreational and therapeutic settings. Kate is interested in creating community through multi-modal therapeutic collaborations, and in how art therapy transforms maladaptive attachment styles and treats trauma. She has her BA in Art with a concentration in oil painting from Asbury College in Wilmore, KT.

Heidi Bardot, ATR-BC, is Director of the Art Therapy Graduate Program at the George Washington University in Washington, DC. She has published, presented, and conducted workshops nationally and internationally on issues of grief, resiliency, effects of war, secondary trauma, and creating art therapy programs internationally. Heidi has worked collaboratively with art therapists in Lebanon, Greece, Italy, Austria, Switzerland, Germany, and France. She created the GW Summer Abroad art therapy diversity courses and service learning programs in France, India, and South Africa. Clinically, she has worked with hospice programs helping children, adolescents, and adults deal with grief and loss issues through art therapy home visits, groups, workshops, and camps.

Donna Betts, PhD, ATR-BC, is an Assistant Professor in the George Washington University Graduate Art Therapy Program in Washington, DC. An active scholar, she has researched, published, and presented on a range of topics (see http://donnabettsphd.wordpress.com). Donna is Director of the International Art Therapy Research Database, www.arttherapyresearch.com. She is the principal investigator on *An Art Therapy Study of Visitor Reactions to the United States Holocaust Memorial Museum Experience*, for which she was co-recipient of the American Art Therapy Association 2012 Research Award. She is also the principal investigator on *The Warrior Stories Platform: A Graphic Novel Authoring Tool* in Washington, DC, and co-investigator on the study *Île ga Bruidhinn: Community-Based Gaelic Language Revitalization* in Nova Scotia, Canada.

Daniel Blausey, MA, LCAT, ATR-BC, is a Boulder, CO based art therapist, artist, and psychotherapist and the founder of Studio Blue: Art + Psychotherapy, LLC. Previously working in New York City, Newark, NJ, and Miami, FL, Daniel has successfully designed, implemented, and directed several mental health programs. Previous NYC settings include GMHC/Gay Men's Health Crisis, the oldest AIDS service organization, and The Door, a premier comprehensive youth agency. Since the mid-1990s, his areas of clinical focus include art therapy with adolescents and young adults, HIV/AIDS, childhood sexual abuse, adult sexual victimization, and the LGBTQ community. Daniel is an adjunct faculty member at Naropa University's Graduate School of Psychology in the Art Therapy concentration of the Transpersonal Counseling Psychology Degree Program.

Charlotte Boston, MA, ATR-BC, has provided art therapy services for more than 25 years in the mid-Atlantic area of the United States. The range of her experiences includes various populations aged 5 to 90, inpatient, military, and residential, with a broad range of psychiatric diagnoses. She has served in roles such as director of expressive therapy, clinical director, supervisor, consultant, and lecturer. Charlotte has presented and published on multicultural issues in art therapy locally and nationally, to include the film *Wheels of Diversity: Pioneers of Color*, which she co-produced. She is currently Secretary of the American Art Therapy Association Board of Directors and has served on various AATA committees. She is also an adjunct professor at the George Washington University's Art Therapy Program in Washington, DC.

Deni Brancheau, Ed.S, ATR-BC, received her Master's in Art Therapy from George Washington University in 1989. She received her ATR in 1991 and earned Board Certification in 1995. In 1998, she received her Advanced Professional Certification in Administration and Special Education from the Maryland State Department of Education. Deni earned her degree of Education Specialist from GW in 2009. She has been active in the fields of mental health and special education since 1989. During that time she has worked as an art therapist, supervisor, school administrator, and program director. Deni has been on the faculty of the Graduate Art Therapy Program at George Washington University since 1995. She maintains a private practice and pursues her interest in art whenever possible.

Tracy Councill, ATR-BC, serves as Art Therapy Program Director in Pediatric Hematology-Oncology at Georgetown University Hospital's Lombardi Comprehensive Cancer Center, and is also Program Director of Tracy's Kids, a non-profit organization that supports art therapy programs in five pediatric oncology treatment centers. She started the art therapy program at Lombardi in 1991, helping children and families use the creative process to navigate the challenges of illness and treatment. Prior to starting the program at Lombardi, she was an art therapist at Walter Reed Army Medical Center in DC and at Dominion Hospital in Falls Church, VA. Tracy is a lecturer in Art Therapy at the George Washington University, where she earned her Master's in Art Therapy in 1988. She earned a BFA in Painting and Printmaking from Virginia Commonwealth University in 1978. Tracy continues to be an active artist; block prints and painting are her favorite media. Her interests include gardening, music, and travel. Cambodia, Ireland, France, and Ethiopia are among the beautiful places she has visited.

Michelle L. Dean, MA, ATR-BC, LPC, CGP, HLM (DVATA), is a nationally recognized expert in treating individuals who have eating disorders. Her nearly 20-year work history includes co-founding The Center for Psyche & the Arts, LLC, in Lansdowne and Berwyn, Pennsylvania, as well as working at nationally recognized eating disordered programs in the Philadelphia area. Michelle is a highly regarded presenter and an advocate for the use of art therapy and therapeutic art-based educational programs, and has authored of several publications including the children's book, *Taking weight problems to school* (JayJo Press, 2005) and the chapter, "Preserving the self: Treating eating disordered individuals who self-injure with art therapy" in *Creative Arts Therapies with Patients who have Eating Disorders*, edited by S. Brooke (Charles C. Thomas, 2008), as well as several other publications currently in press. Her work has earned several awards, including the Delaware Valley Art Therapy Association's Innovations in Art Therapy Award (2007), The Ronald E. Hays Presenter's Award (2009), and the Honorary Life Member Award (2012).

Cheryl Doby-Copeland, PhD, ATR-BC, LPC, LMFT, was trained at Pratt Institute and Howard University, and has been an art therapist for 35 years. She currently works for the DC Government Department of Mental Health in an early childhood treatment program, where she provides individual and family art/play therapy. She has past experience working with adolescent, adult, and geriatric psychiatric patients, and juvenile detainees. Cheryl is a part-time faculty member of the George Washington University Graduate Art Therapy Program in Washington, DC, where she has taught courses in multicultural diversity and family/marital art therapy. Since 1978, she has actively worked to promote multicultural competence in art therapy.

Mimi Farrelly-Hansen, ATR-BC, LPC, is founder and former director and faculty member of Naropa University's graduate program in Transpersonal Counseling Psychology and Art Therapy. Having worked in the art therapy field for over 30 years, she currently maintains a small private practice in Longmont, CO, where she is also active as an exhibiting painter, published poet, retreat facilitator, and advisory board member of a center for persons with brain disorders. Mimi's book, *Spirituality and Art Therapy: Living the Connection*, was released in 2001.

Linda Gantt, PhD, ATR-BC, is Executive Director of Intensive Trauma Therapy, Inc. (ITT) in Morgantown, WV, an outpatient clinic for post-traumatic stress disorder (PTSD) and dissociative disorders. She has a Master's in Art Therapy (George Washington University) and a Doctorate in Interdisciplinary Studies (University of Pittsburgh). She developed the Formal Elements Art Therapy Scale (FEATS) for measuring diagnostic information in patient drawings. Linda has been an art therapist for 30 years and is board-certified by the Art Therapy Credentialing Board. In addition to her clinical experience she served as the President of the American Art Therapy Association and the Chair of the National Coalition of Creative Arts Therapies.

Lisa Raye Garlock, ATR-BC, is on the faculty of the Art Therapy Program at the George Washington University in Washington, DC. As Clinical Placement Coordinator, she helps students find internship placements, develops new sites, and organizes supervisor's workshops. She has traveled widely, including co-leading groups of students in a diversity course in Chennai in recent years. Lisa majored in Printmaking at the Rochester Institute of Technology, with minors in Textiles and Painting, and received her Master's in Art Therapy from Nazareth College of Rochester. She has worked with adults, adolescents and children in hospitals, schools, community-based organizations and shelters. She recently received her ATCS (supervisor credential) and is planning to offer supervision to those working towards their ATR. She has presented on art therapy topics, facilitated workshops in the US and abroad, and exhibits her artwork locally and nationally. Lisa works in a variety of art forms, including glass beads, jewelry, painting, mixed media, and textiles, and is working on a series of paintings inspired by her travels to India.

Emmy Lou Glassman, MA, ATR-BC, crafted a unique high school art therapy program in Fairfax County Public Schools, located in a suburb of Washington, DC, by integrating strict government mandates with well-founded art therapy theories and practices. Emmy

Lou has lectured at public schools, universities, and conferences, about the positive role that art therapy can play for students when adjusting to the world around them. She served as a clinical field supervisor to graduate art therapy students for the George Washington University in Washington, DC, and has been an adjunct faculty member there and at the Corcoran School of Art + Design graduate education program where she continues to instruct. Emmy Lou has done private art therapy work with clients of all ages and continues to supervise new and established art therapists.

David Gussak, PhD, ATR-BC, is Professor and the Chairperson for the Florida State University Department of Art Education and is the Clinical Coordinator for its Graduate Art Therapy Program. David has presented extensively internationally, nationally and regionally on art therapy in forensic settings and working with aggressive and violent clients. He has published extensively on various topics, but most significantly on art therapy within the forensic milieu. His research studies on the benefits of art therapy in prison settings have been well received and all of these articles can be found on the website www.arttherapyinprison.com. Dave is also the co-editor and contributing author for the book *Drawing Time: Art Therapy in Prisons and Other Correctional Settings* with Dr. Evelyn Virshup, and *Art Education for Social Justice* with Dr. Tom Anderson, Kara Hallmark, and Alison Paul. He is also the author of *Art on Trial: Art Therapy in Capital Murder Cases* (Columbia University Press). He is currently co-editing the Wiley-Blackwell *Handbook of Art Therapy* with Dr. Marcia Rosal.

Paula Howie, ATR-BC, LPC, is a registered, board-certified art therapist and a licensed counselor in DC and VA. She worked in and directed the Art Therapy Service at Walter Reed for 25 years. She was given a Special Recognition Award in 2002 from the Secretary of Defense for her contribution to the treatment of survivors of 9/11 and the Walter Reed Commander's Civil Service Award in 2002. She has been a part-time faculty at the George Washington University in Washington, DC, since 1982, where she currently holds the title of Associate Professorial Lecturer. Paula has held numerous positions in the American Art Therapy Association, including that of President from 2005 to 2007. She was awarded the AATA Clinician Award for Adults in 1999. Paula currently maintains a private practice in the Washington, DC area where she focuses on the treatment of trauma. Her art therapy publications include those on working with trauma, independent practice, and the future of art therapy practice. She has made numerous presentations, and was invited to lecture in South Korea in 2004 and 2006. Since her retirement from Walter Reed, in addition to private practice and teaching, she has been actively pursuing her passion for watercolor painting.

Jennie Kristel, MA, CET, RMT, is an expressive therapist in private practice, an Adjunct Professor at Burlington College in Vermont, and is on the Board of Directors at the Centre for Playback Theatre. For over 20 years, Jennie has practiced in clinical and non-clinical settings, using the expressive arts and Playback Theatre, with diverse populations such as individuals in hospices, the homeless, and adults with developmental disabilities. Since 2003 she has worked in South Asia teaching expressive therapies and Playback Theatre through local non-governmental organizations, counseling centers, and universities, while working on a wide range of therapeutic and social justice issues including trauma, disability issues, and women's rights. Jennie hones her artistic muse through her love of printmaking.

Marian Liebmann, OBE, has worked in art therapy with offenders, women's groups, and community groups. She is currently a member of the Inner City Mental Health Team in Bristol, UK, where she has developed work on anger issues, with asylum seekers and refugees. She lectures on art therapy at several universities in the UK and Europe. She also works in restorative justice, mediation, and conflict resolution, and has run workshops on art, conflict, and anger in many countries. Marian has written/edited ten books, most recently *Art Therapy and Anger* (2008). In 2010 she was awarded her PhD by publications from Bristol University, and in 2013 she was awarded an OBE in the Queen's New Year Honours, for services to art therapy and mediation.

Linda Levine Madori, PhD, is a two-time Fulbright Scholar, a professor, and author of a book on a creative arts approach to brain stimulation titled *Therapeutic Thematic Arts Programming*, 2007 (TTAP Method.com). Her second book, *Transcending Dementia Through the TTAP Method: A New Psychology of Art, Brain and Cognition*, 2012, documents research on the TTAP Method® with older adults and those with Alzheimer's disease. Findings include enhanced cognition, increased social stimulation, and dramatically reduced health care costs due to documented reduction of aggressive behaviors and falls. Linda authored a Certification Training Course in 2009, available to health care professionals nationally and internationally. She has been recognized for her excellence in teaching, program development, training, and health care advocacy, and received the St. Thomas Aquinas Board of Trustees' Award in 2011, the Distinguished Service Award in the health care field from New York State in 2010, and the New York State Most Innovative Program Award in 2008. Contact Dr. Levine Madori for information at Linda@Levinemadoriphd.com.

Reshma Malick, M.Phil, is a psychologist working as a counselor at the T. T. Ranganathan Clinical Research Foundation, Chennai, India. Her role involves conducting re-educative classes for clients and their family members, conducting relapse prevention and management programs, and training professionals who work in the addiction management field. She also supervises students who undertake arts-based therapy courses. She has undergone training in arts-based therapy conducted by the World Centre for Creative Learning Foundation (WCCLF), in Pune, India.

Catherine Hyland Moon, MA, ATR, is an Associate Professor in the Art Therapy Department at the School of the Art Institute of Chicago. She is the author of *Studio Art Therapy: Cultivating the Artist Identity in the Art Therapist* and editor of *Materials and Media in Art Therapy: Critical Understandings of Diverse Artistic Vocabularies*. She has practiced art therapy for over 30 years, working in settings ranging from an inpatient psychiatric hospital to a community-based studio. Her current practice is focused on the collaborative development of community studios in Chicago and therapeutic art programs for children in East Africa.

Audrey Di Maria Nankervis, ATR-BC, is an Adjunct Associate Professor and Rotating Chair in George Washington University's Art Therapy Program in Washington, DC, where she has lectured since 1978. She consults for Save the Children's HEART program, which trains teachers in countries ravaged by war or natural disasters to provide children with arts-based curricula. Audrey received the American Art Therapy Association's Clinician Award for her work with children. She served as the Chairperson of the AATA's Education and Publications Committees and as Secretary of the Art Therapy Credentials Board, which oversees the credentials of approximately 4000 art therapists. She and her husband Ken Nankervis divide their time among Washington, DC, Audrey's childhood home in New Hampshire, and Ken's native Australia, where they have three children and seven grandchildren.

Katharine Phlegar, ATR-BC, is an art therapist for Tracy's Kids in the Center for Cancer and Blood Disorders at the Children's National Medical Center in Washington, DC. Tracy's Kids is a non-profit organization that provides art therapy services to patients and their family members in pediatric oncology treatment centers. Katherine received her Master of Arts in Art Therapy from the George Washington University in 2010 and her Bachelor of Arts in Studio Art from Davidson College in North Carolina in 2008.

Sangeeta Prasad, MA, ATR, is an art therapist with over 20 years of experience working in the United States and India. She has worked with children and adults with serious mental illness. She has presented in both the United States and India, and enjoys working in both countries. Sangeeta helped create a Summer Abroad program for George Washington University, Washington, DC, to give institutions in India an opportunity to use art therapy. Through her work, she hopes to bridge the information gap between countries that have already established art therapy programs and those in which art therapy is just beginning to take root. She self-published her first book, *Creative Expressions: Say it with Art*, to introduce the concepts of art education and art therapy to parents, teachers, and counselors in Southeast Asia. Sangeeta hopes to inspire others about art therapy through her art, writings, and teachings, and through her work with the Prasad Family Foundation and Bambino Educational Trust.

Shanthi Ranganathan, MD, is the founder of the T. T. Ranganathan Clinical Research Foundation, now known popularly as the TTK Hospital, a pioneering institution committed to the treatment and rehabilitation of people addicted to alcohol and drugs. A therapist, trainer, consultant, and author, she is a recipient of the Padma Shri Award, instituted by the Government of India; the United Nations Vienna Civil Society Award (1999); and the Colombo Plan Award (2003), recognizing her outstanding services in the field of addiction research and treatment. She has undergone training in arts-based therapy conducted by the World Centre for Creative Learning Foundation (WCCLF) in Pune, India.

Valery Shuman, MAAT, LCPC, ATR-BC, received her Master's in Art Therapy from the School of the Art Institute of Chicago in 2002. She has worked at Heartland Health Outreach in various capacities since 1998, primarily with formerly homeless participants with co-occurring mental health and substance use concerns. She now serves as the Associate Director of Heartland's Midwest Harm Reduction Institute, providing training and technical assistance to organizations moving toward a harm reduction approach. She has taught at the School of the Art Institute and Mount Mary College in Milwaukee. Valery's interests include applying art therapy in a harm reduction setting, and working to reduce the stigma associated with having a mental illness or a substance use disorder.

Barbara Sobol, LPC, ATR-BC, CTT, is a graduate of the George Washington University Master's Program in Art Therapy and is a Professorial Lecturer in that program. Over the course of 30 years as a teacher and as a clinician in both the public and private sectors, she has developed specialties in family therapy and trauma. In her published writing, presentations, research, and particularly in her direct service to clients, she explores the vulnerability of children to the effects on attachment arising from the intergenerational transmission of trauma. In 2012, Barbara was awarded the American Art Therapy Association's "Clinician of the Year" honor for her work in family art therapy.

Louis Tinnin, MD, did his undergraduate and medical school training at the University of Chicago. He was trained in psychiatry at the University of Cincinnati and received post-graduate training at the National Institute of Mental Health in the United States. He is a diplomat of the American Board of Psychiatry and Neurology and Professor Emeritus in Psychiatry at West Virginia University. Louis founded the Trauma Recovery Institute in Morgantown, West Virginia, where innovative treatment in psychotraumatology was developed and tested. His current interest is in brief treatment procedures for the medical and psychiatric consequences of trauma.

Subject Index

Author Index